HANDBOOK OF UNUSUAL NATURAL PHENOMENA

HANDBOOK OF UNUSUAL NATURAL PHENOMENA

Compiled by

WILLIAM R. CORLISS

Illustrated by John C. Holden

ANCHOR BOOKS
Anchor Press/Doubleday
Garden City, New York
1983

HANDBOOK OF UNUSUAL NATURAL PHENOMENA was originally published in a hardbound edition by The Sourcebook Project in 1977. This is the first Anchor Press edition, and it is a revised and expanded edition.

Anchor Press edition: 1983

Library of Congress Cataloging in Publication Data

Corliss, William R.
    Handbook of unusual natural phenomena.

    Includes indexes.
    1. Earth sciences—Miscellanea. I. Title.
        QE53.C66   1983   550
                AACR2
            ISBN: 0-385-14754-6
Library of Congress Catalog Card Number 78-22625

CONTENTS

HANDBOOK OF UNUSUAL NATURAL PHENOMENA

1

LUMINOUS PHENOMENA

The primary sensory channel for detecting unusual natural phenomena will always be the human eye. Nothing catches the attention faster than a mysterious light. Who hasn't jumped at a nearby flash of lightning or pondered a far-off light moving through the night sky? Was it just an airplane or some phenomenon unknown to science? Most strange lights, of course, turn out to have easy scientific explanations, but this chapter will demonstrate that some luminous phenomena still tax the ability of today's science to account for them.

The lights described here are self-luminous; like light bulbs they shine through the release of internal energy rather than the reflection of light from the sun, moon, or some other external source. This category includes ordinary lightning, the auroras, meteors, marine phosphorescence, and other luminous displays that manufacture their own light. Halos, rainbows, mirages, and phenomena that depend upon reflected light are covered in the next chapter.

The earth's atmosphere absorbs sunlight and streams of subatomic particles (plasma) spewed out by the sun. This influx of solar energy fuels many of our luminous phenomena. Various electrical and chemical processes in the atmosphere convert solar energy into lightning, the auroras, St. Elmo's fire, the Andes glow, and the host of curious and beautiful luminous phenomena that are discussed in this chapter. A meteor transforms its energy of motion into light as it burns out in the upper atmosphere. Down on the earth's surface, the incredible geometrical displays of marine phosphorescence probably draw their energy from minute organisms in the seawater. Finally the earth itself is a reservoir of energy. The energy of earthquake action sometimes ignites the sky with electric flashes, glows, and moving balls of light. Gases escaping from the earth's crust may be converted into soft lambent flames called will-o'-the-wisps. Nature is profligate with energy and has discovered many ways to turn it into visible light.

Genuine mysteries surround most of the luminous phenomena described in this chapter. For example:

- The precise energy sources of some phenomena are unknown.
- Ball lightning, normal lightning, and the so-called ghost lights sometimes display prankish, uncanny behavior that seems to transcend objective science.
- Some auroras and meteors are accompanied by hisses and humming sounds that cannot be explained by ordinary sound propagation.
- Many light displays, such as the Andes glow, seem influenced by solar activity—and no one knows why.
- Some auroras, most marine phosphorescent displays, and a few electric discharge phenomena manifest themselves as curious geometrical patterns (wheels, parallel bands, rings, etc.) that are most difficult to account for.
- Ghost lights, ball lightning, marine light displays, and other phenomena are closely tied to the murky problems of human perception and the role of the mind. Indeed, we already know that some lights, such as those that astronauts see when pierced by cosmic rays, do not truly exist.

The rich lode of luminous phenomena provides a fertile ground for scientific exploration. Unfortunately, the controversial aspects of the phenomena and the highly subjective nature of many of the observations make this a risky field for scientists to tackle.

Auroralike Phenomena

Auroras are luminous displays of the northern skies in the northern hemisphere and of the southern skies in the opposite hemisphere. The repertoire of "normal" auroral displays is remarkable, ranging from an unimpressive dull greenish glow just tinting the northern sky to kaleidoscopes of flickering red, yellow, and bluish flames, and arches that fill half the heavens. The eerie involuted draperies, the silently flashing displays, and the cavorting flames called the "merry dancers" grip the beholder today and inspired awe and legend in primitive people.

Despite all our modern research with spacecraft and instrumented rockets, the auroras have not yielded up all their mysteries—not even the "normal" auroras. Auroras are loosely associated with solar activity and geomagnetic storms, so we know that the gusts of electrically charged particles emitted by the sun (the solar wind) help in some way to "set fire" to the polar heavens. Beyond these generalities, there is much we do not understand. In particular, the anomalous or abnormal auroras reveal even deeper layers of ignorance about one of nature's most spectacular manifestations.

To begin, auroras of uncommon form, such as those that paint the starlit sky with misty north-south bands (usually six in number), pose serious problems in explanation. Are there regularly spaced conduits in the upper atmosphere through which electrical currents flow? Also, how do some rare auroras approach the earth's surface, even to the point of engulfing observers in a luminous mist? Conventional wisdom has it that all auroras weave their luminous magic well above 100 km. altitude. The abundant records of auroral "fogs," crackling and hissing sounds, and the acrid odor of ozone detected during exceptionally energetic auroral displays demonstrate that some auroras may record the slow discharge of terrestrial electricity to the upper atmosphere. It is as if a temporary hole had been punched in the earth's protective magnetic field and had short-circuited the earth to the solar system's dynamo, the sun. There are also puzzling observations linking auroras to daytime cloud formations—to thunderstorms, earthquakes, and mountaintop glows. That the earth is electrically active cannot be denied—it is a part of an enveloping cosmos seething with energy.

Auroras, although frequently strange and inexplicable, are accepted denizens of the night skies, but there exist even stranger luminous displays that may or may not be related to auroras. What could cause an electric-blue, all-sky flash or expanding ghostly bubbles of pale light many times the size of the moon? What could cause the entire sky to glow so brightly that the finest newsprint can be read outdoors at midnight? For want of a better category, such phenomena are included with anomalous auroras.

NARROW SKY-SPANNING AURORAL ARCHES

August 21, 1903, Cranberry Lake, New York: Frederick Campbell relates how he was camping in the Adirondack wilderness, when "at half past nine, I was suddenly summoned out of doors to witness a spectacle such as I had never looked upon before nor had ever heard or read of. The heavens were spanned by two great bows of light, crossing each other near the zenith by a wide angle. The one was the familiar Milky Way, or Galaxy, then in its glory, no moon being present. The other was a remarkable archway of light, comparable with the Galaxy in width, but much brighter, and seemingly, stretching from horizon to horizon" (*Pop-*

ular Astronomy, 11: 484, 1903). Well-formed auroral arches are rare in the temperate zone. Exceedingly well-defined and bright arches, often with waves propagating along the arch, may be created by temporary magnetically focused rings of electric current circling the globe.

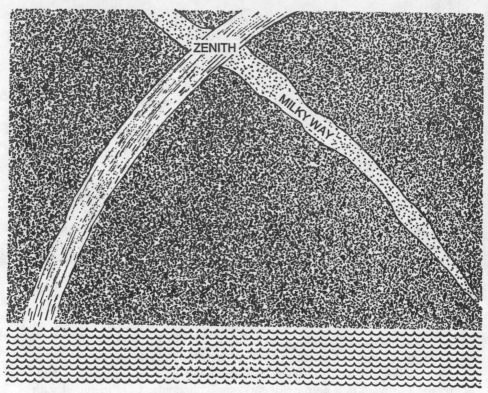

Arch of auroral light crossing the Milky Way

SEARCHLIGHT-LIKE SHAFTS OF LIGHT ON THE HORIZON (AURORAL PILLARS)

Today, when one sees a shaft of light in the sky, one automatically identifies it as an advertising gimmick. Fifty years ago, only nature lit up the skies in this fashion. Just how nature fashions an auroral pillar is a mystery. Probably electrically charged particles in the upper atmosphere form a partial ring around the earth or are somehow short-circuited to earth. Captain William Noble, an English astronomer, relates in his observation of August 28, 1883: "I was just coming out of my observatory when, on the ENE. point of the horizon beneath the Pleiades, I saw a bright light. My first thought was that the moon was rising, but an instant's reflection sufficed to remind me that she would not be up for the next two hours. As I watched the light becoming brighter and brighter, I saw that it threw a kind of radial illumination upward" (*Knowledge*, 4: 173, 1883). Captain Noble appended a sketch to his report that showed the typical searchlight beam structure of this variety of auroral pillar.

On May 8, 1837, R. H. Bonnycastle was startled to observe an intense, parallel-sided pillar of light rising up from the Bay of Toronto. Bonnycastle was looking east across the Bay and realized that the apparition might be a moon pillar caused by light from the rising moon reflected off ice crystals in the atmosphere. He checked this possibility and found that the moon had risen hours earlier (*American Journal of Science*, 1: 32: 393, 1837). This was likely an auroral pillar or incomplete auroral arch.

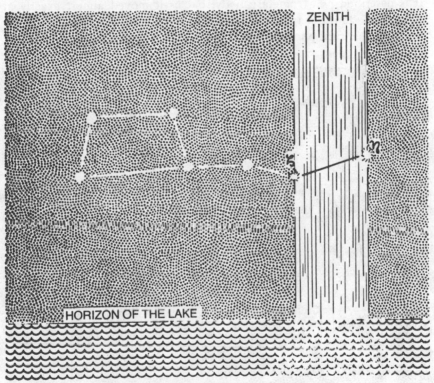

A *straight-sided auroral beam or auroral pillar*

MOVING PATCHES OF LIGHT (AURORAL METEORS)

November 17, 1882: A spectacular, torpedo-shaped cloud of whitish light swept across the skies of northern Europe. For several months thereafter, considerable debate as to the nature of this startling luminous wave appeared in the scientific literature. Many scientists termed it an auroral "meteor," for it cruised purposefully across the sky like a large meteor. One observer described it thus; "a cloud of whitish light, shaped like a torpedo, passed from the southeastern to the northwestern horizon. . . . It was of nearly uniform brightness. Its length was nearly ninety degrees. . . . It passed across the heavens in about two minutes. It is described as a cometary body, but as it moved almost exactly at right-angles to the magnetic meridian, there can be very little doubt that it was an electrical phenomenon" (*Knowledge*, 2: 419, 1882).

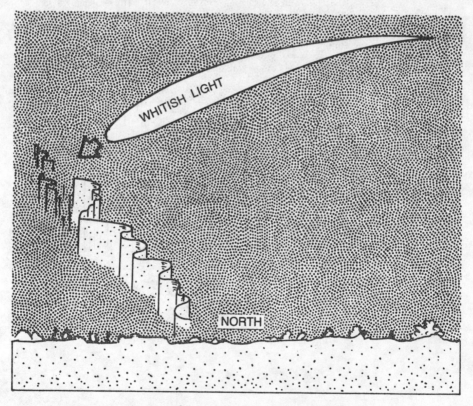

An auroral "meteor" drifting across the sky

A more bizarre version of this type of phenomenon was seen from Cincinnati in 1849. "A bright streak of light shot suddenly up from the verge of the horizon, and after attaining an altitude of about 45°, burst asunder, and spread over the whole surface of the heavens, making everything for an instant plainly visible. It was followed by five other bursts of light, all of equal splendor, and rising from near the same place" (*Scientific American*, 4: 193, 1849).

Very likely the auroral meteors are disturbances moving through the upper atmosphere and causing it to glow rather than true meteors of rock and metal. Gusts of solar wind are suspect, as are moving atmospheric disturbances called gravity waves. Alan W. Peterson has recently photographed in the night skies over Arizona several drifting luminosities that resemble the 1882 phenomenon (*Applied Optics*, 18: 3390–93, 1979).

AURORAS WITH INEXPLICABLE (AND IMPROBABLE) APPENDAGES

Nature really indulges her taste for the macabre when she begins decorating the standard auroral arches and streaks with bobbing spheres and triangles. There is nothing in auroral theory that explains the following two observations—except to say they are "vagaries."

September 12, 1881: A passenger on the steamship *Atlantic* off the Newfoundland coast was watching a normal aurora in the north when he spied two hazy streaks in the southeast with remarkable appendages. "From the upper streak were suspended, by small cords of light, a number of balls, brighter than either of the streaks, which were continually jumping up and down in vertical lines, much like pith balls when charged with electricity" (*Nature*, 26: 160–61, 1882).

August 21, 1903: "The spectacle seemed almost to overstep the modesty of nature," wrote A. F. A. King about the aurora he observed from York Harbor, Maine. To the north a magnificent auroral arch framed a more conventional display of auroral streaks. Along this arch "there appeared what might easily be likened to a string of tremendous comets. These pennants of light, however—unlike comets—were more brilliant at their bases, less at their apices. . . . They were constantly changing, appearing and disappearing, but not very rapidly. . . . Surprise, delight, admiration, and awe—these were the feelings that thrilled with pleasure those of us who witnessed the sublime and mysterious scene—a scene that few of us will ever see again" (*Popular Science Monthly*, 63: 563, 1903).

AURORAS THAT PENETRATE CLOSE TO THE EARTH'S SURFACE

On some cold, crystalline Arctic nights, the blazing auroral light seems to press closer and closer to the endless tracts of ice and snow. Many explorers tell tales of low auroras, even of being enveloped in a sea of ethereal white fog. Impossible, say most scientists—auroras never descend below 50 km. height and are usually hundreds of kilometers above the surface. Nevertheless some testimony is emphatic that a few rare auroras do reach down to the surface, seeming to make some sort of electrical contact by precipitating the electricity introduced into our atmosphere by the sun. In some respects the low auroras resemble the mountaintop glows with their soft luminescence and beams of light. Both may be diffuse exchanges of electricity between the earth and the upper atmosphere.

In 1901 while exploring Alaska, J. Halvor Johnson observed "an un-

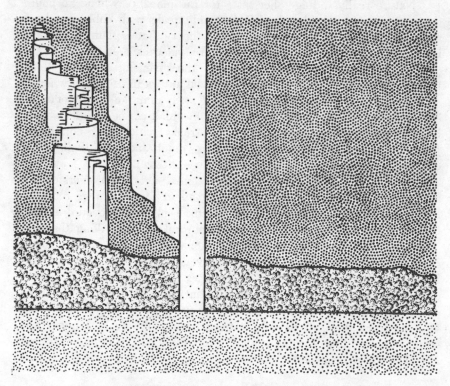

An aurora penetrates close to the earth's surface in Alaska.

mistakably low aurora, which was visible between himself and a mountain about half a mile distant, rising to about 1,200 feet above his own level. Moreover, on this and but one other occasion he heard sounds accompanying the aurora" (*Nature,* 127: 341, 1931).

In the winter of 1917–18, members of a government radio station encamped in the Arctic "were enveloped in a light mist or fog-like substance in the aurora; a hand extended could be seen as if in a coloured fog and a kaleidoscope of colors was visible between the hand and the body. It was impossible to feel this visible fog or mist, and there was no dampness. By stooping close to the ground it was possible to see under this light which did not go below four feet from the ground" (*Nature,* 127: 342, 1931). This and the preceding observation were used by the pioneer geophysicist, S. Chapman, to demonstrate the reality of low auroras.

But low auroras are not confined to the Arctic wastelands. During the winter of 1908–9, Floyd C. Kelley, then attending Trinity College in Hartford, Connecticut, observed "a magnificent aurora. The light effects gave me the impression that the atmosphere was filled with fog and someone was illuminating it by playing a searchlight back and forth. The effect was very striking because the display was so close to the ground that I seemed to walk right through the illuminated fog" (*Nature,* 133: 218, 1934). Kelley also heard swishing sounds that kept time with the flickerings of the aurora.

MAN-MADE AURORAS

During the last century the electrical nature of the aurora was questioned. To demonstrate that electricity (still regarded as a rather mysterious "fluid") was involved, Selim Lemstrom, a Scandinavian scientist, tried to lure an aurora down to a mountaintop in Lapland. He strung several miles of wire atop posts set on the summit of a small mountain. A luminous shaft rose over the mountain whenever a strong natural aurora prevailed (*Science,* 4: 465, 1884). In essence, Lemstrom apparently created a low-level aurora by helping nature complete an electrical circuit between earth and the upper atmosphere.

In March 1976 an equivalent experiment was performed with rockets high above Alaska. By releasing metallic barium at high altitudes, scientists extended the range of an existing aurora. "An effect which appeared to be a pulsating aurora was observed to be associated with explosive releases of barium vapor near 250-km. altitude, but only when the explosions were in the path of precipitating electrons associated with the visible aurora" (*Nature,* 267: 135, 1977).

NORTHERN LIGHTS IN THE SOUTHERN SKY

Auroras generally occur in a ring-shaped area close to the earth's magnetic poles. During particularly strong magnetic storms, caused by solar activity, this ring expands, and the incongruous sight of the aurora borealis may be seen toward the south by northern residents.

M. A. Veeder reported such a displaced aurora on March 30, 1894. Observing from Lyons, New York, the aurora "consisted of flickering, irregular patches which filled the entire heavens from [the] zenith down to the southern horizon, there being nothing whatever to be seen in the usual location of aurora toward the north. . . . Southward in Pennsylvania the entire sky was more or less covered with flickering patches and masses of light, and still further south the aurora was seen toward the north exclusively" (*American Meteorological Journal,* 11: 77, 1894).

DO AURORAS CAUSE THUNDERSTORMS OR VICE VERSA?

The thunderstorm is one of nature's mechanisms for relieving electrical imbalances between the earth and upper atmosphere. A giant storm may extend into the stratosphere, creating in effect an electrical conduit right down to the earth's surface. The observation of auroras above thunderstorm centers would bolster the suspicion that thunderstorms may be triggered in part by incursions of solar electricity into the atmosphere. Some thunderstorm statistics tend to support this surmise, but direct observations of thunderstorm auroras are scarce.

On February 4, 1893, J. Ewen Davidson reported an aurora apparently springing up from the top of a far-off thunderstorm near Queensland, in tropical Australia. "I was sitting on the lawn watching the distant flashes, when suddenly a patch of rosy light—5° to 6° in diameter—rose up from above the thunderstorm and mounted upwards, disappearing at an elevation of 40°–45°. There were about twenty to twenty-five of these patches in the course of half an hour; they took from one to two seconds to mount and were not associated with any particular flash. . . . There were also occasional streamers, sometimes bifurcated, of 2° in breadth, which shot up in the same way as the auroral streamers, which I have seen both in the arctic and antarctic zones" (*Nature,* 47: 582, 1893).

THE STRANGE RELATIONSHIP BETWEEN AURORAL STRUCTURES
AND DAYTIME CLOUDS

"The records of the great nineteenth-century Arctic expeditions contain many accounts of 'clouds' becoming aurorae after dark and aurorae becoming 'clouds' at dawn. Indeed, A. Paulsen regarded the presence of such clouds as an indicator of daylight aurorae; the opinion has also been expressed that the aurora is a material object; the clouds luminous by night and white by day; are an aerosol, formed in the ionosphere" (*British Astronomical Association, Journal*, 73: 234, 1963).

Ciceley M. Botley, an indefatigable researcher of old scientific reports, summarized the aurora-cloud connection in the preceding paragraph. Could the auroras have more substance to them than the glowing, rarefied gases stipulated by geophysicists? A curious bit of northern folklore claims that silken threads sometimes fall during intense auroral displays! Surely the auroras are not that substantial, but upper atmospheric disturbances could well create conditions conducive both to auroras and high-level clouds. Meteor trails in particular might seed the upper air with long columns of ionized particles that could serve as cloud condensation nuclei. Like the barium released from rockets, the meteor trails might also focus auroral activity.

PARALLEL LUMINOUS BANDS IN THE NIGHT SKY

Meteor trails are scattered too haphazardly to blame for the infrequent appearances of "banded sky." What natural force could coerce several meteors to pursue parallel courses across the whole firmament? Yet there must be some geometrically inclined cause-and-effect relationship at work because too many observers have seen these faintly luminous, ghostly patterns in the night sky. Here is a typical report from Cumberland, England, by W. B. Housman, dated September 9, 1932: "There was a very definite display of banded sky on this date. Irregular bands, fainter and narrower than the Galaxy, radiated from horizon points at [bearing] 50° and [bearing] 230°, but were almost entirely absent from W. area of the sky. About 6 bands were counted at 0030, the most conspicuous and broadest following closely the ecliptic" (*British Astronomical Association, Journal*, 44: 27, 1933). Six bands are often counted. No explanation can be offered for this improbable phenomena, but there might be some connection with the twilight bands and the aligned cirrus cloud bands described in Chapters 2 and 3.

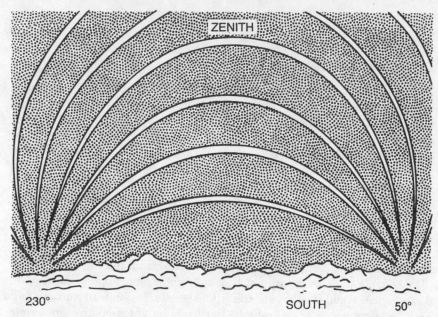

Two-dimensional representation of the banded-sky phenomenon

ABNORMALLY BRIGHT NIGHTS

Huddled in light-drenched cities and shielded by split-levels, people today can hardly be connoisseurs of the varying nighttime levels of weak natural illumination. Perhaps a few shepherds in remote areas are aware that some nights are brighter than others. Scientists have confirmed this phenomena with sensitive instruments and explain it in terms of varying levels of airglow. Airglow is caused in part by sunlight scattered around the curvature of the earth and the solar wind impacting the upper reaches of the atmosphere and causing air atoms to radiate light. But nocturnal airglow, although well-verified, is too feeble to account for the following spectacular observations.

Col. A. F. Wrotnowski was camped on a houseboat in the middle of a large lake in southeastern Florida in 1886. "I awoke a little before 3 A.M. and noticed that it was very light, and as there was no moon, got up and went out on the deck, and to my surprise saw everything illuminated with a pale greenish light so intense that we could read by it. . . . The illumination lasted fully an hour and gradually faded away to normal" (*Popular Astronomy*, 29: 448, 1921).

The English scientific journal *Nature* reviewed the major geophysical phenomena recorded in recent times in a weekly column during the early 1930s. Singled out was the nighttime luminosity that first appeared on January 7, 1831. "Owing to the presence of a kind of luminous mist, print could be read at midnight in Italy and Germany. The abnormally light nights continued for a considerable period" (*Nature*, 125: 33, 1930).

In the absence of any other obvious natural light source, abnormally bright nights must be ascribed to the airglow, possibly enhanced by charged particles emitted by a large solar flare. Some terrestrial events, however, have caused remarkable sky glows, although they were localized in the sky. The 1908 Tunguska Event (or Siberian meteor) and the 1883 eruption of Krakatoa were both associated with glowing skies.

LOCALIZED GLOWING AREAS IN THE NIGHT SKY

Having broached the subject of the 1908 Tunguska Event, let us see what *Nature* reported in its issue immediately following the Siberian cataclysm and well before news of the meteor reached the civilized world. "Brilliant sky glows were observed in many parts of the United Kingdom on the night of June 30 and on several succeeding nights, the phenomenon being apparently at its maximum intensity on the night of July 1. The whole of the northern part of the sky, from the horizon to an altitude of about 45°, and extending to the west, was suffused with a reddish hue, the colour varying from a pink to an Indian red, whilst to the eastward of north the colour was distinctly a pale green. No flickering or scintillation was observed on the reddened sky, nor was there any tendency to the formation of the streamers or luminous arch characteristic of the aurora. . . . A special feature of the phenomenon was the prolongation of twilight, extending almost to the following daybreak, and from the experience cited by many observers in various parts of Great Britain the light at midnight was sufficient to allow of fairly small print being read without any aid from artificial light" (*Nature*, July 9, 1908, and *Royal Meteorological Society, Quarterly Journal*, 34: 202, 1908). Current speculation attributes the Tunguska Event to a miniature comet. Whatever it was, it and possibly dust or gas accompanying it continued to affect a large portion of the earth's atmosphere days after the explosion in Siberia.

Most localized sky glows are never correlated with other phenomena and thus remain mysterious. The first of the following examples may be some unrecognized variety of auroral activity, but the second defies explanation.

On October 9, 1931, W. B. Housman, an English astronomer, reported that "a misty, white light filled the northern horizon, obliterating the Zodiacal Band limit on the northern side, and so intense that it almost obliterated the Galaxy itself, where it arched up on the northern side. The sky itself was cloudless and filled with stars which shone through this strange nebulosity. . . . It filled a great segment—perhaps a fifth of the sky" (*Journal of the British Astronomical Association*, 43: 48, 1932).

Mr. D. Nicholson, third officer of the M.V. *Sussex*, was on watch on October 13, 1951, as the vessel cruised 300 miles east of the Brazilian coast. "Between sunset at 1954 G.M.T. and 2040," he wrote, "a reddish glare spread from the western horizon until it covered the sky half-way to the zenith over an arc of 90°. The glare was reflected on the sea surface and combined with the silvery light from the moon gave an eerie effect which was most unusual" (*Marine Observer*, 22: 196, 1952). Post-sunset sky glows are often caused by volcanic dust in the upper atmosphere, but no eruptions were correlated with this event.

PATCHES OF LIGHT THAT MOVE AROUND THE HORIZON
(THE SO-CALLED WEATHER OR STORM LIGHTS)

Back before radio or TV weather forecasts, farmers and other weather-conscious people relied upon portents that seemed to verge on witchcraft. Clouds and wind were prominent indicators of future weather, as one might expect, but many claimed that lights on the horizon also told of severe weather on the way. Such luminous weather signs are summarily dismissed today; who could see them anyway amidst all the man-made sources of illumination? Objectively, though, active weather systems do penetrate far into the upper atmosphere and may stimulate airglow or weak auroral activity. A farmer of a century ago might well have seen such illumination hundreds of miles away.

Professor Cuthbert P. Conrad saw "weather lights" on the evening of February 26, 1884, at Fayetteville, Arkansas. A violent snowstorm followed the apparition. He wrote, "I have watched these 'weather lights' in this locality for four years. . . . The appearance is that of a rosy red to white light appearing above the horizon, 5°, 10°, and even 30°, and all the way from northeast around to the southwest . . . fading out and reappearing in the northwest, west, or southwest. These lights invariably precede a change in the weather—either rain or snow" (*American Meteorological Journal*, 1: 81, 1884).

Similar lights have been seen moving along the horizon in recent years in remote areas, but no attempt has been made to correlate such phenomena with weather changes. On October 8, 1954, G. S. Forbes was on watch aboard the S.S. *Perim* in the Arabian Sea en route to Aden. He described his experience this way: "Just after the sun had disappeared below the horizon, bright patches of light were seen to travel around the horizon in a clockwise direction. . . . Each wedge was seen to sink into the horizon and start again" (*Marine Observer*, 25: 213, 1955).

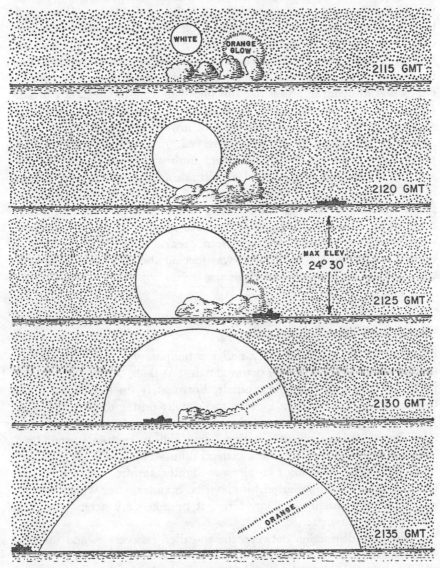

Ghostly white expanding disk observed at sea off the African coast

HUGE, GHOSTLY, EXPANDING DISKS OF LIGHT

Spacecraft launches beginning in the 1950s have added several new varieties of luminous phenomena. Weird lighting effects are often noted by the crews of ships plying the Atlantic off Cape Canaveral. As the hot gases from the rockets expand in the near-vacuum of the upper atmosphere, glowing areas blossom forth and are sometimes grotesquely deformed by winds. Spacecraft-linked phenomena should always be considered when studying sightings like this one seen from the deck of the S.S. *Osaka Bay* on June 22, 1976: "At 2113 GMT a pale orange glow was seen to be coming from behind a bank of towering cumulus to the west. At 2115 a ghostly white disk was observed. . . . At 2125 the disk had grown to such an extent that the lower limb was touching the horizon and the upper limb had reached an altitude of 24° 30′. . . . light from behind the cloud was becoming elongated, like a searchlight beam, as the disk sank. . . . By 2140 the disk had disappeared completely, but the beam of light was visible for a further five minutes . . ." (*Marine Observer*, 47: 66, 1977). Was this light from a rocket launch at Cape Canaveral? Possibly, but the *Osaka Bay* was just off the coast of Africa, several thousand miles away from Florida.

THE FALSE DAWN

Seafarers have occasionally noted a temporary brightening of the eastern sky a couple of hours before dawn, but their observations rarely find their way into scientific journals. Fortunately, meteorologist J. H. Cumming was driving from London to Torquay during the wee hours of January 7, 1933, and he recorded a modern observation of the elusive false dawn. "It became so light that I was able to see the surrounding countryside. . . . The light was a general diffused light with no apparent focal point, but I should say it was lighter toward the south and east. . . . this condition lasted for about 20 minutes, after which period, and about as suddenly as it appeared, it became dark again" (*Meteorological Magazine*, 71: 189, 1936).

The only distinction between the so-called false dawn and the all-sky glows mentioned earlier is that the former seems to appear regularly about two hours before the real dawn. So few reliable observations exist to confirm this purported schedule that the false dawn should perhaps be left to sailors' tales and an occasional poet.

ALL-SKY LIGHT FLASHES

In contrast to the weakly confirmed false dawn, many well-verified observations of sudden flashes of light covering the entire sky exist. Such phenomena vary from a brilliant, electric-blue flash to a flickering purple one. Some unknown agency trips a planet-sized "flash cube," releasing considerable luminous energy.

Astronomers at a Smithsonian-affiliated observatory in India described the extraordinary sky brightening of June 9, 1970: "The total local sky suddenly brightened up to an intensity comparable to that of the Milky Way during these summer months" (James Cornell and John Surowiecki, *The Pulse of the Planet*, New York, 1972, p. 73). The most spectacular recent observations of this incredible phenomenon were made in western Alaska on May 15, 1972. "The sky suddenly brightened to what eyewitnesses call daylight intensity, remaining illuminated for approximately two seconds. . . . It appeared suddenly, 'like a flashbulb,' changing in color from bluish through green to white, fading to orange or reddish. . . . Two observers claim to have seen two closely spaced flashes" (*Sky and Telescope*, 44: 19, 1972).

The prime candidate for a natural flashbulb is a large meteor. A big chunk of space debris flashing into incandescence above a cloud layer would certainly bathe the entire countryside in a bright light. But the brightenings detailed above took place under clear skies when a meteor (and usually its long-enduring trail) could hardly be missed by laymen, much less by trained observers. Nuclear atmospheric tests might do the job, but they too would be readily correlated with the event. Possibly a blast of solar wind slamming into the upper atmosphere would suffice; but to be honest the real stimulus or energy source for all-sky flashes has not been found.

Ball Lightning

Thousands of people have seen ball lightning, and hundreds of scientists have written about it. Nevertheless it remains as inscrutable as ever. Science admits the objective reality of these strange, mobile globes of light, but has been unsuccessful at explaining their origin or their explosive demise.

One reason ball lightning resists explanation is that its nature is so variable. It may be as small as a pea or as large as a house. It may be violet, red, or yellow, or may even change colors during its brief life. The shape of ball lightning is usually spherical, but rods, dumbbells, spiked balls, and other shapes have been sighted. Sometimes ball lightning appears to have internal structure; strange appendages may accompany the main body of the phenomenon.

Ball lightning is a dynamic thing. It may glide silently and disinterestedly past an observer or it may inquisitively explore a room as if directed by intelligence. While many of these enigmatic apparitions dematerialize silently, most seem to explode violently. One has to hedge about the location of the sound because the actual explosions sometimes seem to occur elsewhere—outside the house in which the ball has appeared, for example. This observation, plus the frequent materialization of ball lightning in closed rooms and metal aircraft, suggests that the process of electrical induction may be involved in some cases. In other words, electrical forces from an enveloping thunderstorm may create a glowing ball of plasma in the air inside a closed container similar to the St. Elmo's fire induced on pointed objects. When the electrical forces disappear (usually with a peal of thunder), the ball lightning vanishes. Observers, however, have no doubt that something palpable has visited them because the room is usually filled with the smell of electricity (ozone) and there may be considerable material damage.

Strangely, ball lightning rarely hurts people seriously, even though it may follow and hover around them. Ordinary lightning in contrast kills many. This may be a misleading observation because ordinary lightning is much more common than ball lightning.

There is no such thing as a standard description of ball lightning. If pressed for such information, one would have to say that most ball lightning is spherical, yellowish (perhaps with a fringe or hazy halo), and exists for only five to ten seconds, disappearing with a detonation. But this description glosses over the incredible scope of this phenomenon, as detailed in the following eyewitness accounts.

No reasonable explanation exists for ball lightning. Glowing spheres of plasma created by natural electromagnetic forces have been proposed and found wanting. Others have suggested antimatter meteorites, violent chemical reactions in the atmosphere, and even intense cosmic radiation. The sheer difficulty in accounting for ball lightning has led some scientists to claim that all such observations are illusory—aberrations of the eye and brain. But photographs of ball lightning do exist and we must come to terms with the reality of this phenomenon. Perhaps the intense electrical forces occurring during some thunderstorms somehow distort our space-time continuum and provide a fleeting glimpse into some unknown cosmos. Ball lightning is strange enough to stimulate such wild thoughts.

"ORDINARY" BALL LIGHTNING

Although no ball lightning is really "ordinary," it is best to begin with some less bizarre cases. On November 10, 1940, E. Matts reported a fair-weather instance of ball lightning from England: "I was working at the far end of my garden; the weather was normal, no rain, no signs of thunder. Suddenly I seemed to be in the centre of intense blackness and looking down [I] observed at my feet a ball about 2 ft. across. It was of a pale blue-green colour and seemed made of a mass of writhing strings of light, about 1/4 in. in diameter. It remained there for about 3 seconds and then rose, away from me, just missing a poplar tree about 3 ft. away. It cleared the houses by about 20 ft. and landed at the rear of the *Weavers Arms* on the Bell Green Road, a distance of about 1/4 mile. There was a loud explosion and much damage was done to the public house" (*Weather*, 19: 228, 1964).

R. Clark was walking along a road in West Yorkshire, England, when he was overtaken by a thunderstorm. "After one lightning discharge there appeared a ball of light, 'electric' blue in the centre with an ill-defined yellow fringe, the whole being about 18 in. in diameter. It first appeared from beneath the tree branches on my side of the road, perhaps 20 yards away, and approached slowly with a staggering, undulating motion, but keeping approximately to the same height under the trees. As it approached me, it crossed the road gradually and then, when almost opposite me, turned back across the road and slightly backward, passed through the lodge gates where I lost sight of it" (*Weather*, 20: 134, 1965).

On August 8, 1975, the following display occurred in England during a vigorous thunderstorm: "The witness was [in] the kitchen of her house in Smethwick, Warley, at about 1945, when a sphere of light appeared over the cooker. The ball was $\cong 10$ cm. across and surrounded by a flame-coloured halo; its colour was bright blue to purple. The ball moved straight towards the witness at an estimated height of 95 cm. from the ground. Burning heat was felt, and there was a singeing smell. A sound something like a rattle was heard. . . . 'The ball seemed to hit me below the belt, as it were, and I automatically brushed it away from me and it just disappeared. Where I brushed it away there appeared a redness and swelling on my left hand. It seemed as if my gold wedding ring was burning into my finger.'" A hole 4 by 11 cm. was made in the woman's dress, but without charred edges (*Nature*, 260: 596, 1976).

Ball lightning with stringlike surface materializes in an English garden.

BALL LIGHTNING WITH PROJECTING RAYS

The inclination of some theorists is to explain ball lightning as a hot ball of plasma (i.e., a mixture of ions and electrons) that retains its spherical shape due to confining electromagnetic fields—a sort of globular magnetic bottle. At the very best, these magnetic bottles (assuming this explanation is on the right track) are very leaky. The numerous sightings of spiked ball lightning underscore this, as do the following examples of balls surrounded by projecting rays.

Mary Ethel Hunneman was sitting on a second-story, glassed-in porch watching a thunderstorm at Fitzwilliam, New Hampshire, on August 10, 1937. "Coincident with a crash of thunder, the fireball appeared. . . . It just came out of space and seemed to move directly toward the window and then fell as though to enter the cellar of the house. It was a round, bronze, glistening ball with gleaming rays shooting from the top and sides; by its beauty and brilliance reminding one of an ornament at the top of a Christmas tree" (*Science*, 86: 244, 1937).

Even stranger was a deformed ball described by R. J. Davis, who witnessed the display in 1920 in Johannesburg. "I observed a ball of lightning rolling slowly up an incline about 50 cm. (20 inches) above and parallel to the sloping ground. This ball of light was about 50 cm. in diameter with irregular saw-tooth streaks of light around it, and had a comet-like tail. The ball continued until it met a dry-stone terrace wall, when it exploded in a flash of flame leaving an acrid smell" (*Journal of Meteorology, U.K.*, 2: 290, 1977).

ROD-SHAPED LIGHTNING: A PARTICULARLY VIOLENT SUBSPECIES OF BALL LIGHTNING

Ball lightning frequently explodes violently upon disappearing, and in so doing it may sometimes cause extensive damage. The rod-shaped

Rod-type ball lightning materializes in the sky over Burlington, Vermont.

variety, however, always seems to detonate with considerable violence. In 1907 William H. Alexander was standing on the corner of Church and College streets in Burlington, Vermont, engaged in conversation with two other gentlemen. The trio was startled by a tremendous explosion. "Raising my eyes and looking eastward along College Street, I observed a torpedo-shaped body some 300 feet away, stationary in appearance and suspended in the air about 50 feet above the tops of the buildings. In size, it was about 6 feet long by 8 inches in diameter, the shell or cover having a dark appearance, with here and there tongues of fire issuing from spots on the surface resembling red-hot unburnished copper. . . . When first seen it was surrounded by a halo of dim light, some 20 feet in diameter" (*Monthly Weather Review*, 36: 310, 1907).

MINIATURE BALL LIGHTNING (SMALLER THAN ONE INCH)

In contrast to the rather malevolent-appearing rod form of ball lightning, the pea-sized variety is benign. In fact, these tiny glowing spheres seem almost playful, materializing mysteriously inside closed rooms and resembling some sort of electrostatic parlor trick. Evidently, miniature ball lightning is some sort of electrical induction phenomenon—i.e., intense electrical fields generated by outside storms create (in some unexplained way) small globes of ionized air. Two of these curious manifestations are reported in the following paragraphs. The reader should compare them to typical St. Elmo's fire phenomena in the next section.

Two English ladies were sitting at a table during a rainstorm with the window open. "As one of the ladies took up a knife to cut bread, the ball of light was seen to flash past the knife (without touching it) on to the table, travelling a distance of about 9 in. at an average height of about 3 in. from the table. . . . When the ball touched the tablecloth, it 'went out with a spitting sound,' leaving no mark or trace of any sort. . . . As to the appearance of the ball itself, it was 'about the size of a pea, the light encircling it being about the size of a golf ball. The light was intensely bright, like electricity. Too dazzling to see through'" (*Nature*, 109: 106, 1922).

W. J. Humphreys, a meteorologist fascinated by ball lightning, reported this example from America: "Mrs. Ames was standing on a rug during a thunderstorm with her hand at her waist, one finger more or less extended. I was about five feet away and noticed the air between her finger and the floor was quivering so that it looked just like the hot air over a field. I noticed something rise slowly from the floor up towards her finger, and then there was for an instant a small oblong fireball about the size of a pecan attached to her finger. It was not very bright and ap-

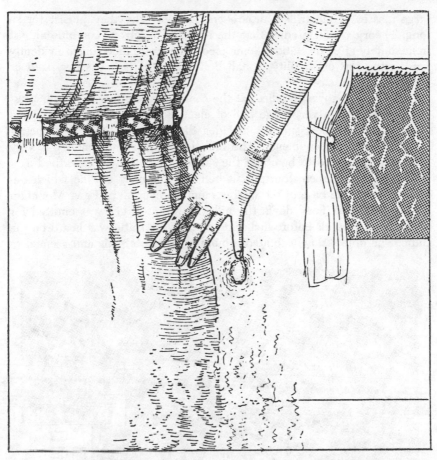

Miniature ball lightning attached to a woman's finger

peared to shine through a haze. There came a flood of lightning outside, and then the fireball disappeared" (*American Philosophical Society, Proceedings,* 76: 613, 1936).

GIANT BALL LIGHTNING (LARGER THAN FIVE FEET)

At the large end of the size spectrum, ball lightning seems to merge with electric induction displays, such as the "electric bath" an observer once experienced in Yellowstone Park (see the next section). But like miniature ball lightning, the macroscopic variety seems harmless, being little more than a floating cloud of electrified air. Scientifically, giant ball lightning cannot be dismissed so lightly, for we do not know how such large masses of electrified air are created nor why they persist for so long. Theory would predict that the ions and electrons combine almost immediately after formation. Some electromagnetic mechanism evidently lends some sort of stability to ball lightning, whether it is pea-sized or the size of a house.

On June 8, 1977, an officer at the coastguard station at Dyfed, West Wales, observed a very large ball of electrified air. Note that the radio static and bounciness support the idea that the large balls are electrostatic induction phenomena. "The ball lightning phenomenon was very large and estimated to be about the size of a bus. It was described as a brilliant, yellow-green, transparent ball with a fuzzy outline which descended from the base of a towering cumulus over Garn Fawr Mountain and appeared to 'float' down the hillside. Intense light was emitted for about three seconds before flickering out. Severe static was heard on the radio. The object slowly rotated around a horizontal axis and seemed to

Large luminous sphere materializes during an intense thunderstorm.

'bounce' off projections on the ground. It was noticed that cattle and seabirds in the immediate vicinity became disturbed" (*Journal of Meteorology, U.K.,* 2: 271, 1977).

On July 5, 1975, near Albany, New York, S. Colucci made these observations during an intense thunderstorm from an observatory atop a 200-ft. building. "Over a three-second interval, four distinct lightning strokes, each following the same path, hit the building, and during this time an unmistakable fireball was seen near the ground an estimated 5 meters [16 ft.] to the west of the point of impact of the lightning stroke. The ball was very bright, fuzzy in appearance, equal in brightness to the lightning stroke, and orange-yellow in color. Apparently, the ball was quite large, its size estimated to be approximately 5 meters [16 ft.] in diameter." The ball appeared during the first of the four strokes and vanished after the last, remaining bright and steady during the period (*Weather,* 31: 68, 1976).

BALL LIGHTNING THAT MATERIALIZES INSIDE ENCLOSURES

One of the spookiest aspects of ball lightning is its ability to materialize inside rooms, even in all-metal aircraft, often with no evidence of penetration anywhere. This characteristic alone suggests that some, if not all, manifestations of ball lightning are induction phenomena, for electromagnetic lines of force can penetrate enclosures, just as TV and radio signals do. Once again though, scientists are stymied when it comes to explaining the stability of the ball and its strange antics.

One of the more curious incidents occurred on August 25, 1965, in Dunnellon, Florida. Mr. and Mrs. Robert B. Greenlee and a Mrs. Riggs were relaxing on their fiberglass-screened, roofed patio. There was thunder in the distance and a slight drizzle. "Mrs. Greenlee had just swatted a fly when a ball of lightning the size of a basketball appeared immediately in front of her. The ball was later described as being of a color and brightness comparable to the flash seen in arc welding, with a fuzzy appearance around the edges. Mrs. Riggs did not see the ball itself, but saw the flyswatter 'edged in fire' dropping on the floor. The movement of the ball to the floor was accompanied by a report 'like a shotgun blast.' . . . with respect to the fly, Mrs. Riggs commented, "You sure got him that time" (*Science,* 151: 634, 1966).

R. C. Jennison, a British scientist, was flying Eastern Airlines en route from New York to Washington during an electrical storm on March 19, 1963. The aircraft was "enveloped in a sudden bright and loud electrical discharge. . . . Some seconds after this a glowing sphere a little more than 20 cm. [8 in.] in diameter emerged from the pilot's cabin and passed down the aisle of the aircraft approximately 50 cm. [20 in.] from me, maintaining the same height and course for the whole distance over which it could be observed." The ball seemed to move at about 1.5 meters [5 ft.] per second (*Nature,* 224: 895, 1969).

FIREBALLS THAT SEEM TO RISE FROM THE SEA

Electrical phenomena often visit ships at sea because they are essentially sharp projections on an otherwise featureless surface—almost like lightning rods—and a magnet for electrical activity. St. Elmo's fire frequently decorates the masts and spars, and many ball-lightning reports come from ship's logs. One odd type of ball lightning has been reported several times at sea. This type seems to rise right out of the water and to ascend into the atmosphere. Generally ball lightning descends from clouds or simply materializes. Most reports of sea-born ball lightning are ancient. UFO investigators often list them as examples of extraterrestrial vehicles' leaving some secret undersea base for the outer cosmos. However, the two classic cases cited below display nothing beyond the "ordinary" capabilities of ball lightning.

On November 12, 1887, in the North Atlantic off Cape Race, "a large ball of fire seemed to rise out of the sea to a height of about 50 feet, coming against the wind close up to the ship, and then running away to the southeast, lasting altogether about five minutes" (*Nature,* 37: 187, 1887).

In 1845, from the brig *Victoria* in the Mediterranean: ". . . without any appearance of bad weather; her topgallant and royal masts suddenly went over the side, as if carried away by a sudden squall; and two hours after, it blew very hard from the south and east, but suddenly again fell calm, with an overpowering stench of sulphur and an unbearable heat. At this moment three luminous bodies were seen to issue from the sea at a distance of about half a mile from the vessel, which remained visible for about 10 minutes . . ." (*Reports of the British Association for the Advancement of Science,* 1861, p. 30).

BALL LIGHTNING WITH UNUSUAL SHAPES

The preceding cases of ball lightning definitely place this phenomenon in the "strange" category. But the strangest is yet to come. Up to this point, admittedly with some stretching of the laws of electromagnetism, ball lightning seemed almost within our ken—almost a phenomenon science could handle. But here are three bizarre cases, selected from many, that place the total phenomenon beyond the pale of reason. Here we verge on the real unknown territory. No UFO sighting could be stranger. These are in fact UFO's with ball-lightning tendencies. The first is reported in a recent reputable scientific journal, the latter two from about a century ago when reports of UFO's were nonexistent.

On August 15, 1975, Miss M. E. MacArthur witnessed an incredible species of ball lightning outside her home in Argyllshire, Scotland. The shape of the lightning, especially the tail, is the critical element in this observation. "I call it a bulb of lightning, it was opaque; it may or may not have been lit inside. It would be 9 inches in length, slim, dome-shaped. I saw it from my chair as the fire come down in front of the kitchen window; it did not touch the ground; it hovered about 9 inches above. . . . Attached to the bulb was a long white crinkly tail, not an unearthly white, 1 yard or more in length, 1 inch or slightly more in width. It was like the old-fashioned watered silk ribbon we used to buy in the draper's shop. The tail kept to the end of the bulb, also kept slightly higher; it did not fall down as a ribbon would have done. Bulb and tail snuffed out like a candle, leaving no trace. That was the end of the thunderstorm" (*Journal of Meteorology, U.K.,* 1: 310, 1976).

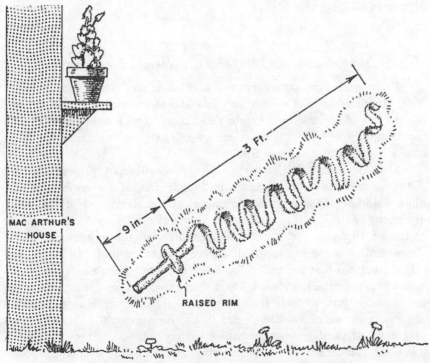

Ball lightning with a curious ribbon attached

On January 31, 1882, near Zurich, Switzerland, ". . . a noise was first heard; then one saw a snow-white lump floating in the air, apparently hardly 50 metres (166 feet) above the ground; a thin sulphur-yellow strip then branched northwestwards, but presently contracted again into [a] ball shape, the whole suddenly disappearing with a play of red, white, and green colour" (*English Mechanic*, 35: 32, 1882).

November 30, 1872: T. L. M. Cartwright of Banbury, England, was leaving his house about five minutes after a vivid flash of lightning and peculiar rolling thunder. "My gardener called me to come quickly and see the ball of fire. I was unfortunately half a minute too late, but I have seen four persons who saw it from different points and who all agree they heard a whizzing, roaring sound like a passing train, which attracted their attention, and then saw a huge revolving ball of fire travelling from 6 ft. to 10 ft. off the ground. The smoke was whizzing around and rising high in the air, and a blast of wind accompanied it, carrying a cloud of branches along and destroying everything in its way. The havoc done is very considerable—large trees bodily uprooted, others broken off about 10 ft. from the ground. . . ." The "ball" was attended by a sulphurous odor and ultimately seemed to vanish without a sound (*English Mechanic*, 16: 309, 1872).

Slow, Luminous Discharges of Natural Electricity

Everyone is familiar with *fast* discharges of electricity, such as lightning. More rare are the *slow* flows of natural electrical currents. In these, the passage of electricity is gentle and almost soundless in contrast with the thunderbolt. Nevertheless, the slow-discharge phenomena are often luminous and strangely beautiful.

Slow electrical discharges usually proceed from projections and sharp points, such as ships' masts, radio antennas, and even fingers held aloft. Pointlike structures concentrate electrical fields and, if the fields are strong enough, will permit a weak flow of electricity from the point to the air. In damp and stormy weather, high-voltage power lines sometimes exhibit eerie luminous discharge effects around insulators and other structures that are called "corona discharges" because of the bluish glows that are usually present. The natural analogue of corona discharge is St. Elmo's fire. Reports from ships at sea and mountaintop scientific observatories tell of St. Elmo's fire in the form of cold lambent flames and auras streaming from instruments, guy wires, and even people's heads. St. Elmo's fire also appears infrequently in snowstorms and sandstorms as the falling and blowing particles transfer electricity between earth and air like the omnipresent Wimshurst electrostatic machines in high school physics labs.

Corona discharges and St. Elmo's fire are not particularly mysterious to physicists; they, therefore, constitute a good starting point for a journey into more controversial territory.

The next stop is a truly spectacular one: the so-called Andes glow or, more generally, the mountaintop glow. Since many mountains pierce the atmosphere with sharp projecting surfaces, the appearance of slow electrical discharges from their peaks is not especially surprising. It is the scale of the process that is awe-inspiring: the sheets of flame and aurora-like beams of light projecting into the stratosphere may be visible for hundreds of miles. Where does this mountain electricity go? To outer space? And why are the mountaintop glows often enhanced during major earthquakes? No one has really studied this phenomenon.

On a smaller, less violent scale, intense electrical storms may create patches or waves of luminous electrical activity that engulf humans in their paths, electrically shocking them or wrapping them in a garment of St. Elmo's fire. In some ways these surface displays resemble the luminous marine displays, such as the phosphorescent wheel described later in this chapter.

Much more mysterious are the glowing enigmatic toy-balloon–like spheres that seem unrelated to ball lightning. These floating, cavorting bubbles may not even be electrical in origin. Whatever they are, modern science has paid little attention to them—perhaps because providing an explanation is so difficult.

Earthquake lights are seen on occasion near quake focal points and may take the form of auroras, mountaintop glows, and ball lightning. Recent scientific observations indicate that earthquake shock waves can be transmitted by the atmosphere up into the ionosphere. These atmospheric disturbances may help create low-conductivity paths for earth-space electrical discharges. The ball lightning, the sheets of flame issuing from the ground, and other localized luminous phenomena may be generated by large-scale piezoelectric effects (i.e., the generation of electricity by stresses on crystals such as quartz). An alternative explanation of earthquake lights involves the spontaneous ignition of natural gas liberated by movements of the earth's crust.

Violent volcanos and tornados also display unusual lights. Normal lightning and ball lightning are to be expected in violent storms, but what is the origin of the peculiar shafts of light in tornado funnels and the strange glowing patches in and above the storm clouds? The precise role of electricity in tornado action, if any, is highly controversial. Superficially at least, the long shafts of light seen in the cores of some tornados resemble huge fluorescent lights and may actually arise from the much larger-scale glow discharge of electricity in these naturally formed tubes.

The earth is a gigantic electrical machine. The constant turmoil of the atmosphere, its bombardment by the solar wind, the intense forces squeezing its surface rocks—all conspire to create a wide spectrum of curious and poorly understood luminous effects.

ST. ELMO'S FIRE: A FAMILIAR DISCHARGE PHENOMENON

Shakespeare wrote about it. Melville had Captain Ahab tame it in *Moby Dick*. The soft, glowing plumes and jets of corona discharge have fascinated humans from time immemorial. Superstitious dread of St. Elmo's fire has subsided as science has learned about the flow of electricity from sharp projections into the atmosphere, particularly during

St. Elmo's fire adorns a man on top of Pike's Peak

stormy weather. The first situation described below is the typical manifestation of St. Elmo's fire. One cannot avoid associating St. Elmo's fire
with the mountaintop glow described a few pages later on. St. Elmo's fire
is simply a miniature variant of the Andes glow.

Sergeant L. M. Dey, signal officer at the summit of Pike's Peak,
wrote the editor of *Scientific American* in 1882 about the fascinating
effects of electric discharge at high altitudes. The weather station equipment was covered with "brushes" of light. "In placing my hands over the
revolving cups of the anemometer [wind gauge]—where the electrical
excitement was abundant—not the slightest sensation of heat was discovered, but my hands instantly became aflame. On raising them and
spreading my fingers, each of them became tipped with one or more
beautiful cones of light, nearly three inches in length. The flames issued
from my fingers with a rushing noise . . . accompanied by a crackling
sound. There was a feeling as of a current of vapor escaping, with a
slight tingling sensation. The wristband of my woolen shirt, as soon as it
became dampened, formed a fiery ring around my arm, while my mus-
tache was lighted up so as to make a veritable lantern of my face"
(*Scientific American*, 47: 16, 1882).

During a powerful thunderstorm in France during 1879, a whole
forest was lit up with corona discharge (also called brush discharge).
"The sun was hidden and the country covered with thick darkness. At
this moment the pine forest round St. Cergues was suddenly illuminated
and shone with a light bearing a striking resemblance to the phosphorescence of the sea as seen in the tropics. The light disappeared with
every clap of thunder, but only to reappear with increased intensity until
the subsidence of the tempest" (*English Mechanic*, 29: 622, 1879).

A German farmer driving along a narrow road on May 14, 1896, encountered a remarkable instance of St. Elmo's fire. While driving along a
section of road with a wire fence on each side, ". . . his attention was attracted by a bright light behind him. On looking around he saw fire balls
about the size of a man's hand travelling towards him along the wire on
both sides. In a moment they were abreast of the carriage, and then
travelled along with it *pari passu*, while brush discharges and audible
crackling, as from a large electric machine, were observed to proceed
from the fireballs towards, apparently, the iron parts of the carriage. Vibrations of the wires could be distinctly heard, and a torrent of sparks
sprang over from the fences to the carriage and horses. The frightened
horses now ran away, but they could not shake off their fiery escort till
the fences were interrupted by gaps on each side" (*Royal Meteorological
Society, Quarterly Journal*, 22: 295, 1896).

*Luminous electrified spheres race along fence wires to pace
horse-and-carriage.*

HOW BLOWING SNOW AND SAND CREATE ELECTRICAL DISCHARGE EFFECTS

March 3, 1964, Tucson, Arizona: During an unusual (for this locale)
snowstorm, as observed from an 80-ft.-high building, "short flashes of
'lightning' were seen to be occurring at intervals estimated to be about
15–20 seconds and at random places around the town. The flashes continued throughout the storm, until the snow ceased at about 11:30 P.M. . . .
The flashes of 'lightning' contained several unusual features: They appeared to be single, short flashes of light without the 'flicker' normally associated with lightning. They were less intense than normal lightning
and were not observed to cast sharp shadows. Moreover, thunder was
not heard at any time, nor could correlation between the flashes and
'static' over the radio be found" (*Weather*, 19: 291, 1964).

Long sparks rise from gypsum dunes in New Mexico.

On May 11, 1971, while measuring atmospheric electricity at the White Sands National Monument in southeastern New Mexico, A. K. Kamra made a fascinating observation of earth-to-air electric discharge from the gypsum dunes. A strong wind was blowing as a thunderstorm passed over the site. "Electric sparks were observed extending from the top of the sand dunes up into the air, terminating at a height of a few metres. At least five sparks, all on different dune tops, were observed within the period 1510 to 1600 MDT. These sparks extended straight up, and no branches were observed" (*Nature*, 240: 143, 1972).

MOUNTAINTOP GLOWS: LARGE-SCALE ELECTRIC DISCHARGES FROM
EARTH TO THE UPPER ATMOSPHERE

If the gypsum dunes just described are magnified to the size of the Rockies or Andes, the scene is set for a corona discharge on a much larger scale. The electrical principles involved, however, are the same. Weather conditions establish a high voltage between the mountaintop and the upper air; corona discharge ensues.

Beginning with small mountains, consider the electric discharge effects seen by the watch on the S.S. *Tribulus* as it approached Madeira, in the eastern Atlantic, on June 7, 1954. ". . . the island was completely covered with low cloud. . . . On arriving within 16 miles of the island the cloud rapidly lifted and numerous white flashes were observed at frequent intervals on various mountain peaks. At the time of these occurrences, the cloud was clear of the island, although there was some Sc [stratocumulus clouds] to the NW. After the flashes had continued for some 20 min., a low rumbling was heard like distant thunder" (*Marine Observer*, 25: 95, 1955).

The Andes glow is one of nature's most spectacular luminous phenomena. Yet few know of it. One of the rare studies was published in 1971 by two American geophysicists, Ralph Markson and Richard Nelson. "'Andes Glow' or 'Andes Lights' are terms used to describe illumi-

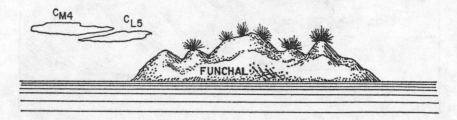

Apparent electrical discharges from peaks on the island of Madeira

nation seen at night in the vicinity of certain mountain peaks. While the majority of reports have come from the Andes mountains of Bolivia, Chile, and Peru, the phenomenon has also been reported in the European Alps, Mexico, and Lapland, and presumably could occur in many mountainous regions under favourable conditions. While sometimes thought to be lightning, for lack of a more obvious explanation, the interesting property of these light displays is that they can occur under cloudless skies. Sometimes they are but one single flash, while at other times they may persist intermittently for hours. On occasion, a periodicity has been noted in the time between flashes. At their most spectacular they have been described as '. . . not only clothing the peaks, but producing great beams which can be seen miles out at sea'" (*Weather*, 25: 350, 1971).

ELECTRIFIED PATCHES THAT MOVE ALONG THE EARTH'S SURFACE

September 1949, Yellowstone Park, Wyoming: William B. Sanborn had just stepped out of his car to watch a violent electrical storm several miles away. "It was then that I noticed a bluish light coming from over the low ridge to the west of Swan Lake. My first thought was of a fire, perhaps caused by lightning. I watched the ridge for a moment and was amazed to see what can best be described as a hazy patch of blue light coming down the hill slope toward the flats around the lake. It was then that I observed a very low lead-gray cloud moving swiftly above the patch of light. . . . When the patch was but a few yards away, I noted a sudden calm in the air and a marked change in temperature, as well as what I believe was the odor of ozone. . . . The patch which actually was a static field, enveloped my immediate area. . . . It kept low to the ground, actually 'flowing around' everything that it came in contact with, coating it with a strange pulsating light. Each twig on the sagebrush was surrounded by a halo of light about 2 in. of diameter" (*Natural History*, 59: 258, 1950).

J. B. A. Watt reported a similar low-level electrified cloud in Midlothian, England, on July 23, 1885. ". . . a party of four of us were standing at the head of the avenue leading to this house when we saw a feebly-luminous flash appear on the ground at a distance of some thirty yards down the avenue. It rushed towards us with a wave-like motion, at a rate which I estimate at thirty miles an hour, and seemed to envelope us for an instant. My left hand, which was hanging by my side, experienced precisely the same sensation as I have felt from a weak galvanic battery. About three minutes afterwards we heard a peal of thunder. . . . Another of the party says that he observed what seemed to be a luminous cloud running up the avenue with a wavy motion. When it reached the party, it rose off the ground and passed over the bodies of two of them, casting a sort of flash on their shoulders" (*Nature*, 32: 316, 1885).

Evidently, electrified patches are quite mobile, being in effect miniature, slightly luminous clouds. The wavelike pattern of the Midlothian display resembles some of the marine phosphorescent displays that feature moving parallel bars (p. 79).

LUMINOUS·BUBBLES IN THE ATMOSPHERE

Let us now turn to another spherical luminous phenomenon: luminous bubbles. So unlikely and unreasonable are these that three specific instances are reported below to better substantiate the phenomenon. The bubbles have the mobility of ball lightning but apparently do not explode or burn. Lightning and thunderstorms are always nearby, so the bubbles are probably electrical in nature—a ghostly and insubstantial cross between ball lightning and will-o'-the-wisps.

August 17, 1876, was a hot oppressive day at Ringstead Bay on the English coast. Sheet lightning flashed in the distance. "Between 4 and 5 P.M., two ladies who were out on the cliff saw, surrounding them on all

sides and extending from a few inches above the surface to two or three
feet overhead, numerous globes of light, the size of billiard balls, which
were moving independently and vertically up and down, sometimes
within a few inches of the observers, but always eluding their grasps;

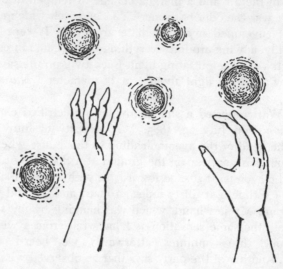

Luminous spheres float just out of reach at Ringstead Bay, England.

now gliding slowly upward two or three feet, and as slowly falling again,
resembling in their movements soap bubbles floating in the air. The balls
were all aglow, but not dazzling, with a soft, superb iridescence, rich and
warm of hue, and each of variable tints, their charming colors brightening the extreme beauty of the scene. . . . Their numbers were continually fluctuating; at times thousands of them enveloped the observers,
and a few minutes afterward the numbers would dwindle to perhaps as
few as twenty, but soon they would be swarming again, as numerous as
ever. Not the slightest sound accompanied the display" (*Symons's
Monthly Meteorological Magazine*, 32: 127, 1898).

On December 18, 1922, Lionel Smith-Gordon, residing near Salisbury, England, saw the bubbles and described them as a form of ball
lightning. "The phenomenon took the form of balls of bluish, misty
flame, which either hovered stationary or darted about the heavens in a
curiously irregular manner. Vivid lightning of the ordinary kind accompanied the display, which must have lasted at least two hours" (*Meteorological Magazine*, 57: 336, 1922).

Dr. C. G. R. Jennings, of Glenora, New York, recalled his encounter
with luminous bubbles while walking home at dusk as follows: "The air
was sultry and there were flashes of heat lightning on the horizon. When

I came to what we called in New England the village green, I saw a remarkable exhibition of what I assumed to be static electricity. There were some twelve or more round balls of luminescence bouncing around in the most undisciplined manner in all directions. They would apparently strike the ground, then bounce up in the air in the lightest and most buoyant fashion. They looked to be about the size of a football" (*American Mercury*, 26: 69, 1932).

EARTHQUAKE LIGHTS

Like ball lightning, earthquake lights are accepted as real by many geophysicists, although their acceptance is somewhat grudging, primarily because the mechanism of generation is unclear. The testimony of history is almost overwhelming in support of a great variety of luminous phenomena appearing before, during, and just after intense earthquakes. The November 2, 1931, Japanese quake was especially violent and generated many observations of earthquake lights. "With this earthquake, the lights were usually described as beams radiating from a point on the horizon, as like lightning or a searchlight turned to the sky, and as of a blue or bluish colour. They were seen before the earthquake by 26 observers, during it by 99, and after it by 22" (*Seismological Society of America, Bulletin*, 63: 2177, 1973).

Radiating beams of light during a Japanese earthquake

The variability of earthquake lights was demonstrated by the January 20, 1941, shock on Cyprus. "A bright flash associated with the earthquake was seen from the eastern and central parts of the island." After the quake itself, one Nicosia Hodja, standing on a minaret for morning prayer, "saw a brilliant reddish object like a huge globular lightning moving slowly toward the east. . . . There is strong evidence that [the] direction of the flash was pointing to the epicentral area" (*Nature,* 149: 640, 1942). The widely seen bright flash resembles some of the all-sky flashes discussed previously.

LUMINOUS PHENOMENA IN SEA ICE AND WATERFALLS

Some earthquake lights are probably due to the electricity created when crystalline materials in the earth's crust are suddenly stressed. Called piezoelectricity, this well-known effect is used in phonograph pickups and other technical applications. The sudden increase in stress on solids and liquids also generates light in unexpected places. Ice-breakers, for example, sometimes create phosphorescence and flashes of light in sea ice as they ram through it (*Nature,* 24: 459, 1881). Here a phenomenon called triboluminescence is probably the cause. This luminous effect occurs when some solids (viz., sugar cubes) are rubbed together. Again, at the bases of waterfalls, the violence of the falling water is sufficient to cause mysterious flashes of light via some unexplained mechanism associated with the sudden violent compression of water and entrained gases (*New Scientist,* 19: 399, 1963).

FLASHING ARCS DURING VOLCANIC ERUPTIONS

Air also becomes luminescent when suddenly compressed. An impressive consequence of this effect is sometimes seen around the orifices of violently active volcanos. The sharp detonations create spherical shock waves that expand upward and outward. On April 7, 1906, Frank A. Perret and Professor Matteucci were skirting the southern flank of Vesuvius during one of its especially violent phases. "The frequency of the explosions varied from approximately one every three or four seconds to at least three per second. Although powerful, they were very sharp and sudden in their nature, and at the instant of each—but before it could be sensed by the eye or ear—a thin, luminous arc flashed upward and outward from the crater and disappeared into space. Then came the sound of the explosion and detritus above the lip of the crater. The motion of translation of the arcs, while very rapid in comparison with that of the detritus, was not above the limits of easy observation and there could be no doubt as to the reality of the phenomenon, which was repeated some hundreds of times" (*American Journal of Science,* 4: 329, 1912). In

Flashing arcs expand away from erupting cone of Vesuvius.

Chapter 2 a similar phenomenon will be described in which the firing of artillery pieces causes spherical atmospheric disturbances. The artillery arcs, however, seem to be due to shock waves changing the air's index of refraction rather than the actual emission of light.

ELECTRICAL DISCHARGES INSIDE TORNADOS

Any farmer from America's "tornado alley" (Oklahoma and Kansas, primarily) will testify to the extreme violence of a tornado vortex. Tornados are associated with electrical storms. Scientists have been arguing for years as to whether storm electricity helps spawn tornados and whether electrical effects are important attributes of the funnels. The first eyewitness account is descriptive of obvious electrical activity inside a funnel. The second bit of testimony is even more interesting since it describes long vertical light columns (like "neon tubes") associated with tornado funnels. The tubes tie in with occasional observations of auroralike columns above distant thunderstorms (p. 10).

A farmer living near Greensburg, Kansas, on June 22, 1928, had the rare "privilege" of looking right up into a tornado funnel while standing at the entrance of his cyclone cellar. "As I paused to look I saw that the lower end, which had been sweeping the ground, was beginning to rise. I knew what that meant, so I kept my position. I knew that I was comparatively safe and I knew that if the tornado again dipped I could drop down and close the door before any harm could be done. . . . At last the great shaggy end of the funnel hung directly overhead. Everything was as still as death. There was a strong gassy odor and it seemed that I could not breathe. There was a screaming, hissing sound coming directly from the end of the funnel. I looked up and to my astonishment I saw right up into the heart of the tornado. There was a circular opening in the center of the funnel, about 50 or 100 feet in diameter, and extending straight upward for a distance of at least one-half mile, as best I could judge under the circumstances. The walls of this opening were of rotating clouds and the whole was made brilliantly visible by constant flashes of lightning which zigzagged from side to side" (*Monthly Weather Review*, 58: 205, 1930).

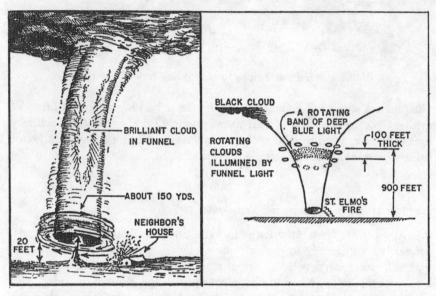

Luminous phenomena observed during a Blackwell, Oklahoma, tornado in 1955.

The May 25, 1955, tornado at Blackwell, Oklahoma, was a particularly strong tornado. Lee Hunter saw the light-column effect vividly. "The funnel from the cloud to the ground was lit up. It was a steady, deep blue light—very bright. It had an orange color fire in the center from the cloud to the ground. As it came along my field, it took a swath about 100 yards wide. As it swung from left to right, it looked like a giant neon tube in the air or a flagman at a railroad crossing. As it swung along the ground level, the orange fire or electricity would gush out from the bottom of the funnel, and the updraft would take it up in the air causing a terrific light—and it was gone!" (*Journal of Meteorology*, 14: 284, 1957).

UNEXPLAINED LUMINOUS STRUCTURES IN STORMS

Hurricanes and thunderstorms are machines in the sense that they feed on some source of energy and have complex structures that help sustain them and even make them grow larger. The hurricane, for example, is a heat engine dependent upon temperature differences between the sea and atmosphere. The role of electricity in storm dynamics, particularly in thunderstorms, is debatable. Is electrical activity just a side effect or is it a dynamo that helps keep the machine going? This question cannot be answered now, but there are unusual electrical structures in some of the more violent storms. On occasion, these structures glow and flash, revealing some unrecognized organization within the storm. They also betray our ignorance of some storm processes and the part played by electricity.

Herbert L. Jones has labeled one of these elusive structures the "tornado pulse generator." He described the tornado of May 25, 1955, near Blackwell, Oklahoma. Radio equipment indicated that intense electrical activity was nearby. But precipitation was fifteen miles away according to radar. Jones expected to see considerable lightning in the direction of the storm. "Much to the disappointment of the author at that time, how-

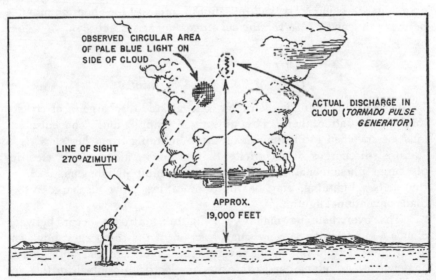

Luminous components of the postulated "tornado pulse generator"

ever, there was no apparent electrical activity whatsoever except for an odd flashing of a patch of illumination in the top section of the thundercloud . . . a flashing that appeared as a circular patch of light on the side of the cloud structure between the observer and the center of action where the electrical activity appeared to be. At that time these patches of light appeared as circular patches of pale blue illumination for an estimated time of two seconds; this circular area would then become dark for another estimated two seconds and again would reappear" (*Weatherwise,* 18: 78, 1965).

A more enigmatic luminous structure appeared over a cloud bank in New Zealand on February 29, 1936. M. D. Laurenson was watching the progress of the storm from a distance when he became aware of a glowing light. "Some minutes later, a bright flash from the north lit up the sky, and I was more than amazed to realize that the glowing light actually proceeded from the upper surface of a black bank of cloud. The time was then 10:15 P.M. and the glowing light had been practically steady for five minutes. By steady, I mean that it had stayed in the same position, no movement right or left, up or down. . . . Before I had time to conjecture what that could mean, I witnessed one of the most weird and uncanny sights I have ever seen. It suddenly seemed to pulsate, it took a definite shape as a molten ball of soft light; but although in itself not dazzling to the eyes, [it] threw off an indescribably bright, greenish-white light, or rather radiance. The radiance lit up the whole of the upper surface of the cloud bank and showed the ball of light balanced on a finger of cloud." The ball pulsated in intensity for about 15 minutes before fading away (*Meteorological Magazine,* 71: 134, 1936).

Unusual Forms of Lightning

Ordinary lightning is the rapid, concentrated discharge of electricity through the atmosphere. The adjectives "rapid" and "concentrated" must be specified to distinguish ordinary lightning from the "slow" and "diffuse" discharges of electricity that occur in auroras and electric-discharge phenomena. Actually, some lightning phenomena, such as thunderless lightning, may be forms of diffuse glow discharge rather than conventional lightning.

The overwhelming majority of lightning strokes occur between clouds and the earth. A very small fraction of the discharges, however, reach upward from the clouds towards the ionosphere and outer space. Somewhere high above the earth exists an electrical terminal for this upward-directed "rocket lightning." (Could auroras and mountaintop glows use the same unseen terminal?)

A singular and most impressive form of lightning is pinched or bead lightning, which some view as the progenitor of ball lightning. Terrestrial experiments with strong electric currents in gases demonstrate that an electric current may magnetically constrict or pinch itself. Bead lightning may begin as ordinary lightning which ends up strangling itself with its own magnetic field, breaking up into many brilliant beads.

Long horizontal strokes of lightning pose a different kind of problem because there seems no obvious reason for lightning to digress 5 miles parallel to the surface when the ground is only a thousand feet straight down. Do certain areas, perhaps because of geological conditions, have a special attraction for lightning and attract it from afar?

Rarely lightning will strike the earth without warning and with no clouds in sight. In such cases, an electric charge must accumulate in the atmosphere without the usual accumulation of water vapor in the form of visible clouds. Little is known about these invisible concentrations of electrical charge. All we know is that "bolts out of the blue" do occur.

Thunder is usually considered inseparable from lightning, but the strangely weak and fitful "heat lightning" so common on sultry summer nights is often silent. On these occasions, the whole sky may flicker eerily for hours like a defective fluorescent bulb. This lack of sound confirms the opinion that heat lightning is nothing but the diffuse discharge of electricity rather than distant thunderbolts.

Sounds other than thunder sometimes precede nearby lightning strikes. The rapid build-up of electrostatic forces in the lightning's target area creates corona or brush discharge from twigs and other sharp objects to the air. Momentary hisses and buzzes, like those heard in conjunction with St. Elmo's fire, may build up until the electrical stresses are relieved suddenly by the sharp crack from the lightning stroke.

Lightning shadowgraphs or lightning pictures have been reported on surfaces exposed to intense light. The intense light from the flash may cause some temporary chemical reaction on the surface that freezes the silhouette for a few moments. Another graphic (and rather gruesome) effect of the thunderbolt is the "lightning figure" or veinlike pattern occasionally seen on the bodies of those struck by lightning. In less sophisticated times, lightning figures were said to be the shadowgraphs of nearby trees on the skin. Today's thinking is that they are simply the result of the branching, veinlike flow of electrical currents on the body's surface. Nevertheless the literature contains some strange stories.

Finally lightning is an unpredictable prankster, smashing a house to bits one moment and then delicately cracking eggshells but leaving the thin membrane underneath intact. It may carefully avoid a child playing on the floor and then melt all the wiring in the house. These mischievous acts are probably beyond the ken of science.

ROCKET LIGHTNING (FLASHES FROM LOW CLOUDS TO THE UPPER ATMOSPHERE)

November 19, 1951: Captain H. S. Wood of the M.V. *Ajax* bound for Aden observed a typical exhibition of rocket lightning in the Arabian Sea. "A brilliant greenish explosion, bearing 015° (T) [True], seemed to occur behind a large Cu [cumulus cloud], lighting it up and in particular illuminating its outer edges for about two seconds; at the same time a fiery shaft, similar to a brilliant rocket, shot up to a height of about 18°. This was visible for about one second and then seemed to extinguish itself in a downward direction" (*Marine Observer*, 22: 194, 1952).

A somewhat different display of rocket lightning was seen from the M.V. *Geesthaven* on October 13, 1967, by several of the ship's officers. As in the preceding case, bright flashes seemed to provide the stimulus for the ascending lightning bolts. The natures of the precursor flashes and the rocket lightning itself are not known. "At 0215 GMT lightning of unusual character was seen in the southeast. Instead of travelling downwards toward the sea it began at an elevation of about 35° and travelled upward to an altitude of 45° to 50°. In some respects it resembled a firework display. No thunder was heard" (*Marine Observer*, 38: 173, 1968).

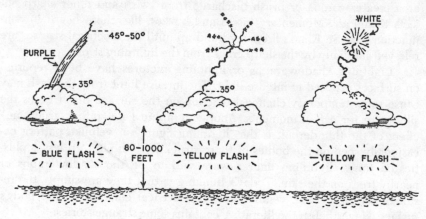

Rocket lightning with subcloud flashes

The rocket lightning reported from the M.V. *Trewidden*, in the South Atlantic, on February 16, 1964, exhibited the branchlike structure so common in the usual downwardly directed lightning displays. Nevertheless, these discharges proceeded upward from the clouds, apparently terminating in the atmosphere itself. "Between 0030 and 0130 GMT very vivid lightning was observed to the westward, shooting upwards from a bank of Cb [cumulonimbus] cloud" (*Marine Observer,* 35: 9, 1965).

PINCHED OR BEAD LIGHTNING

J. F. Steward reported a typical instance of bead lightning in 1894 from Colorado. "Today while driving over the country amidst a terrific thunderstorm, I observed many fine flashes, one instance of which deserves particular mention. Two substantially parallel flashes, somewhat wavy, seemed to pass toward the earth. Length about 40°, distance apart about 7°, both brilliant, but not blindingly so. Both, as lines of light, vanished instantly, but the one to the right broke into a multiplicity of what seemed to be spheres. This string of beads, as it seemed, appeared to be formed of material furnished by the original flash" (*Popular Astronomy,* 2: 89, 1894).

The breaking up of a lightning flash into nonspherical segments was vividly described by R. W. Gill, the second officer of the S.S. *Salvador*. It

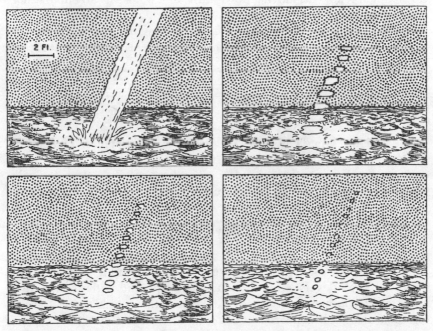

Anomalous lightning flash hits ocean and then breaks up into segments.

was July 26, 1929, in the Balboa Channel off the Pacific coast of South America. "At 2.15 a flash of lightning on the port hand appeared to enter the sea about 100 yards from the vessel. It appeared as a stream of molten metal being poured from a height into the sea and of about one to two feet wide. It first made [a] most peculiar shattering noise (as a china plate would make upon a stone floor); then, as it broke up the noise became a sizzling sound (as fat being thrown on a fire). Breaking up it appeared as a disjointed spinal column and the sea as if water was being poured into it" (*Marine Observer*, 7: 146, 1930).

STEPWISE LIGHTNING

A peculiar case of induced lightning occurred on October 17, 1956. Two officers on the S.S. *Oronsay* in the mid-Atlantic saw a cloud struck by one bolt emit a secondary bolt, evidently a consequence of the first flash. "Lightning started to flash from a point slightly behind the Ci [cirrus clouds] and traveled in a path about 30° from the vertical in an absolutely straight line, at what seemed to be a comparatively slow speed, towards the small Cu [cumulus cloud]. It appeared to enter the Cu and then reappear, moving downwards in a different direction at normal speed. The lightning track from the Cu, which had a greenish glow when 'hit,' did not seem to be so wide as the original one" (*Marine Observer*, 27: 208, 1957). The first flash apparently originated in the clear sky.

HORIZONTAL LIGHTNING: BOLTS THAT STRIKE FAR FROM THE CLOUD OF ORIGIN

Electricity normally follows the path of least resistance. The path of lightning is (with minor twists and turns) from a cloud directly to the earth below. When a bolt wanders miles horizontally before it finally makes contact with the earth, unusual atmospheric conditions must reduce the electrical resistance along the path taken. Moisture and particulate matter in the air could encourage such deviations.

Several spectacular examples of horizontal lightning exist. One was seen from the deck of the S.S. *Caltex Edinburgh* in the Pacific on May 14, 1965. "At 2040 GMT, a single jagged flash of lightning was seen coming from a well-developed Cb [cumulonimbus] cloud with anvil, several miles to the southwards. Instead of following the normal cloud-to-earth direction, this flash appeared to begin in a horizontal direction, curving to earth a considerable distance to the east and well clear of the cloud itself" (*Marine Observer*, 36: 53, 1966).

On July 16, 1873, in Hereford, England, W. Clement Ley described a horizontal flash that could have easily been misinterpreted as lightning

Horizontal lightning digresses 5 miles over Hereford, England.

from a clear sky. "I was standing in my garden watching the distant lightning, when a flash left the cloud 2 or 3 miles to W.N.W. of this place, passed almost directly overhead, but a little to the N.E., and descended upon Hereford, traversing in a horizontal direction a space of about five miles of clear blue sky, devoid of cloud. . . . The inhabitants of Hereford, few of whom had noted the distant storm, were greatly startled by the terrific flash and clap under a clear sky and brilliant sun" (*Symons's Monthly Meteorological Magazine*, 8: 106, 1873).

LIGHTNING FROM A CLEAR SKY

As suggested above, a few cases of lightning from a clear sky may actually originate in clouds miles from the point of contact with the earth. Nevertheless there are many instances of lightning when no clouds are in sight or clouds are much too far away. According to electrical theory, somewhere in the clear sky there must exist an invisible concentration of electrical charge. The same sort of unseen electrical terminal must also exist for rocket lightning, mountaintop glows, etc. The character and origin of this invisible electrode are unknown.

W. Williams witnessed one of these bolts from the blue on Cyprus on July 21, 1952. "I was riding along the foothills to the south of Mount Troodos at an elevation of about 3,000 feet . . . when straight in front of me I distinctly saw this flash. It was exactly similar to the ordinary flash usually seen against a dark thundercloud. It was followed by a very sharp crash of thunder, so that there can be no doubt it was an electric discharge. Heavy thunderclouds were then forming on the high mountains to the side, and low thunder was rumbling continuously, but the flash was quite away from these clouds and where the sky was entirely blue" (*Royal Meteorological Society, Quarterly Journal*, 36: 126, 1910).

On July 21, 1952, Lt. Donald Baskin was flying near the Panama Canal Zone in an aircraft trailing a small steel cable attached to a cloth sleeve. "I was flying on a heading of 270 degrees magnetic, and off in the distance (about 50 miles) I noticed a flash of lightning. About two minutes later the plane I was flying was struck by lightning. The plane lurched and I was blinded momentarily. The lightning struck the plane on the left side of the nose and travelled down the side to the rear. It passed to the small cable at the rear of the plane and completely demolished it by burning it to a crisp. . . . There were no clouds of any type present at my location" (*American Meteorological Society, Bulletin*, 33: 348, 1952). Possibly the towing of the sleeve generated an electrical charge on the plane that was discharged by the lightning.

COLORED LIGHTNING

The color of a lightning flash or any electrical spark depends largely upon the atoms and molecules in the discharge path. The flow of electrical current stimulates these particles to emit light, each species producing its own characteristic wavelengths. Almost all lightning is white or yellow, but most other colors are also on record. No one has discovered which molecules (probably impurities in the air) produce the abnormal colors. An interesting sidelight involving the color of lightning is that some forest rangers maintain that red lightning is much more likely to set forest fires.

May 7, 1976, from D. J. Hammond on the outskirts of Northampton, England: ". . . the flashes were of kaleidoscopic beauty—coloured patterns, mostly of pink, orange, and red, in the form of shimmering streamers. There was an occasional flash giving a bluish, irregular, nebulous appearance. The flashes were vivid, yet not the slightest rumble of thunder could be heard" (*Journal of Meteorology, U.K.*, 1: 295, 1976).

H. H. Stephenson of Brantford, Ontario, reported that "during a thunderstorm last night [October 6, 1927], a flash of lightning started from the top [as] white, and about half-way down turned to a vivid green" (*Nature*, 120: 695, 1927).

An unusual display of flashes of varied colors was observed by Frederic Pincott in August 1890 in England. "At about 3.30, while looking from a window due east, a flash occurred stretching upward far towards the zenith as a jagged yellow line. While looking with interest at the cumulus cloud from which it seemed to spring, a second flash occurred in the same region. It seemed in shape an oval yellow patch with a brilliant blue line down the centre. After an interval of a few seconds a third flash occurred, which seemed to start from the same spot in the sky and to stretch away horizontally to my right hand. It was of a bright red colour" (*Knowledge*, 13: 237, 1890).

THUNDERLESS LIGHTNING

On sultry summer evenings, the flicker of heat lightning often appears on the horizon. No sound is heard; little or no rain falls. Even when the clouds move overhead and the whole sky is filled with flashings, almost complete silence prevails. A rare cloud-to-earth stroke may break the strange stillness, but the cloud-to-cloud flickers are mostly quiet, almost like auroras. The cloud-to-cloud discharges are slow and diffuse—evidently most are not energetic enough to generate enough noise to be heard on the ground. Heat lightning may put on more spectacular performances, exhibiting some features of energetic auroras.

Dr. Walter Knoche, a well-known German meteorologist reported such an anomalous display while on the Rio Paraguay, South America. It was during a violent, rainless thunderstorm, on October 3, 1927, featuring red and beaded lightning. "Dr. Knoche tells also of various anomalous phenomena seen during the display, including curious, rapidly moving orange-colored discharges, which he says resembled cylindrical masses of glowing gas; flashes that revolved like pinwheels; and, at one period of the storm, hundreds of luminous arcs crowded together near the zenith, so dazzling in their brilliancy that he had to close his eyes. Strange to say, this spectacular display went on for hours without thunder" (*American Meteorological Society, Bulletin*, 12: 130, 1931).

The following display was seen in Shanghai on July 19, 1899. "The northern sky was in an almost constant blaze of light. Flashes came sometimes from two centres, as though there were an elliptical area of disturbance, from whose foci were sent forth the shafts of lightning. At times these flashes would take the opposite course and starting from the circumference make their way to the foci. Though the lightning reached within twenty-five degrees of the zenith, and were [was] vigorous enough in all conscience, yet nothing but the faintest rumbling could be heard" (*Nature,* 60: 511, 1899).

LIGHTNING SOUNDS OTHER THAN THUNDER

As the electrical tension between thundercloud and earth builds up prior to a discharge of lightning, strong electrical fields appear around sharp points, particularly tree branches and shrubbery. Just before lightning strikes, electrical current may be emitted into the air from these points. This is termed a brush discharge, and peculiar buzzing or ripping sounds may accompany it. Luminous phenomena such as St. Elmo's fire may also attend brush discharge, but it usually goes unnoticed because only a fraction of a second separates a brush discharge from the lightning stroke.

A click or "vit" sound is the most common precursor. However, Captain J. Burton Davies reported a curious variation while on the deck of the S.S. *Hurunui* in the North Atlantic on June 30, 1921. ". . . a terrific electric storm was played about the ship. . . . On three occasions the officer of the watch and myself were momentarily completely dazzled by flashes, and it appeared that immediately before the flash we heard a tearing noise as of canvas being ripped violently. . . . The fact that the noise was heard before the flash seems to indicate that it may have been caused by a brush discharge" (*Nature,* 116: 98, 1925).

Brush discharge was doubtless responsible for the eerie sounds heard by J. E. Belasco and his wife, who were sitting by an open window at Blenheim Gardens, England, on April 28, 1934. "We did not see the actual discharge as it was on the other side of the house. The illumination from it was, however, brilliantly white (no rain was falling) and was accompanied by a peculiar sound as if of the noise of something swiftly rushing through the air across the garden from north to south or the swishing of a long whip. This sound was also heard by my wife, who describes it like that of a sudden rush of wind, although there was almost a calm. This was followed almost immediately by a terrific crash of thunder" (*Meteorological Magazine,* 69: 91, 1934).

LIGHTNING SHADOWGRAPHS AND LIGHTNING FIGURES

Lightning unquestionably casts vivid shadows—a sort of natural superflashbulb. But is the light from the flash strong enough to create short-lived shadowgraphs on surfaces? The first instance presented below seems to answer "yes" to this question. The second example, though, is incredible and smacks of a hoax.

1904, the North Atlantic: ". . . the second officer of the Hamburg–America liner *Galicia* observed the following phenomena, which he carefully noted. . . . In advance it may be remarked that all the wood- and ironwork about the bridge had been painted gray. In chang-

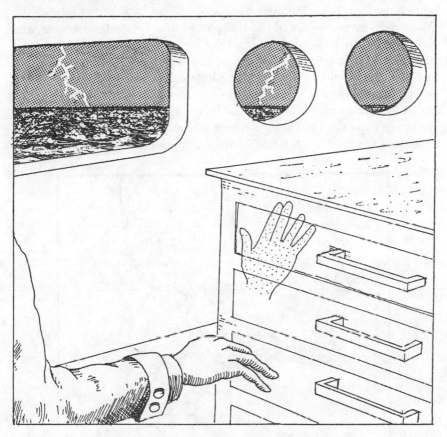

Vivid lightning creates shadowgraph of hand.

ing his position he casually removed his hand from a cabinet of the bridge immediately after a particularly brilliant flash of lightning, and what was his astonishment to notice an exact counterpart of it in silhouette upon the cabinet, and to add to his amazement the picture remained imprinted fully five minutes. Such a spectacle was well calculated to incite the officer to further observations, which he carried out with like results. Among others he placed an observation instrument upon the cabinet, and waiting his opportunity removed it just after a vivid flash, to find the shadowgraph perfect in detail" (*Scientific American Supplement*, 57: 23679, 1904).

Thomas Logan was an eyewitness to this rather unlikely event. The time was July 1851, Washington County, Maryland. Some sheep had taken shelter under an oak tree during a thunderstorm. "On a limb or branch of the tree sat a robin, directly over the sheep; a flash of lightning struck the tree, the robin, and the sheep, killing both of the latter. . . . When we arrived, we found the sheep dead, lying upon the left side, and found the dead body of the robin lying upon the right or upper side of the sheep. Capt. Ressley, who owned the sheep, ordered his servants to skin the sheep, which they did immediately, and when they came to the spot on the right, and which was the upper side, where the body of the robin had fallen and where we had found it, they noticed a strange appearance and called our attention to it. To our no small astonishment, we found on the inside of the skin of the sheep and also on the flesh of the

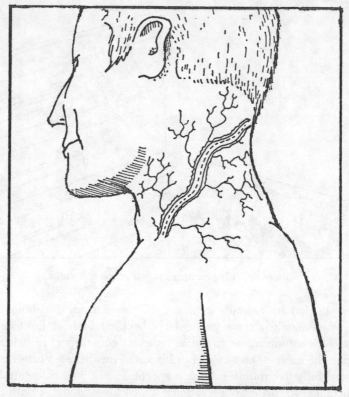

Typical veinlike pattern of a "lightning figure"

body of it, a perfect picture of the robin, even to the fine fringes of the feathers of its wings" (*Scientific American*, 21: 214, 1869).

The robin tale, whatever its accuracy, resembles the well-verified lightning figures found on humans struck by lightning. On September 14, 1919, a man walking in Finsbury Park, London, was struck by lightning and extensively burned. A physician who examined the body described the "lightning figure" he discovered. "From the right shoulder and across the chest and down to the lower front of the abdomen, impressions of branches and leaves were clearly imprinted on the skin, showing like an X-ray plate how certain rays of light were impeded by the branches and foliage, whilst others made the contour of these" (*Symons's Meteorological Magazine*, 54: 104, 1919). The branchlike pattern is more likely due to the electricity following the body's veins or paths of least resistance.

On June 9, 1883, again in England, four boys were taking refuge in a stable during a thunderstorm when lightning hit a yew tree at the back of the stable. All of the boys received severe shocks. "One of the boys had got such a shock in his arms that he asked if they were off. His jacket was removed to see if there was any visible cause of the pain he seemed to suffer, when it was found that the impression of the yew-tree branches was as distinct on his arms and body as if there had been a prepared surface and struck off in the camera. Each of the boys presented more or less similar appearances. During the course of two days the appearances had all left their skin, and all the boys have fully recovered" (*Symons's Monthly Meteorological Magazine*, 18: 82, 1883).

PRANKS AND CAPRICIOUS ACTIONS OF LIGHTNING

The pranks of lightning are difficult to categorize as well as hard to fathom. There seems no rhyme or reason to some of the things lightning does. To begin, about 1902, in Iowa, a Dr. Enfield described the damage done to a house struck by lightning. "After the occurrence, a pile of dinner plates, twelve in number, was found to have every other plate broken. It would seem as if the plates constituted a condenser under the intensely electrified condition of the atmosphere" (*Nature*, 66: 158, 1902). Why *every other* plate?

On January 5, 1890, in County Mayo, Ireland, a lightning bolt completely wrecked a kitchen. "All objects of glass or china in the room were upset, but only a few of them were broken; a corner was cut clear off a glass ink bottle, without spilling the ink, &c. The most extraordinary occurrence was what happened to a basket of eggs lying on the floor of the room. The shells were shattered so that they fell off when the eggs were put in boiling water, but the inner membrane was not broken. The eggs tasted quite sound" (*Royal Meteorological Society, Quarterly Journal,* 17: 18, 1891). Lightning can be rather fastidious in some circumstances.

Lightning created an expanding circle of death in Vernon, France, about 1873. "Five or six years ago lightning struck a garden planted with gooseberry bushes and cherry trees, making a very deep hole, the orifice of which was not 10 cm. in diameter. Subsequently everything died round about. The death circle enlarged year by year. It is now 7 metres in diameter and has just reached a cherry tree planted twelve years ago, which has died like the rest" (*English Mechanic,* 27: 214, 1878). The fatal effects of lightning on vegetation are usually instantaneous.

On June 8, 1972, lightning drilled a neat circle in a window pane in the Meteorology Department at the University of Edinburgh. "The result was an almost circular hole of dimensions 4.9 cm. by 4.6 cm., and an

Artist's rendition of a prank played by lightning in Germany

irregular crack which ran across the pane from the bottom of the hole; the pane broke along this crack while it was being removed. The 'missing' circle of glass was found intact inside the room; the edge of this piece and also that of the glass surrounding the hole had a fused appearance, and this was smooth to the touch, on the *inner* side of the pane" (*Weather*, 28: 160, 1973).

Prof. L. Weber has described an even more bizarre window incident that occurred in 1886 in Germany at Ribnitz during a violent thunderstorm. ". . . the lower pane of a window on the first floor was broken by lightning, and a jet of water was thrown upwards through the aperture to the ceiling, where it detached part of the ceiling, and this, falling with the water, broke a small cigar table below. Three bucketfulls of water were afterwards taken from the room. The hole in the window was like that from a bullet." The origin of the water jet remained a mystery to the investigators (*Nature*, 33: 396, 1886).

In a later chapter, some instances of animals falling from the sky will be presented. Some of these "animal falls" are probably due to meteorological conditions, as in this 1875 case from California. As hail began to fall and lightning flashed, thousands of geese rose from shallow ponds in the area. "They went up and up, apparently to rise above the fearful cloud. It was nearly dark, and those who saw them rise thought no more of it until morning when they began to find dead geese, and hear of hundreds being picked up by the neighbors. Some 700 were found. . . . The heads were badly torn and their bills split into fragments" (*Popular Science Monthly*, 6: 378, 1875).

Meteorlike Luminous Phenomena

Conventional meteors are those streaks of light in the night sky that we commonly call "falling stars." Very rarely meteors are so large that they are not completely burned up by atmospheric friction and impact the earth's surface as meteorites—usually with impressive visible effects. Most, however, explosively fragment at high altitudes or silently burn to near nothingness, the residual dust floating slowly and unseen to the surface.

A few meteors follow different patterns. The really great meteoric displays have nearly worldwide effects, such as the 1908 Tunguska Event and the 1913 North American meteors described below. The phenomena attending these events are decidedly nonconventional. In 1908, matter released by the Tunguska Event created spectacular sunsets for months as well as jostling scientific instruments around the world. The great 1913 meteor "procession" was eerie in its deliberateness and precise order of march.

There are also meteors that inch their way across the sky with difficult-to-explain slowness. Others deviate from the normal straight or slightly curved trajectory and trace inexplicable spirals or change course sharply. More awe-inspiring are low-level meteorlike luminous phenomena that emulate ball lightning or miniature tornados. The dividing lines between these three classes of phenomena become distressingly vague here. If something palpable remains—a meteorite—we class the phenomenon as meteoric and hope for the best.

Seeds and insects high in the air and illuminated by the bright sun may sometimes resemble showers of tiny meteors if seen through a telescope. These so-called "telescopic meteors" have reasonable explanations in most—but not all—cases. Defying this rationality are the so-called "sleeks" and mysterious streaks of light that sometimes appear disturbingly close to observers. Auroral, electrical, and physiological mechanisms have been proposed for these phenomena, but no one has really investigated them.

A few meteors are heard before they are seen. A swish, a buzz, or a whir attracts the observer's attention—he looks up and sees a meteor flashing across the sky. The physical problem is that these meteors are usually scores of miles high, and there is simply not enough time for the meteor sound to reach the observer. Such meteor sounds should not be confused with the legitimate thunderlike rumblings and detonations often heard well after the meteor has passed. An electromagnetic effect may cause people to think they hear these anomalous noises. The resemblance to auroral sounds is also manifest.

A few terrestrial electrical effects have been attributed to the passages of meteors, but the cases are few and not clear-cut. Electrical effects are not impossible, but a ball of fire that electrically shocks an observer might well be ball lightning instead of a true meteor.

THE 1908 TUNGUSKA EVENT

The most celebrated meteoric event of recorded history occurred on the night of June 30, 1908, near the Tunguska River, some 500 miles north of Lake Baikal, Siberia. ". . . in mild weather and a cloudless sky, a large bolide or fireball rushed along in the general direction from south to north over the basin of the River Yenissei in central Siberia. The fall of the mass onto the earth was completed by the appearance of a column of fire raised over the *taiga* [virgin forest]—and observed from a distance of 400 km. at Kirensk—by three or four powerful thunderclaps and a crash, recorded at a distance of more than a thousand kilometers from the center of the fall. To distances of some scores of kilometers around the center of the fall, these waves blew down the trees of the *taiga* in an eccentric-radial direction, tops outward, and were so powerful that they set into motion the baromicrographs of western Europe as well as those of North America and other countries. . . . Huge masses of the finest substance, sprayed by the meteorite in its flight through the atmosphere and raised by the explosion in the earth's crust (due to the cosmic speed of the impact of the meteorite), caused the heavy blanket of dust in the upper layers of the atmosphere, and the formation, at a height of from 83 to 85 km., of 'silvery clouds' (light clouds), and dust screens on the 'ceiling' and in the lower layers of the stratosphere. Thus were produced those remarkable phenomena called 'night dawns,' which were of incomparable beauty. . . ." (*Popular Astronomy*, 45: 559, 1937). The sky brightening was remarked upon all over Europe (see pp. 12–13).

"One eyewitness, S. B. Semenov, a farmer at Vanovara some 60 km. away, told L. A. Kulik, who investigated the meteor first in 1927, that he was sitting on the steps outside his house around 8 A.M., facing north, when a fiery explosion occurred which emitted so much heat that he could not stand it: 'My shirt was almost burnt on my body.' However, the fireball did not last long. He just managed to lower his eyes. When he looked again, the fireball had disappeared. At the same time, an explosion threw him off the steps for several feet, leaving him briefly unconscious. After regaining his senses, a tremendous sound occurred, shaking all the houses, breaking the glass in the windows, and damaging his barn considerably" (*Nature*, 206: 861, 1965).

The 1908 event was no ordinary meteoric encounter. No crater has ever been found, although considerable destruction to the forests was evident even years later. Reports of abnormal growth of vegetation and lingering excess radioactivity persist. Apparently, the "meteor" was not a conventional meteor but perhaps an icy comet, or a bit of antimatter—or according to some more recent sensationalist literature an exploding nuclear-powered alien spaceship! Whatever this enigmatic object was, it must have dragged considerable dust and debris along with it to cause the extended period of bright night skies in Europe.

FORMATIONS OF METEORS

Less than five years after the Tunguska Event, on February 9, 1913, a spectacular procession of large meteors cruised in a slow deliberate manner across eastern North America. The puzzling aspects of this overflight are the great distances involved, the multiple bodies, their slow and stately movement, and the curious discipline maintained by the members of the procession. If seen today, these meteors would be claimed as an overflight of UFO's. Indeed, most observers did note an uncanny, artificial quality about the 1913 procession.

"As seen from western Ontario there suddenly appeared in the northwestern sky a fiery red or golden-yellow body, which quickly grew larger as it approached, and had attached to it a long tail; observers vary in their descriptions as to whether the body was single or composed of three or four parts with a tail to each part. This body or group of bodies moved forward on an apparently perfectly horizontal path 'with peculiar, majestic, dignified deliberation; and continuing its course without the least apparent sinking towards the earth, it moved on to the south-east, where it simply disappeared in the distance!' After this group of bodies had vanished, another group emerged from precisely the same region. 'Onward they moved, at the same deliberate pace, in twos or threes or fours, with tails streaming behind them, though not so long or bright as in the first case.' This group disappeared in the same direction. A third group followed with less luminosity and shorter tails.

"In reading some of the communications from the numerous observers, the extraordinary feature of the phenomenon seems to have been the regular order and movement of the groups. Thus some compared them to a fleet of airships with lights on either side and fore and aft; others to a number of battleships attended by cruisers and destroyers; others to a brilliantly lighted passenger train travelling in sections and seen from a distance of several miles.

"Mr. J. G. MacArthur writes: 'There were probably thirty or thirty-two bodies, and the peculiar thing about them was their moving in fours, threes, and twos, abreast of one another; and so perfect was the lining up, you would have thought it was an aerial fleet maneuvering after rigid drilling. About half of them had passed when an unusually large one hove in sight, fully ten times as large as the others. Five or six would appear in two detachments, probably five seconds apart; then another wait of five or ten seconds, and another detachment would come into view. We could see each detachment for probably twenty or twenty-five seconds. The display lasted about three minutes. As the last detachment vanished, the booming as of thunder was heard—about five or six very pronounced reports'" (*Nature*, 92: 87, 1919).

In the South Pacific en route to Melbourne, the entire crew of the *Halifax Star* watched incredulously as a formation of bright lights with tails rose and set, never appearing to burn out, and taking a full 90 seconds to traverse the sky. Since the great majority of meteors survive only a fraction of a second and cross only a small arc of the sky, the 1913 meteors and the flight seen from the *Halifax Star* seem to have violated all the laws of meteorites and must have been essentially temporary satellites of the earth.

At approximately 1610 GMT, on October 15, 1976, the ship's company of the *Halifax Star* saw a bright light appear in the northern skies. "It rose rapidly, and it was then noted that it comprised several leading lights, all of a very bright nature. It came from the north through an arc, reaching a zenith of about 35° and then appeared to set ahead of the vessel in a southeasterly direction. At its zenith it was easily the brightest object in the sky and the particularly vivid tail could be seen. This appeared to consist of smaller but also brilliantly lit particles and was about 15° in length, with a magnitude greater than that of Venus (−3.4) which had just set" (*Marine Observer*, 47: 176, 1977).

METEORS THAT FLY ERRATIC COURSES

Although meteors are inanimate objects, they can vary to some degree their flights through the atmosphere. Inclusions of gas or volatile materials will be heated by atmospheric friction and then expand like rocket fuel, throwing the meteor off course. A slowly rotating meteor with an irregular surface may wobble noticeably as it progresses. Lastly, meteors grazing the earth may skip off the upper atmosphere like flat stones from a pond surface. Meteors do not necessarily behave rationally; they are not perfect spheres of solid rock and metal.

From the astronomical notebooks of B. J. Hopkins: "1879, Oct. 20, 10 h. 49 m. G.M.T.: Observed a bright yellow meteor, which described a zigzag path with two bends. Appeared between alpha and beta *Cameli*, disappeared near theta *Persei*" (*Royal Astronomical Society, Monthly Notices*, 46: 27–28, 1885).

An undulating meteor was observed by the second officer of the S.S. *Hector*, en route from Adelaide to Aden, on November 14, 1960. "At 2046 GMT a meteor of unusual brilliance was observed ahead and moving in azimuth from 310° to 295°, approximately, at a mean altitude of 4°. Its flight was slower than usual, though it was in view for only 2 seconds, but it was nevertheless remarkable in that its track showed a dip and a climb, as shown in the accompanying sketch" (*Marine Observer*, 31: 189, 1961).

On August 10, 1972, a huge meteor bounced off the earth's atmosphere over the western United States and Canada. "From the ground it was seen as a blazing ball of fire, a metallic bluish-white in colour (like a carbon arc or welders torch) moving slowly ($\cong 15$ km/s^{-1}) across the sky, leaving behind a train which persisted for about an hour and looked rather like a smoke trail." Satellite-borne instruments picked up this me-

A meteor with an undulating path seen over the Indian Ocean

teor, providing evidence that fixed its mass at about a million kg. (1,000 metric tons). "If this meteor had hit the ground, it would have produced a crater with a diameter of about 200–300 meters. The failure of this meteor to impact, however, is a much rarer occurrence and can only happen to the larger meteoroids (mass greater than a few grams). The 'bouncing' meteoroids enter the atmosphere almost tangentially. . . ." This meteoroid apparently bounced off the atmosphere and flew back into space (*Nature*, 247: 423, 1974).

SLOW OR LAZY METEORS

Slow meteors are usually those overtaking the earth. They seem to inch along the firmament, but subsequent calculations prove that they are traveling at speeds expected when pursuing the earth. Such a meteor overtook the earth over Oregon on April 17, 1934. "A beautiful reddish meteor, followed by a long train, floated in from the ocean and over the mid-Oregon coastline at 9:35 P.M., April 17, 1934. Its seeming leisure caused a newspaper to dub it the 'Lazy Meteor.' Travelling almost east-south-east, it finally disappeared over a point well in the state of Nevada. Many reports from widely separated observers were received. All indicated that it seemed almost to crawl and to bore its way across the sky. . . . Many reported that the meteor was in sight fully a minute. Unreasonable as it may seem, the writer is certain that it lasted 25 to 30 seconds. The calculated projected path was over 300 miles in length. This fact would indicate a reasonable speed for a fireball overtaking the earth" (*Popular Astronomy*, 45: 277, 1937).

A curious meteor passed over Broken Hill, Northern Rhodesia, on April 28, 1938. "It was luminous, orange in colour, and roughly pear-shaped, with a round head 'about the size of a football,' and a tapering tail from which sparks or streamers emerged as from a firework. . . . The object moved slowly across the sky from south to north and was lost from view after about *half an hour* [emphasis supplied]. Soon afterwards there was a loud detonation which caused a perceptible earth tremor" (*Meteorological Magazine*, 73: 244, 1938). The viewing time of 30 minutes does not seem reasonable in light of known meteor velocities.

METEORS AT VERY LOW LEVELS

According to theory, meteors should not behave like those described below. In fact these apparitions do not seem to be meteors, ball lightning, or any known, scientifically acceptable phenomena. They are UFO's but are doubtless purely natural. Because they are apparently beyond our ken, they will be discussed in some detail.

The first phenomenon has meteorological overtones and might be some rare form of whirlwind or tornado. It was observed in 1872, in England. "The people living near King's Sutton, Banbury, say that about one o'clock on Saturday they saw something like a haycock revolving through the air, accompanied by fire and dense smoke. It made a noise resembling that of a railway train, but very much louder, and travelled with greater rapidity. It was sometimes high in the air, and sometimes near the ground. It passed over the estates of Colonel North, M. P., Sir W. R. Brown, Bart., and Mr. Leslie Melville-Cartwright, whose park wall it threw down to the foundation in several places, and at one place for upwards of sixty yards" (*Nature*, 7: 112, 1872).

On February 28, 1904, the crew of the U.S.S. *Supply* in the North Atlantic were startled to see a very low-level formation of meteors. "The meteors appeared near the horizon and below the clouds, travelling in a group from northwest by north (true) directly toward the ship. As they approached the ship, they appeared to soar, passing above the clouds at an elevation of about 45°. After rising above the clouds, their angular motion became less and less until it ceased, when they appeared to be moving directly away from the earth at an elevation of about 75° and in direction west-northwest (true). . . . When sighted, the largest meteor was in the lead, followed by the second in size at a distance of less than twice the diameter of the larger, and then by the third in size at a similar distance from the second in size. They appeared to be travelling in echelon, and so continued as long as in sight. . . . The largest meteor had an apparent area of about six suns. It was egg-shaped, the sharper end for-

Formation of three meteors (?) dips below clouds and then roars off into space.

ward. This end was jagged in outline. Its after end was regular and full in outline. . . . The meteors were in sight over two minutes and were carefully observed by three people, whose accounts agree as to details" (*Monthly Weather Review*, 32: 115, 1904). Meteors do not appear below cloud level and survive for long.

Even more incredible was the object carefully observed by F. W. Keppler and two companions while duck hunting on October 29, 1936, near Lake Butte des Mortes, Wisconsin. "We were facing north watching a large raft of duck, when from the east, seemingly low over the water, came a rocket black formation throwing sparks of various colors, which shot across our front and seemed to disintegrate in the north-west" (*Popular Astronomy*, 44: 569, 1936).

IMMENSE FORMATIONS OF "METEORS" SEEN THROUGH TELESCOPES

Amateur astronomers as well as an occasional professional are sometimes deceived by seeds, birds, and debris floating in the upper atmosphere. The sunlight glinting off airborne seeds will mimic a colossal flight of bright meteors through the telescope. An experienced astronomer quickly adjusts his focus and discovers that these "meteors" are actually very near the earth's surface instead of far out in space. These so-called telescopic meteors can put on impressive performances, as in the following testimony.

William Read was observing Mercury's approach to the sun on September 4, 1850, through his telescope. "I observed, passing through the field of view, in a continuous stream, a great number of luminous bodies. . . . When I first saw them, I was filled with surprise and endeavored to account for their strange appearance by supposing that they were bodies floating in the atmosphere, such as the seeds of plants, as we are accustomed to witness them in the open country about this season; but nothing was visible to the naked eye. . . . They continued passing, often in inconceivable numbers, from 1/2 past 9 A.M., when I first saw them, almost without intermission, till about 1/2 past 3 P.M., when they finally became fewer, passed at longer intervals, and then finally ceased. The bodies were all round, with about the brightness of Venus, as seen in the same field of view with them; and their light was white, or with a slight tinge of blue; and they appeared *self-luminous.* . . . They passed with different velocities, some slowly, and others with great rapidity; and they were various in size. . . . I tried various [eyepiece] powers on them, and used both direct and diagonal eyepieces; but with every one I employed they showed the same appearance, being as sharply defined as the planet Jupiter, without haze or spot, or inequality of brightness" (*Reports of the British Association for the Advancement of Science*, 1852, p. 235).

"SLEEKS" AND DARTING GLEAMS OF LIGHT

Astronomers are ever alert for unusual luminous phenomena. A few declare that they are on very rare occasions startled by a sudden streak of light appearing extremely close at hand. Dubbed "sleeks" in the older literature, they were described as follows by W. F. Denning, the renowned English authority on meteors: "They exhibit exceedingly swift motion, give an impression of extraordinary nearness and show no heads, trains, or streaks. In fact they are mere gleams of white or bluish-white light, seemingly quite close, and very dissimilar to the ordinary meteors which are probably what their appearances suggest—viz., solid bodies in a state of combustion and dissipation. The special kind, to which I have alluded, is somewhat rare and perhaps I have not seen more than one or two in every 500 meteors of normal type and they certainly suggest electrical origin. . . . On March 19, 1914, Mrs. Fiammetta Wilson recorded two of them as 'appearing quite near,' moving terribly rapid and suggesting little lines of light rushing close to one like a lighted wire" (*Popular Astronomy*, 22: 404, 1914).

Additional testimony comes from Vincent Anyzeski, a Connecticut observer. "From time to time I have become aware of faint wisps of light that flashed into view and startled me into thinking, for the instant, that I have [had] seen a meteor. These wisps were extremely faint and nebulous, as if a piece of auroral streamer had swished across the sky. . . . They appeared to assume many shapes, and their flight extended up to twenty degrees in 0.2 second, tho some may have travelled as long as 0.5 second. They were from 1° to 10° long, and 1/2° to 3° broad, flashing into view quite in their entirety as to shape. They appeared from very few to 20 an hour, being especially numerous on three nights of slight auroral activity. One out of ten appeared directly in my line of vision. Lastly, they were more numerous in the early hours of the night, before midnight" (*Popular Astronomy*, 54: 203, 1946).

Anyzeski attributes sleeks to natural electrical phenomena, but another possibility exists. Astronauts often report seeing streaks of light, even with their eyes closed. Cosmic rays passing through their heads seem the most likely stimulus and may well also explain some of the elusive streaks observed by astronomers.

UNUSUAL LUMINOUS EFFECTS CREATED BY ROCKETS AND SPACECRAFT

Ascending rockets punch detectable holes in the ionosphere and are sometimes heard hundreds of miles away. Rockets that release this much energy must also produce visible effects as the engine's hot exhaust gases expand into the rarefied upper atmosphere and ionosphere. High-altitude winds blow the glowing exhaust plumes into fantastic shapes visible over great distances.

The NASA *Centaur 2* launch on November 27, 1963, instigated several reports of strange luminous phenomena from ships far off the Florida coast. On the M.V. *Wendover*, bound from Dakar (Senegal) to Cape Town, the captain and many of the crew were treated to a spectacular show. "At first a small, white spherical cloud with a bright centre was seen bearing 230° at an altitude of 40°. It rapidly enlarged and assumed the form of perfectly defined concentric circles of light. The circles reached a maximum of 5° radius from altitude 40° to 50° and the greatest brightness was equal to that of a full moon. As the object passed across the sky, heading approximately 310°–130°, the concentric circles became elliptical, with a 'catherine-wheel' effect which gave the impression of anticlockwise rotation. When the body passed ahead of the vessel, the surrounding cloud of light dissolved and became [the] single bright

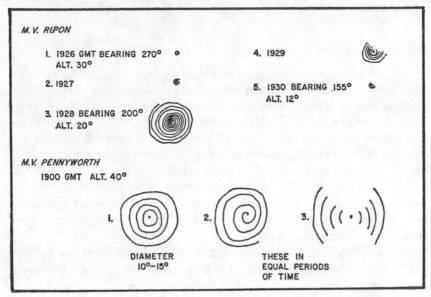

Unusual luminous phenomena caused by a spacecraft launch

white light usually associated with artificial satellites" (*Marine Observer,* 35: 20, 1965).

Sketches of the phenomenon were submitted to the editor of the *Marine Observer* by the captains of the M.V. *Pennyworth* and the M.V. *Ripon,* also in the North Atlantic well off Cape Canaveral.

THE PECULIAR PHENOMENON OF DOUBLE METEOR TRAILS

"Enduring meteor trails that appear at a height of about 85 km as double lines of light have been reported for more than a century, the first being Newton's in 1869. Although the dual appearance, which has been seen in the telescope within a few seconds of trail formation and by the naked eye after about 1 min. is not due to the separate occurrence of separate trails, no explanation has yet been offered for the phenomenon. The peculiar formation almost certainly results from the expanding meteor trail assuming the shape of a hollow cylinder. . . ." The observer's eye would see the expanding outer walls of the cylinder as two separate lines (where the material in the trail is densest at the outer edges) separated by the thin, essentially invisible central section (*Nature,* 270: 588, 1977).

INEXPLICABLE HISSES AND BUZZES ASSOCIATED WITH METEORS

High-level meteors are usually silent, expiring quietly many miles above the earth's surface. Larger objects that penetrate farther down into the denser air frequently detonate under the action of atmospheric heating. Rumbles like those of a high jet follow the passage of large meteors by many seconds, the exact time of sound arrival depending upon the height of the meteor. Such sounds are normal and to be expected. But dozens, perhaps hundreds, of reports relate that hisses and buzzing sounds were heard before or instantaneously with the visual sighting. Sound cannot travel this fast, and scientists were long wont to dismiss these observations as imaginary or due to psychological effects. (See Chapter 6 for further discussion.)

On April 10, 1902, a bright fireball streaked across Northern Ireland. Mrs. Martin of Dunsink reported her experience. "While walking down the fields my attention was attracted by a rushing noise above my head, and glancing up I saw a beautiful pear-shaped object, with a tail about six times as long as the head, going in a northerly direction. . . . Before I saw the object and all the time I was watching it, which could only have been for three or four seconds, I distinctly heard a rushing sound" (*Knowledge,* 25: 142, 1902).

In August 1910, Robert Speirs was hiking toward Krugersdorp, South Africa. "I started my ten-mile hike to Krugersdorp. When I had gone about a third of the way, I heard a screaming, whirring sound, and the sky to the north of me became all illuminated as if from a battery of floodlights. I had never seen such a thing before, and I immediately put my hand to my head to make sure I had not been struck by a native's knobkerry [wooden club], at the same time whipping out an Iver Johnson .32 to spoil the fun. As I swung around to face the associated tribes of Shangaano [Shangani], Zulus, Swarzis, etc., I saw instead a meteorite at about an angle of 45° to the northwards of me, almost as big as a basketball and apparently white-hot and going at some speed" (*Popular Astronomy,* 39: 107, 1931).

Despite the deliberate avoidance of this subject by most scientists, a possible physical mechanism exists for near-instantaneous, nonvisual detection of a large meteor far overhead. Electromagnetic waves emitted by the ionized meteor plowing through the atmosphere arrives at the ground with the speed of light. Some individuals are sensitive, in some unexplained way, to sharp electromagnetic bursts. For example, some hear nearby radar transmitter pulses as distinct clicks. Conceivably, people thus sensitive to electromagnetic bursts might also "hear" meteors before the real sound arrives.

TERRESTRIAL ELECTRICAL EFFECTS APPARENTLY RELATED TO METEORS

The passage of a meteor through the atmosphere understandably leaves a trail of ions (electrical charges) and in addition provides the meteor itself with a net electrical charge. Thus there may be scientific grounds, although such speculation is admittedly rather farfetched, to suggest that meteors cause noticeable electrical effects on the earth's surface as their electrically charged masses induce current flow on the ground.

The first recorded account of electrical meteors does not stretch commonsense greatly. On March 24, 1933, C. W. Coyle was en route from Albuquerque to Amarillo. "When first seen by him, the meteor was very low; it seemed to be rising in the east and appeared like a floodlight gradually being turned on. Then it seemed to be coming directly toward him, rapidly increasing in brilliancy and leaving a long trail behind. . . . In passing, the meteor seemed to be lower than the airplane, which was flying at an elevation of about 7,000 feet. . . . The passing of the meteor created an electrical effect, which appeared in the radio set of the pilot, resembling frictional static sometimes carried by dust in the air. This effect lasted for a little while after the meteor had passed" (*Science, 78:* 58, 1933).

The village of Lachine, near Montreal, was the target of a most unusual meteor on July 7, 1885. "Mrs. Popham was seated upstairs in her house, sewing, when all of a sudden the apartment became illuminated with a blinding flash of light. The lady instantly glanced out of the window, when to her astonishment she beheld a huge mass of fire descending towards the earth in a diagonal direction. . . . Simultaneous[ly], as it seemed to Mrs. Popham, she received a paralysing shock that affected her from head to foot, as if the entire contents of a highly-charged battery had been discharged into her body at once." Many people in the nearby village also experienced an apparent electrical shock (*Symons's Monthly Meteorological Magazine,* 18: 120, 1883). The magnitude and scale of the reported electrical effect is difficult to account for. Some psychological factor may have been at work, as is often the case in traumatic events. (The magnetic effects of meteors are discussed in Chapter 7.)

Nocturnal Lights

Nocturnal lights are not associated in any obvious way with conventional meteors, electrical storms, or violent weather. The name "nocturnal light" had its origin in the UFO literature, but most nocturnal lights, such as the will-o'-the-wisps, seem to have prosaic, natural origins. The characteristics of the class are: small size (a few feet in diameter on the average); flamelike or globular shape; appearance at low levels, usually just a few feet off the ground; strange movements that may be categorized as "playful"; and a soft eerie light. Of all the luminous phenomena reported in this book, nocturnal lights are most closely related to psychic phenomena, and they may in some cases have no objective existence.

Nocturnal lights are divided into five groups:

- *Will-o'-the-wisps*—these are softly glowing flames or luminous bubbles, usually associated with swamps and decaying organic matter. Combustible natural gases are believed to be the source of will-o'-the-wisps, although the flames are almost always described as cold. Will-o'-the-wisps may move about vertically and horizontally in an erratic fashion. Serious scientific studies are nonexistent.
- *Ghost Lights*—these are lights, generally spherical, almost always moving just above the ground, sometimes disappearing upon approach and reappearing nearby. Because they occur repeatedly and reliably in the same localities, they often have local names—viz., the Ozark Spooklight. Ghost lights may seem inquisitive or playful and may actually approach the curious observer, at least according to many reports. Some ghost lights may actually be will-o'-the-wisps, but most that have been investigated seem to be created by the unusual refraction (atmospheric bending) of lights from distant automobiles and towns, although considerable dissension persists on this count. Since some ghost lights have histories that predate modern electric lights and autos, this explanation may not be the only one. Seagoing ghost lights, such as the renowned Bay Chaleur Fireship, are more likely due to electrical activity of some kind, although the possibility of natural gas bubbles erupting from ocean-bottom sediments and igniting cannot be ruled out.
- *Hot Natural Flames*—these natural lights are caused by combusting gases released from the earth, as contrasted to the usual cold flames of will-o'-the-wisps. Flames from burning coal seams would logically fall into this category but are excluded as uninteresting.
- *UFO-like Lights*—these distant, bright, starlike lights move, flash, and on occasion change color. The great majority of UFO's are of

this type, and most can be explained as tricks of refraction, celestial objects, balloons, advertising planes, hoaxes, etc. The unexplained residual cases, though, seem to have no easy explanations. Like some ghost lights, UFO-like lights may approach the observer and maneuver in mysterious ways.

· *Physiological and Psychic Lights*—these are lights that have no objective existence because they are created by visual problems, cosmic rays, optical illusions, and hallucinations. The eye and the brain of the observer combine to produce an impressive repertoire of phenomena that simulate external lights but exist only in the mind of the affected observer.

COLD, GROUND-LEVEL FLAMES AND LIGHTS (WILL-O'-THE-WISPS)

Few scientific observations of will-o'-the-wisps are on record. Perhaps they are disdained as having little to offer the ambitious scientist. To one who studies unusual natural phenomena, however, they are irresistible. Mobile, colorful, and ethereal, will-o'-the-wisps have a ghostlike quality.

In 1927, in Bohemia, the German scientist H. H. Sven, looking out over a swampy tract of land, saw "four small bluish phosphorescent flames. They were of the height of a candle flame and a diameter of about an inch and were constantly hopping up and down. Near them appeared a flame of about three feet in height of a yellowish-green color and diameter of about a foot. The light of the flames was sufficient to read the face of a watch and make notes, but they had no heat when touched" (*Science*, 68; *sup. xii*, October 5, 1928).

The astronomer Bessell did not consider will-o'-the-wisps beneath his notice. He reported hundreds playing over a German peat marsh on December 2, 1807. "They consisted of numerous little flames which appeared over ground which was covered in many places with standing water and which after they had glowed for a time disappeared. The color of these flames was somewhat bluish, similar to the flame of the impure hydrogen which is prepared by the action of dilute sulphuric acid on iron. Their luminosity must have been insignificant, since I could not observe that the ground under one of them was illuminated nor that the great numbers of them which frequently appeared at the same time produced a noticeable brightness. . . . As regards the number of flames which were visible at one time and as regards the period of burning, I can not speak with certainty since both conditions were quite variable. I can only estimate as some hundreds the number visible at a time, and a quarter of a minute as the average period of their luminosity. The flames frequently remained quiet in one position, and at other times they moved about horizontally. When motion occurred, numerous groups of the flames seemed to move together" (*Scientific Monthly*, 9: 362, 1919).

An interesting correlation between will-o'-the-wisps and weather changes was noted by F. Ramsbotham, residing in Sussex, England. "For some years now, since I have been living at the Warren, Crowborough, in Sussex, I have, in common with many others, been struck by seeing Will-o'-the-Wisp, or *Ignis Fatuus*, playing about in the evening at various times, sometimes in one place, sometimes in another, and sometimes two at once, but not in the same place. Now I have observed that these appearances always coincide with unsettled weather, that is, that bad weather has invariably followed their appearance—in fact, it is quite a storm warning to us, as bad weather is sure to follow sooner or later, generally sooner. On Saturday, September 26th, 1891, one of my brothers and myself watched one for some time, and last night (October 1st) it appeared in the same place and was visible for quite half-an-hour. It does not dance about, but now and then takes a graceful sweep, now to quite a height, and then makes a gentle curve downwards, after sparkling and scintillating away for ten minutes or more" (*Royal Meteorological Society, Quarterly Journal*, 17: 260, 1891). Weather changes bring changes in atmospheric pressure that could force gases out of the ground. If escaping gases were phosphorescent, will-o'-the-wisps would be born.

CLOSE ENCOUNTERS WITH PRANKISH, LOW-LEVEL LIGHTS (SPOOKLIGHTS)

In Bolivia, the following spooklight appeared regularly near a military encampment close to a temporary swamp. To solve the mystery, "the military were posted around the square, and we waited from 10 o'clock till 12 or 1 in an atmosphere bathed in the brilliancy of a full moon. Only twice was it seen by me, but then very distinctly: the first time some little distance off, but the second quite close. On the first occasion the light started up from the ground with the brightness and speed of a rocket, and then again descended to the earth with equal velocity but less splendour: on the second we caught sight of it as it directly, but gently, approached along the road, upon which, running to intercept it, and stumbling at every step over rough and swampy ground, we managed to arrive within 3 yards of the glowing vision as it slowly glided at a level of about 5 feet from the earth. It presented a globular form of bluish light, so intense that we could scarcely look at it, but emitted no rays and cast no shadows; and when about actually to grasp the incandescent nothingness, suddenly elongating into a pear-shape tapering to the ground, it instantly vanished; but on looking round up it rose again within 50 yards, but this time we could not overtake it, as it bounded over a hedge, then over trees, and finally disappeared in an impenetrable swamp" (*Journal of Science*, 19: 447–54, 1882).

The Esperanza light, like so many spooklights, has generated its share of folklore. Native to La Salle County, Texas, the phenomenon has been described by J. W. Blackwell. "This light on the Esperanza Creek, this Will-O'-the-Wisp, appears to be about the size of the headlight on an automobile. It travels at various speeds, and at a distance of from one to three feet above the ground. It has been seen in all kinds of weather conditions, and at all seasons of the year, at all hours from dusk till dawn. . . . Night travelers along this road have seen the mysterious light as far out as six or eight miles from the crossing of the creek and have been followed by it beyond the creek. Only travelers on horseback or in horse-drawn vehicles see the light, which may approach the traveler from either side. It comes within twenty steps before it stops. When the traveler's horse stops, blinded by the light, the light retreats and meanders along, crossing the road back and forth in front of the traveler. Sometimes the light slowly recedes until it can scarcely be seen, but it returns at great speed. After crossing the creek, the light continues to follow for a few miles, but always returns to the river at the mouth of the creek, and goes straight up and then down and disappears" (*Texas Folklore Society, Publications*, 17: 118, 1941). Quite obviously, the Esperanza light cannot be a run-of-the-mill will-o'-the-wisp. This type of spooklight has no scientific explanation.

TWO WELL-KNOWN SPOOKLIGHTS

No discussion of spooklights would be complete without the famed Brown Mountain Lights. Melville Chater mentioned them in a *National Geographic* tour of North Carolina. "From three points near Linville there may be witnessed a curious and, some North Carolinians insist, as yet unexplained phenomenon, known as the Brown Mountain Lights. These appear with fairly dependable regularity and at all seasons, especially on dark nights. They have been variously described as 'globular, glowing red, like toy fire-balloons,' or 'a pale white light with a faint halo around it,' or 'not unlike a star from a bursting skyrocket.' As a rule, they appear singly in succession, rising over Brown Mountain's level ridge, then suddenly winking out. Often several lights appear simultaneously. While their average duration is from 15 to 60 seconds, they have been seen stationary over the ridge for 10 and even 20 minutes before extinguishment." The Brown Mountain Lights are usually ascribed to the refraction of distant automobile and locomotive headlights. Other researchers believe they may have a piezoelectric origin, like earthquake lights, because the area is seismically active (*National Geographic Magazine*, 49: 51–78, 1926).

The Hornet, or Ozark Spooklight, is a permanent resident on a country road nine miles south of Joplin, Missouri. So persistent is the Hornet Light that *Popular Mechanics* commissioned Robert Gannon to track it down in 1965. "Ahead of us a golden light flashed into view, as though someone a half mile away had switched on a reading lamp. It seemed to jiggle, to wobble back and forth, diminishing and brightening. When I let myself, I could imagine it was rushing at me, then quickly receding. It *did* look like a ball of fire; the edges were blurred and constantly changing. We could see its reflection in the car hood. It jiggled around for a few minutes, then blinked out. . . . A few minutes later the light appeared again, exactly as before, down at the end of that canyon of trees. I started my stopwatch. The light shimmered for four minutes, 20 seconds, then disappeared again." Gannon concluded that the Ozark Spooklight was unquestionably the result of the refraction of automobile lights by layers of air at different temperatures (*Popular Mechanics*, 124: 116, September 1965).

FIRESHIPS, OR SPOOKLIGHTS AT SEA

The Bay Chaleur Fireship, seen off New Brunswick, Canada, is almost as famous as Missouri's Hornet Light. The automobile-light explanation does not suffice here because the light is seen over the water. Professor W. F. Ganong found the descriptions of this apparition so intriguing that he made a detailed investigation. "After an examination of all the evidence, it appears to the author plain (1) that a physical light is frequently seen over the waters of Bay Chaleur and its vicinity; (2) that it occurs at all seasons, or at least in winter and summer; (3) that it usually precedes a storm; (4) that its usual form is roughly hemispherical with the flat side to the water, and that at times it simply glows without much change of form, but that at other times it rises into slender moving columns, giving rise to an appearance capable of interpretation as the flaming rigging of a ship, its vibrating and dancing movements increasing the illusion. This is doubtless a manifestation of *St. Elmo's fire*, but the compiler of these notes is not aware of any reports of similar phenomena, of such frequency in one locality, and of such considerable development" (*Science*, 24: 501, 1906). Natural gas escaping from the Bay's sediments should also be considered here.

Other fireships exist. Doubtless they would be called UFO's today.

Here is a multiple-witness report from the H.M.S. *Bacchante* plying the waters off Australia. "At 4 A.M., the Flying Dutchman crossed our bows. A strange red light, as of a phantom ship, all aglow, in the midst of which light the masts, spars, and sails of the brig, 200 yards distant, stood out in strong relief. As she came up, the lookout man on the forecastle reported her as close on the port bow, where also the officer of the watch from the bridge clearly saw her, as did also the quarterdeck midshipman, who was sent forward at once to the forecastle. But on arriving there no vestige nor any sign whatever of any material ship was to be seen, either near or right away to the horizon" (*Scientific American*, 54: 279, 1886). Could this be a case of mass hallucination? It is an incredible tale, with no feasible natural explanation.

HOT NATURAL FLAMES

To bring the reader back to objective reality, there is a class of palpable phenomena amenable to reasonable explanation.

On June 5, 1902, on the seashore at Blundell Sands, H. T. Dixon and several others observed the escape of self-igniting gas from mud deposits. "The evening was dull and grey, a strong northwesterly wind was blowing in from the sea and the tide was flowing in. In the distance we first saw smoke with frequent jets of fire bursting forth from the mud of

Jets of flame rise from a mud flat.

a shallow channel. Drawing near, we perceived a strong sulphurous odour, and saw little flames of fire and heard a hissing sound as though a large quantity of phosphorous was being ignited. It was impossible to detect anything which caused the fire, only the water where the flames appeared had particles of a bluish hue floating on the surface. The area over which the tiny flames kept bursting forth was about 40 yards. A gentleman present stirred up the mud with his walking stick, and immediately large yellow flames nearly 2 feet in length and breadth burst forth" (*Nature*, 66: 151, 1902).

September 1, 1905, Kittery Point, Maine: "On the evening of Friday, September 1, the guests at the Hotel Parkfield were startled by the appearance of flames rising from the beach and from the surface of the water, an event of so remarkable and unusual a character as to excite great curiosity and some alarm. The conflagration occurred between seven and eight o'clock in the evening, and lasted for upwards of forty-five minutes. The flames were about one foot in height. They were accompanied by a loud and continuous crackling noise which could be distinctly heard one hundred yards away, while at the same time there was a very strong liberation of sulphurous acid fumes which penetrated the hotel. . . . One guest of an investigating turn of mind secured some of the sand in his hand, but was obliged to drop it on account of the heat. When some of the sand was taken into the hotel and stirred in water, bubbles of gas were liberated and produced flame as they broke at the surface in contact with the air" (*Science*, 22: 794, 1905).

UFO-LIKE LIGHTS

On February 24, 1893, Charles J. Norcock was aboard the H.M.S. *Caroline* in the North China Sea bound for Japan's Inland Sea. About 10 P.M., when the ship was 16 miles south of Quelpart Island, "some unusual lights were reported by the officer of the watch between the ship and Mount Auckland, a mountain 6,000 feet high. It was a windy, cold, moonlit night. My first impression was that they were either some fires on shore, apparently higher from the horizon than a ship's masthead, or some junk's 'flare-up' lights raised by mirage. To the naked eye they appeared sometimes as a mass; at others, spread out in an irregular line, and, being globular in form, they resembled Chinese lanterns festooned between the masts of a lofty vessel. . . . As the ship was passing the land to the eastward at the rate of seven knots an hour, it soon became obvious that the lights were not on the land, though observed with the mountain behind them." The lights were also observed the following night. "A clear reflection or glare could be seen on the horizon beneath the lights. Through a telescope the globes appeared to be of a reddish colour and to emit a thin smoke" (*Nature,* 48: 76, 1893). Norcock thought these lights might be a form of St. Elmo's fire. This is doubtful because of the clear winter weather and absence of surfaces to provide coronal discharge.

During the 1970s, *Physics Today* published several letters from puzzled scientists who had seen randomly occurring lights in the sky. The observers were quite sure about what they saw but had no feasible explanations. Bruce S. Maccabee related one instance that occurred near a Washington, D.C., military facility in full view of three competent witnesses. "The witnesses reported seeing two bright, apparently self-luminous, circular objects at midday when the sky was cloudless, empty of aircraft, balloons and so on, and the visibility was about 20 miles according to the weather records of the date and time. The objects were observed to descend 'from the blue' one after the other, and remain at a fixed angular altitude for a time estimated to be a minute or more. During this time the observers noted faint dark rings about the central bright regions. The second appearing object then executed a left-right, zig-zag motion, and then rose rapidly 'straight up.' Moments later the first appearing object also began a rapid uniform, apparently vertical ascent" (*Physics Today,* 29: 90, March 1976).

LIGHTS OF POSSIBLE PHYSIOLOGICAL OR PSYCHOLOGICAL ORIGIN

When bright streaks are seen in closed, darkened rooms, the choice of natural explanations dwindles to near nothing. Meteors, auroras, and most other luminous phenomena verge on the impossible as explanations. Ball lightning frequently appears indoors but not in the form of bright streaks. Before musing further, consider the observation of Delores J. Galera, of the University of London Observatory. "I was lying in bed, in a darkened room, when I saw a bright streak of light to my extreme right. Had I seen this streak in the sky, I would undoubtedly have called it a meteor and would have described it as: colour, white; magnitude, 11.5; speed, fast; length, 20° arc; width, 1/2°. However, it started from just below the ceiling and disappeared before it reached the floor. It did not move with my eye, but carried on falling as I looked up at it. I have seen minor bright spots and flashes before and have always regarded them as mere optical defects, but this streak was very real and in fact, its appearance startled me" (*New Scientist,* 47: 351, 1970). Other astronomers have reported similar darting gleams of light or "sleeks" (see pages 63–64), but not indoors. Quite possibly this is another case of a "visible cosmic ray."

Physical scientists have long ignored the claims that intense emotional situations seem to call forth luminous displays, seemingly from the dark depths of the human mind. "Psychic lights," as they are termed, were seen in great numbers during the great Welsh religious revival of 1905. Many accounts were collected by A. T. Fryer. Especially interesting are those lights that apparently attended Mrs. Jones, one of the preachers. A man caught up in the revival fervor reported his experience to Fryer. "My wife and myself went down that night specially to see if the light accompanied Mrs. Jones from outside Egryn. We happened to reach Llanfair about 9:15 P.M. It was a rather dark and damp evening. In nearing the chapel, which can be seen from a distance, we saw balls of light, deep red, ascending from one side of the chapel, the side of which is in a field. There was nothing in this field to cause this phenomenon—i.e., no houses, etc. After that we walked to and fro on the main road for nearly two hours without seeing any light except from a distance in the direction of Llanbedr. This time it appeared brilliant, ascending high into the sky from amongst the trees where lives the well-known Rev. C.E. The distance between us and the light which appeared this time was about a mile. . . . In a few minutes afterwards Mrs. Jones was passing us home in her carriage, and in a few seconds after she passed, on the main road, and within a yard of us, there appeared a brilliant light twice, tinged with blue. . . . Perhaps I ought to say that I had an intense desire to see the light this night for a special purpose; in fact I prayed for it, not as a mere curiosity, but for a higher object, which I need not mention. Some will ridicule this idea, but I have a great faith in prayer" (*Society for Psychical Research, Proceedings*, 19: 148, 1905). Fryer's report was 81 pages long and consisted almost entirely of eyewitness accounts. A proper conclusion would be that not all luminous phenomena have an objective existence.

Oceanic Phosphorescent Displays

Ships that ply the Indian Ocean, particularly the waters leading to the oil-sodden lands around the Persian Gulf, frequently encounter dazzling phosphorescent seas. As Kipling described it, the ship's wake is "a welt of light that holds the hot sky tame." Huge globes of light rise from the depths and explode on the surface. Wavetops sparkle, porpoises resemble luminous torpedoes, and broad geometrically precise corridors of light stretch from horizon to horizon. Buckets lowered into these glowing seas prove that marine organisms are the cause of most phosphorescent displays.

Phosphorescent ship wakes are mundane and unimpressive compared to the vast rotating wheels of light and the other fantastic luminescent displays encountered in these same seas. Ridiculed as wild sailors' tales for centuries, ships have reported hundreds of bona fide geometrical displays since World War II. Mariners tell of great spokelike bands of light seemingly spinning about some distant hub. Occasionally, two wheels will overlap, simultaneously turning in opposite directions about separate hubs. Expanding rings of light and bright whirling crescents may also engulf ships in the Persian Gulf area. Crews that see these fantastic apparitions do not soon forget them. Scientists, alas, have generally ignored them.

One's first reaction is to explain the wheels of light and related geometrical displays in terms of marine bioluminescence stimulated by natural forces that, like the wake of a ship, leave behind glowing evidence of their passage. Sound waves emanating from submarine disturbances have been the most popular type of explanation offered. But what combination of seismic waves can stimulate overlapping, counterrotating wheels or hundreds of spinning phosphorescent crescents? Furthermore, there are several well-attested cases where the luminous displays have been seen in the air well above the sea's surface. This fact, together with the persistence of the phenomena (a half an hour or so) and the complex nature of the displays, suggests that we look for other stimuli, perhaps even for nonbiological sources of light.

The physical forces that create the auroras and the Andes glow may also be at work here. To illustrate this possibility, the luminous "mist" seen during some low-level auroras resembles the aerial phosphorescence in some marine displays. The curious interaction of radar with marine phosphorescence is also suggestive. Also, the self-generated, collective behavior of marine organisms should not be ruled out. Travelers in the tropics, for example, tell amazing accounts of the synchronized flashing of immense assemblages of fireflies. Could marine bioluminescent organisms indulge in such cooperative action—and if so, why?

Many other questions can be asked about marine phosphorescent displays. Why are they concentrated in the Indian Ocean to the near exclusion of other seas where bioluminescence is also common? Where does the mysterious *te lapa* (Polynesian underwater lightning) fit in? Unfortunately, the answers are hard to come by in this field which has attracted so little scientific interest.

STATIONARY PHOSPHORESCENT BANDS

Stationary luminous bands are more widely distributed than the remarkable moving displays seen in the Persian Gulf and Indian Ocean.

Phosphorescent marine organisms frequent most oceans and could well be stimulated to create long parallel lanes of light where ocean currents meet or where subsurface waves (internal waves) intersect the surface. The following report is from Captain Yon A. Carlson of the S.S. *Dover* 35 miles off Mobile Light in the Gulf of Mexico on October 24, 1908: "The ship ran suddenly in a streak of light coming from the water which alternated blue and green, the colors being so brilliant that the vessel was lighted up as if she were covered with arc lights with colored globes. A half-mile streak of dark water and a blackness that settled like a pall over the ship followed, and a second streak of the same brilliant-hued waters was encountered. The second streak was about as wide as the first one, and when the ship ran out of it, the same black waters and a night of exceptional blackness were also encountered. . . . Each of the streaks and the intermediate streak of black water was about half a mile wide" (*Monthly Weather Review,* 36: 371, 1908).

In contrast to the above observation, the luminous band encountered by the S.S. *Koranna* in the Arabian Sea on May 30, 1926, was composed of many separate sources of light switching on and off. The strength of the light sources and the regularity of its pulsations are remarkable. "The belt was first sighted as a line of phosphorescent water stretching across the horizon ahead from east to west. As the ship approached the area, it presented a curious scintillating effect. On passing through it, it was found to be a belt about half a mile in width extending to the horizon in an east and west direction. The effect at close quarters was as though thousands of powerful beams of light directed upwards from under water, each illuminating a patch of some twenty to thirty square yards of sea surface, were being switched on and off alternately, independently of each other. If any of these patches were watched, the intervals of light and darkness were found to be of surprising regularity, about 1 to 1 1/2 seconds" (*Marine Observer,* 3: 70, 1926).

MOVING PHOSPHORESCENT BANDS

When luminous bands move along the sea's surface, either some external stimulus must be at work, causing the marine organisms to light up, or the organisms are engaged in some mysterious cooperative action with a purpose we cannot even guess. The speeds of these bands greatly exceed the swimming velocities of any bioluminescent organisms.

A letter from A. A. Carnegie on the S.S. *Patrick Stewart* cruising in the Gulf of Oman in 1906 provides a typical description. "At 10:30 P.M. I was on watch, and noticed ahead of the ship a bank of apparently quiescent phosphorescence. . . . When we got to within twenty yards of the whitish water, I saw it break into life and light—shafts of brilliant light came sweeping across the ship's bow at a prodigious speed, which might be put down as anything between sixty and two hundred miles an hour. Then we steamed into the light, and the effect was weird to a degree. It was just as if a large gun with a rectangular muzzle were shooting bars of light at us from infinity. These light bars were about twenty feet apart and most regular; their brilliancy was dazzling. They first struck us on our broadside, and I noticed on our lee side that an intervening ship had no effect on the light beams; they started away from the lee side of the ship just as if they had travelled right through it" (*Royal Meteorological Society, Quarterly Journal*, 32: 280, 1906).

The next sighting took place on September 28, 1959, on board the S.S. *Stanvac Bangkok*, then in the East Indian Archipelago. "The first indication of anything unusual was the appearance of white caps on the sea here and there, which made me think that the wind had freshened, but I could feel that this was not so. Then flashing beams appeared over

Parallel phosphorescent bands rush toward a vessel, phosphorescent wheel in the background.

the water, which made the officer on watch think that the fishing boats were using powerful flashlights. These beams of light became more intense and appeared absolutely parallel, about 8 ft. wide, and could be seen coming from right ahead at about 1/2-sec. intervals. At the time, I thought I could hear a swish as they passed, but decided that this was imagination. . . . When this part of the phenomenon was at its height, it looked as if huge seas were dashing toward the vessel, and the sea surface appeared to be boiling, but it was more or less normal around a fishing vessel when we passed fairly close." Many of these moving-band displays seem to appear at the commencement or conclusion of the wheel-type displays described farther on. The swishing noises may be psychological in origin, but there seems to be an intriguing resemblance to the sounds reported during low-level auroras (*Marine Observer,* 30: 128, 1960).

PHOSPHORESCENT DISPLAYS SEEN IN THE AIR ABOVE THE SEA

Scientists universally attribute marine phosphorescent displays to bioluminescent organisms. Unfortunately for this theory there are several carefully observed cases of luminous waves sweeping along the surface several feet above the water. In this respect, the waves emulate the auroral fogs and the occasional ground-hugging electrical clouds that have been reported. Could marine phosphorescent displays be auroral in origin or could they possibly be related to earthquake lights?

Two aerial phosphorescent displays will now be described from among those on file. The first was seen by five officers of the S.S. *Dunkery Beacon* cruising in the Gulf of Aden on May 13, 1955. "Shortly after leaving Aden for Suez, bright pulsating waves of light having a period of 1.5 sec. were observed emanating from the sea in close proximity to the ship. They were travelling in a direction of 070° for some distance and extended to a height of about 12 ft. above the sea. This phenomenon was definitely not caused by the proximity of shore lights; there was no sign of phosphorescence in the sea at the time of observation" (*Marine Observer,* 26: 78, 1956).

The venerable *Monthly Weather Review* printed another account of aerial luminescence in 1908. The report came from the steamer *Counsellor,* then in the Gulf of Siam. "The steamer past thru [*sic*] a small field of remarkable phosphorescent patches in the form of a kind of vapor lying above the surface of the water in lengths of 500 to 1,000 feet and breadths of 100 feet approximately, and about 15 to 20 feet in depth to the surface of the water. At distances of 1 to 2 miles, these 'streaks' appeared like shining silver (no moon was shining) and were first taken to be shoals of fish, but on passing directly thru one, it had all the effect of a slight luminous fog" (*Monthly Weather Review,* 36: 371, 1908).

MARINE LIGHT WHEELS

Of all the marine phosphorescent phenomena, the vast rotating wheels of light have perplexed scientists the most. Hundreds of such wheels are on record; and no one has a reasonable explanation for these incredible geometric displays.

S. C. Patterson, second officer of the S.S. *Delta*, forwarded this observation made in the Malacca Strait: "I noticed shafts of pale yellow light moving rapidly over the surface of the water. During the major part of the time, the shafts seemed to move round a centre—like the spokes of a wheel—and appeared to be about 300 yards long, the appearance being very similar to that of the reflection of a powerful electric quick-flashing light (of the type of Ushant) thrown on the clouds on a clear dark night" (*Royal Meteorological Society, Quarterly Journal*, 33: 294, 1907).

Armin Roth, second officer of the W.M.S. *Olympic Challenger*, filed a report from the Gulf of Oman, dated November 5, 1953, concerning an aerial phosphorescent wheel. "In about 1 metre above the surface of the water there are suddenly appearing quickly moving bands of light (similar to fog). They have an extension of about two nautical miles and they are in a rotating motion, wheeling around from the right to the left (clockwise) and passing the ship at rather regular intervals. The centre of motion seems to be at a distance of about one nautical mile from the ship" (*Marine Observer*, 24: 233, 1954).

Three intersecting wheels of light; one spinning clockwise, two counterclockwise

Any theory purporting to explain these wheels of light must confront the numerous observations of several intersecting wheels seen spinning together about separate centers and in varying directions.

April 24, 1953, from the M.V. *Rafaela* in the Gulf of Siam: "Faint flashes of light with oscillating movements were observed on the sea. The flashes gradually increased in strength until at 0230 they suddenly changed into rather intensive rays of light moving around centres lying near the horizon. Three groups of rays were present, as shown in the sketch. . . . The beams were curved with the concave side in the direction of the movement, and were passing the ship continuously with a frequency of about three a second; they looked more like glowing shafts than beams of light. Reflections on the ship were clearly visible. The Chinese quartermaster became panic-stricken, left the wheel, and did not return until he had been called three times." The display lasted 20 minutes (*Marine Observer*, 23: 74, 1954).

EXPANDING PHOSPHORESCENT RINGS

The versatility of the unknown geometer creating the marine displays seems unbounded. This sighting, dated April 17, 1956, comes from

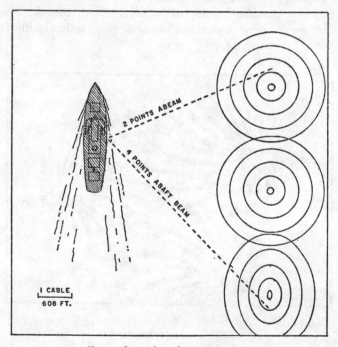

Expanding phosphorescent rings

R. G. Broderick, third officer on the S.S. *San Leopoldo* in the Persian Gulf. "A strange effect was noticed on the sea surface about 2 miles away on the port bow. On approaching the area, large bands or ripples of faint light appeared to be travelling in a confused way across the surface. Further inspection showed that these bands were spreading out from several central points distributed fairly evenly over an area about 2 miles across, in the same way as the circular ripples produced by raindrops in a puddle of water. Each band was about 70 yd. wide and had a faint white light. They spread, in unison, from the various central points, at intervals of a little more than 1 second. They travelled at a considerable speed, so that by the time one circular band was formed the previous one was vanishing, at a radius of about 1/2 mile" (*Marine Observer*, 27: 92, 1957).

An interesting variation of this geometry was observed on October 14, 1960, from the S.S. *British Energy*, then in the Gulf of Oman. "At 2130 GMT three very fast outward-moving rings of light were seen emanating suddenly from three separate vortices which were spaced about three cables apart in a straight line parallel to the ship's fore and aft line, and about five cables distant on the starboard side: the positions of the vortices in the water appeared to remain unchanged. The first two appeared almost simultaneously and produced circular rings, at a frequency of about one second or slightly less. The third appeared a minute or so later and produced elliptical rings which were moving much faster than the others" (*Marine Observer*, 31: 184, 1961).

PHOSPHORESCENT PATCHES MOVING IN CIRCLES

On May 30, 1956, the following report came from the M.V. *British Caution* in the Persian Gulf. The first portion of the display consisted of moving parallel bands of luminous patches. After several minutes, "the parallel line formation disappeared and the patches were seen to be moving fairly slowly in an anticlockwise direction round circles of from 100 ft. to 300 ft. in diameter. When the vessel passed through a circle, the patches of light disappeared on reaching the ship's port side and reappeared in the same formation on the starboard side. . . . The patches on the starboard side were small, about 1–2 ft. in diameter, and were rotating in circles of about 20 ft. [in] diameter" (*Marine Observer*, 27: 92, 1957).

Spinning groups of phosphorescent patches

RADAR-STIMULATED SPINNING CRESCENTS

The theory of an electromagnetic origin of marine phosphorescent displays is encouraged by observations such as this one from the M.V. *British Premier* sailing in the Gulf of Oman on November 30, 1951. "The ship's radar apparatus had been switched on with a view to checking her position, when, in the same instant that this gear became operative, most brilliant boomerang-shaped arcs of phosphorescent light appeared in the sea, gyrating in a clockwise direction to starboard and anticlockwise to port, but all sweeping inwards towards the ship from points situated from five to six points on either bow and some two miles distant, and conveying the impression that they ricocheted from each other on meeting at the ship's bows and then turned and travelled away astern to similar points which were equidistant on either side and about four points on each quarter" (*Marine Observer*, 22: 190, 1952).

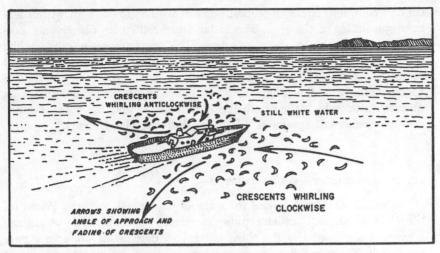

CRESCENTS
WHIRLING ANTICLOCKWISE

STILL WHITE WATER

CRESCENTS WHIRLING
CLOCKWISE

ARROWS SHOWING
ANGLE OF APPROACH AND
FADING OF CRESCENTS

Radar-stimulated, moving patterns of spinning crescents

OTHER RADAR-RELATED DISPLAYS

This sighting took place on February 9, 1953, on the S.S. *Strathmore* in the Gulf of Oman, which was engulfed by a display of phosphorescent waves. "At 0152 the waves reached their maximum brilliance, appearing to travel from the starboard quarter to the port bow. On switching off the radar, the phenomenon ceased close to the ship, but it was still faintly discernible on the port beam about 2 cables away. At 0157 the radar was switched on again. The phenomenon did reappear close to the ship but only faintly and soon disappeared altogether" (*Marine Observer*, 24: 8, 1954).

Even stranger are those situations where false radar echoes seem connected with phosphorescence. How can bioluminescent organisms in the water give rise to radar echoes? Consider this 1977 report from the M.V. *Ebani* in the North Atlantic: "Throughout the day various spurious echoes had periodically appeared on the radar screen. The echoes, which resembled those of small clusters of fishing vessels, rarely closed to the vessel to less than a range of 8 n. miles before disappearing from the screen. At 2200 another such cluster appeared on the radar screen directly ahead at a range of 10 n. miles. This cluster began to spread out on either side of the bow and a number of stronger echoes appeared in it until it gave an impression similar to that expected from a coastline. The echoes behaved as stationary objects and closed to a range of 5.5 n. miles when they again began to spread out until the ship was at the centre of a complete circle of echoes, none of which closed with within less than 5 n. miles of the ship. The radar appeared to be functioning normally throughout. At about this time, the sea took on a milky white colour and the beam from the Aldis lamp revealed a mass of luminescent organisms each about the size of a flashlight bulb—yet each clearly distinguishable from the other. This phenomenon continued for about 45 minutes, after which time both the luminescence and the various spurious radar echoes disappeared" (*Marine Observer*, 48: 20, 1978).

FLASHING ZIGZAG STREAKS OF LIGHT

The S.S. *Dara* was bound for Karachi on August 30, 1949. When off the Gulf of Kutch, "brilliant phosphorescence in lightning-like zig-zag form was observed [by the third officer] in patches of about a square mile each. These patches seemed to have a slight directional movement WNW., but the zig-zag phosphorescence flashed from left to right in a WNW.–ESE. direction" (*Marine Observer*, 20: 139, 1950).

TE LAPA: UNDERWATER LIGHTNING

In 1974 the *National Geographic* featured Polynesia in one of its numbers. One of the writers was aboard the *Isbjorn* listening to a Polynesian sailor explain one method of navigating across the great stretches of ocean separating the Pacific islands. The technique employs *te lapa*, an underwater light display possibly related to the other forms of marine phosphorescence. " 'Then look.' Tevake pointed over the side. 'No, not on top, deep down. You see him all same underwater lightning.' The phrase was apt. Streaks, flashes, and momentarily glowing plaques of light kept appearing well below the surface. Tevake explained that *te lapa* streaks dart out from directions in which islands lie. The phenomenon is best seen eighty to a hundred miles out and disappears by the time a low atoll is well in sight. He stressed that it was quite different from ordinary surface luminescence" (*National Geographic Magazine*, 146: 751, 1974).

WHITE WATER OR MILKY SEA

Although devoid of eye-catching movement and structure, the milky sea is nonetheless an impressive spectacle. Sometimes it seems like a luminous fog hugging the surface of the sea; in other cases the light seems to come from great depths. It is an eerie phenomenon, having some characteristics in common with arctic whiteouts where visible reference points, such as the horizon, are blotted out.

Many accounts exist. Here is one from an English gentleman en route to South America in 1871. "While lying becalmed a couple of degrees south of the equator, I had the opportunity of observing the grand phenomenon of a luminous sea, and I must say that of all the phenomena I have witnessed, none gave me greater pleasure than that alluded to. About 10 P.M. the luminosity commenced, and the whole of the sea, from the centre we occupied to the horizon all around, appeared to be one mass of phosphorescent light. Even the stars above seemed dimmed, and the sails of the ship were brightly illuminated, while every cord in the rigging was clearly distinguishable. I drew up a bucketful of the water from alongside and found that directly the bucket touched the water the phosphorescence suddenly ceased for a few minutes in the immediate vicinity of the ship. For about ten minutes the water in the bucket was as dark as ink, but after that time again shone out, though immediately [when] a finger was dipped in, it again became dark" (*Knowledge*, 2: 438, 1882).

2

OPTICAL AND RADIO ANOMALIES IN THE ATMOSPHERE

The atmosphere plays many curious optical tricks, from sideways mirages to all-red rainbows to radar "angels." The venerable laws of optical reflection, refraction, and color dispersion are adequate to explain the great majority of these frequently breathtaking displays of colors, shadows, halos, and distorted images. Undoubtedly, the same laws will ultimately explain most of the rarer phenomena described below, but the theoretical attempts made so far have not been completely satisfactory. How can one account for elliptical halos, kaleidoscopic suns, long-delayed radio echoes, and all the trickery of mirages?

Actually, only a few scientists take much interest in atmospheric optical phenomena nowadays. They are for the most part content that these atmospheric anomalies can be brought into the fold of the scientifically explained with little effort, that we already know all that is really important about light, color, and the propagation of radio waves in the atmosphere. This attitude is, of course, smug and dangerous. Some of the ephemeral phenomena of this chapter pinpoint areas of genuine scientific ignorance—perhaps not so much ignorance of the basic laws of optics as of the fine structure of our atmosphere and its interfaces with the earth's surface and outer space.

It is regrettable that so many of the irregular atmospheric phenomena transpire at sea, on mountaintops, in the reaches of the Arctic, and in other remote places. Only a favored few witness these natural nuances of sunlight and moonlight. By necessity, this chapter is mainly the testimony of mariners, explorers, and those who frequent the remote, open places of the world.

Unusual Halos and Mock Suns

Misty rings around the sun and moon are rather common—a fixture of weather lore. The most frequently observed halos have radii of 22° and 46° and are readily explained in terms of the reflection and refraction of sunlight or moonlight from two different shapes of ice crystals in the atmosphere. Rare halos with different radii as well as various arcs and tangents are also recognized—all fairly well understood in terms of meteorological optics; that is, understood as reflections and refractions from other types of crystals falling in different orientations through the atmosphere. Despite the power of optical theory, many other halo phenomena cannot be accounted for. They are, as modern parlance has it, "unrecognized!" How can optics explain offset and noncircular halos? Even perfectly square halos have been reported! All manner of peculiar and unexplained arcs grace otherwise normal halo displays. Deviations from theory are many and varied. Of course, ice crystals come in many shapes and sizes, and the atmosphere itself is plagued with irregularities. Conceivably, if we knew all the conditions, meteorological optics might come up with reasonable explanations. Nevertheless, the many departures from "recognized" displays make it clear that there are significant gaps in our understanding of natural light and color phenomena.

PRIMER ON THE COMMON HALOS

Cicely M. Botley, an indefatigable collector of data on unusual atmospheric and astronomical phenomena, prepared the following summary of the most-often-seen halos for the British magazine *Weather:*

"Halo phenomena are due to refraction and reflection of the light of the sun or moon by ice crystals; they are often very complicated and diverse owing to the variety of crystal forms and the large possible number of refractions and reflections. Refraction phenomena, especially those due to sunlight, are sometimes beautifully coloured.

"[The following illustration is] . . . a schematic drawing of some of the most common halo phenomena. It is well to know these so as to be able to recognize unusual forms when they occur.

"A. The common halo of 22° radius, formed by refraction in hexagonal crystals at a 60° angle, and which may be seen, entire or in part, on about 200 days of the year. This halo enjoys an enormous reputation as a sign of bad weather, which, as it is often seen in the cirrostratus in front of a depression, is not unfounded; it also occurs, often in fragments,

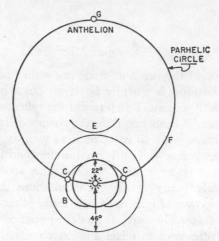

The common halos, arcs, and mock suns. See text for explanations.

in fine-weather cirrus. It is usually not well coloured, appearing as a narrow whitish ring, reddish on the inside.

"B. The circumscribed halo, oval in shape, which may surround the 22° ring when the sun is higher than 29°. At lower altitudes it breaks up into upper and lower arcs of contact. Uncommon, but to be looked for, is a curved bar across the upper contact arc—the Parry arc. Anomalous contact arcs are sometimes to be seen.

"C. The mock suns or parhelia of 22°, which are two bright patches, often brilliant and beautifully coloured and sometimes with long white 'tails,' on a level with the sun. They often appear by themselves and arise when the axes of the ice crystals in large number are vertical. They are on the halo at low altitudes, but as the sun rises they recede from it and sometimes become connected with it by the arcs of Lowitz.

"D. The halo of 46°, due to refraction at 90° in hexagonal ice crystals oriented at random. It is not common and is faint, though the colours are better than in the common halo. It has parhelia and certain contact arcs, but these are rare.

"E. What has been described as the 'most beautiful of all halo phenomena,' the circumzenithal arc, which appears as a miniature rainbow, red towards the sun and parallel to the horizon, a few degrees above the summit of the 46° halo when this is visible. Often this arc appears alone. It is not infrequent but somewhat transient, so it is not well known. Three or four times it has been seen as a complete circle. It arises from refraction through crystals, shaped like plates or umbrellas, with vertical axes floating in a stable position.

"F. The parhelic circle, a white ring passing through the sun parallel with the horizon and due, as its lack of colour shows, to reflection from the side faces of crystals floating with axes vertical. On it are the parhelia, those already mentioned and others, notably those at 90° and 120°. Other odd ones also occur and, if possible, the distances of these from the sun or moon should be carefully measured with instruments.

"G. Opposite the sun, on the ring, is the very uncommon anthelion through which may pass certain arcs. The parhelic circle is often fragmentary" (*Weather*, 18: 5–6, 1963).

HALOS OF RARE RADII AND WITH UNUSUAL APPENDAGES

On April 24, 1935, at Wick, Scotland, T. J. McGuiness observed a very small halo inside the common 22° halo. "A_1 and A_2 were the first parts to appear, then the small halo marked $B_1B_2B_4B_5$, and finally the arcs of the halo C_1C_3 (probably the 22° halo) with the upper arc of contact C_2. Mr. McGuiness reports that the whole was brightly coloured 'like a rainbow with the shaded part white' and that the radius of the inner halo and the difference between the radii of the two halos were both equal to approximately 4 1/4 inches measured with a pencil at arm's length. The brilliant colours at so many points are exceptional and confirm that this was not an ordinary display." The inner halo may have

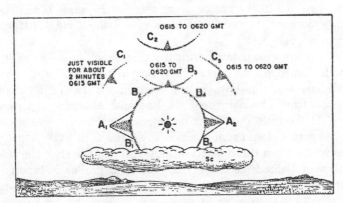

An anomalously small halo with many points of color

been the extremely rare 15° halo (*Meteorological Magazine*, 70: 114, 1935).

D. H. Mobberley, an officer aboard the M.V. *Herefordshire,* had the good fortune to record a common 22° lunar halo flanked by two inexplicable arcs. At the time of the sighting (September 16, 1962), the vessel was in the Indian Ocean bound for Colombo, Ceylon. "Between 1945 and

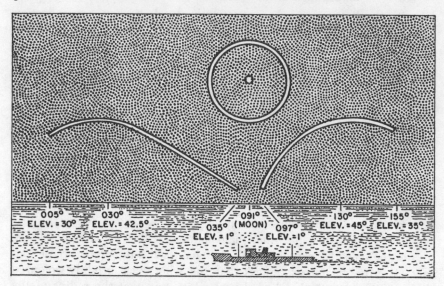

A common 22° halo flanked by unusual arcs

2000 GMT a complete halo, pale silver blue in colour, was seen round the moon, age 17 days, altitude 60°, bearing 091°. The inside radius of the halo was 21 1/2° and the outside 23°. Two asymmetrical arcs having the dimensions shown in the sketch were seen at the same time. They had the same colour as the halo, but were of a paler shade" (*Marine Observer*, 33: 125, 1963).

Mock moons appear less frequently than mock suns, but rarity is not the issue in the following observation; rather it is the strange and unaccountable cones of light projecting horizontally from the moon. The sighting was from Thornaby-on-Tees, England, March 7, 1931, by a Mr. Hobday. "At the time stated the moon was very bright and surrounded by a large narrow ring. From the moon two shafts of light extended, one east, one west. When these shafts of light reached the ring, the colours of the rainbow appeared; then the shafts of light gradually tapered away. The remarkable thing about it all was the distinctness of the rainbow colours, which were as clear as such seen during summer showers. The shafts of light were exactly similar to the beam from a searchlight" (*Meteorological Magazine*, 66: 160, 1931). The cones may have been distorted "moon dogs."

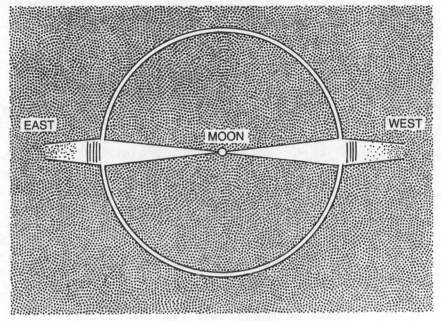

A lunar halo with horizontal cones of light

CROSSES IN THE SKY CREATED BY HALO PHENOMENA

If the horizontal shafts of light described in the preceding observation are bisected by a vertical shaft—a so-called *sun pillar*—the result is an aerial cross within a circle. One can imagine the awe engendered in more primitive times by such an apparition. However sophisticated we may be scientifically, the genesis of the horizontal arms of the cross is not fully understood, although the vertical, sun-pillar portion is. F. S. Davenport reports a cross-in-the-sky seen from Jerseyville, Illinois, on December 30, 1880. "There appeared, at the hour stated, two very brilliant mock suns intersected by a well defined, slightly iris-colored, bright circle, having the sun as its center. This circle was divided into quadrants by four brilliant rays of white light, radiating apparently from the sun, two horizontally and two vertically, the horizontal rays intersecting the mock suns and extending some distance beyond. . . . The most remarkable part of this interesting phenomenon was the appearance of a brilliant inverted crescent near the zenith, subtending from cusp to cusp an angle of about 14°. The colors were disposed in prismatic order and as brilliant as those of the most beautiful rainbow I ever saw; the red outside, toward the sun; the violet inside." The inverted crescent is probably the circumzenithal arc (*Scientific American*, 44: 52, 1881).

A somewhat different cross (often two crosses, one above the other) is created when a vertical sun pillar intersects the upper and lower portions of a normal halo. R. V. Lendenfeld encountered this phenomenon twice in March 1881 while atop Alpine peaks. "The phenomenon is a combination of two rings of light, one of which has its centre in the line connecting the observer with the sun, and appears to have the same dimensions as the large ring sometimes observed round the moon and the sun at low levels. The other ring has its centre in the observer and passes through the zenith and the sun. Both rings are pale, the latter paler than the former, and not visible near the northern horizon. Where the two rings intersect each other, they are much brighter than elsewhere; and so it appears at first sight, if one does not look carefully, as if there were merely two bright crosses, one below and one above the sun, the arms of both crosses being vertical and horizontal." The first circle is a normal solar halo, while the second is apparently a greatly elongated solar pillar, also formed by sunlight reflecting off ice crystals in the atmosphere (*Nature*, 43: 464, 1891).

EXTRAORDINARY MOCK SUNS (SUN DOGS)

The laws of optics predict that the atmospheric ice crystals that cause the common halos will also produce bright patches of light to the right and left of the true sun on the halo ring. Sometimes the rest of the halo ring is very faint and these patches stand out vividly. Such mock suns and mock moons are not at all unusual when halo conditions prevail. Almost all are located 22° or 46° from the sun. There are, however, many rare and unusual mock-sun reports—some at unusual angular distances, others notable for their multiplicity or lack thereof.

An inexplicable one-sided mock sun at a radius of 3° 30′ from the true sun was observed by several passengers aboard the motorship *Fairstar* in the Sea of Timor on June 15, 1965. "About 10 minutes before sunset, Mrs. N. S. noticed to her surprise a second sun, much less bright than the real one, somewhat to the left, but at the same height above the horizon. There was nothing at the symmetrical point to the right." A photograph was taken and subsequent measurement revealed that the mock sun was 3° 30′ away from the real sun. Most mock suns are 22° away from the sun. This is not a known halo phenomenon (*Weather*, 21: 250, 1966).

Another one-sided mock sun was observed at an angle of 10° from the true sun from the S.S. *Manchester Civilian* off the English coast on

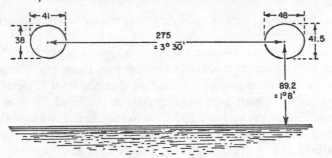

Detailed measurements of a one-sided mock sun

February 16, 1926. "The phenomenon was first seen at 15 h. 46 m. GMT when the true sun, with an altitude of 14° and bearing of 227° was shining brightly with good limb in medium sextant shade, and a heavy squall was moving from west to south-southeast, with the upper edge of the cumulonimbus cloud at a point vertically below the sun and having an altitude of 8°. The phenomenon was an uncoloured image of the true sun at the same altitude and at an angular distance of 10° to the left, certainly not 22°. It was fairly well defined, sufficiently so for an azimuth

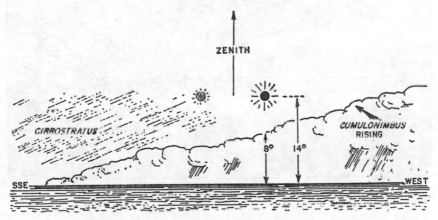

This one-sided mock sun was 10° rather than the usual 22° away from the true sun.

bearing, but not enough for anything but a doubtful sextant altitude. The image had the appearance of the true sun shining through denser layers of cloud, although the cirrostratus was fairly uniform in density, with a slightly mottled appearance. No image was seen to the right of the true sun, and probably, though not certainly, the corresponding position to the right of the sun was already occupied by the moving cumulonimbus. No halo or mock-sun ring was observed" (*Meteorological Magazine*, 61: 91, 1966).

The two foregoing observations pose a double mystery: Why were the angular distances so unusual and why was there not a companion mock sun on the other side of the true sun, as the laws of optics stipulate? Now an even more perplexing riddle is proffered by a mock sun that rises well after the real sun and thus cannot have the same altitude— an apparent theoretical impossibility. The testimony reported is that of Rev. Charles Lane of Kent, England. "The sun appeared to have already risen, and to be about 3° above the horizon, showing a sickly face through a bank of fog; and from the northern limb of the sun there streamed upwards a broad ray of creamy light. . . . Mr. Lane noticed the time, which was 7:15 A.M.—too soon by 33 minutes . . . for the sun-

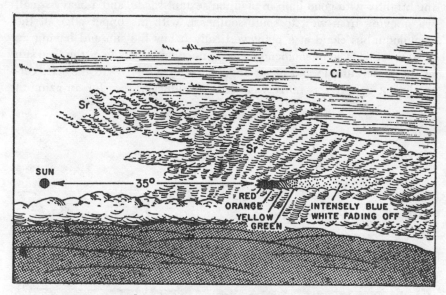

A mock sun with a vividly colored, cometlike tail

rise of the almanac. . . . The ball of the mock sun was well defined (its form distinctly globular) for fully fifteen minutes; it then began gradually to disappear; and it entirely vanished in the first beams of the real luminary of day." Mock suns should be at the same altitude as the real sun (*Meteorological Magazine*, 64: 84, 1929).

Ordinary mock suns sometimes display rainbow colors, but R. Scott has described a vivid, spectral, cometlike mock sun. Scott viewed this curiously shaped mock sun in North Wales, on December 12, 1952. "I first noticed a very brilliant patch of light at 1510 on December 12, 1952, and was immediately impressed by its brilliance and colouring, the latter being most vivid and noticeable. The patch appeared, as indicated in the sketch, rather like a comet with a brilliant tail. The 'nose' ranged rainbow fashion from deep red to green; then followed an intensely blue-white tail which faded off into the background of cloud" (*Meteorological Magazine*, 82: 155, 1953).

Two mock suns are customary, but under extraordinary conditions additional bright patches may be seen. On December 30, 1880, the residents of Sauk Center, Minnesota, were treated to a fantastic halo display with eight mock suns. "The sky was clear, save that the air was full of floating frost crystals that gave a leaden aspect to the heavens around. The sun, as I .have tried to represent, was surrounded by a double halo, both very perfect and distinct in outline. To the right and left of the sun and on the rim of the first halo were very bright parhelia or mock suns. Passing through the sun and these mock suns and around the whole dome of the heavens, seemingly, at about 20° from the horizon, was a great circle of light. This had the appearance of the large ring of Saturn —very bright and about 1/4 of a degree [15'] in width. Again about 15° from the rim of the outer or second halo and in the path of this circle of light, were other parhelia on either side of the sun; and on the opposite side of it from the sun was another or third parhelion. This circle was very brilliant, describing a diameter of about 100°. Intersecting this bright circle, at the points of the two parhelia, passed a somewhat less brilliant ring of light in the form of an ellipse, with its longest diameter some 130° and the short one 80°. At the northern end of the ellipse were three parhelia" (*Scientific American*, 44: 68, 1881).

NONCIRCULAR HALOS

Halo theory does not allow for noncircular halos. But the theory is based upon a uniform veil of identically shaped ice crystals suspended or slowly falling in the upper atmosphere. Complications arise when a mixture of different crystal forms prevail or when the crystal distribution is localized. Even allowing for such departures from the ideal, theorists are generally at a loss to explain the strangely shaped halos described below.

The most common distortion squeezes the ideal circular halo into an ellipse, with its long axis vertical. R. E. W. Butcher, third officer on the S.S. *City of Brisbane* reported seeing a 40° by 30° halo in the North Atlantic on July 8, 1958. "The halo shown in the sketch was seen from 1200 to 1230 G.M.T. It was silvery in appearance, against the 7/8 layer of white Cs [cirrus] cloud present" (*Marine Observer*, 29: 116, 1959).

On February 25, 1901, C. M. Broomall saw a small elliptical lunar halo at Media, Pennsylvania. "There was visible in this locality a lunar halo of rather unusual form. . . . This phenomenon consisted of an elliptical ring around the moon with axes apparently about six degrees and

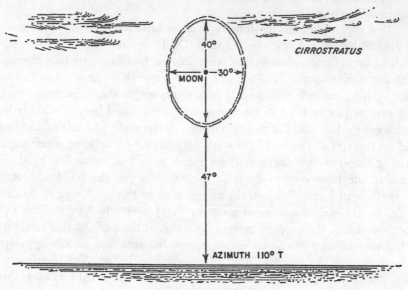

A rare elliptical halo

nine degrees respectively. The principal axis of the ellipse was vertical while the terminator of light on the moon's surface made an angle of about 45 degrees with the horizon. The moon was about half way down in the southwest and half full" (*Science*, 13: 549, 1901).

It is possible that some sort of unusual atmospheric refraction distorted the halos, but in both cases the halos were well above the horizon where atmospheric distortion is not common.

Certainly some form of transient atmospheric distortion or mixing of crystal forms can be invoked to explain the gradual transformation of a teardrop-shaped halo into a circular form. The third officer and quartermaster of the M.V. *Patroclus* observed such a transformation on September 15, 1976, while en route from Los Angeles to Balboa, Canal Zone. "At 0730 GMT an unusually shaped lunar halo was observed to the NNE. The moon, at its gibbous phase, had a 14° halo which projected outwards to a point about 28° from the centre. The appearance was that of a very large tear drop. . . . The phenomenon lasted for about 20 minutes, after which time the elongation gradually diminished until a perfect 14° halo was achieved" (*Marine Observer*, 47: 110, 1977).

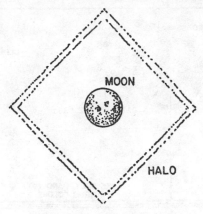

An inexplicable square halo

On January 21, 1913, Lewis Evans saw a most improbable, well-defined square lunar halo. There is nothing in meteorological optics that can account for such a strange apparition. The sighting was made from the R.M.S. *Balmoral Castle*, then in the equatorial Atlantic. "The halo was square with quite straight sides and the angles quite sharp, and I estimated the length of each side of the square at 3 diameters of the moon." The halo was dull yellow and persisted most of the night (*Royal Meteorological Society, Quarterly Journal*, 39: 154, 1913).

OFFSET HALOS

Since the sun or moon is the source of light for halo phenomena, the various circles, arcs, and mock suns and moons are almost invariably centered on these heavenly bodies. When a halo is centered elsewhere, the meteorologist instinctively looks for another light source. Offset rainbows, for example, are not especially rare and can almost always be explained in terms of the sun's image being reflected from a body of water and thus creating a second bright source of light. Unfortunately, the offset halos and arcs introduced in the following reports do not have this easy explanation. Some of the color phenomena, too, are difficult to explain.

On June 13, 1954, on the northern Italian coast, a naturalist and chemical engineer made a detailed report of a complex and puzzling halo display. "We first noticed a circle of darker sky, concentric with the sun, at 11.45. At noon we noticed the second circle (same diameter as the first); it was paler than the first, and its circumference cut the centre of the sun. The peripherae of both circles were concentric rings of spec-

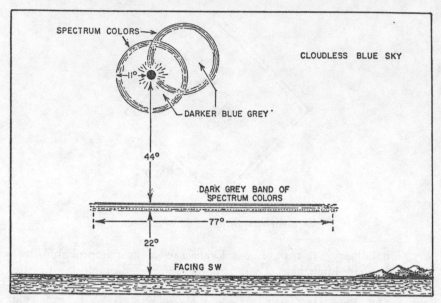

Normal halo with an offset halo intersecting the sun

trum colours (unfortunately I did not note the positional order of the colours). At 1210 we noticed the horizontal bar of dark grey 'cloud' in front of us, between the almost overhead sun and the horizon; it was composed of horizontal layers of the spectrum colours (again, unfortunately, I did not note the positional order of the colours). Meanwhile the two circles overhead maintained their position in relation to the sun, but were gradually becoming fainter." An offset halo should have an offset light source, but none was observed (*Weather*, 10: 359, 1955).

Another offset halo, this time a lunar halo, was observed by D. J. A. Pritchard from the M.V. *Port Chalmers* in the Caribbean. "A distinct lunar halo of radius 22° was observed. The halo was obscured from time to time by Cu [cumulus clouds]. At 0640 an arc of a second halo, of apparently slightly larger radius, appeared. It intersected the primary and the outer perimeter passed to within about 2° of the moon, as shown in the sketch." No explanation can be given for the slightly larger offset halo, if indeed it was a true halo (*Marine Observer*, 21: 16, 1951).

A similar halo phenomenon, but with the offset halo a complete circle, was reported from both Tokyo and Yokohama on January 29, 1882. "At first I was under the impression that the figure was slightly elongated on the outer circle—that is to say, the distance from the centre of the moon to the edge of the first halo was less than that from the edge of the first halo to the farthest point in the second; but on drawing it I am

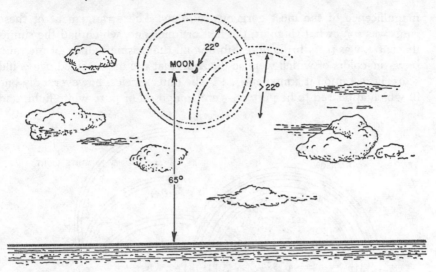

Normal 22° lunar halo with a larger offset halo

convinced that this was an optical illusion. The lower part of the second halo intersected the lower horn of the moon in a peculiar way, as given in the drawing" (*Knowledge,* 1: 521, 1882).

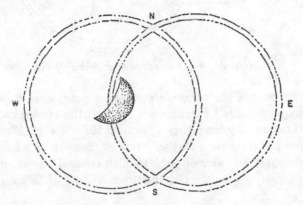

Offset halo intersects the moon.

As if a single offset halo were not enough to pique the imagination, Alfred T. King reported a "halo or corona of great splendor" that appeared over Greensburgh, Pennsylvania, on August 28, 1841. King's halo consisted of several offset halos to the right of the primary halo. "This phenomenon consisted of from three to five circular belts or zones of light, one of which emulated, in appearance, the splendor and magnificence of the most gorgeous rainbow. The arrangement of these rings was somewhat singular; the first or inner one, which had the sun as its centre, was *truly* brilliant, exhibiting all the prismatic hues of the rainbow, the colors of which were so dazzling that the unprotected eye could scarcely rest upon it a moment. . . . The outer circles, however, only one of which appeared to be perfect, were composed of pure white light, and

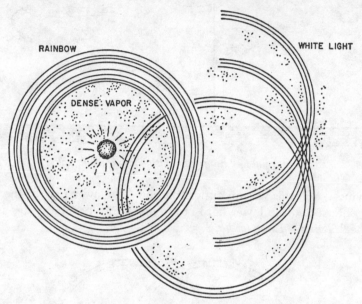

Multiple offset halos seen over Pennsylvania

had for their centres the circumference, or a point near it, of the inner ring. Consequently, their circumferences, if all the circles had been perfect, would necessarily have passed through the apparent situation of the sun. I mentioned, however, that only one of these rings was perfect; the others were concentric arcs of circles which crossed one another, as seen in the accompanying diagram" (*American Journal of Science*, 1: 40: 25, 1841).

But even the Greensburgh phenomenon pales beside an extraordinarily complex system of halos and arcs that appeared over the Indian Ocean on May 29, 1963. "Between 1515 and 1520 GMT, when the moon was at an altitude of 60° and bearing 302°, the halo complex shown in the sketch was observed. The halo (a) and the arc (b) formed first; x and y appeared at the time when a and b touched. The arc z formed when x and y moved outward and joined; the whole system faded when z lay along the top of a" (*Marine Observer*, 34: 73, 1964).

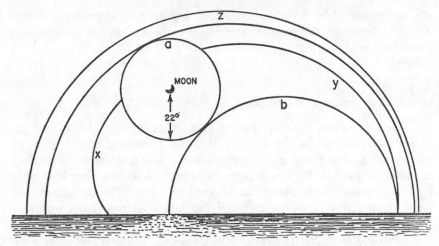

An extraordinarily complex display of offset lunar halos and arcs

At the risk of supersaturating the reader's appetite for static halo phenomena, one final item from my collection illustrates in a single display: (1) a double halo, (2) a mock sun, (3) a mock-sun pillar, and (4) a

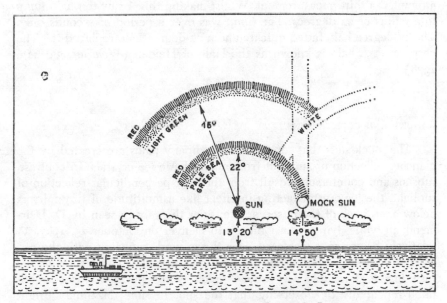

A double halo, mock sun with pillar, and offset arc

curious offset arc. The display was highly colored and most impressive. Mock-sun pillars are extremely rare and when they do occur are generally accompanied by a real sun pillar, as was seen in 1957 in the South Atlantic; therefore, this unusual apparition embodies several puzzling aspects (*Marine Observer*, 28: 17–18, 1958).

MOVING AND JUMPING HALOS

The atmosphere is a dynamic milieu. As it changes, halos and associated phenomena brighten and fade away. Conceivably, the types of ice crystals could change rather suddenly too and transform one variety of halo into another. Such a change could explain the jumping halo seen by D. J. Wadsworth in Manitoba on April 30, 1977. "The cumulonimbus were moving from west to east and the glaciated tops from north to south. In the glaciated sheet a weakly coloured halo was visible. Using a home-made theodolite [surveyor's instrument], I undertook a routine measurement of the angular radius of the halo. To my surprise the value was 15° from the sun to the inner edge of the halo, with about a 1/2° [30′] spread of the spectrum, blue to the outside and red to the inside. I checked the instrument and made a second measurement, having doubted my first. This confirmed my first observation but, still not sure, I attempted a third measurement. Whilst making this, I saw the halo *jump* to a radius of 22 degrees. The *jump* was over a period of seconds only. The 15-degree halo faded quickly and a 22-degree halo replaced it." The very rare 15° halo is known as the Halo of Heiden (*Weather*, 33: 113, 1978).

SUBSUNS AND COUNTERSUNS

The mock suns that sometimes accompany halos are created by the glancing reflection of sunlight from atmospheric ice crystals. In contrast, subsuns and countersuns result from the near-perpendicular reflection of sunlight, the ice crystals acting in effect like a multitude of tiny mirrors below or in back of the observer. Consider the subsun seen by D. Deirmendjian while flying from Chicago to Denver on October 15, 1967. "A relatively bright spot was seen near the ground, traveling with the aircraft at what appeared to be the position for specular reflection of the sun's image. That this was indeed precisely the position was corroborated repeatedly by observing that the spot became dazzlingly bright whenever it passed over a small body of water (ponds, rivers, etc.). . . . The spot appeared only *between clouds* where there might have been some tenuous haze, but disappeared again in larger cloudless areas over bare terrain and vegetation." The bright spot was probably created by the reflection of the sun by a layer of ice crystals under the aircraft (*Applied Optics*, 7: 556, 1968).

Another countersun was observed by Stephen Gauss in 1958 at Marblehead, Massachusetts. "I saw a golden-brown glow in the sky directly opposite the sun. This glow, about four to six degrees in diameter, remained visible until the sun had completely set." This glowing patch was probably a countersun or anthelion caused by the reflection of sunlight by ice crystals located directly opposite the sun (*Sky and Telescope*, 17: 596, 1958).

BISHOP'S RING AND GREAT VOLCANIC ERUPTIONS

For almost two years after the cataclysmic eruption of Krakatoa in the East Indies on August 27, 1883, the entire planet was treated to spectacular sunsets. In addition, the sun was often surrounded by a colored corona quite different from the common ice-crystal halos. This apparently new phenomenon was designated a Bishop's Ring, after a scientist who provided one of the first descriptions. "Bishop's Ring is a circumsolar corona formed of two parts: around the sun is a limb of bluish silver flashing, having a radius of about 10°; it is surrounded by a copper-red circular band of about 20° in width, the radius of the middle of this band being about 15°. The copper circle on the inner side is mixed with the silver limb, on the outer side with the blue sky, the contours being badly defined, especially the exterior, and this gradual decrease of colour gives a strange appearance to the blue of the sky" (*Observatory*, 26: 431, 1903).

In 1902 and 1903, some twenty years after Krakatoa, both the spectacular sunsets and the Bishop's Ring reappeared. This time there was no exceptional volcanic action. The "new" Bishop's Ring was described as follows: "A glare around the sun merging into a faint smoky red or purple ring 5° to 10° wide, with the maximum color about 30° from the sun, has been observed here during the past two weeks. . . . *January 9* [1903]—at 9 to 10 A.M. yesterday morning and again at 10 A.M. today the ring about the sun resembling a faint Bishop's Ring was visible. . . . At 10 A.M. a whitish glare surrounded the sun out to about 20°, when it showed a ring of slightly yellow light; outside of this, at a distance of 25° to 30° from the sun, was a ring of faint smoky red or purple light visible out to a distance of about 40° from the sun" (*Science*, 17: 150, 1903).

In 1914 more remarkable sunsets appeared along with the Bishop's Ring. This time a volcano in the Aleutians had erupted and provided an easy explanation. Unfortunately the whole business of the Bishop's Ring and the Krakatoa sunsets is complicated by scattered reports of remarkable sunsets *before* the Krakatoa eruption. (See page 139.) There seem ample grounds for believing that volcanic matter was not necessarily the only cause of the fabulous sunsets and appearances of Bishop's Ring. Could extraterrestrial matter have been injected into the atmosphere, as may also have been the case with the Tunguska Event?

KALEIDOSCOPIC SUNS

On January 9, 1923, at Cork, Ireland, there occurred a solar phenomenon that seems well beyond the capacity of atmospheric optical theory to explain. The observer, a Joseph Mintern, termed it a kaleidoscopic sun. The name fits. The phenomenon is so improbable that one would seriously question the veracity of Mr. Mintern if similar reports did not exist. Here is Mintern's testimony. "A friend shouting to me to hurry out, I saw the sun behaving in a most unusual fashion; now surrounded by bright red, flashing rays in all directions, then changing to yellow in which the body of the sun, though more clearly visible, appeared to dance and shift about here and there in a radius of about 5°; again, changing to green, the rays flashing as in the red—all these changes taking place in less time than it takes to write. . . . Of all the beauties seen I should think the quickly changing mock suns the most beautiful as they flashed here and there faster than it was possible to count them. The colours were so brilliant and dazzling that even after I had come indoors anything I looked at appeared a mixture of all the colours seen." The changing rays and shifting mock suns may have arisen from sheets of falling ice crystals of different geometries (*Meteorological Magazine*, 58: 10, 1923).

In June 1885, several residents of Birmingham, Michigan, saw a similar display just before sunset. "The sky was clear with the exception of a few clouds of the cumulonimbus order a few degrees above and to the northward of the sun. Suddenly there appeared a peculiarly weird and hazy condition of the atmosphere. There was an indescribable commingling and general diffusion of all the hues of the rainbow. During this state of things there appeared in the sky, on the earth, and on the trees, innumerable balls of decomposed light, presenting all imaginable colors and apparently of about the size of a bushel basket. They were uniform in size and appearance. The phenomenon was confined to that region of sky about the sun, extending but a few degrees each side of it. It lasted about twenty minutes, when it disappeared as suddenly as it came" (*American Meteorological Journal*, 3: 486, 1887).

The kaleidoscopic suns bring to mind the famous 1917 "Miracle of Fatima" seen in Portugal by many thousands of people. This event has not been described in the scientific journals examined to date, but Charles Osborne gives a good discussion of the event in *Catholic World*, 169: 208–15, 1949. The similarities between the "dancing sun" of Fatima and kaleidoscopic suns are strong.

Brocken Specters, Glories, Heiligenschein

A wild tale has long circulated about a giant specter seen by mountain climbers on the Brocken, a German mountain. As the story goes, there was once a climber working his way along a precipice who suddenly saw an immense human figure rise out of the mists toward him. In his fright he lost his footing and fell to his death. Doubtless this is just a story, but the Brocken specter does exist, not only on the Brocken but wherever shadows are cast upon mist, fog, and fine water droplets.

That one's shadow can be seen, even in giant proportions, on a wall of white mist is not surprising. Some features of the phenomenon, however, are more difficult to explain. A common feature of the Brocken specter is the "glory" or concentric rings of color centered on the observer's head. As many as five complete, rainbow-colored rings have been observed. There is controversy as to whether these glories have the same origin as the solar coronas (i.e., refraction and reflection from water droplets) or whether optical diffraction and interference are at work.

Curious things happen inside the glories. Sometimes, an observer can see only his own shadow; at other times, nearby persons are also visible. Some glories are elliptical rather than circular. Glories may be distorted by the approach of another person. Another unusual feature is the appearance of dark streaks that seem to radiate from the observer's arms and other linear objects. There is much that is difficult to explain in terms of conventional optics.

A phenomenon similar to the Brocken specter can be seen when the sun is low and the observer's shadow is cast upon a field fresh with dew. He sees his head's shadow surrounded by a luminous halo called *heiligenschein*. As with the colored glory, the observer sees only his own head with a halo while others nearby see only theirs. *Heiligenschein* is attributed to rainbowlike reflections and refractions inside spherical dewdrops, but the spectral colors overlap (as in fogbows) so that the bow is white.

GIANT BROCKEN SPECTERS

A typical Brocken specter was seen by the famous French astronomers E. M. Antoniadi and C. Flammarion in 1896. They had been making stellar measurements at Flammarion's observatory at Juvisy, when an incredibly dense fog enveloped them. "On stepping out to the terrace adjoining the dome to see what was going on, I was very agreeably surprised to see my shadow some 200 feet high, as thrown on the mist by a strong lamp, rise up to the zenith! It was a very curious spectacle indeed. Every movement of the hand or head was faithfully reproduced by the phantasm. But only the head and shoulders of the figure were neatly delineated. The remainder of the body was exceedingly indistinct. Giant rays of a grey colour radiated from the head (the eyes as a centre) in all directions, and expecially from the projecting parts of the figure, the ears, shoulders, corners of the hat, &c., to a very great distance from the centre of emanation." The giant proportions of the specter are common, but the gray rays are rare and puzzling (*British Astronomical Association, Journal*, 7: 79, 1896).

GLORIES OR BROCKEN BOWS

On August 4, 1893, a party climbing Gausta Mountain, Norway, saw well-defined glories or Brocken bows. "We mounted to the flagstaff in

Brocken specter with encircling glories projected on a fog bank

order to obtain a better view of the scenery, and there we at once observed in the fog, in an easterly direction, a double rainbow forming a complete circle and seeming to be 20 to 30 feet distant from us. In the middle of this we all appeared as black, erect, and nearly life-size silhouettes. The outlines of the silhouettes were so sharp that we could easily recognise the figures of each other, and every movement was reproduced. The head of each individual appeared to occupy the centre of the circle, and each of us seemed to be standing on the inner periphery of the rainbow" (*Nature*, 48: 391, 1893).

On July 12, 1875, a party was ascending Snowdon, an English mountain. H. J. Wetenhall reported their experiences as follows: "Drifting toward us, when very near, the cloud dropped over the eastern shoulder of the mountain just where it dips toward Capel Curig. As we stood watching, great was our surprise and delight as we beheld painted upon it, not the *arc-en-ciel* with which we are familiar, but a complete and prismatic circle, apparently about thirty feet in diameter, in the very centre of which we ourselves were depicted, the image being somewhat enlarged but clearly defined; as we arranged the party in groups, or bowed to each other, every form and movement was faithfully reproduced in the picture" (*Nature*, 12: 292, 1875).

TWO FAMOUS BROCKEN SPECTERS AND THEIR GLORIES

Possibly the most famous Brocken specter is not to be found in the Alps but rather atop Adams Peak in Ceylon (Sri Lanka). This is another "giant" Brocken specter, and again there are the inexplicable projecting lines. Ralph Abercromby ascended the peak in 1886 with instruments to ascertain the nature of the phenomenon. "The morning broke in a very unpromising manner. Heavy clouds lay all about, lightning flickered over a dark bank to the right of the rising sun, and at frequent intervals masses of light vapour blew up from the valley and enveloped the summit in their mist. Suddenly, at 6:30 A.M., the sun peeked through a chink in the eastern sky, and we saw a shadow of the peak projected on the land; then a little mist drove in front of the shadow, and we saw a circular rainbow of perhaps 8° or 10° diameter surrounding the shadow of the summit, and as we waved our arms we saw the shadow of our limbs moving in the mist. Two dark lines seemed to radiate from the centre of the bow, almost in a prolongation of the slopes of the Peak. . . . Twice this shadow appeared and vanished as cloud obscured the sun, but the third time we saw what has apparently struck so many observers. The shadow seemed to rise up and stand in front of us in the air, with rainbow and spectral arms, and then to fall down suddenly to the earth as

Brocken specter of the Desert View Watch Tower at Grand Canyon, Arizona

the bow disappeared. The cause of the whole was obvious. As a mass of vapour drove across the shadow, the condensed particles caught the shadow and in this case were also large enough to form a bow. As the vapour blew past, the shadow fell to its natural level—the surface of the earth. An hour later, when the sun was well up, we again saw the shadow of the Peak and ourselves, this time encircled by a double bow. Then the shadow was so far down that there was no illusion of standing up in front of us" (*Nature*, 33: 532, 1886).

A similar sight can be seen on occasion from the Desert View Watch Tower, Grand Canyon, Arizona. "The spectre consists of a series of colors which arc or bow around the shadow of the tower. Yellow was innermost, with reds and purples forming the intermediate and outer bands. Cloud particles diffused the colors along their adjacent edges and formed many interesting blends. Later in the same day, the spectre shifted and was centered over the shorter shadow of the *kiva* section of the tower" (*Science*, 119: 164, 1954).

LUMINOUS HALOS AROUND THE SHADOWS OF HEADS (HEILIGENSCHEIN)

On December 4, 1912, L. L. Fermor was stationed in the Central Provinces of India. He encountered a typical example of *heiligenschein*. "I had set out on field work at dawn, with my colleague, Mr. H. Walker, and two *chaprasis* (Indian servants). I happened to be watching our shadows as we passed along the edge of a field of young green wheat, when, to my surprise, I noticed a halo of light round the shadow of my own head and neck. Looking at the other shadows, I was still more surprised to see that only my shadow was invested with this halo. I directed the attention of Mr. Walker and the *chaprasis* to the phenomenon and found that each could see a halo round his own head only. . . . The sun was at low altitude on our left, and the wheat was soaking wet with dew on our right." The resemblance to the Brocken specter is obvious. Both are created by veils of water droplets (*Nature*, 90: 592, 1913).

Stephen F. Jacobs, a physicist, recalled a curious, somewhat different, self-centered shadow. "The following example of such a phenomenon excited my curiosity even when I was very young: standing on the end of a diving board over deep water, the sun behind me, I often wondered as I studied my shadow on the water's surface about the rays which seemed to emanate from my head. They radiated from a spot between my eyes, and the rays seemed to glisten and to rotate like the spokes of a wheel, generally rotating continuously in one direction. When a friend would join me, we would both see the rays coming from our own heads. This phenomenon is observed sufficiently seldom to elude investigation, for it is not a very striking effect and requires: (1) deep water, over three feet depending on the nature of the bottom; (2) sunshine; (3) suspended particles, such as algae or minerals; (4) relatively quiet water." The rotating rays are apparently caused by sunlight first refracted by small waves and then reflected from suspended particles (*American Journal of Physics*, 21: 234, 1953).

Rare Rainbows and Allied Spectral Phenomena

Everyone knows the rainbow and just about everyone also knows that it is produced by sunlight falling on a veil of raindrops. In more scientific terms, the sunlight (or moonlight) is dispersed into the spectral colors by reflections inside the transparent raindrops. Two internal reflections create the primary bow; three reflections produce the larger, rarer secondary bow with a reversed color sequence. Such commonplace rainbows are excluded here as unmysterious, but this still leaves us with offset rainbows, red rainbows, white "fog" bows, cloudbows, and many other intriguing color phenomena associated with natural water droplets.

How do all these variations of the rainbow phenomenon arise? The classical rainbow situation may be complicated by several things. Most important is the presence of an additional source of light usually due to the reflection of sunlight off a body of water. Displaced rainbows are just one result; one can imagine water ripples introducing additional effects. A second source of distortions is a low sun, whose light has lost some of the shorter wavelengths (violets and blues) due to scattering through a long atmospheric path. The presence of thin, intervening sheets of rain can also create extra spectral phenomena. Even with these possible complications understood, many rainbow phenomena cannot be explained with conventional rainbow theory using any combination of perturbing situations.

Since droplets of water represent the source of spectral bows, we should look for colored bows on cloud tops (from aircraft or mountaintops, of course), on fields covered with dew, and wherever nature spreads out layers of transparent, spherical droplets. In searching for rainbowlike phenomena, one must not be led astray by the closely related halos and glories described earlier in this chapter—although sometimes even an expert may be perplexed as to how to classify an enigmatic strip of prismatic color in the sky.

UNUSUAL MULTIPLE RAINBOWS

The common varieties of multiple rainbows have the same center, just like the garden-variety multiple halo. On rare occasions, though, additional bows will form slightly displaced vertically. A triple rainbow of this type was seen in the Indian Ocean on November 26, 1961, by the officers of the M.V. *City of Khartoum.* "At 0030 GMT a line squall was observed ahead of the vessel, moving approx. SE'S; a single rainbow was seen to form which very clearly showed the colours of the spectrum. Ten minutes later, as the vessel was passing through the line squall, then lying NE'N–SW'W, a triple rainbow was seen directly ahead. All three bows had the same order of colours—red on the outside and violet inside." A meteorologist commented on this observation as follows: Rainbow A is the common primary; rainbow B is probably caused by sunlight reflecting off the water to form a bow with a raised center; rainbow C is similar to the common secondary rainbow except that its colors are not reversed as they should be. Rainbow C is therefore anomalous (*Marine Observer,* 32: 185, 1962).

Less perplexing is the eccentric display reported by Mackaeg in 1873 from England. It was described as consisting "of two rainbows, eccentric to each other, even at the same time, seen a few evenings since, just before sunset. An explanation of the phenomenon is simple. A magnificent rainbow was being refracted from a dense shower, when a narrow (if I may use the term) shower came in front of the denser, showing a rainbow on itself, but not intercepting, only refracting the sun's rays on and from the further shower" (*English Mechanic,* 16: 410, 1873).

HORIZONTALLY OFFSET AND INTERSECTING RAINBOWS

One might term the first example below "classical" in that the rainbow display is simple and easily explained. It will serve as a convenient reference point indicating where our science of meteorological optics is successful. The place is Solway Firth, Scotland. J. Crichton relates his August 12, 1930, sighting. "I observed an unusually brilliant primary rainbow together with a secondary with numerous spurious bows on the underside of the southernmost portion of the primary. . . . The impor-

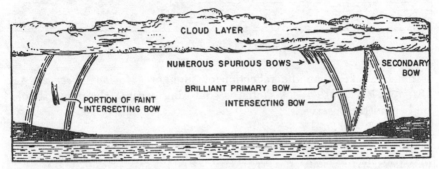

Primary and secondary rainbows with spurious and intersecting bows

tant part, however, of the observation was the appearance of an intersecting bow between the southern extremity of the primary and the secondary bow. . . . The colours of the intersecting bow were brilliant and of the same order as those of the primary. . . . Such an intersecting rainbow arises from the presence of two sources of parallel rays. In the present instance one set was that coming directly from the sun giving the primary and the secondary bows and the other set from the image of the sun in the bay to the westward of the point of observation" (*Meteorological Magazine*, 65: 213, 1930).

Officers of the S.S. *Helenus* saw an offset or intersecting rainbow in the Indian Ocean on August 31, 1963. The interesting feature here is that it is nighttime and these are lunar rainbows. "Directly after a shower of rain had passed, at 2315 GMT, a bright lunar rainbow was seen, having an altitude of about 25°. A very pale bow, which seemed to have a larger radius, intersected the first bow as shown in the sketch. Both were of very short duration enabling a measurement of the altitude of the bright bow, only, to be made. Neither bow showed any colouring." Lunar rainbows, which are rare, are usually uncolored. Offset lunar rainbows are even scarcer because the reflection of moonlight off the surface of water

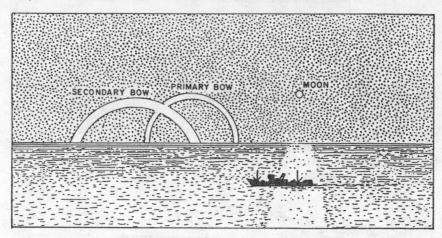

Lunar rainbow with intersecting arc

is much weaker than the reflection of sunlight (*Marine Observer*, 34: 181, 1964). The observer's sketch is confusing because the moon should be behind the observer.

RAINBOWS WITH SPURIOUS WHITE ARCS

Like halos, rainbows are sometimes accompanied by spurious arcs. "Spurious" here generally means inexplicable, for meteorological optics has had little success in this area. A simple instance occurred off the Florida coast on October 31, 1950. The observer was P. A. A. James, third officer of the M.V. *Laguna*. "Off Mollasses Reef an arc of a rainbow was observed extending from right to left for approximately a quarter of a semicircle. At the same time a white arc intersected the other. . . ." There is no accepted explanation for the white arc (*Marine Observer*, 21: 215, 1951).

A much more complex spectral display appeared to the crew of the M.V. *Arabistan* in the South Atlantic in 1956. "At 0802 GMT during generally cloudy conditions giving light showers of rain near the vessel, the end of a rainbow of large radius was seen on the horizon, the rest of the bow being hidden by low [clouds] (sketch 1). The band was 4° wide and fairly bright. Reading from the inside, the colors were red, yellow, green, blue, yellow, white, pink, and red. The sun was then clear of cloud. At 0805, the color sequence from the inside was yellow, purple, blue, green, yellow, orange, and red. By now the sun was shining through thin As [altostratus clouds]. At 0806, during showers in the area, the bright, white ends of a second bow became visible inside the

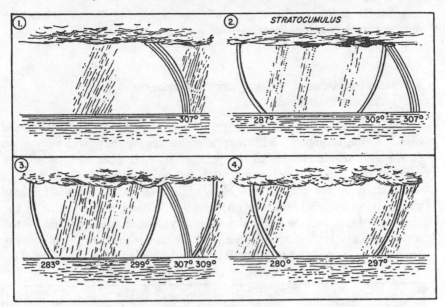

Rainbow with abnormal colors and shifting white arcs

rainbow (sketch 2). . . . At 0813 yet another fainter white bow, 2° wide, appeared outside the others. The bearings were then as shown in sketch 3." The rainbow colors are abnormal and the white arcs cannot be accounted for by conventional rainbow theory (*Marine Observer,* 27: 210, 1957).

PILLARS AT THE ENDS OF THE RAINBOW

There may be no pots of gold where rainbows seem to intersect the earth's surface, but sometimes one sees peculiar vertical pillars of light tangent to the ends of rainbows. Rainbow pillars were observed by a Mr. Bowman from the steamer *Commodore* making her way up the estuary of the Clyde, in Scotland. First a brilliant rainbow formed with several supernumerary bows below. (Supernumerary bows are created by optical interference and, while curious, are not mysterious.) Next "I . . . observed a faint perpendicular light on the north side of the primary bow and apparently in contact with its outer margin and as though diverging from it in a tangent. By degrees this shot up higher and acquired the prismatic colours, which were clearly in the same order as in the primary bow, though fainter. Shortly afterwards a similar tangent was seen on the opposite side, in all respects corresponding, both extending upwards to about the height of the large bow" (*Reports of the British Association for the Advancement of Science,* 1840, part 2, p. 12).

A STRANGE DARK-COLORED SPACE BETWEEN PRIMARY
AND SECONDARY RAINBOWS

In the evening of July 20, 1947, a brilliant primary rainbow formed over Urbana, Illinois. In addition, "a secondary rainbow was very plain above and outside the arc of the primary bow. In this, as is usual, the order of the colors was reversed, with the red at the bottom and green above. It is uncommon for the blue, indigo, and violet bands to show above the green, and this was no exception. However, the width of the secondary bow, even without the blues, was about equal to that of the whole primary bow. Between the primary and secondary bows the sky appeared to be lacking in light. It was dark, leaden gray in color." This

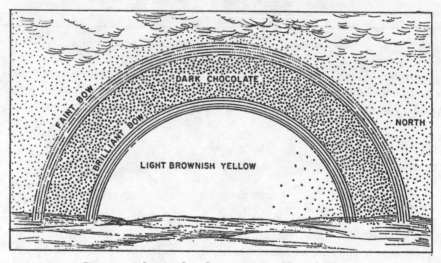

Primary and secondary bows separated by a dark area

dark region is most curious and not accounted for by the usual rainbow theory. Possibly the primary and secondary bows somehow interfered with each other to create the dark band (*Science,* 106: 225, 1947).

The strange dark band has been noticed before. A "Mr. B." made the following report from Leeds, England, on the evening of August 19, 1875. "The entire plane enclosed by the inner rainbow, except a portion towards the north, was of uniform light brownish-yellow colour, unchecquered by any other colour or shade. On the other hand, the plane between the two rainbows, especially toward the south, was of a uniform dark chocolate colour, forming a conspicuous and somewhat startling contrast to the lighter-coloured expanse enclosed by the inner rainbow. The lines of demarcation were sharp and defined, adding to the force of the contrast" (*English Mechanic*, 21: 616, 1875).

RADIAL STREAKS IN RAINBOWS

The first item mentions crepuscular rays crossing a bright double-rainbow display and optically interacting with a third colorless band. Crepuscular rays are almost always seen near sunset and sunrise when fanlike rays of light seem to stream through cloud formations. (Crepuscular rays are treated in more detail later in this chapter since their explanation is not pat.) Here the main questions revolve around the nature of the colorless bow and the peculiar interaction with the bright rays. The observation took place in the Indian Ocean on July 14, 1958. At 0215 GMT primary and secondary rainbows were seen. "Inside the primary, on the righthand side and parallel to it, a portion of a colourless bow, which persisted for 5 minutes, extended from the horizon—the spacing

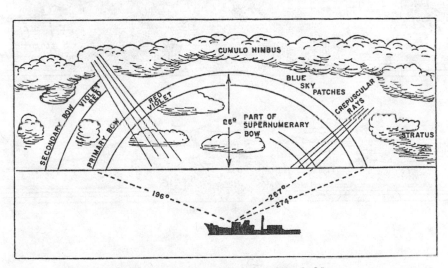

A double rainbow with unexplained radial beams

between the two bows being 7° of arc. A number of crepuscular rays crossed the primary and secondary, while another set crossed the primary and the colourless bow. A very interesting feature was the well-marked band of colouring that occurred in the place where the crepuscular rays and the colourless bow overlapped. The order of the colouring was the same as in the primary bow—i.e., with red on the outside" (*Marine Observer*, 29: 114–15, 1959).

MALFORMED RAINBOWS POSSIBLY CREATED BY REFLECTIONS FROM ROUGH WATER

On September 13, 1955, a distorted rainbow was observed from the S.S. *Thalamus* in the North Atlantic. "At 1115 G.M.T. a light rain shower passed overhead and travelled in a w'ly [westerly] direction. When about a mile away, bearing 280° T, a brilliant coloration was observed on the cloud (sketch 1), approximately 300 yards long. In the sketches the letter *a* denotes a brownish-orange colour, *b* a greenish tinge, and *c* turquoise blue. After about 3 minutes the lefthand side of the ellipse seemed to merge into the other side until only a 'hump' of one colour remained (sketch 2). After a further 2 minutes the coloration was ob-

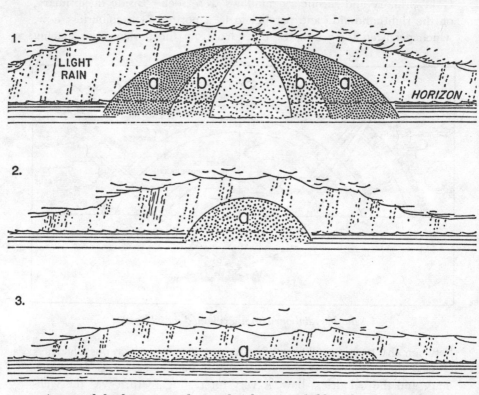

A spectral display seen in the North Atlantic, probably a distorted rainbow

served to be flattening and lengthening into a thin band (sketch 3), which completely disappeared after a [still] further 2 minutes" (*Marine Observer*, 26: 147, 1956).

A wildly deformed rainbow (if it can be dignified with that name) appeared to the crew of the M.V. *Phemius* on July 31, 1973, then in the Coral Sea. ". . . at 0250 GMT a horizontal distribution of the spectrum was observed . . . the base of the phenomenon being at sea level. The sky was completely clouded over with Sc and Cu [stratocumulus and cumulus clouds]. The ship's course was 191° T. while the phenomenon bore 170° T.; the sun bore about 360° T. There were showers of rain visible near the vessel but no precipitation at the time of observation." This may have been a rainbow derived from the image of the sun on an ocean distorted by a smooth swell (*Marine Observer*, 44: 110, 1974).

RED RAINBOWS AT SUNSET

Red sun and sky at sunset and sunrise are common. The light from the low sun must travel nearly horizontally along a much longer atmospheric path than when the sun is high in the sky. The atmosphere scatters the short wavelengths (blues, violets, etc.) leaving mainly the reddish colors in the direct beams. If rainbow conditions prevail at sunset, the resulting display will also be devoid of the shorter wavelengths—that is, the display will be mostly red. A typical red bow was seen by H. Harries at Hove, England, on July 30, 1922. "I observed over the sea about 20° of the southern end of a very remarkable rainbow—a pillar of a dark red colour, the red so intense that none of the other prismatic colours could be detected. The western sky at this time was gorgeous in brilliant yellow gold, the sun itself being hidden by a cloud bank. Gradually the red pillar stretched up and curved over until by 19 h. 47 m. it reached to a point above the South Downs and about 150° from the sea" (*Meteorological Magazine*, 57: 246, 1922).

DYNAMIC RAINBOWS

Theoretically a rainbow should appear stationary to the observer. Its direction is fixed by the line connecting the sun and the observer. Thus optical theory has no ready explanation for the moving colored arcs seen by L. E. Watson in the Outer Hebrides on December 16, 1952. The shifting wind indicated that a weather trough had just passed. ". . . the wind dropped slightly and the rain became intermittent, and during this period a faint but complete rainbow was observed at 1125 between Ben-

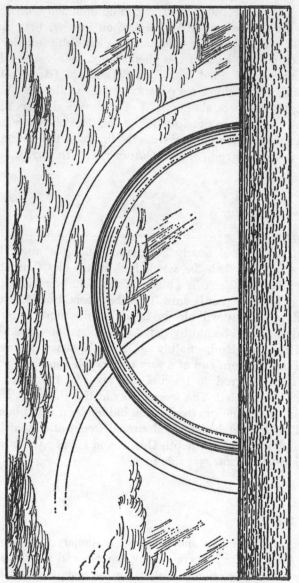

Double lunar rainbow with an intersecting arc

becula and North Uist. At 1135 an arc formed in the opposite direction to the original bow which had faded and now had only an arc composed of the western half of the bow, red being uppermost in both arcs. [In] subsequent developments . . . red [is] uppermost in all the arcs . . ." (*Meteorological Magazine*, 82: 218, 1953).

UNUSUAL LUNAR RAINBOWS

Moonlight is so weak compared with sunlight that lunar rainbows are exceedingly scarce and, when they are seen, they are usually colorless. The colors appearing in the two cases of lunar rainbows described below are therefore unusual in their own right. The unexplained extra bows, arcs, and asymmetries make the sightings even more remarkable.

On November 10, 1948, the following phenomenon was observed from the S.S. *Corinthic* in the North Atlantic: "Two complete lunar rainbows were observed and one arc of a third bow. The lower complete bow showed the spectrum colors very distinctly, but the upper bow and remaining arc were white." The offset white arc is not explained by the optical theory of rainbows (*Marine Observer*, 19: 188, 1949).

On January 1, 1953, from the M.V. *Glenhank* off the Seychelles: "A lunar rainbow was observed with clear colours—violet, yellow, and green.

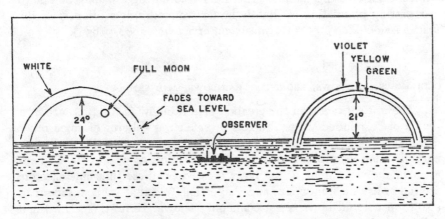

A lunar rainbow opposite the moon (the normal situation) plus an inexplicable white arc near the moon

This formation remained pronounced for a few minutes only. A second arc which formed beside the full moon was white and higher in the sky than the first, although its arch was not so wide and tended to fade near sea level." The white arc near the moon cannot be accounted for by ordinary rainbow or halo theories (*Marine Observer*, 24: 13, 1954).

WHITE RAINBOWS OR FOGBOWS

G. H. Pickering saw a representative fogbow from the S.S. *Saxon* as it was passing through thick fogbanks in the North Atlantic on January 7, 1928. "A single halo was observed at intervals, opposite the moon—i.e., 180° [from it]. The angle between the horizon and upper limb varied in size from about 6° to 10°, the lower limb appearing to reach the side of the ship." Fogbows form when the sun or moon shine on minute droplets of water suspended in the air. The fog droplets are so small that the usual prismatic colors of the rainbow merge together to form a white arc opposite the sun or moon. True halos form around the sun or moon (*Marine Observer*, 6: 11, 1919).

"Besides the ordinary fogbow which can frequently be seen, a fainter or supernumerary one may also be observed on rare occasions. This bow is smaller than the primary and separated from it by a space of about three degrees. It consists of a ring of green succeeded on the inside by a ring of red light, each being about half a degree in breadth and concentric with the principal bow. . . . The latter was sometimes irregular, owing apparently to the presence of small needles or lines of grey or whitish light crossing the arc." The inner colored fogbow may be due to a coexisting population of slightly larger water droplets (*Report of the British Association for the Advancement of Science*, 1884, p. 656).

CLOUDBOWS, DEWBOWS, BROADCAST RAINBOWS, AND SANDBOWS

The critical factor in the creation of a rainbow is the presence of a region of suspended water droplets or reflecting spheres of some other material. Clouds, dewy fields, misty lake surfaces, waterfalls, and other natural situations provide such screens of droplets as well as the customary rain showers. Some of the bows created by these unusual reflectors are rather astonishing in size and shape. The fact that such surfaces can also form colored bows is not commonly known. Here, then, is a small collection on nonrain bows.

Geophysicist James E. McDonald reported seeing a gigantic horizontal cloudbow when en route to Honolulu from Los Angeles on September 19, 1961. "About 10 o'clock Honolulu time, I noted from my port window that we were accompanied by a luminous arc below the aircraft. My first, wrong, impression was that I was viewing some kind of ice-crys-

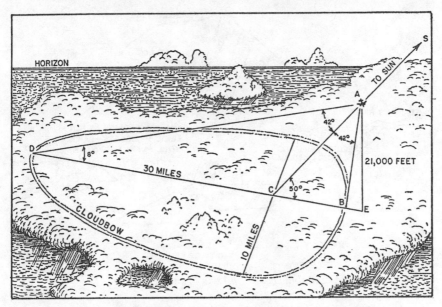

HORIZON

TO SUN'

S

A

42°

42°

21,000 FEET

D

8°

30 MILES

C

50°

B

E

CLOUDBOW

10 MILES

Giant cloudbow seen from an aircraft above the clouds

tal halo involving both reflection and refraction since it had the almost colourless luminosity characteristic of the majority of halos. However, in a moment of further scrutiny, I noted that it seemed to originate on the cloud deck whose tops we had earlier penetrated at about 8,000-ft. altitude. Its true nature was then unambiguously revealed when I noted further that here and there along its course it assumed a most vivid rainbow banding where I was looking down through breaks in the 8,000-ft. deck to where the trade cumuli were raining. . . . Having recognized its real nature, I scanned along the expected arc far to the north of our flight path, and was pleased to find that the luminosity, though very pale in the distance, constituted well over half of a full bow from my vantage point." Subsequent calculations indicated that the cloudbow or horizontal rainbow was an ellipse 30 by 10 miles in size (*Weather*, 17: 243, 1962).

W. T. Donnelly was aboard his yacht on Lake Monroe, Florida, on January 22, 1922. "This morning when I came out on deck soon after sunrise, I noticed toward the east a remarkable phenomenon on the water. A band of prismatic colors, familiarly known as the rainbow, seemed to extend on the water, commencing about one third of the way across the lake and reaching to the shore. This phenomenon persisted and at the present time, 9:30 A.M., is truly remarkable" (*Natural History*, 22: 372, 1922). For a possible explanation, see the next item.

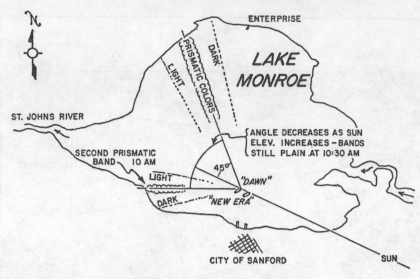

Rainbow colors on Lake Monroe, Florida

A similar horizontal bow was seen by H. M. Reese on a Missouri lake, *circa* 1919. "The bow was seen about nine o'clock according to the daylight-saving bill, or eight by the usual local railroad time. Its appearance was about as shown in the accompanying figure. AB is the western shoreline of the lake, about 200 yards away. The bow was complete except in the following particulars; the part near S was hidden by the shadow of the observer and that of the boat in which he sat; and the part PRQ was inverted, like a reflection of what should have been the crest,

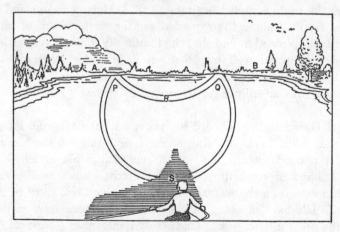

Horizontal rainbow cast on a Missouri lake

the part near R being somewhat less bright than the rest. . . . Though the bow was very brilliant, no trace of a second bow was visible." The observer examined the lake surface and found tiny droplets of water on the surface remaining from a fog that had hung over the lake during the night. The lake was very calm and surface tension kept the droplets from being assimilated by the lake. Thus perfect rainbow conditions were produced (*Science,* 50: 542, 1919).

Perhaps the most unusual bow of all had nothing to do with water. The locale was the Great Salt Lake, Utah; the time, May 16, 1901. "On the evening of May 16, the writer was crossing the main ridge of Antelope Island—the largest land body within the area of the Great Salt Lake. As he began the descent on the eastern slope, there appeared between the island and the mainland what seemed at first glance to be a segment of a brilliant rainbow of unusual width. It was evident, however, that no rain was falling in that direction. Clouds were gathering in the south and west, but the sun was yet unobscured. A wind setting toward the mainland had lifted from the dry flats large quantities of the 'oolitic sand,' with which the lake bottom and the recently dried patches on this side of the island are covered to a depth varying from a few inches to several feet. This so-called 'sand' consists of calcareous spherules, fairly uniform in size between the limits of No. 8 and No. 10 shot. The oolitic bodies are polished and exhibit a pearly luster. It would seem that the outer spherical surfaces reflected the light in such a manner as to produce the bow. The colored column appeared almost to touch the lake bed, and its ends subtended with the observer an angle of about 40°. The prismatic colors were distinct, the red being outside—i.e., away from the sun. In apparent width the column was fully double that of the ordinary rainbow. A fainter secondary bow was plainly visible beyond the primary, with the colors in reverse order. The phenomenon was so brilliant as to attract the attention of all members of the party, and it remained visible for over five minutes; then, as the sun sank lower, it rapidly died away. The production of a color bow by reflection from the outer surfaces of opaque spherules is a new phenomenon to the writer. It is inexplicable on the principle of refraction and total reflection from the interior of transparent spheroids, according to which the rainbow is generally explained" (*Science,* 13: 992, 1901).

Low-Sun Phenomena

As the sun sinks toward the horizon, the amount of atmosphere between it and the observer increases rapidly. The longer path that light must travel through the capricious atmosphere introduces new kinds of phenomena. Images of astronomical objects are distorted grotesquely, multiplied, and painted with various unlikely hues. The bending of light waves (refraction) by the different layers of air performs this magic. Still closer to the horizon, clouds and mountain peaks intercept and further distort the sunlight, giving rise to the well-known, fan-shaped crepuscular rays as well as more exotic phenomena. The horizon itself may act as a sharp opaque edge that casts shadow bands on the earth (through the process of optical diffraction) or may spread out the spectral colors of the sun (through the process of dispersion). The famous green ray, or green flash, of the setting sun is due to the phenomenon of dispersion. Even with the sun below the horizon, sunlight may be reflected into the observer's eyes by high altitude dust and ice crystals. Solar pillars and twilight bows may result. And as night draws near, the shadow of the earth itself is sometimes seen cast upon the upper atmosphere as it advances relentlessly from the east. Most of these low-sun phenomena also occur at sunrise, but in reverse, of course.

Many low-sun phenomena are well understood, such as the solar pillar, which is merely sunlight reflected halolike from atmospheric ice crystals. Other phenomena, though, are curious and enigmatic. The green ray and the crepuscular rays, for example, have long been considered as "explained." The stock explanations, however, seem simplistic when the full ranges of these phenomena are considered. Some green rays seem purely subjective; others are real and can be photographed. And to call the mysterious antisolar rays "extended crepuscular rays," as is the current scientific policy, is extrapolating a known effect too far. Even the famous Krakatoa sunsets of 1883–84 have a mysterious dimension. How could they have been seen months before the actual eruption of Krakatoa—and then episodically for many years afterward? Were these spectacular sunsets (and sunrises) truly caused by the volcano's dust? And then we have the Alpenglow and iridescent landscapes, to say nothing of unexpected spectral bows at sunset and sunrise. Low-sun phenomena are not only very beautiful but they severely try the mettle of meteorological optics.

COLOR FLASHES FROM RISING AND SETTING ASTRONOMICAL BODIES

The long-debated green ray is almost always associated with the setting and rising sun. Actually, it also appears occasionally when the moon and Venus rise and set. This is not surprising because they too are bright celestial objects, and the laws of optics play no favorites. Nevertheless, a few lunar and Venusian flashes have unusual features.

On March 11, 1962, the M.V. *Journalist* was off Somaliland when the third officer recorded a noteworthy green flash from the setting moon. "At 1947 GMT, the moon, which was crescent-shaped was seen to be a dark red colour as it sank toward the horizon. When the left-hand cusp was disappearing below the horizon, a pale green flash was seen through 7 × 50 binoculars. There was no flash when the right-hand cusp disappeared." Conditions favorable to the green flash are obviously transitory (*Marine Observer,* 33: 20, 1963).

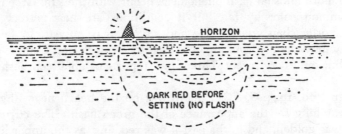

Green flash from a cusp of the setting moon

Under exceptionally clear atmospheric conditions, T. W. Edmunds observed a green flash when Venus was setting over the Indian Ocean on June 23, 1975. This phenomenon was preceded by curious color changes due to changes in refraction. "When the planet was slightly above the horizon, it appeared red, but on examination through binoculars it was in fact alternating from red to orange and back again. At the moment the planet set, the colour immediately changed to bright green and a small bright green flash was observed, lasting about 1 second." Jupiter when setting has also exhibited the green flash (*Marine Observer,* 46: 69, 1976).

A remarkable red flash at moonrise appeared to the second officer of

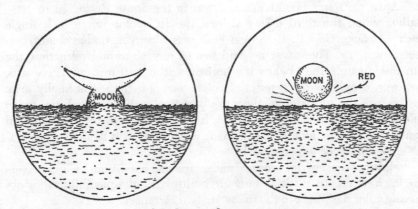

Red flash from the rising moon

the M.V. *Deseado* in the North Atlantic on May 19, 1960. Also out of the ordinary was the gross distortion of the shape of the rising moon due to anomalous refraction near the horizon. "The moon on rising at 0339 GMT was seen, when examined through binoculars, to have assumed the distorted appearance shown in the sketch. As the lowest part of the limb cleared the horizon a brilliant red flash was observed which lasted for 1 1/2 seconds approx." (*Marine Observer*, 31: 68, 1961).

The more unusual flash phenomena occur with the sun. Green is the most common color by far, but if conditions are near-perfect wavelengths shorter than green (blue and violet) may appear. In fact, the green ray may change from green to blue to violet during a single observation—but only very rarely. Three brief reports of nongreen flashes follow.

August 20, 1943: S. E. Ashmore was on the beach near Rhyl, England, watching for the appearance of the green flash. "The cirrus near the sun was golden, and in the east it was red. Just as the upper limb of the sun was disappearing, its colour appeared a beautiful blue, a trifle bluer than the deepest sky-blue seen with maritime polar air in spring." Blue wavelengths are shorter than green and consequently more easily absorbed in the atmosphere; thus blue flashes are correspondingly more rare (*Meteorological Magazine*, 76: 21, 1947).

January 3, 1960: The watch on the M.V. *Port Macquarie* in the South Pacific were lucky enough to see a rare purple flash. Purple/violet wavelengths are even shorter than blue, so purple flashes are extremely uncommon. "As the sun was setting at 0733 GMT, small segments appeared to break away and turned purple. The sun was a very bright white at sunset, there being little trace of any red colour. As it went down below the horizon there was a bright purple flash of a 2-to-3-seconds duration" (*Marine Observer*, 31: 21, 1961).

April 12, 1957: The M.V. *Otaki* was in the South Pacific en route to Balboa when the third officer viewed the full color range in a single flash. "At 0053 G.M.T., the green flash was observed under almost perfect conditions. There was no evidence of any abnormal refraction, the sun sinking uniformly below the horizon without distortion. There was, however, a more striking series of colour changes than is normally seen. Just before the top edge of the sun's disc finally disappeared, the green colouration quickly changed to blue, from pale blue to intense blue and finally to a purple, almost violet, shade as the last rays of light vanished" (*Marine Observer*, 28: 76, 1958).

Multiple flashes may occur under special conditions. Cloud layers can in effect create artificial horizons, multiplying the possibilities for observing color flashes, as in the following two instances.

The fourth officer of the M.V. *Coptic* recorded successive red and green flashes on August 21, 1952, in the North Atlantic. Note that a red flash may appear momentarily as the sun emerges below a cloud layer because the red rays are bent the most by the atmosphere and therefore appear first to the observer. (The red flash may be considered the "reverse" of the green flash!) "As the sun's lower limb, altitude 35′, ap-

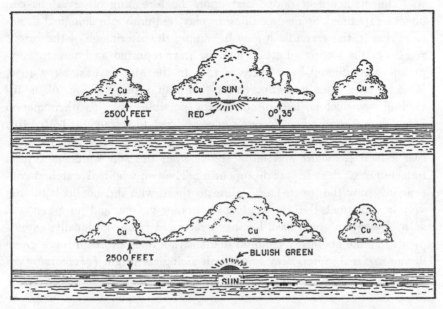

Red flash below a cloud followed by green flash from the horizon

peared to emerge at 2208 G.M.T. from the base of a large [cumulus cloud] (estimated at 2,500 ft.), a brilliant red flash was observed. As the sun's disc sank below the horizon (2215), a brilliant bluish-green flash was seen from its upper limb" (*Marine Observer*, 23: 144, 1953).

December 4, 1962, from the S.S. *Ceramic* in the South Pacific: Three green flashes. "Near sunset at 0130 GMT, three brilliant green flashes were seen as the sun's upper limb sank below three separate layers of Sc [stratocumulus clouds]" (*Marine Observer*, 33: 188, 1963).

Lastly, under extraordinary conditions the green flash may be prolonged for several minutes. In 1930 "Admiral Byrd observed the green colour for as long as thirty-five minutes in Antarctica as the sun rolled along the horizon" (*Nature*, 135: 992, 1935).

It is a remarkable fact that the green ray may be created by a nearby artificial horizon—at least if the following account is accurate. "I remember that, some twenty years ago, at Portpatrick, I happened to be on the east side of a breakwater as the Sun was setting. The whole disk of the Sun was still above the horizon but, by stooping, the top of the breakwater could be brought upwards across the Sun. At the instant when the disk was just covered, the Green Flash was seen. It could be repeated as often as one wished by performing the necessary gymnastics" (*British Astronomical Association, Journal*, 71: 35, 1961).

The modicum of doubt cast upon the foregoing observations can now be explained. Some green flashes may be purely physiological in nature; that is, the green flash may be simply the afterimage of the bright red tip of the setting sun. C. Vaughan Starr reported an interesting experiment conducted by a party of four in the Middle East *circa* 1930. "One evening when expecting to see this flash, a party of four of us, including two doctors, had discussed the possibility of this phenomenon being due to some effect in one's eyes and not to refraction: to try this out two of us watched the sun carefully until it had set, while the other two looked eastward and on a signal from the sun watchers turned quickly just as the sun was disappearing. The two who had watched continuously saw the green flash, while to those who did not look till the very last moment, the sun went down orange-yellow, and no green was seen." Since the green flash has been recorded photographically, experiments like the one just recounted demonstrate that, although some green flashes are real, others may have a physiological origin (*Meteorological Magazine*, 64: 290, 1930).

TRICKS OF REFRACTION: MULTIPLE SUNS, MOONS, AND PLANETS

The layered structure of the atmosphere near the horizon transforms the familiar sun and moon into grotesque shapes and colors them with unnatural tones. It is easy to brush off these low-sun effects as due only to atmospheric vagaries—curious but hardly world-shaking phenomena.

A double sun probably caused by anomalous refraction near the horizon

In the potpourri of refraction oddities that follows, it is clear that there are some remarkable effects which should be investigated.

A double sun was seen off Cape Finnesterre (Spain) from the M.V. *Lotorium* on March 2, 1954. "Two suns were observed at sunset, the [second] image being above the true sun" (*Marine Observer*, 25: 31, 1955). The diagonal displacement of the second sun suggests unusual conditions of refraction.

Multiple segments of the setting sun appeared above the true sun at Saughall, England, on June 15, 1936. "At the time the sun was below a band of altocumulus lenticularis with the elevation of the centre of the sun about 8°. The sun appeared as a deep red orb while above it were two segments of a circle, also deep red in colour. The upper and smaller segment was at a distance of approximately 2° from the upper limit of the sun and the second was about midway between this and the sun." Such multiplication of objects near the horizon is rather common where there exist layers of air with different densities. See also the section on mirages (*Meteorological Magazine*, 71: 139, 1936).

On December 7, 1957, in the South Pacific, the third officer of the M.V. *Port Auckland* recorded a multiple crescent moon. "At 1000 G.M.T., when at an altitude of 35°, the whole of the moon's disc was very faintly visible, due to 'earthshine,' in addition to the crescent which was

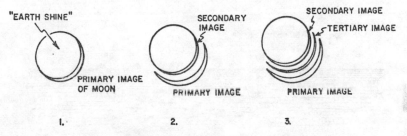

Atmospheric refraction multiplies moon's crescent.

of normal brilliance. At 1007, the crescent appeared to become attached, and occupied a separate position, a small distance away from the moon's disc. At the same time, another crescent, slightly thinner than the original one, took its place; it was just as distinct and had the same colour. At 1010 the separation between the two crescents increased further and at 1012 a third narrow crescent appeared between the other two. It was just as clearly defined and of the same colour as those which preceded it" (*Marine Observer*, 29: 177, 1959).

Mirage action combined with abnormal refraction often produces weird lunar shapes. A series of strangely distorted images of the rising moon appeared *before* actual moonrise to the watch on the S.S. *Beaver-ford* in the North Atlantic on October 28, 1961. "Between 2321 and 2326 1/2 GMT, the rising moon, which was very red in colour, assumed the shapes shown in the sketches. The true time of moonrise was some 5 minutes later, the moon then having an entirely normal appearance" (*Marine Observer*, 32: 182, 1962).

Distortions of the moon (still below the horizon) caused by atmospheric refraction

Venus was treated in a curious manner by the atmosphere in the Gulf of Aden on November 11, 1965. According to the log of the M.V. *Delphic*, "At 1744 GMT when Venus was about to set, bearing 237°, it changed from a yellowish-white to red. Shortly afterwards the planet appeared double, i.e. with a red image a short distance beneath the true disc. The image was below the horizon line and it gradually rose to meet the horizon as Venus decreased in altitude. At the moment of disappear-

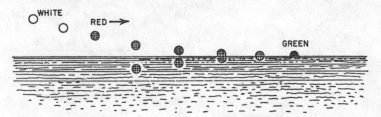

As Venus sets, atmospheric refraction doubles and colors the image.

ing, the two red discs coalesced for an instant and changed to a light green colour" (*Marine Observer*, 36: 183, 1966).

August 24, 1959, from the S.S. *Devon* in the Indian Ocean: The lights of distant ships appeared magnified and the stars were scintillating more than usual. "When the moon had risen to 15 minutes altitude and was clear of the cloud, its lower limb was seen to scintillate with a brilliant scarlet colour. The coloured rim gradually contracted in length and the last of the scarlet disappeared when the moon was at an altitude of about 1°." This phenomenon probably originated in a low-level temperature inversion (*Marine Observer*, 30: 135, 1960).

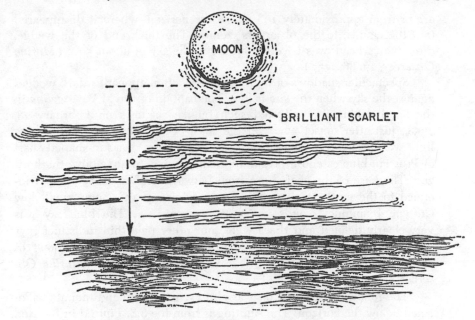

MOON

BRILLIANT SCARLET

1°

Moon's lower edge scintillates with brilliant purple.

SHADOW OF THE EARTH AND OTHER STRANGE SHADOWS CAST UPON THE SKY

Lord Deerhurst was rowing down the Púnguè River in Portuguese East Africa on December 9, 1891, with two friends. "From the east we noticed a light blue streak in the sky very little darker than the blue of the heavens; it was narrow at first, but gradually became broader and extended, getting darker as it did so (it got darker from the east, the densest part being in the eastern horizon), eventually passing between us and the moon and being lost in the west at the point where the sun was going down. This streak seemed quite transparent and deepened, when fully up, from a very light blue in the west to almost indigo in the east. It passed, seemingly, between us and the clouds, and you could distinctly see them through it, also the moon." A fairly typical observation of the earth's shadow thrown upon the sky at sunset (*Royal Meteorological Society, Quarterly Journal*, 18: 147, 1892).

A particularly sharp shadow of the earth was cast upon the South Pacific sky on April 6, 1956. It was seen from the M.V. *Wanstead* and recorded thus: "A wedge-shaped piece of sky, in the E., was coloured deep blue, almost purple, and the sky on either side of the wedge was a very pale blue. The wedge was extremely well defined and covered an

arc of from approximately 10° above the horizon, where it disappeared
into the clouds, to the observers' zenith. The thick end of the wedge,
directly overhead, was covering an arc in the sky of about 50°" (*Marine
Observer*, 27: 86, 1957).

Spectacular shadows of high mountains often appear as dark wedges
against the sky when the sun is low. The captain of the M.V. *Angelina* in
the South China Sea reported such fanlike shadows on February 28,
1958, "just after sunset when off the coast of Viet Nam, a peculiar blue
light was observed in the western sky in the form of a fan-shaped shaft
of Prussian blue extending from approximately 4° to 40° above the horizon. The base of the shaft bore from between 264° and 269° and it inclined to the north at an angle of approximately 15°. Some small low
Cu-type [cumulus] clouds were also present. . . . The blue ray was
very clearly defined and there were four other pale thin indistinct rays
lower down to the north." The shafts may have been the shadows of
clouds or of high mountains in the interior of Viet Nam (*Marine Observer*, 29: 14, 1959).

The following observation was also ascribed to inland mountains located below the horizon. The sighting is from the S.S. *Pipiriki* in the Red
Sea bound for Suez. On November 11, 1947, "at about 1450 the sunset
glow broke up, leaving blue sky from horizon to zenith in the sector between W. × S. and SW. On the W. × S. bearing, the division between
bright orange glow and blue sky was at right angles to the horizon,
whereas on the SW. bearing the orange glow was at an angle of 20° to the
horizon. . . . When the phenomenon was at its best, the summit of Jebel
Aduali could be seen between the two sections of orange light" (*Marine
Observer*, 18: 193, 1948).

ANTISOLAR RAYS: FAN-SHAPED BANDS IN THE EAST AT SUNSET

One would not expect to see distinct, well-formed optical phenomena in the darkening east as sunset nears. This controversial occurrence
is exemplified by a report of antisolar rays from the S.S. *Loch Ryan* in
the North Atlantic on January 29, 1959. "Before sunset, when the sun
was 7° above the horizon, bearing 246°, several bands showing a darker
colour than the sky, which was rose pink, were observed to be radiating
from a point just below the horizon diametrically opposite to the sun
(see the sketch)." These bands may be shadows of clouds thrown across
the sky, but this phenomenon also exhibits complexities that cast doubt
on this simplistic explanation, as subsequent items will show (*Marine
Observer*, 30: 19, 1960).

In Ethiopia's pollution-free skies, twilight bands and antisolar rays are unusually vivid. The development of these bands is reminiscent of the banded-sky phenomenon mentioned in Chapter 1 and is just as enigmatic. Pierre Gouin, who was director of the Geophysical Observatory at Addis Ababa provides a definitive description of the bands. "In Ethiopia, at sunset, the lower part of the eastern horizon is normally pink. This

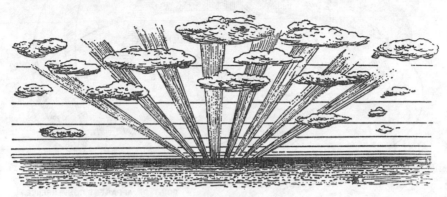

Antisolar rays in the east at sunset

pink layer moves up, because [it is] better delineated as a dark segment develops underneath it; it soon becomes an antitwilight arc with a horizontal extent of some 180 degrees. Three to five minutes after the upper limb of the sun has disappeared below the western horizon, from a point 4 to 5 degrees above the *eastern* horizon and in the centre of the antitwilight arc, dark blue bands suddenly radiate in all directions through the pink-coloured sky, progressively over the whole hemisphere and converge towards a focus apparently lower under the *western* horizon than the actual position of the sun. Then the blue bands slowly vanish from the east, covered by the earth's shadow advancing westward. The number of dark blue bands may vary from one to seven or nine. . . . The pattern is usually observed to be more or less geometrically perfect, from October to the end of December in the Addis Ababa region. Although it is more spectacular when the sky is clear, the clearness of the sky is not a guarantee that, on a particular day during that period, the phenomenon will take place." The recurring geometric precision and the appearance of the bands on cloudless days argue against cloud shadows being the source of the bands (*Weather*, 23: 70, 1969).

The reverse situation may occur at sunrise. The November 15, 1913, observation of Captain A. Lucke from Port Saïd, Egypt, illustrates this. "Crepuscular rays were seen in the west at sunrise. Sunrise was normal,

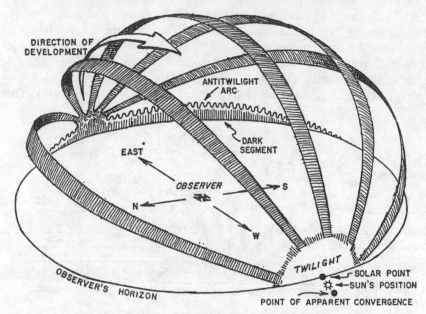

Dark bands spread across the sky at sunset in Ethiopia

the moon being 10° above the western horizon. The fanlike rays were suddenly seen below the moon, spreading out from a point considerably below the horizon to a distance of approximately 17° above it (sextant angles), the dark space between the pearly rays distinctly darkening the clouds above mentioned. The rays were irregular in positions and numbers, and their upper edges indistinct in form, the lower being, on the contrary, sharply defined." About 14 rays were counted in the west. There were no rays above the rising sun in the east (*British Astronomical Association, Journal*, 24: 112, 1913).

The astronomers E. M. Antoniadi and C. Flammarion both saw curious rays crossing the sky at sunset on September 12, 1894, at Juvisy, France. The rays were white and two in number. "The sun was very nearly setting, when all of a sudden, two very narrow lines, like telegraph wires, but *white*, originating from a point of the western horizon *near* the sun, rose in a gentle curve toward the east, attaining on the south their maximum height (20°) above the horizon. The lines were probably parallel, but owing (apparently) to perspective, their distance, which was over the south some 1° apart, was only half that amount in the vicinity of the sun." These rays seem to be neither halo phenomena nor crepuscular rays (*Knowledge*, 18: 205, 1895).

An even more puzzling optical phenomenon was seen in the North Pacific on April 17, 1974. Most of the ship's company of the M.V. *Man-*

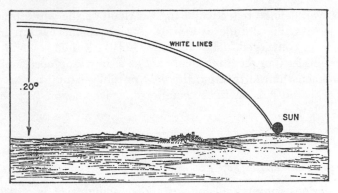

Two anomalous white arcs cross the sky at sunset.

chester Concept viewed the spectacle of a sky-spanning arch of colored rays. The report termed the rays "crepuscular," but the colors suggest otherwise. "At about 1930 SMT (0930 GMT), shortly after sunset, the sky was observed to be divided into two distinct halves by what appeared to be crepuscular rays. These rays spread from the western horizon across to the eastern horizon in a band approx. 5° wide. The sky was deep blue and the rays were arranged in the order of pale green, pale orange, cream, pale orange, and pale green. At the time of sunset there were, on the western horizon, medium and towering Cu [cumulus] clouds, the eastern horizon being clear. By following these rays across to

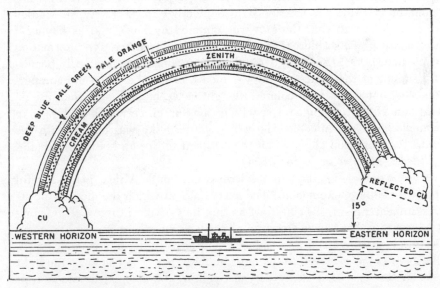

Colored arcs connect a cloud with its (supposed) reflection.

the east, a well-defined reflection of the Cu cloud on the western horizon
could be seen at an altitude of approx. 15° above the eastern horizon
where the rays converged." The "reflection" of the cumulus cloud in the
east is incredible. Can the atmosphere act as a mirror on occasion? Antisolar phenomena hint at this, but the only possible natural mirror would
be a veil of ice crystals, as in the countersun phenomenon (*Marine Observer*, 45: 68, 1975).

THE SO-CALLED KRAKATOA SUNSETS

The glorious sunsets and long-extended twilights of late 1883 and
most of 1884 captured the attention of laymen and scientists alike. So
spectacular were these phenomena that scientists were pressed to pre-
pare a rather dogmatic explanation and then to defend it in the face of
contrary evidence. First, let us consider the general characteristics of
the displays, as related by the editor of the *Sidereal Messenger*, an astronomical journal of the day.

"For the past two months and more, varied and most brilliant sunsets have attracted the attention of foreign observers, and full notes of
these extraordinary phenomena have appeared in the current numbers of
their scientific periodicals. A few citations from *Nature* and *Knowledge*
must suffice for our present purpose. Dr. J. Arnold saw the *Sun* as a blue
globe, [on] September 2, and after dark [he] thought the town on fire
from the brightness of the sky. [On] September 10, 11, 12, W. R. Manley
of India reported that the *Sun* was dimmed by haze, and as having a
decidedly greenish-blue tinge. From Nice, November 15, information
came to Mr. A. C. Ranyard of England describing extraordinarily beautiful sunsets at that place during the month of October. The most important fact noted was that 'colored twilight lasted much longer than usual!'
Captain Noble of England speaks of similar observations and says in
Knowledge, November 8: 'The whole western sky was ablaze with the
most vivid crimson glow; albeit the *Sun* had set for an hour and a half'"
(*Sidereal Messenger*, 2: 291, 1883).

John Ballot, residing in the Transvaal, South Africa, made careful
records of the phenomenon. "The exact date on which the glow made its
first appearance in this country I am not in a position to give. It is, however, certain that it *was observed* so early as the 5th of September, 1883.
From about the 7th of September it had already become a noted peculiarity after sunset, even to the most unobservant. The colour of the light
was at the first of a sickly greenish-yellow, but deepened into a cop-
perish-red as the evening advanced: the light was strong enough to cast

a deep shadow against a wall or anything else, if an object was held close to it. . . . But I will not attempt to describe any of the gorgeous cloud effects thus produced. They are beyond my powers of description. A few concluding remarks will be devoted to the order in which the glow is generally formed. . . . Soon after sunset the usual twilight appears, which remains visible for a short while; as it gradually contracts and fades, everything seems to be settling down for the approaching darkness. The rosy glow over the point of sunset rapidly contracts; only a thin rim of red remains visible on each side, with a small arc of red marking the point of sunset. The observer will now begin to notice a peculiar bluish-white glare forming a few degrees above the arc of red and extending some distance upwards. . . . The fading rim of the first twilight forms itself into a long, narrow brownish belt, stretching along the horizon, caused, no doubt, by the denser layers of haze and vapour lower down. Immediately above this belt and just below the bluish-white glare, there remains an apparent blank; this blank is but slowly filled up by the new glow. . . . As the glow spreads outwards, above the white glare, it seems to acquire a strong tinge of purple, which gradually fades into a violet near the borders of the spreading luminosity" (*English Mechanic*, 39: 185, 1884).

To explain the long series of unparalleled sunsets and afterglows, scientists pointed to the colossal eruption of Krakatoa in Java, in late August 1883. The immense quantities of dust thrown up into the atmosphere supposedly traveled on stratospheric winds around the world, creating the unparalleled sunset phenomena. But there were doubters: "Certainly the whole question of the glorious fore- and afterglows which have prevailed is shrouded in mystery. Ice granules at a great height would produce these beautiful phenomena; but why should they be . . . so intermittently persistent, seems an insoluble puzzle. That the Krakatoa eruption had as much—or as little—to do with them as the Queen's tumble down stairs at Windsor in the previous March is indisputable. They had been noted, among other places, in South Africa in February, 1883, whereas the terrible Javan eruption did not occur until August 27 in that year." The author, a noted astronomer, notes later that the specially formed Krakatoa Committee of the Royal Society refused to admit such early observations as evidence (*English Mechanic*, 43: 29, 1886).

The afterglows returned again in 1891, with additional unexpected and unpredictable recurrences for at least two more decades. If the sunset-glow–producing dust was from Krakatoa, where was it during the intervening years—in outer space?

THE BRIGHT NIGHTS FOLLOWING THE TUNGUSKA EVENT

Some of the luminous phenomena accompanying the Tunguska Event (the Siberian meteor) have been mentioned in Chapter 1. An interesting feature pertinent to the present subject was the protracted twilight that occurred for several days. "On the night of June 30, and to some extent on the nights succeeding, brilliant sky-glows were observed in various parts of the country and lasted throughout the night. At 9 h. 30 m. P.M. at Greenwich on June 30, the sky along the northwest and north horizon was of a brilliant red, in fact there was what is usually termed a 'brilliant sunset,' the only peculiarity being that the brightness stretched more to the north than is usual, and endured, so that at one o'clock in the morning it extended well across the north of the horizon, and the northern sky above was of a brightness approaching that of the southern sky at the time of Full Moon. The light, indeed, was sufficient to take photographs of terrestrial objects. . . . It happened that the Sun was in a state of activity at the time, as shown by a large prominence on the southwest limb, and this gave strength to the suggestion that it was an auroral display, but spectroscopic observations fail to give any evidence of this. A long-lasting solar halo was seen in the forenoon and afternoon of June 30 and another on July 1." At the time this was written, the fact of the Siberian meteor or Tunguska Event was unknown in Western Europe (*Observatory*, 31: 325, 1908).

The similarity of the Krakatoa and Tunguska twilight phenomena open the possibility that the earth may on occasion encounter clouds of dust either associated with meteors or perhaps blown into space by terrestrial volcanic activity. Krakatoa's colossal explosion may have been violent enough to do this, the recurring sunsets could then be explained in terms of repeated encounters with the dust clouds. This surmise is, of course, on the fantastic side and does not account for the pre-eruption appearance of brilliant sunsets.

PECULIAR ARCS OF COLOR IN THE WEST AFTER SUNSET

Colored arcs dominate all rainbow displays and many halo phenomena as well, but a third, more mysterious class of arcs is associated with the setting sun. The three twilight spectral displays detailed below have no ready optical explanations.

On December 31, 1954, the captain and fourth officer on the M.V. *Timaru Star* saw strange colored rays form over the Indian Ocean shortly after sunset. ". . . a very noticeable set of violet rays were seen, which reached an altitude of 47° and extended over a considerable arc. Immediately above the horizon the sky was bright orange, obscured in parts by Sc and Cu. Above this was an arc of approximately 5° of greenish-white,

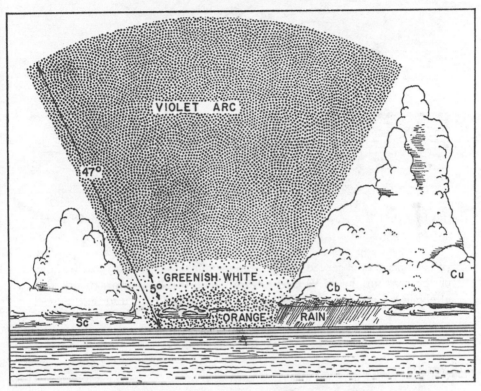

Colored rays after sunset over the Indian Ocean

topped by the violet rays, which became most noticeable 15 min. after sunset; they retained maximum brilliance for a further 10 min. and then commenced to fade. Within another 10 min. the rays were invisible." The colors are in the order of the spectrum, but there is no explanation of this sort of phenomenon (*Marine Observer*, 25: 216, 1955).

April 21, 1954, in the West Pacific: The report is from J. K. Marshall, third officer of the M.V. *Ajax*. "The sun set at 0900, and at 0930 a beautiful rainbow effect was seen in the W. [west], although the arc did not appear to have the sun as centre. It consisted of a greenish patch surrounded by three red quarter arcs enclosing two spectra. These arcs lasted for about 3 min." The spectral order is the reverse of the preceding phenomenon. No explanation is available here either, especially for

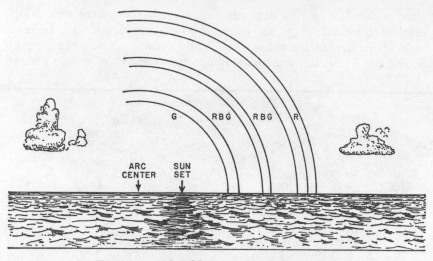

G ⋅ RBG RBG R

ARC   SUN
CENTER   SET

Eccentric rainbowlike arcs appear after sunset.

the fact that the phenomenon was not sun-centered (*Marine Observer*, 25: 103, 1955).

An evolving color display with moving shadows and an expanding yellow disk was observed in the Mediterranean on July 6, 1964, by some of the crew of the M.V. *Great City*. "At 1915 GMT approx., but definitely after sunset, the rings shown in the sketches appeared on the west-

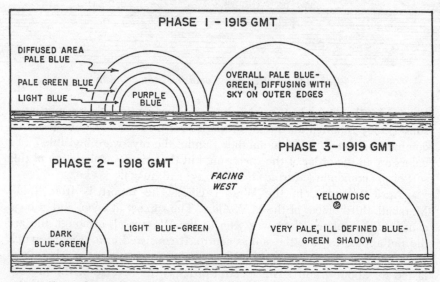

PHASE 1 – 1915 GMT

DIFFUSED AREA
PALE BLUE

PALE GREEN BLUE

LIGHT BLUE

PURPLE
BLUE

OVERALL PALE BLUE-
GREEN, DIFFUSING WITH
SKY ON OUTER EDGES

PHASE 3– 1919 GMT

PHASE 2 – 1918 GMT

FACING
WEST

YELLOW DISC

DARK
BLUE-GREEN

LIGHT BLUE-GREEN

VERY PALE, ILL DEFINED BLUE-
GREEN SHADOW

Expanding yellow disk and spectral display over the Mediterranean

ern horizon in the direction where the sun had set. They were distinct and the colour differentiation was well defined, but the shadow to the right was less so, though plainly seen. Within a short space of time the whole complex expanded, became lighter in colour and began to merge. With no apparent warning, a yellow disc appeared superimposed upon the very light shadow. It is stressed that the disc appeared and did not rise from the horizon. It rapidly diffused, increasing in size and becoming pale in colour until it finally merged with the now rapidly dispersing blue-green shadow" (*Marine Observer*, 25: 123, 1965). Halos and mock suns come to mind, but mock suns do not disperse like the disk described above.

THE ALPENGLOW: MOUNTAINS THAT SHINE AFTER SUNSET

In clear weather, in the Alps, the Rockies, and other regions with high peaks, mountaintops may appear to glow long after sunset. This radiance, called the Alpenglow, is not to be confused with the mountaintop glows (Chapter 1) seen in the same areas. The former is optical in origin; the latter electrical. However, the optical details of the Alpenglow phenomenon are undetermined, being vaguely ascribed to light from the sun below the horizon that is reflected back to earth from a high-altitude layer of dust. Here is a typical description of the Alpenglow. "In fine weather the following sequence of events may be noted: When the sun has sunk nearly to the observer's horizon, the peaks to the eastward begin to have a reddish or golden hue. This fades gradually, but in a few minutes, when the sun is a little below the observer's horizon but the peaks are still bathed in direct sunlight, an intense red glow begins down the slopes and moves upward to the summits. This is identical with the rosy 'twilight arch' that in clear weather rises from the eastern horizon as the sun sinks below the western; and it is bordered below by the blue shadow of the earth. Now, for a few minutes, the peaks are in the earth-shadow; their rocks and snows assume a livid appearance, aptly described by the inhabitants of the vale of Chamonix, whence the phenomena in question are well seen on the summits of Mont Blanc, as the 'teinte cadavéreuse.'

"Presently occurs the remarkable phenomenon known as 'recoloration' or 'afterglow.' In Chamonix it is called 'the resurrection of Mont Blanc.' The peaks, from which all color had faded, again assume a rosy tint; but this time gradually and without any sharp line of demarcation between the glow and the shadow beneath. The recoloration is by no means a daily occurrence—in fact, it is rather uncommon—and it varies greatly in appearance and duration. Sometimes it lasts until an hour after sunset, and it passes away from below upward. Very rarely a faint second recoloration may be seen. All these phenomena may be seen, in reverse order, at sunrise, though they are less common then than at sunset. They are known, collectively, as the 'Alpenglow.'" The Alpenglow is generally explained as due to sunlight scattered back to earth from dust high in the atmosphere (*Scientific American,* 108: 482, 1913).

STRANGE FLUORESCENCE OF THE LANDSCAPE AT LOW SUN ANGLES

Some unusual tricks are played by the atmosphere at sunrise and sunset. The light illuminating the landscape has been largely stripped of the shorter wavelengths by the atmospheric scattering of the blues and greens. When conditions are just right (we do not know what "just right" really means here), the landscape seems to glow, fluoresce, or become iridescent. We shall recount two slightly different descriptions of the phenomenon from a much larger collection of sightings.

M. F. Folie of the Belgian Academy was in the mountains near Zermatt (Switzerland) in the early morning of August 18, 1892. "On our right, towards the east, on the steep flanks of the mountains which enclose the valley of Viege, rose a group of fir trees, the highest of which projected themselves against the azure of the sky, at a height of 500 meters above the road. While I was botanising, my son exclaimed, 'Come and look: the firs are as if covered with hoar-frost!' We paid the most scrupulous attention to the phenomenon. To make sure that we were not misled by an illusion we made various observations, both with the naked eye and with an excellent opera-glass. It was observed that not only the distant trees, but those lining the road, glittered in a silvery light, which seemed to belong to the trees themselves, and that the insects and birds playing round the branches were bathed in the same light, forming an aureole round the tops of the trees, somewhat resembling the light effects observed in the Blue Grotto" (*Nature,* 47: 303, 1893).

On October 1, 1953, in England, W. E. Richardson recorded an allied experience. "The hills near Alston, Cumberland, were capped with low cloud and this extended over the entire sky. . . . Quite suddenly this same continuous cloud sheet glowed a coppery-red, presumably due to the fact that it was of no great thickness and above it a brilliant red sunset was taking place. However, the extraordinary consequence of this reddening of the sky was to be seen in the landscape, for the fading greens of the trees and meadows had been transformed to a brilliance which might be described as 'fluorescent.' So brilliant were these greens that I developed a mild headache from the strain of observing" (*Weather,* 10: 29, 1955).

SUNRISE AND SUNSET SHADOW BANDS

A well-known optical effect is produced by intercepting part of a beam of light with a sharp-edged opaque obstruction. A screen on the other side of the obstruction will display a shadow fringed by light and dark bands. This optical phenomenon is called diffraction. Nature can reproduce this experiment when the sun sets behind a mountain range. Ronald L. Ives once actually saw natural diffraction bands. "At sunset, when looking eastward over flat barren terrain, from a point having a higher angular elevation than the sun, faint, eastward-moving shadow bands, several miles wide and extending an unknown, but relatively great, distance to the north and south, have been observed on several occasions. These bands were seen, in each instance, just as the sun dipped below the local horizon. Duration of the phenomena was less than 30 seconds. Estimated rate of eastward motion of the nearest shadow band was 40 miles per hour. Recession of the bands seemed to accelerate with distance." These sunset bands resemble the shadow bands seen during solar eclipses, but it is believed that they are really due to diffraction even though theoretical calculations do not correspond with what is observed (*Optical Society of America, Journal*, 35: 736, 1945).

C. Rozet, a French scientist, made a study of these natural shadow bands in 1905. He placed a white screen facing the sunrise and the mountains. "The bands were easily seen and were generally straight, parallel, and not at all likely to be confounded with the irregular shadows produced by convection currents near the screen. . . . (*a*) The orientation of the dark bands, on a screen of perpendicular rays, is constantly parallel to the part of the mountain edge over which the sun is rising or setting. (*b*) The direction of their displacement is always perpendicular to their orientation but may be in one of two directions, direct or retrograde. (*c*) The velocity of the motion of the bands varies considerably from time to time, which may have some relation to the force of the wind, as the most rapid movements occur during high winds, and the slow ones during calm weather." The diffraction of light around a sharp edge produces bands, but the complex motion of the sunrise/sunset shadow bands and their relationship with weather conditions thwarts any easy optical explanation (*Knowledge*, 3: 457, 1906).

The Magic of Mirages

Many mirages are associated with the sea. Landfalls and other ships are seen long before they actually poke above the horizon. Inverted images of ships and shorelines, frequently greatly distorted and even replicated, are very common. Good mirages appear less frequently over the land. Flat plains, deserts, and ice fields are the best places to hunt for these atmospheric apparitions. The most common mirage of all is that of the sky seen in the air against the background of a hot road surface. But let us talk of less mundane things: great but nonexistent cities in the sky, sideways mirages, mirror mirages, and tricks of the atmosphere that are hard to explain.

Mirages sometimes display highly magnified objects. Islands and cities, hundreds and perhaps thousands of miles away and well below the horizon, appear larger than life in the sky. To magnify in this fashion, the atmosphere must behave like a lens—several lenses in the case of multiple mirages. Just how magnifying lenses of air are formed and how they can persist for so long are hard to explain. While some mirages are blurred and fuzzy, others show distant scenes with great clarity—something expected only from rigid, precisely ground glass lenses. Also like glass lenses, the mirage lens focuses its image in a very restricted area. Moving one's head up, down, or sideways a few feet may defocus and destroy the mirage. Lateral or sideways mirages also tax the science of meteorological optics because they require the formation of vertically oriented layers of air at different densities. Gravity should quickly destroy these layers, as if they were playing cards standing on end. Yet sideways mirages are rather common, with a record of nine replications of a scene spaced out side by side.

One of the strangest of all mirages—one that seems impossible to atmospheric optics—is the mirror or reflection mirage. Several observations exist where a scene is apparently reflected in the sky as if some giant mirror had been erected, with the observer between the real object and the reflected image. These images are not shadowlike Brocken specters but well-defined images. Can the atmosphere capriciously construct prisms and mirrors, as well as lenses, to confound us?

The question no conventional meteorologist will admit into the discussion is whether some images seen in the sky might not be mirages at all, but rather visual projections through time and/or space that are completely divorced from real objects. Are all the visions of armies, unidentified cities fair, idyllic countrysides, and ghost ships really extant in this space-time continuum, or do we verge here on the parapsychological? How much does the human mind embellish unusual natural phenomena?

THE FATA MORGANA

In 1773, the Dominican friar Antonio Minasi described a type of mirage seen across the Straits of Messina known as a Fata Morgana. Minasi's description was given wide circulation and adopted as a synonym for this variety of mirage. The unusual name is derived from the legend of the fairy sister of King Arthur, Morgan le Fay, whose magic created visions of cities and harbors that lured seamen to their deaths. Indeed, the Fata Morgana does seem to conjure up fantastic visions of ethereal cities and bucolic countrysides, but most of these scenes are simply atmospheric distortions of commonplace objects. It is fitting to begin this section on unusual mirages with Minasi's classical account.

"When the rising sun shines from that point whence its incident ray forms an angle of about 45 degrees on the sea of Reggio, and the bright surface of the water in the bay is not disturbed either by the wind or the current, the spectator being placed on an eminence of the city, with his back to the sun and his face to the sea—on a sudden he sees appear in the water, as in a catoptric theater [a hall of mirrors], various multiplied objects, such as numberless series of pilasters, arches, castles well delineated, regular columns, lofty towers, superb palaces with balconies and windows, extended alleys of trees, delightful plains with herds and flocks, armies of men on foot and horseback, and many other strange figures, all in their natural colors and proper action, and passing rapidly in succession along the surface of the sea, during the whole short period of time that the above mentioned causes remain. But if, in addition to the circumstances before described, the atmosphere be highly impregnated with vapor and exhalations not dispersed by the wind nor rarefied by the sun, it then happens that this vapor, as in a curtain extended along the channel to a height of about thirty palms and nearly down to the sea, the observer will behold the scene of the same objects not only reflected from the surface of the sea, but likewise in the air, though not in so distinct and defined a manner as in the sea." At times, three images of this rare but famous mirage are seen, one above the other. The buildings and landscapes are actually magnified portions of the Sicilian coast across the Straits. Rocks and coastline are greatly expanded and distorted, allowing one's imagination to see many objects not truly there (*Scientific American*, 106: 335, 1912).

Fata Morganas are actually more common in colder climes, as related in the following account from Firth of Forth, Scotland, 1871: The

The classical Fata Morgana seen across the Straits of Messina

power of the mirage to create fantastic, artificial-appearing shapes is confirmed here. "The early part of the day had been warm, and there was the usual dull, deceptive haze extending about half-way across the Firth, rendering the Fife coast invisible. The only object on the Fife coast, indeed, which was brought within the range of the refraction was Balconic Castle on the 'East Neuk,' which appeared half-way up the horizon, and in a line with the Isle of May. The most extraordinary illusions, however, were those presented by the May island, which, from a mere speck on the water, suddenly shot up in the form of a huge perpendicular wall, apparently 800 or 900 feet high, with a smooth and unbroken front to the sea. On the east side lay a long, low range of rocks, apparently detached from the island at various points, and it was on these that the most fantastic exhibitions took place. Besides assuming the most diversified and fantastic shapes, the rocks were constantly changing their positions, now moving off and again approaching each other. At one time, a beautiful columnal circle, the column seemingly from 20 to 30 feet high, appeared on the outermost rock. Presently the figure was changed to a clump of trees, whose green umbrageous foliage had a very vivid appearance. By and by the clump of trees increased to a large plantation, which gradually approached the main portion of the island, until within 300 or 400 feet, when the intervening space was spanned by a beautiful arch. Another and another arch was afterwards formed in the same way, the spans being nearly of the same width, while the whole length of the island, from east to west, seemed as flat and smooth as the top of a table. At a later period the phenomena, which were constantly changing, showed huge jagged rifts and ravines in the face of the high wall, through which the light came and went as they opened and shut, while trees and towers, columns and arches, sprang up and disappeared as if by magic" (*Symons's Monthly Meteorological Magazine*, 6: 98, 1871).

On April 15, 1949, the second officer of the M.V. *Stirling Castle*, then in the English Channel, reported a type of mirage that is usually responsible for double images of low-altitude stars and planets, some terrestrial ghost lights, and probably more than a few UFO reports. "A vessel was picked up about 4 points on the port bow, about 20° forwards of the bearing of the moon. With binoculars, the lights of the vessel appeared to be duplicated for short periods. This duplication was symmetrically opposite to the true lights. . . . When the upper lights merged with the lower lights, they appeared to form vertical strips of light. The distance of the vessel was about 5 miles." Certainly this mirage differs from the classical Fata Morgana, but the multiplication and apparent elongation of the images originate in the same optical process that so grossly distorts distant shorelines and in doing so paints nonexistent cities in the sky (*Marine Observer*, 20: 63, 1950).

MIRAGES THAT BEND FAR AROUND THE CURVATURE OF THE EARTH

That one can occasionally see a bit over the horizon via the mirage effect is well accepted by science. But when the image of a distant object or landscape is enlarged several times while remaining sharp and distinct, then science has some explaining to do. Three examples of magnifying, over-the-horizon mirages are presented below in order of increasing unbelievability.

On May 9, 1937, the M.S. *Hauraki* was plying the South Pacific bound for Papeete. "At 5:05 P.M. A.T.S. (0321 G.M.T., May 10) the islands of Tahiti, Mooréa, Huahine Iti and Raiatéa were seen. Only the peaks of Raiatéa and Huahine Iti were visible, but Tahiti and Mooréa were plainly recognizable. Very heavy rains have been experienced for four hours previously, ceasing at 4:30 P.M. A.T.S. The horizon cleared from east to north and showed with unusual sharpness and clearness some time before the mirage came into being. Tahiti gave the appearance of being 35 miles distant, when in reality Tahiti Peak was 210 miles away" (*Marine Observer,* 15: 52, 1938).

The Arctic is famous for magnifying mirages. Captain Robert A. Bartlett of the schooner *Effie M. Morrissey* was headed for Iceland in the summer of 1939, when he discerned peaks on that island long before he should have under normal conditions. "On July 17, the schooner was from its noon observation in sunshine found to be in latitude 63° 38′ N. and longitude 33° 42′ W. The ship's three chronometers had been checked daily by the Naval Observatory signal, and the air was calm and the sea smooth. At 4 P.M. with sun in the southwest, the remarkable mirage appeared in the direction of southwestern Iceland. The Snaefells Jokull (4,715 feet) and other landmarks well known to the captain and the mate were seen as though at a distance of twenty-five or thirty nautical miles, though the position of the schooner showed that these features were actually at a distance of 335 to 350 statute miles. . . . Captain Bartlett writes: 'If I hadn't been sure of my position and had been bound for Reykjavik, I would have expected to arrive within a few hours. The contours of the land and the snow-covered summit of the Snaefells Jokull showed up almost unbelievably near' " (*Science,* 90: 513, 1939).

During June and July of each year, if we are to believe all the legends and stories, a famous and inexplicable mirage appears in Alaska. It resembles the classical Fata Morgana, which is simply the optical distortion of nearby features, but many claim it is instead an extreme example of a long-distance, magnifying mirage. Called "The Silent City of Alaska," it is said to appear on the gigantic glacier of Mount Fairweather. "This phenomenon has engaged the attention of scientists, and up to the present time it has baffled all investigation. The scene has been known to the Alaska Indians of the locality for generations, and has been a common subject of speculation among them. . . . The phenomenon is seen between 7 and 9 o'clock between June 21 and July 10, and the scene never varies excepting for slight changes in the buildings and other prominent landmarks. It is believed that the mirage is a representation of the city of Bristol, England. That it is a seaport is shown by the mast of a vessel, while a tower, an exact duplicate of that of St. Mary Redcliff, appears in the background. . . . The distance between Bristol and Mount Fairweather is about 2,500 miles. The longest distance a mirage has been seen hitherto is 600 miles" (*Royal Meteorological Society, Quarterly Journal,* 27: 158, 1901).

MULTIPLE-IMAGE MIRAGES

In the preceding paragraphs, we have seen that the stratified, everchanging atmosphere can multiply and distort objects in fantastic ways. Multiple-image mirages are most likely created by several separate lenslike layers of air which magnify distant scenery with little distortion and present the viewer with a multiplex panorama, like some gigantic television set gone awry. The lighthousekeeper at Cape Wrath, Scotland, a Mr. Anderson, saw such a multiple-image mirage on December 5, 1922. This mirage was notable because it was highly sensitive to the position of the observer's head. "Mr. Anderson focussed his telescope on a sheep, which was grazing on top of a conical hill (height about 200 feet) about a quarter of a mile away, and immediately noticed an unusual appearance in the atmosphere around. On swinging the telescope slightly upward, he observed that a belt of the atmosphere appeared to be land and sea, giving a perfect representation of the whole of the coast line from Cape Wrath to Dunnet Head. The appearance in the mirage was an exact replica of what would have been seen from a distance of about 10 miles out to sea. In a direction south of the lighthouse there were three representations of the mirage one above the other, with sea separating each pair. The entrance to Loch Eriboll and the other bays could be seen and easily recognised in the main mirage, though Cape Wrath itself was rather indistinct. . . . The mirage was practically invisible to the naked eye, and was only visible from a very restricted area.

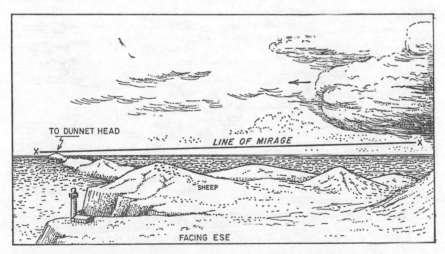

The terrain at Cape Wrath where a multiple mirage occurred

Mr. Anderson states that it was not visible at a distance of 20 yards either way from his original position, but was still visible 4 or 5 yards from that point" (*Nature*, 111: 222, 1923).

The following abstract demonstrates that the optics of mirages can be very complex indeed; each of the multiple images requires its own lenslike layer of air. "Multiple-image mirages have been observed many times. The greatest number of images, eight, on record is for an 1869 observation of the superior mirage. The greatest number of images previously recorded for the lateral mirage was three. A nine-image lateral mirage has now been photographed. It is suggested that the multiplicity of images is primarily related to the nature of the heat transport from a vertical surface" (*American Geophysical Union, Transactions*, 53: 274, 1972).

LATERAL OR SIDEWAYS MIRAGES

On June 14, 1956, a double sun was observed by the second officer of the M.V. *Salaverry*, then in the North Atlantic, bound for Curaçao. Double suns are occasionally due to anomalous halo phenomena—i.e., the one-sided mock sun, as described earlier in this chapter. In this instance, however, the subsequent merging of the two suns suggests a sideways mirage created by unstable vertical masses of air at different densities. "Shortly before sunset, with the sun at an altitude of 2° 35′, bearing 298°, twin suns were observed side by side, quite clearly separated. The image

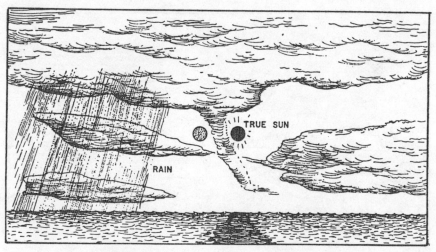

A double sun possibly created by a sideways mirage

was to the right of the true sun, there being no distortion of either. The phenomenon persisted for 2 minutes, after which the image gradually elongated in the direction of the true sun, eventually merging with it within 1/2 minute" (*Marine Observer*, 27: 84, 1957).

"At 17 h. 5 m. G.M.T. on October 11th [1927], the sun had fallen behind the Snowdon range [in Wales], and the range was backed by a large golden fleecy cloud, on which was outlined a dark, well-defined shadow of Snowdon, persisting for some five or ten minutes. I find it difficult to understand how the shadow was cast in the direction of the sun, as the cloud was manifestly on the far side of the hills, the atmosphere was clear, and the eastern sky was almost cloudless. At 17 h. 20 m. the cloud had disappeared, and the western horizon was clear except for some distant striations, when suddenly there appeared over Crib Goch a streaky golden outline of its summit, which faded out after perhaps 15 seconds or half a minute" (*Meteorological Magazine*, 63: 15, 1928).

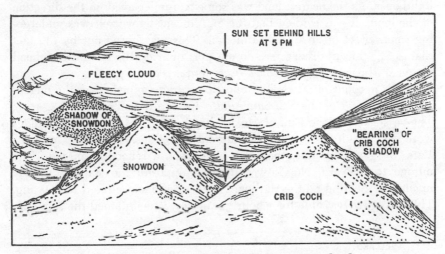

Sideways mirage in the Snowdon Range, England

MIRROR OR REFLECTION MIRAGES

This type of mirage is not recognized by most meteorologists, for it seems to contradict the principles of atmospheric optics. Nevertheless, several apparently legitimate observations of mirrorlike reflections occur in the annals of geophysics. Three such instances appear below; a fourth was reported in conjunction with twilight bands earlier in this chapter.

On December 2, 1961, A. J. Child aboard the M.V. *Glengyle* en route to Port Saïd in the Red Sea observed peculiar refraction effects.

Between 1440 and 1445 GMT, "a Blue Funnel ship was seen on the horizon towards the south at 1440, with the funnel much enlarged due to refraction; simultaneously a 'watery-looking' image of the same vessel was seen on the horizon in the WNW. At 1443 the sun was obscured by hills some 63 miles distant and 3,000–7,000 ft. high. The vessel and its image now looked larger than they did 3 minutes previously. The image disappeared at 1445, which was, by calculation, the time of sunset" (*Marine Observer*, 32: 183, 1962).

The apparent reflection of a lighthouse appeared on November 26, 1963, to the second officer of the S.S. *Bravo* off Cape St. Vincent, Spain. "At 0315 GMT, when the vessel was 4 miles due south of the Cape St. Vincent light, a false loom was seen on the reciprocal bearing of the lighthouse, which was so real in appearance that one would have expected the light itself to have been sighted in that direction at any moment. The loom was flashing every 5 seconds, as does the St. Vincent lighthouse. As the nearest land was some 240 miles away in the direction of the loom, it was evident that the St. Vincent light itself was undergoing some effect of abnormal refraction. This was borne out by the fact that as St. Vincent drew astern on our port quarter, the loom drew ahead on our starboard bow" (*Marine Observer*, 34: 180, 1964).

This account of a possible reflection mirage appeared in the meteorological record of the S.S. *San Adolfo* for the date February 14, 1936. The vessel was in the Gulf of Mexico headed for Tampico. Two mirages were seen simultaneously but in different directions. One was a "normal" Fata Morgana, but the other may have been a reflection mirage. "The mirage to seaward, No. 1, was directly opposite the sun and slowly opened its bearing on the starboard bow, as the sun altered its bearing. This mirage was visible for 1 hour 5 minutes; it maintained the same ap-

Unusual mirage resembling the classical Fata Morgana in Gulf of Mexico

pearance throughout and always bore directly opposite the sun. It appeared as two headlands forming an entrance to a bay or harbour, and trees were clearly visible, also hills in the background. The fronts of these headlands were a sandy colour" (*Marine Observer*, 14: 11, 1937).

HORIZON UNDULATIONS AND SURGING MIRAGES

On March 29, 1948, G. G. Pegler on the M.V. *Silverwalnut*, then near the Cape of Good Hope, saw a "bump" move along the horizon. "The phenomenon first appeared at 1400 G.M.T. and lasted for 7 minutes, during which period the whole horizon in this direction appeared to be traversed by an enormous swell. The 'crest,' with slight variations in shape, moved steadily along the horizon from south to west and finally merged into the usual horizon line. The remainder of the horizon was clear and completely undistorted throughout" (*Marine Observer*, 19: 10, 1949).

Kenneth Sinclair was lighthouseman at Fair Isle Lighthouse, Great Britain, in April 1919. He reported a peculiar moving mirage, now termed a "surging mirage": "Coming from the east toward the station about 8 A.M., I observed peculiar shades flittering at about an altitude of 22 to 30 degrees in the western sky. The sun was very bright and the sea carried a deep roll, so to speak, with a glassy surface, both of which, I consider, played an important part in this phenomenon. By the eye alone I could form no conception, so [I] resorted to the telescope. By its aid, to my great surprise, I could see spread out a panorama wonderful to behold. The islands of North Ronaldshay, Sanday, and Westray were stretched out mapped and clothed in their natural beauty, against the curve of the western sky. But this most astonishing phenomenon increased in interest when I observed a reversed view, equally as clear, of North Ronaldshay and part of Sanday only, immediately under, as if growing from one base; and, as sure as the timely rise and fall of the fountain ball, so did this strange sight rise and fall as if governed by the movement of some sighing bosom. Each movement downwards seemed to separate each object at its base, and growing more distorted on the upward movement things gradually assumed their natural aspect, when I could make out many of the houses on North Ronaldshay, Star Point Lighthouse, and farms on Sanday, also Noup Head, Westray" (*Meteorological Magazine*, 58: 12, 1923).

Some mirages seem extraordinarily sensitive to the location of the observer, both in the horizontal and vertical directions. The multiple mirage at Cape Wrath described previously displayed this feature, as did the following apparition of May 1, 1949, at Hunstanton Beach, England. "The phenomenon occurred between N. and NE. at a distance of about 1,300–1,500 yards from us. . . . A dark smooth sheet of water changed sharply at this distance to a bright silver-blue, spreading towards the open sea and merging with the sky, no horizon line being discernible in this direction. The display was mainly over the sea since the beach narrowed in that direction. Most probably it was a distant wide sector of the beach with objects and people on it reflected. We could distinctly see little human figures walking to and fro far out on the sea but the 'permanent' objects changed positions with time very little, and this was probably due only to the motion of the sun. . . . With a decrease of the angle of view—i.e., by bending down to about 3 feet—the bright surface spread a little towards us; the objects and the illusive walkers faded and then completely vanished. The other people present on the beach over which we watched the mirage did not disappear. With an increase of the angle of view, the objects reappeared and the people again walked on the sea. By standing on small rocks (3–4 feet), it all became more clearly defined" (*Weather*, 40: 234, 1949).

Curious Shadows and Obscurations

Disturbances propagating through the atmosphere may become visible in unexpected ways. Shock waves from explosions and supersonic jet aircraft, usually undetectable by the eye, are sometimes traced across the sky with geometric precision if atmospheric conditions are just right. There is nothing mysterious about this; aeronautical engineers photograph shock waves every day in wind tunnels using optical instruments to detect the different air properties of the compressed shock waves. Yet naturally visible shock waves are rare and, because they are usually seen under the stress of battle, quite disconcerting to the observer.

Definitely more mysterious are the common solar-eclipse shadow bands that engulf observers along the path of totality. Usually explained away either as shadows of ripples in the atmosphere (analogous to those in the bottom of a wind-ruffled swimming pool) or diffraction patterns caused by light bending around the edge of the moon to form, through optical interference, a series of parallel shadows. A long series of coordinated observations of eclipse shadow bands has demonstrated that neither explanation seems correct. So what are they? There is no accepted theory. Perhaps they are related in some way to an unexplored fine structure woven into the atmosphere. For example, the long-lived "aerial blobs" described here hint at some sort of unseen fabric, often quite regular in its structure, cast like an invisible net across the clear sky.

VISIBLE SOUND WAVES

On September 26, 1917, Frederick A. Saunders was stationed in France with an American regiment 400–500 yards in front of a battery of 6-inch guns. The sun was obscured by heavy fog. "Soon after the attack opened, I had occasion to go to the top of one of the hills which flanked our position, and at a certain definite level above the battery a very considerable disturbance in the fog was noticeable after each discharge of the heavy rifles behind me. The visibility was such that the flash of the discharge could not be seen, but each time before the report reached us a band of greater density was clearly visible in the fog, moving with great rapidity up the valley toward us in the form of an arc. Its arrival was simultaneous with that of the sound of the discharge. This arc of greater fog density was perhaps six feet from its anterior to its posterior edge and of about the same depth. It followed closely an altitude of some sixty or seventy feet above the floor of the valley and was clearly visible from both above and below that plane, but no similar phenomena were visible in any other plane" (*Science*, 52: 442, 1920).

A similar phenomenon appeared to V. S. Taylor in 1944, at Anzio, Italy, on the Allied beachhead. "During and immediately after intense A.A. fire under conditions of virtually clear sky, with the sun behind the observer, concentrically disposed wave-ripple arcs could be seen passing away from the barrage zone, in the portion of the sky about 45° forward of the observer. The acute compression of the atmosphere peripheral to the bursting shells caused the compression zones to be sufficiently altered in refractive index to produce an optically visible phenomenon when refracting undiffused sunlight" (*Nature*, 155: 388, 1945).

In Chapter 1, "flashing volcanic arcs" were described. It is possible that instead of being self-luminous, these arcs are merely optical effects similar to those observed in England, in 1944, by the British as German bombs rained down. "Such waves have been seen by observers of nearby explosions and have been described as 'a faint but distinct line in the form of a seemingly perfect arc centered on the spot where a bomb has disappeared.' These effects are connected with the explosion wave within a few hundred yards of the explosion itself, and it seems that the curved line represents the hemispherical wave of compressed air. In this case the optical effect might arise either from evaporation of water droplets in cloudy sky or even as a refraction (mirage) effect from the relatively steep gradient of air density" (*Nature,* 154: 738, 1944).

Supersonic aircraft can emulate the optical effects created by artillery and bursting bombs. On October 15, 1971, a California resident was watching military jets. "It was about 5:45 P.M. Pacific Daylight Time on October 15, 1971, with the sun about 3° above distant hills and the sky quite cloudless. An aircraft perhaps 5,000 feet above Edwards Air Force Base passed almost overhead toward the setting sun. As it receded, two concentric well-defined dark semicircles appeared below and slightly be-

Visible shock waves created by a supersonic aircraft

hind the craft. These arcs rapidly expanded symmetrically to at least six times their original size, maintaining their spacing and sharpness. The total optical impression, which lasted only a fraction of a second, was of a double ripple in the sky that expanded away from the aircraft. It was immediately followed by the double concussion effect of a sonic boom" (*Sky and Telescope,* 44: 205, 1972).

RIPPLES CROSSING CIRRUS CLOUDS AND HALO DISPLAYS

As atmospheric disturbances move through regions containing clouds and ice crystals, optical effects may be noted as water droplets and ice crystals are jostled. Phenomena of this type are quite rare, and frequently the cause of the disturbance is unknown. In the first example, however, the observer was located on a ship off the Normandy coast on

July 30, 1944, when the sounds of battle were omnipresent. Responding to an account of mock-sun ripples, M. Blake wrote, "R. White suggests that the ripples he saw passing through a mock sun may have been caused by sound waves, although he was unable to verify this. The phenomenon I observed can much more confidently be attributed to sound waves. The entry in my diary for 30 July 1944 states in part 'Plentiful tufts, bands, and patches of cirrus and cirrocumulus moving from the west, seemingly very high. In mock sun at 1930 see concussion waves from firing on front passing through cirrus.' I can recall many features of the display quite clearly. I noticed it initially with the naked eye and then examined it through binoculars. The mock sun was the southern or left-handed parhelion of the 22° halo. It was in a patch of cloud and was quite brilliant in contrast with nearby blue sky. I do not remember any other parts of a halo being visible. The phenomenon took the form of dark parallel bands moving rapidly from bottom left to top right of the sun dog, i.e., from south to north. I think that the ripples showed themselves most clearly in the red part of the parhelion, but this association with red in my mind may be a caprice of memory. At any rate I can recall a clear picture of moving bands within which the luminous pink colour was momentarily extinguished allowing the blue of the sky to show through the tenuous cloud. Through binoculars, in fact, the striations of cloud appeared to flicker on and off as a ripple passed. Ripples crossed the mock sun at irregular intervals every few seconds. I cannot recall whether they came in closely associated groups, like ripples from a stone dropped into a pond, or singly; I do remember that most were quite faint, but that every now and then there would be a stronger impulse apparently originating from a point farther east than the others" (*Weather*, 32: 276, 1977).

In more peaceful times, R. Scott, at Kitt Peak National Observatory, Arizona, reported strange waves moving through cirrus clouds on February 3, 1977. "My attention was caught by a patch of sky which displayed a wave-pattern moving apparently at high speed from west to east. The pattern contrast was very low; it was the motion that made it visible. My notes suggested that the pattern may not have been purely sinusoidal, but rather more of a square-wave pattern or that it at least contained some higher harmonics. The wavelength was of the order of one degree, and the orientation of the troughs was north-south. I would not rule out that the velocity was that of sound. The phenomenon lasted for about three seconds, vanished, and then reappeared for perhaps a couple of seconds more." No source for the disturbance was suggested (*Weather*, 33: 38, 1978).

On December 15, 1976, B. J. Burton reported from Chelmsford, England: "While observing an upper arc of contact to the 22° halo, a num-

ber of closely spaced grey bands were seen rapidly crossing it from left
to right, roughly north to south. . . . The dark bands were first seen for
about ten seconds. There was then a period of about 15 seconds when no
bands were seen. More bands then appeared for about 5 seconds. During
the interval the attention of three colleagues was summoned, two of
whom are trained meteorologists. All three witnessed the second sighting
and confirm my own observations. During the first sighting an estimated
30 or so bands crossed the arc of contact, there being about 5 to 10 bands
visible at any time. The bands appeared greyish in colour and did not
have a sharp outline. They were narrow, appeared to be straight, parallel, and regularly spaced. They moved steadily, taking an estimated two
seconds to cross the arc of contact" (*Journal of Meteorology, U.K.*, 2:
233, 1977).

SHADOW BANDS SEEN DURING ECLIPSES

Long before supersonic aircraft and aerial bombs, astronomers were
perplexed by shadow bands sweeping the landscape before and after
total eclipses of the sun. The simplistic explanations have long prevailed:
the bands are merely shadows cast by atmospheric disturbances or lunar
diffraction patterns. Do the actual observations support this explanation?

On September 22, 1922, Jean L. Chant was following the total
eclipse at Wallal, Australia, and ready with a white sheet to measure
shadow bands. "Suddenly, and before I had expected it, the shimmering,
elusive, wave-like shadows began to sweep over me and the sheet. I
grasped the rod and moved it back and forth until it was parallel to the
crests of the waves as they moved forward. At the same time I began
counting seconds—'one-and, two-and, three-and, etc.'—and I continued
counting up to 150 before totality was announced. I think perhaps I
counted a little too rapidly and, allowing for that, I judge that the
bands began approximately 2 1/4 minutes before totality. They continued to move over me for only a short time, perhaps ten seconds, and then
they were gone! They were faint, thrilling, ghost-like, but definite
enough for me to be sure that I had seen the shadow bands. . . . I took
my position at the second sheet to watch for the shadow-bands again.
They began at 15 seconds after totality and to my surprise they seemed
to come from the opposite direction. They were even fainter than at the
beginning and lasted perhaps five seconds. I moved the second rod until
I judged it was parallel to the crest of the waves. At the beginning of
totality the bands came from west to east, moving in the same direction
as did the moon's shadow as it swept across the earth; at the end they

moved in the opposite direction, or so it seemed to me" (*Popular Astronomy*, 32: 202, 1924).

Notes made by Prof. E. Waite Elder, at Denver, Colorado, on June 18, 1918, cast doubt on the suggestion that atmospheric disturbances create the eclipse shadow bands: "Too cloudy to see shadow bands at beginning of totality; shadow bands about 10 cm. wide and 20 cm. apart! An entry two minutes later reads: Brisk wind from N.W. at end of totality, shadow bands 15 degrees N. of E. travelling 2.5 to 3 meters per second toward S.E. by S. Would this not imply the visibility of shadow bands at mid-totality? It is also interesting to note here that although a brisk wind was behind the shadow bands, they were hardly moving as fast as the shadow bands that we observed at Beacon, N.Y., last year, although there the air was absolutely calm. If the shadow bands are due to surface air currents, why should their motion not be speeded up appreciably by a stiff wind?" (*Popular Astronomy*, 34: 279, 1926).

One of the authorities on eclipse shadow bands, Richard L. Feldman, sums up their peculiarities in the two excerpts that follow. "The critical reader is asked to keep in mind certain peculiarities of behavior of the bands which are demonstrated to exist. (1) It is only at points along the center line of the path of totality that the line of extension of the bands is the same after totality as before; an abrupt difference is always noted elsewhere, this difference approaching a right angle as the locations reporting are farther and farther out from the center line. (2) Although these abrupt changes in extension are noted between pre- and post-totality, an interval which seldom exceeds two or three minutes, nevertheless (and this is important in objecting to the 'air wave' refractionists) *no abrupt changes* during the pre-totality period, or during post-totality, seem ever to have been reliably reported. On the other hand, points near the border of the path of totality have frequently reported *progressive* changes in the direction of extension. (3) The direction of progress of the bands, which is normal, or perpendicular, to their extension, is also normal to the shadow's edge, progressing either toward or away from it, with several reliable reports recorded of stationary bands. . . . (6) It is readily recognizable that the range of speeds of the bands over the ground—reported most often at from 5 to 10 miles per hour—is but the hundredth part of the speed at which the shadow spot races across the face of the globe" (*Popular Astronomy*, 48: 2, 1940).

Thirty-two years later, Feldman wrote: "The records I have collected since 1932, which cover more than a century of solar eclipses, confirm the following definite features of shadow bands: (1) Shadow bands are parts of arcs concentric with the moon's shadow, since observations at any one site show that the bands are tangent to the nearest edge of the shadow. Similarly, at any position on the center line of the eclipse track, bands seen after totality are parallel to those observed before it. (2) The bands are most closely spaced just before and after totality; that is, they crowd inward toward the shadow edge. (3) The speed of translation of the bands is greatest at the beginning and end of totality" (*Sky and Telescope,* 43: 224, 1972).

PECULIAR SHADOW BANDS SEEN ON WALLS

Circa 1906, "the observations were made in Quiberon Bay, during the stay of the North Squadron. During the night exercises, the powerful searchlights from the warships repeatedly rested on the white vertical walls of the buildings on shore. The dark bands, very clear, with an undulating motion, were from 10–15 cm. wide and had a motion of 4.5 metres per second. The wall forming the screen was oriented to the east and was placed perpendicularly to the rays from the projectors, of which the distance was about 3 1/2 kilometres. Under those conditions the bands were displaced from the North to the South. They were best seen at about 10 metres distance. Similar fringes were seen on another wall oriented North-east to South-west, thus being very oblique to the line of rays, and in this case, as before, the shadows moved from right to left" (*Knowledge,* 3: 431, 1906).

Moving shadows may be cast upon a wall by sun shining through a bow window. "Between the frames, where the light passes only through clean glass, there are fairly regularly dark stripes, mostly vertical, but for some panes horizontal. They disappear when the window is opened so that they depend on the glass, presumably some polarization effect resulting from the manufacture of the plate. More puzzling is the fact that these dark lines move, even when the window remains stationary. Sometimes a continuous movement can be traced to the edge of a cloud passing over the sun. But frequently there is considerable slow to-and-fro movement, looking rather like a *moiré* fringe, when there is no cloud in the sky and no visible movement anywhere! The dark lines are not consistent in appearance—sometimes they are even diagonal, but at any one moment of time they are very well defined, remarkably parallel and equidistant" (*New Scientist,* 14: 362, 1961).

OPTICAL PHENOMENA CAUSED BY "AERIAL BLOBS"

Aerial blobs are volumes of air possessing different densities, temperatures, and water contents from the atmospheric sea in which they float. When these blobs are in the path of starlight entering a telescope, portions of the star's image will come to focus above or below the photographic plate. By analyzing these extrafocal images, aerial blobs have been found to have the following properties. "Linear dimensions of aerial blobs have been observed ranging from millimeters to many meters. Blobs may be globular, lenticular, or cylindrical in shape, thus producing sharp pointlike or linelike extrafocal images of stars. Often hundreds of

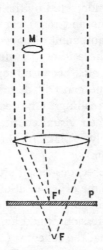

Long-lived "aerial blobs" with different indexes of refraction distort telescopic images.

blobs are quite regularly spaced and drift with the winds at various altitudes up to 50 km. or perhaps higher. . . . A most amazing feature of many aerial blobs is their durability and stability; some of them preserve their shapes for hours" (*Science*, 122: 159, 1955).

Aerial blobs create much of the familiar twinkling and fading of stars. Such blobs may also be the cause of this report of June 8, 1978, from Guyton, Georgia: "At about 6:55 Universal Time, I was making a naked-eye and binocular sweep of the Scorpius region when Antares [magnitude + 0.9] suddenly dimmed to only slightly brighter than Beta Scorpii [magnitude 2.5]. Antares remained dim for about 30 seconds [time] before suddenly returning to its original brightness. While dim, Antares appeared about magnitude 2.3 and much deeper red than usual" (*Sky and Telescope*, 54: 207, 1978).

Anomalies in the Transmission and Reception of Radio and Radar Signals

Our eyes see only a very narrow portion of the electromagnetic spectrum. It is therefore reasonable to assume that the major share of atmospheric anomalies go undetected by the observer not possessing special instruments. When radio and radar came along earlier in this century, the operators of this equipment discovered a whole new universe of atmospheric phenomena. These idiosyncrasies are not as widely known as mirages, rainbows, halos, etc., because they can be detected only by a select few. Of course, no one can call them beautiful or awe-inspiring; they are simply instrument readings. One reads of them in the technical journals. As in the case of their visual counterparts, almost all radio and radar anomalies are probably explainable in terms of reflection, refraction, and frequency dispersion.

The long-delayed radio echoes first detected in the 1920s have received the most publicity, some of it sensational in character. Even in today's overcrowded electromagnetic environment, long-delayed echoes are frequently heard by professionals and amateurs alike. The delays are so long (several seconds) that the reflector (if that is what causes them) must be located outside the moon's orbit. Even alien (extraterrestrial intelligent beings) space probes carrying radio-repeaters have been proposed to explain these echoes. Natural clouds of ionized matter are certainly more likely, but no one knows for sure.

The apparent effects of the positions of the moon and planets upon radio transmission are also quite controversial. For the planets in particular there seems no natural force strong enough to affect terrestrial radio propagation. More likely the culprit is solar activity, as measured by sunspot number, which can also be loosely correlated with planetary positions; but this just transfers the mystery to some unrecognized planetary force that affects solar activity. Here is a genuine scientific puzzle—the possibility of a hitherto undetected physical force!

In the case of radar, human blindness at long wavelengths is particularly frustrating because radars are always detecting "angels" and spurious targets unaccounted for by aircraft, ships, or topographic and meteorological features. Birds and insects, singly or *en masse*, reflect enough radar energy to cause some angels. In addition, the bubble or bloblike constitution of the atmosphere—quite invisible to man—causes additional false radar targets. Nevertheless, some solid-appearing radar targets cannot be accounted for.

LONG-DELAYED RADIO ECHOES

In 1928, after learning that Hals, at Oslo, had observed shortwave echoes delayed by several seconds, the Dutch scientist, B. van der Pol, set up experimental equipment at Eindhoven. No delayed echoes were recorded for several months. "Then suddenly, on October 11, I got a telegram from Prof. Stormer stating that very fine echoes had been heard that afternoon. Thereupon I immediately arranged the same night a series of test signals to be sent consisting of three short dots in rapid succession given every 30 seconds between 20 and 21 o'clock local time. I listened with my assistant to the 120 signals. Thirteen echoes were observed by both of us, the times between the signals and the echoes being: 8, 11, 15, 8, 13, 3, 8, 8, 8, 12, 15, 13, 8, [and] 8 seconds. The [radio] frequency of the echo was always exactly equal to the frequency of the signal, which fact could be easily verified as the signals were 'unmodulated,' and therefore the receiver was kept oscillating. . . . The echoes I heard were rather weak, and though their oscillation frequency could be easily detected to be the same as the frequency of the direct signals, the three dots of the original signal could not be recognised in the echo, the latter being of a blurred nature, except in one case where the echo came in 3 seconds after the signal, when the three dots of the original signal were very plainly audible in the echo as well" (*Nature*, 122: 878, 1929).

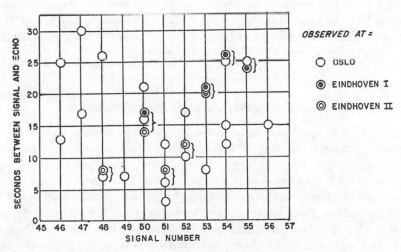

Delays between transmitted radio signals and their echoes

A typical modern instance of long-delayed radio echoes was reported by H. L. Rasmussen. On July 7, 1974, echoes occurred at 1,296 MHz while employing moon-bounce transmission. "On the day in question a series of dots or a single dash were being reflected back from the Moon after 2.6 seconds. Suddenly there appeared a second signal delayed by approximately 2 seconds. This signal had the same characteristics of the moon-bounce signal except that it was weaker. At the time of the observations it was afternoon, the sun was almost due west, and the moon was to the southwest with an altitude of about 30°. Throughout a series of transmissions, the returning moon signal was followed about 2 seconds later by the delayed ghost signal with the same characteristic note of the transmitter." The observer thought the echoes might be from streams of solar plasma (*Nature*, 257: 36, 1975).

Many observations of long-delayed radio echoes (LDE's) followed those of Hals and van der Pol, by both scientists and amateurs (hams). In 1969, Villard et al. summarized the accumulated ham data in *QSR*, a journal published for radio amateurs. "Following is a summary of the conclusions which can be derived from the ham reports taken as a group: (1) multiple-second 'coherent' signal echoes, either phone or c.w. [continuous wave], appear to be real and are observable for short periods of time at highly infrequent intervals, (2) they are audible both on a station's own signals and on signals of other stations, (3) they have been observed at 7, 14, 21, and 28 MHz, but apparently not at higher frequencies, (4) they occur most frequently (or perhaps are most easily heard) when a given band is just 'opening up'—i.e., when skywave propagation to some point on earth is just becoming possible . . . (8) the LDE's appear to be one single echo, rather than several successive ones, (9) no Doppler shift is perceptible . . . (13) the total time interval during which the echo effect can be heard is remarkably short—usually no more than a few minutes" (*QSR*, 53: 38, May 1969).

EFFECT OF ASTRONOMICAL BODIES ON RADIO TRANSMISSION

In the late 1940s and early 1950s, J. H. Nelson of RCA was attempting to discover a method of forecasting shortwave radio transmission conditions. His studies led him to conclude that while solar activity was important, other astronomical conditions were also involved. Here is a brief excerpt from his controversial 1952 paper. "Cyclic variations in sunspot activity have been studied by many solar investigators in the past, and attempts were made by some, notably Huntington, Clayton, and Sanford, to connect these variations to planetary influences. The books of these three investigators were studied and their results found sufficiently encouraging to warrant correlating similar planetary interrelationships with radio signal behavior. However, it was decided to investigate the effects of all of the planets from Mercury to Saturn instead of only the major planets as they had done. The same heliocentric angular relationships of 0, 90, 180, and 270 degrees were used, and dates when any two or more planets were separated by one of these angles were recorded.

"Investigation quickly showed there was positive correlation between these planetary angles and transatlantic short-wave signal variations. Radio signals showed a tendency to become degraded within a day or two of planetary configurations of the type being studied. However, some configurations showed better correlation than others.

"Considerable study was devoted to the most severe degradations and led to the discovery that when three planets held a 'multiple-of-90-degrees' arrangement among themselves, the correlation was more pronounced. These arrangements were called 'multiple configurations'; [they] exist when two planets are at 0 degree with each other and a third planet is 90 degrees or 180 degrees away from them. Also, a multi-

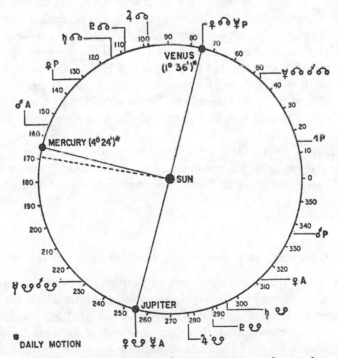

One of Nelson's charts relating radio transmission quality to planetary positions; the astrological overtones are obvious.

ple exists when two planets are separated by 180 degrees with a third planet 90 degrees from each. These multiples are quite common. A more uncommon type of multiple is the case where all three planets are at 0 degree with each other. From the few cases recorded, this type of multiple shows the least correlation.

"Many of the multiples are completed in the space of a few hours, being accompanied by sharp severe signal degradation. At other times, the multiple may take several days to pass, being accompanied by generally erratic conditions during the period" (*Electrical Engineering*, 71: 421, 1952).

Nelson's work was attacked on the basis that the planets exert no known forces strong enough to affect terrestrial conditions, but the astrological overtones of Nelson's papers made the controversy more emotional than usual. (See the accompanying figure, which looks like something out of a horoscope.) The RCA work, however, was done solely for practical engineering purposes without prejudice one way or another.

Nelson's correlations are certainly not without precedent, as illustrated by this notice in *Nature*. "In a recent communication to the Editors, Mr. P. A. de G. Howell, 77 Glandovey Road, Fendation, Christchurch, N.W., New Zealand, claims to have observed during 1938–1939 and 1944–1945, a correlation between the variation in long-distance transmission conditions at short wavelengths and the phase of the moon. It was observed that there was a minimum of background noise at high signal strength with little tendency to fade for about two or three days on either side of full phase, these conditions changing to a maximum of noise with poor signals and fading around the time of new moon" (*Nature*, 159: 396, 1947).

The moon's gravitational attraction does create tides in the upper atmosphere and ionosphere that can conceivably affect radio transmissions; thus the lunar effect is scientifically acceptable whereas planetary effects are not.

A STABLE ELECTROMAGNETIC RADIATION PATTERN OVER THE OCEAN

During the 1960s, off the coast of Southern California, radio receivers charted an unexpected stable radiation pattern. "During a flight-test program performed by LTV [Ling-Temco-Voight] for another purpose, it was recognized that there exists a unique low- and medium-frequency electromagnetic radiation pattern over the surface of the ocean. This radiation pattern appears to be quite stable and is found as variations in the signal from radio stations. Statistical analysis showed a

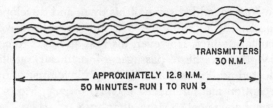

TRANSMITTERS
30 N.M.

APPROXIMATELY 12.8 N.M.
50 MINUTES- RUN I TO RUN 5

Stable radio-signal intensity patterns over the ocean

correlation between patterns taken on consecutive runs over the same area to be as high as 0.9 over a 1-hour period. . . . The accompanying illustration shows two patterns (runs 2 and 5) from two broadcast stations, recorded approximately 20 minutes apart. . . . The day-to-day repeatability is not known." The existence of this relatively stable pattern represents a new phenomenon. No explanation exists at present (*Undersea Technology*, 5: 29, 1964).

UNIDENTIFIED RADIO SIGNALS

"In May and June 1962, Rohan et al., observed unexplained sudden amplitude and phase changes on GBR signals at Salisbury, South Australia. Allan reported similar observations made simultaneously at Lower Hutt, New Zealand. He suspected interfering signals from a powerful transmitter in the vicinity of Australia and operating near 16.0 Kc./s. In April 1963, Allan recorded anomalies on the 18.0 Kc./s. very low frequency transmissions emitted by NBA. . . . Our NBA records of April 1963, taken at Deal (New Jersey), also show phase anomalies with times of observation which agree with the times given by Allan. The anomalies of April 12, 13, and 14 were almost unnoticeable, but the anomaly of April 16 was quite strong. If it was caused by an interfering signal, its frequency had an offset of approximately 7×10^{-7} and its amplitude at Deal could have been as large as 6 dB. below that of the signal from NBA which is located only 3,500 km. south of Deal. . . . Simultaneous observation of numerous phase and amplitude anomalies on the 16.0 Kc./s. GBR signal with practically identical equipment (servo time constant, 50 seconds) at eight widely separated locations in November and December 1965 confirms beyond doubt that the anomalies were caused by an interfering transmitter" (*Nature*, 213: 584, 1967). Although the interfering transmitter could not be identified, little significance was attached to these observations.

John F. Bagby, however, analyzed the 1962, 1963, and 1965 observations reported in *Nature,* added some of his own, and developed a rather startling hypothesis: the interference was due to radio-wave reflection from artificial earth satellites. However, his first attempts to correlate the interference with the overhead passages of artificial satellites failed. Bagby then collected additional data. "During November and December 1965, I made reception measurements of CHU on 7.33 Mc./s. and again found periodic enhancements. More than 90% of them had a very definite pattern which differed from the previous patterns. . . . It was obvious that the time between enhancement periods was different at each succeeding epoch and that the daily advance was also changing. If these enhancements were due to reflexions from the passage of a particular Earth satellite through the upper atmosphere, then that satellite had a changing orbital period. I tried to correlate the various reception enhancements with the osculating orbit of the natural Earth satellite previously discussed in *Nature,* but because I was unable to account for all the various radio enhancement periods as being due to the natural satellite, I put the task aside temporarily." Bagby next assumed that a natural satellite might have a highly elliptical orbit. Analysis of this satellite proved encouraging. It would leave an ionized trail in the upper atmosphere near perigee from which the 16 and 18 Kc./s. signals would be reflected back to earth to cause the observed interference. Bagby's final conclusion was that an ephemeral natural earth satellite could have caused the interfering signals he and others observed.

THE HUMMING EARTH

"The Earth gives off a radio hum at the subsonic frequency of 7.8 cycles per second according to scientists at the Massachusetts Institute of Technology. This hum they believe to be produced by lightning exciting the electrical resonance of the gigantic cavity bounded on one side by the Earth's surface, and on the other by the lower layers of the ionosphere" (*New Scientist,* 9: 763, 1961).

Radar Angels

Just as the human eye sometimes sees things that are not really there, so a radar may pick up false echoes or "angels." Usually such echoes are not really "false" because something tangible but invisible or inconspicuous to the human eye really does reflect the radar pulse. Birds and insects, small as they are, can reflect enough energy to show up on a radar scope. At sea, rips and upwellings roughen the water enough to reflect radar waves back to the antenna and consequently show up as a target. The atmosphere, too, has its bubbles and thin layers of warmer or colder air (called discontinuities) that show up on radar screens. (Atmospheric discontinuities may cause radar UFO's!) There is still much to learn about radar angels. Those associated with phosphorescence in the Persian Gulf (see page 85) are particularly mysterious.

The picture appearing on a radar screen may also be distorted by signals that skip along between the surface and an atmospheric reflecting layer. Ghost or multiple images may result. In another type of radar anomaly, distant mountains may appear nearby if the radar's pulse rate is too fast—the echoes really being from an earlier transmitter pulse rather than the most recent one. Usually a skilled radar operator can recognize most false echoes for what they are, but strange anomalies are always appearing, just as they do in the visual world.

FALSE RADAR TARGETS (DOT ANGELS)

On May 8, 1949, at approximately 0200 hours, the radar of the T.S.S. *Clan Davidson* plying the Red Sea was switched on. "With the 'Heading Marker' checked, echoes were recorded of all ships in the vicinity, but additional echoes were also observed. The false echoes were clear, firm, and constant. One such echo was picked up 10° on the starboard bow at

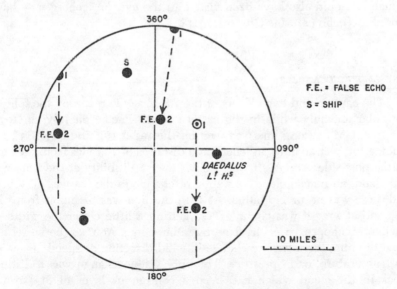

The positions of false echoes on the Clan Davidson *radar screen*

a distance of 10 miles. This echo remained on the same bearing as the distance decreased, though the size of the echo became smaller until at a distance of 3 miles it finally disappeared altogether. Although a strict visual watch was maintained, no object could be seen on this bearing." Near Daedalus Lighthouse, another false echo was picked up with identical results. All real echoes (the Lighthouse and other ships) had proper distances and bearings. No explanation of these false echoes was given (*Marine Observer*, 20: 212, 1950).

The S.S. *Rialto* was in the North Atlantic steaming in dense fog on May 11, 1953. "At approximately 2100 S.M.T. Radar gave echoes on apparent objects that we were unable to identify. Echoes were similar to those given by sea clutter but were in two distinct groups. Firstly, one group to port, distant 1 1/2 miles, and about half an hour later another group, this time to starboard, distant 1/2 mile. Speed was reduced each time accordingly. Nothing was sighted." A current rip (local rough water) may have caused these echoes (*Marine Observer*, 24: 81, 1954).

On May 25, 1960, the S.S. *Marengo* was in the North Atlantic bound for Halifax. "A radar echo was plotted at 0340 GMT, and it was found to be that of a stationary object; no lights were seen, nor were flashing signals answered. The echo was picked up at 9 miles and showed fairly well: it was intermittent at 5.2 miles, the nearest approach, and when abaft the beam it was not detectable beyond 7 miles. The weather was cloudless and there was an auroral glow, but no moon. Visibility was good, with ships' lights being seen up to a distance of 20 miles." Although it should also have been visible to the eye, an iceberg may have caused this echo (*Marine Observer*, 31: 61, 1961).

LINE AND RING ANGELS

The captain and two officers of the S.S. *Arcadia* recorded the following radar anomaly while in the eastern North Pacific on July 20, 1970. "At 1705 GMT a long line was seen on the radar running 005–185°, extending for over 40 miles in length at a distance of 10 miles from the ship on the port side. At 1714 it was 8 miles away. Visibility at the time was very good, no special cloud formation or change in the sea was observed, and there was no precipitation. At 1719 the line was 6.4 miles from the ship and at 1723 it was 5.5 miles. On getting a little closer the width of the line was approx. 1 cable, fixed by radar range. At 1740 the vessel entered the line; there was no change in wind direction or speed, in sea or air temperature, or in pressure. The only visible change was a distinct break in the cloud which had been a continuous layer of St [stratus clouds] at 300 feet with ragged shreds. Through the break could be seen

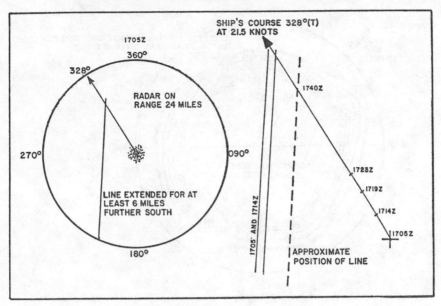

A linear radar angel over 40 miles long

cloud. The radar continued to show this line until 1810 when it slowly faded out." A clear-air discontinuity may have caused this strange linear echo, even though no changes were noted at sea level (*Marine Observer*, 41: 94, 1971).

A similar phenomenon appeared on the radar screen of the M.V. *Glenorchy* in the Red Sea on June 29, 1963. "Between 1430 and 1630 GMT while on passage through the Red Sea, the radar interference shown in the diagram was experienced. It took the form of concentric bands about the ship, generally at a distance of about 6–8 miles away. For the most part there were 8 bands but in some places 12 could be counted. The farthest away was the broadest, 3–4 cables, while the nearest was the narrowest, being about 1/4 cable wide. The spaces between the bands also increased with increasing distance away. The exact shape of the bands was never constant but was at all times changing slowly. Sometimes a part moved toward the ship, sometimes it moved away; occasionally a part would fade or bands would virtually join, at times becoming quite solid." These concentric bands may have been an interference pattern created by two sets of echoes returning from sea waves. One set would come from the direct propagation of the transmitted radar pulse, the second from the reflection of the pulse off a low layer in the atmosphere (*Marine Observer*, 34: 65, 1964).

On January 28, 1973, the M.V. *Otaki* was in the eastern North Atlan-

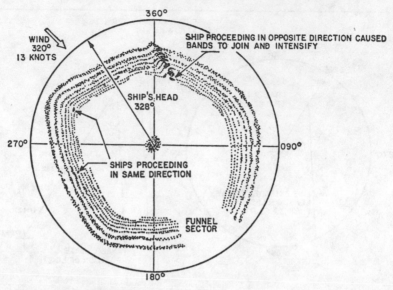

Concentric-ring angels as they appeared on the Glenorchy *radar screen*

tic headed for Capetown. "At 1825 GMT, shortly after coming on watch, a curious effect was observed on the radar screen when the vessel was about 70 miles north of Cape Vert [Cape Verde]. A ring of echoes, similar to land and about 4 miles deep, was forming into a concentric circle about the center spot of the screen. For the first hour or two the echoes varied in diameter from 13 to 15 miles. Ship echoes were still displayed, apparently unaffected. After several hours the echoes became less intense and a second concentric ring formed; shortly afterward the top half of the circles began to fade." These ring echoes may have been created by widespread dust in the atmosphere, a common phenomenon in this area (*Marine Observer*, 44: 13, 1974). (See p. 206 for Cape Verde "dust fogs.")

3

UNUSUAL WEATHER EVENTS

"Weather" is a composite experience of sight, sound, temperature, and sensation of the elements. The phenomena of this chapter are not primarily luminous or acoustic or confined to the sensory channels that form the bases for other chapters. Here we deal with rain, fog, wind, clouds, precipitation, and sunshine—but only when they are anomalous.

Our weather experiences are so widely variable that a phenomenon has to be very strange indeed to gain access to this chapter. The criteria are not so much related to intensity or rarity as they are to unexpectedness and deviations from predictions of meteorological theory. Thus very heavy general rains, even with catastrophic flooding, are excluded, while rain without clouds and "point" rainfall are welcome additions to the chapter.

Several themes that thread their way through most of this book recur once again in this chapter:

1. The importance of electricity in geophysical phenomena.
2. The possibility that some electrical influences may originate in outer space.
3. The influence of the sun, moon, and inbound meteoric material on terrestrial weather.
4. The occasional prankish, frivolous behavior of some meteorological phenomena. This judgment is, of course, highly subjective but it may nevertheless reveal something of importance about man's interface with weather.

Unusual Clouds

Clouds can be classified as unusual if they have peculiar shapes, motions, colors, orientations, or emit unaccountable light or noise. Meteorologists recognize a variety of clouds as "usual" even though they are not fully understood. Lenticular and mammatus clouds, for example, look very strange and even give rise to a few UFO reports. Nevertheless they are recognized cloud species and are omitted here. Rotating ring-shaped clouds and some spectacular roll clouds are included. Although these clouds are doubtless created by atmospheric vortices of some kind, they are neither common nor easy to explain. Cloud arches connecting seemingly independent clouds also pose theoretical problems. Are the arches umbilical in nature, as they seem to be in the occasional reports of waterspouts linking one cloud to another? If so, how do these links form? Some clouds seem to interact in mysterious ways with the earth's magnetic field—the polar-oriented cirrus bands, for example. The physical mechanism here is obscure unless the water droplets forming the clouds are somehow affected by the earth's magnetic field. All in all there are many imponderables in cloud formation and in the subsequent behavior of clouds.

MINIATURE CLOUDS

Normal thunderclouds are well-organized thermodynamic machines miles in extent. Consequently, this report of a miniature thunderstorm by C. S. Bailey is truly incredible. Bailey was staying near the ship canal in Manchester, England, a year or two after World War I. The evening was somewhat oppressive, and the air had become strangely still. "Gazing down the road, I saw a small black thundercloud gathering along the length of the Canal, and about 30 to 40 ft. above it. It was approximately 100 yards long and perhaps 6 ft. thick. As I gazed at this strange formation, a dazzling lightning flash raced through the entire cloud—i.e., parallel to the water—and a bang like the discharge of field artillery followed immediately. About 40 seconds later, another flash and report occurred; then the cloud thinned and dispersed in about four minutes" (*Weather*, 4: 267, 1949).

CLOUDS WITH CURIOUS SHAPES

Several collections of reports dealing with anomalous aerial objects mention an odd circular cloud with a tail observed from the *Lady of the Lake* in the North Atlantic in 1870. Is it an early UFO? "At from 6.30 to 7 P.M. a curious-shaped cloud appeared in the S.S.E. quarter, first appearing distinct at about 25° from the horizon, from where it moved steadily forward, or rather upward, to about 80°, when it settled down bodily to the N.E. Its form was circular, with a semicircle to the northern face near its centre. From the centre to about 6° beyond the circle was a fifth ray broader and more distinct than the others, with a curved end—diameter of circle, 11°, and of semicircle, 2 1/2°. The weather was fine, and the atmosphere remarkably clear, with the usual Trade [Wind] sky. It was of light grey colour, and, though distinctly defined in shape, the patches of cirrocumulus at the back could be clearly seen through. It was very much lower than the other clouds" (*Royal Meteorological Society, Quarterly Journal*, 1: 157, 1873).

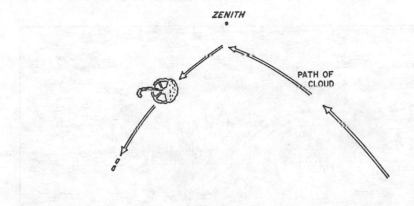

Curious cloud observed from the Lady of the Lake

Modern examples of similar cloud phenomena exist. Many of the crew of the S.S. *City of Liverpool* saw the following apparition over the Red Sea on November 1, 1962. "At 2005 SMT a ball of what seemed to be dense white cloud was seen on a bearing of 260° at an altitude of about 7°. As it approached and passed ahead of the vessel, moving in a NE. direction, it assumed the form of a smoke ring, the apparent diameter of which, when bearing 330°, was about 5 or 6 times that of the full moon. The ring, which became elliptical in shape, was thought to be rotating in an anticlockwise direction" (*Marine Observer*, 33: 190, 1963).

The atmosphere is full of unseen eddies that become visible only when they snatch up a column of dry leaves or, in the following case, create a noticeable ring-shaped cloud. The cloud was seen from the deck of the M.V. *Achilles* in the Gulf of Aden on February 1, 1958. "At 2300 S.M.T. a cloud, in the form of a circle about 1 mile in diameter, was observed lying above and ahead of the path of the ship. When the vessel came nearer, the cloud was clearly seen in the moonlight to be revolving in a clockwise direction. The centre of the circle was completely cloudless." As the *Achilles* steamed beneath the ring, the atmospheric pressure dropped, the sea calmed, and the wind shifted (*Marine Observer*, 29: 19, 1959).

When aircraft seed solid cloud decks with silver iodide, the falling crystals punch a ragged hole in the deck. Nature is more meticulous and sometimes drills almost perfectly circular holes in cloud layers. The me-

One of two holes in a cloud deck over Florida

teorological mechanism is unknown, but the visual effect is startling. On December 1, 1967, two such holes formed over Miami. "Evidence of the anomalous condition that later resulted in the large circular holes was well observed at 0830 EST. . . . At about this time one of us independently noted a distinct downward protrusion of what appeared to be middle cloud below the base of the otherwise uniform altocumulus layer.

By 0900 EST the holes were conspicuous, almost perfect circles. The sketch of the southern hole . . . depicts conditions observed at about 0845 EST. A well-developed cirrus tail extended down from this hole and trailed off approximately west-northwestward." In essence the cirrus tail seemed to pull a circular mass of clouds out of the otherwise solid cloud deck. The diameter of one of the holes was estimated at 4 miles. The observers speculated that some sort of natural cloud-seeding process was at work (*American Meteorological Society, Bulletin,* 50: 157–61, 1969).

CLOUD ARCHES

It is difficult to imagine a meteorological mechanism that would join two well-separated clouds with a narrow arch of cloud. Yet several such situations are on record, as exemplified by the testimony of the third officer of the M.V. *Port Adelaide,* on May 31, 1952. "Two very dark towering Cu [cumulus] clouds bearing 034° appeared to be joined to a single dark towering Cu cloud, bearing 214°, by a narrow band of Cc [cirrocumulus] which stretched across the sky over the ship. This formation lasted about 2 hours before disintegrating. The moon was not visible at the time and the sky was cloudless except for the above formation" (*Marine Observer,* 23: 76, 1953). Note that the configuration of clouds and connecting arch is strongly reminiscent of some of the supposed reflection mirages of clouds mentioned in Chapter 2.

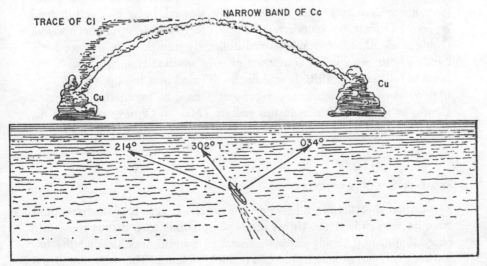

Cloud arch connecting two cumulus clouds

The cloud arches encountered by the R.R.S. *Discovery II* in the South Atlantic were somewhat different. It was November 24, 1933. "About one hour before sunset, an arch of hard clear sky commenced to form slowly and to spread from the S.E. to the N.W. quadrants. This arch had assumed a regular outline by 2115 G.M.T. when the following observations were recorded: 'From two points on the horizon bearing 138° and 304° respectively, an area of hard clear sky arched itself to an altitude of 9°. This maximum angular height was approximately above the sun which set bearing 237 1/2°. Maintaining an almost equal distance with the rim of this arch was another smaller arch with an angular height

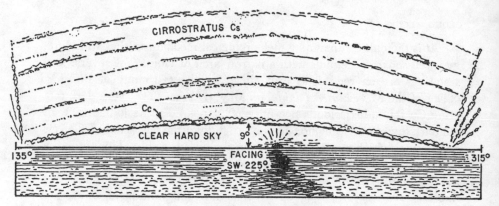

Parallel cloud arches

of 2°. The space between these two arches was packed with cirrocumulus globules which appeared to be closely stowed between well-defined layers of cirrostratus clouds. . . . From the two points on the horizon, bands of cloud radiated and passed obliquely into the sky, the northerly band in both cases being composed of cirrocumulus clouds. These bands became fainter with altitude and finally diffused into the upper sky." The upper cirrostratus bands may represent a case of magnetically aligned clouds, as introduced later in this section (*Marine Observer,* 11: 138–39, 1934).

ANOMALOUS LINES OF CLOUDS

Larger meteors often leave clouds in their wakes that stretch almost from horizon to horizon. Upper atmosphere winds soon distort these into crazy shapes and slowly dissipate them. It is quite possible that the following observation may have been of such a cloud. "This note contains a quoted account of an extraordinary observation made by Captain W. L. Stewart of the British Overseas Airways Corporation, on February 7, 1948, at 11 h. 45 m. UT, while he was flying westbound at an elevation of 10,000 feet, over a point whose equatorial coordinate number (ECN) = + 0209,550, of what was apparently a downwardly concave, cylindrical dust-cloud with a length of near 60 miles" (*Popular Astronomy,* 58: 355–56, 1950).

The advent of satellite cameras with high resolution revealed many curious cloud formations on the earth far below, including many very long linear clouds. Initially, the cloud lines were attributed to ship smoke trails and aircraft contrails. But further research proved that ships and planes were not the sources and that most were due to ocean-temperature gradients (viz., the Gulf Stream boundaries) and various meteorological factors such as the "wakes" of island mountains. Some cloud lines, however, did not succumb to such explanations. One photograph showing some of these unexplained lines "was taken off the coast of Spain and shows a series of anomalous cloud lines. The cause of these cloud lines has not been determined; investigation revealed ships and aircraft were not involved" (*Monthly Weather Review,* 104: 210–13, 1976).

In tropical Australia, residents are occasionally treated to a spectacular linear cloud formation. "Known as the Morning Glory because of its magnificent appearance at sunrise, it is a long horizontal roll of low cloud which appears on the eastern skyline, usually in calm and cloud-

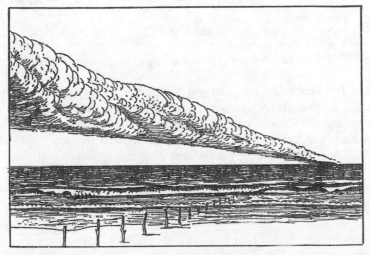

The Morning Glory is an extremely long roll cloud that sweeps in from the sea over Australia.

less conditions, and advances rapidly, like a rolling sea wave, bringing with it a sudden wind squall but rarely any precipitation." The Morning Glory is only 100–200 meters thick and sweeps in as low as 50 meters off the ground. Speeds range from 30 to 70 miles per hour. One aircraft pilot flew along a Morning Glory for 120 km. without finding an end to it. Double Morning Glories are common; as many as seven have appeared in succession. Meteorologists have not come to any conclusions about what actually causes this unusually long linear disturbance (*Weather*, 32: 176–83, 1977).

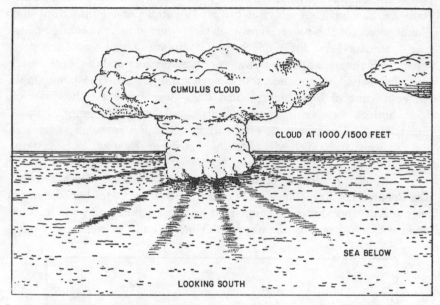

CUMULUS CLOUD

CLOUD AT 1000/1500 FEET

SEA BELOW

LOOKING SOUTH

Radial spokes protruding from the base of a large cumulus cloud

Off the South Devon coast, on November 1, 1937, a pilot carefully observed an inexplicable pattern of radial bands emanating from a large cumulus cloud. "Conditions were mainly fair in the west, but much low cloud and rain [was] encountered on the return journey eastward of Yeovil. It is not improbable that a large cumulus up to 9,000 ft. was quite close to the depression. The pilot was flying at 10,000 ft., and he estimates his distance from the towering cloud to be 12 to 15 miles" (*Meteorological Magazine*, 73: 45–46, 1938).

POLAR-ALIGNED CIRRUS CLOUDS

"Cirrus clouds appear very often in a regular array of parallel bands. Alexander von Humboldt discovered in the course of his meteorological observations in South America and Siberia that these arrays follow frequently the line of the geomagnetic meridian of the locality; he invented the term *bandes polaires* for this phenomenon. Even very casual observations confirm the truth of his statement. He suspected some connexion between the appearance of these 'polar bands' and that of the aurora borealis" (*Nature*, 199: 900, 1963).

On October 22, 1927, T. A. Sergeant on the S.S. *Nagoya*, then in the Mediterranean heading for Suez, recorded a typical display of polar-aligned cirrus. Off Cape Garde he observed a "remarkable cloud formation consisting of radiating streaks of cirrus cloud forming complete, evenly spaced arcs terminating in approximately the true north and south points of the horizon. It gave the sky a wonderful domed appearance and lasted until sunrise" (*Marine Observer*, 5: 203, 1928).

Similar north-south belts appeared over Essex, England, on July 24, 1933. "At 21 h. 20 m. G.M.T. a belt of cirrus cloud was observed stretching across the western sky at an elevation of 35°, from north to south, forming a bow and moving in an easterly direction. This was rapidly followed by a second belt, and between 21 h. 20 m. to 21 h. 50 m. eight belts of cloud travelled across the sky from due west to east. . . . At 21 h. 30 m. four belts were visible simultaneously at elevations of 35°, 55°, 70°,

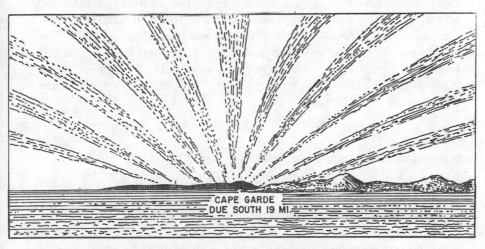

Magnetically aligned cirrus bands looking due south

and 105° from west. All the belts were approximately 1 1/2° in width, the width being even throughout their length. The belts of cloud were whitish in appearance. . . . stars in the path of travel were plainly seen through the cloud, which clearly denotes that the cloud belts were very tenuous" (*Meteorological Magazine*, 68: 186, 1933).

The polar-aligned cirrus bands are obviously very similar to the banded sky phenomenon of Chapter 1. Observers of both phenomena (assuming that the phenomena are different) have noted the connection with auroral streaks, which are also influenced by the earth's magnetic field. Some scientists suggest that these oriented cloud streaks or auroral bands may be induced by the influx of tiny bits of magnetic dust which are somehow channeled by the earth's field.

NOISY CLOUDS

Naturally, thunderclouds and tornado funnels must be excluded from this category as nonanomalous phenomena. Rarely, though, other clouds make rumbling and rattling sounds—and without any obvious discharge of electricity to the ground or within the cloud itself. Yale professor John Zeleny saw such a noisy cloud in July 1931, while on the shore of Caché Lake, Ontario. "It was a chilly morning and the sky was completely overcast with clouds. My attention was attracted by a rumbling sound coming from the west, such as heralds the approach of a heavy thunder storm. As I watched, a very long, low, narrow, tenuous cloud, resembling a squall cloud, appeared above the trees on the opposite shore, moving at right angles to its length. The continuous, rumbling noise, now grown remarkably loud, seemed to come unmistakably from this cloud, whose cross-sectional diameter was only about 200 feet. The cloud passed overhead eastward and was not followed by the expected rainstorm" (*Science*, 75: 80–81, 1932). Zeleny's rumbling cloud resembles a roll cloud and may also be related to the Yellowstone Park electrified cloud described in Chapter 1.

THE OCCULT AND CLOUD DISSIPATION

The ability of the human mind to disintegrate soft, fleecy cumulus clouds is part of occult lore. Strangely enough, clouds do sometimes disappear under unusual conditions, conditions which might be misinterpreted by mentalists. John L. Rich, from the University of Illinois, was watching lazy cumulus clouds drift over the valley of the Illinois River in mid-August 1914. "As a matter of curiosity a particular cloud was selected with the idea of noting its changes of shape and something of its rate of movement. The cloud selected advanced to a point almost exactly overhead, then began to melt away. In a space of less than five minutes it had entirely disappeared. Another and yet another did the same. Finally, an unusually large cloud was selected; but this, too, disappeared on reaching approximately the same point. All advanced in orderly procession from the west till, overhead, they reached a lane of clear sky, then melted away." Rich surmised that the cooler air over the river bottomlands created a region of descending air that dissolved the clouds (*Science,* 40: 851–52, 1914).

Dark Days

A Dark Day is not merely the veiling of the sun by ordinary clouds— they at least let through enough light to conduct the business of the world. On a Dark Day the pall of darkest night descends suddenly, chickens go to roost, and men and women pray and grope for candles, although not necessarily in this order. New England's famous Dark Day of 1780 is typical of the category.

The standard explanation for a Dark Day is smoke from forest fires in the hinterlands. This is reasonable because some Dark Days are accompanied by black rains that are thick with ashes and soot. Wind drives these heavy clouds across the affected region, obscuring the sun more completely than ordinary rain clouds. Sometimes, though, the darkness seems more irrational, descending suddenly without the approach of ominous black clouds. Could forest-fire smoke behave like this? And where did the supposed forest fires rage? In America they were "out west somewhere," set by Indians. In pioneer days, of course, "out west" was devoid of newspaper stringers, and the forests of an entire state could be consumed without easterners knowing of it. While admitting forest fires to be the cause of most Dark Days, we should also ask whether a rare few may not owe their origins to stratospheric or even extraterrestrial clouds of obscuring matter.

NEW ENGLAND'S DARK DAY OF 1780

Some observations made by Nathan Read, a student at Harvard College on May 19, 1780:

"At 10.30—An uncommon degree of darkness commenced.

At 11.00—Darkness still increasing, Mr. Wigglesworth not able to read in a large Bible by a window. . . . Fowls go to roost as at evening. . . .

At 12.21—Darkness still increasing, Mr. W., not able to read the running title of a large Bible. —Candles are in common use. . . . Frogs pipe, and evening birds sing."

The darkness began to decrease at 12:50, and by 3:15 the light level was compared to that on a day with thick clouds (*Weatherwise*, 25: 113–18, 1972).

"The Connecticut legislature was in session at Hartford that day, as the darkness gathered. The journal of the state House of Representatives reads, 'None could see to read or write in the House, or even at a window, or distinguish persons at a small distance, or perceive any distinction of dress in the circle of attendants. Therefore, at 11 o'clock adjourned the House till 2 o'clock, afternoon. In a neighboring room, the governor's council was also in session, and a motion to adjourn was proposed. But Col. Abraham Davenport objected with firm dignity: 'Either the day of judgment is at hand or it is not. If it is not, there is no cause for adjournment. If it is, I wish to be found in the line of my duty. I wish candles to be brought'" (*Sky and Telescope*, 27: 219, 1964).

At some places in New England, the air smelled of a malthouse or a coal kiln. Forest fires in New Hampshire to the north, territory just being opened to settlement, were blamed for the great Dark Day. But other natural phenomena may bring on Dark Days, as in the following item.

At a meeting of the Royal Geographical Society, London, "Mr. Crawford related some particulars respecting the volcanic eruption of the Timboro Mountain in 1814, of which he witnessed some of the effects. At a distance of 300 miles, it was pitch dark for three days; the ashes were carried by the monsoon to a distance of 1,200 miles from the mountain, and for ten days he was obliged to write by candle-light" (*Scientific American*, 9: 35, 1863). Forest fires, volcanos, and intense storms are the primary causes of Dark Days, but not all darkenings are susceptible to these easy explanations.

OTHER SOMEWHAT MORE MYSTERIOUS DARK DAYS

In the afternoon of March 19, 1886, a remarkable atmospheric phenomenon took place at Oshkosh, Wisconsin. "The day was light, though cloudy, when suddenly darkness commenced settling down, and in five minutes it was as dark as midnight. General consternation prevailed; people on the streets rushed to and fro; teams dashed along, and women and children ran in cellars; all business operations ceased until lights could be lighted. Not a breath of air was stirring on the surface of the earth. The darkness lasted from eight to ten minutes, when it passed off, seemingly from west to east, and brightness followed. . . . It seemed to be a wave of total darkness passing along without wind" (*Monthly Weather Review*, 14: 79, 1886).

"A total darkness at about noon which lasted for hours occurred many years back, but within the recollection of people now living, in the city of Amsterdam, the capital of Holland. As I have often been told by trustworthy people, it took place in summer, on a fine bright day; the air was calm and there were no indications of fog. The people in the streets, frightened at such an unusual occurrence, hastened indoors, but the darkness came on so suddenly that many of them lost their lives through walking into the different channels by which the city is divided" (*Notes and Queries*, 2: 4: 139, 1857).

One final old and difficult-to-verify example will suffice. "On the eighteenth of April last, the sun became obscured about noon, in Brazil, although no clouds were visible in the sky. The darkness continued several minutes, and Venus became quite visible to the naked eye. Historians relate that, in 1547 and 1706, like phenomena were witnessed. The cause has been attributed to the passage of clusters of asteroids across the sun's disk" (*Scientific American*, 3: 122, 1860).

Meteorologists record many modern Dark Days, but they are almost always correlated with extraordinary pollution of the air by smoke and industrial wastes. Alas, the romance of the old inexplicable "waves of darkness" seems to have been demolished by modern rationality.

Anomalous Precipitation

What makes precipitation anomalous? The major variables involved are color, shape, size, and intensity. But, as the first group of quotations indicate, any form of precipitation without clouds must also be considered anomalous. True, very fine ice crystals can be precipitated out of clear air when the cold is intense, but where does cloudless rain originate? Throughout this section on precipitation, the very remote possibility that some ice and water may be meteoric should be considered. In other words, some precipitation may originate much higher than normal cloud levels, perhaps even from outside the atmosphere.

Colored rains and snows are rather common. The European "rains of blood" described since history began to be written down are generally blamed on dust blown north from Africa. Black rain is even more common and is ascribed to volcanos, forest fires, or, more lately, urban pollution. The forest fires involved are seldom identified, the same situation prevailing as with the explanation of Dark Days. The conflagrations should be traced via a trail of black rain, but they rarely are.

Uncolored rain can, on occasion, be no less intriguing. Fantastic examples of "point rainfall" or cloudbursts are often noted in the meteorological magazines. The naming of the phenomenon does not explain the unbelievable quantities of water sometimes dumped in very small areas. After reading some of the examples from the literature, the reader may want to classify point rainfall along with falling material (Chapter 4), for the traditional meteorological mechanisms seem wanting.

Hail is notable if it is unusually large or contains inclusions that "shouldn't be there." (Note that isolated ice falls or "hydrometeors" are dealt with in Chapter 4 on falling material.) The great variety of hailstone shapes—crystals, disks, plates, spiked spheres, etc.—indicate the work of unrecognized forces in hail formation. Some of these forces may be electrical in nature. On a larger scale, the peculiar mesh patterns of some hail falls call for explanation in terms of hailstorm dynamics. Finally, the phenomenon of slowly falling hail seems well verified as well as particularly mystifying.

PRECIPITATION FROM A CLOUDLESS SKY

If rain or snow falls without a cloud in sight, some uncommon terrestrial phenomenon is sought first. One cause of cloudless precipitation is extremely low-temperature air high aloft, which squeezes the last bit of moisture out of the air in the form of very fine snow—all without the formation of obvious clouds. Such fine cloudless snow or "diamond dust" is often met with in the polar regions. In warmer climates, where cool and warm, humid air meet, especially near the sea, drizzle seems to come out of nowhere sometimes. Fog or mist generally mark the area of condensation, but they may not be obvious. Even vegetation may provide unexpected local precipitation given the right reason. Not only are there exotic precipitating plants, such as the South American rain tree, but some trees in temperate forests may mimic a light shower on warm fall days. Sap droplets falling from leaf scars may create a steady patter on the forest floor and anyone standing beneath. Needless to say, such false sources of cloudless rain have been eliminated in the accounts that follow.

In Oxfordshire, England, on January 20, 1935, J. S. Dines experienced a steady drizzle from a cloudless sky. "At 9.20 A.M. drizzle was observed; and as the sun was shining brightly, the state of the sky was carefully studied. No cloud was visible although the blue of the sky was somewhat pale and watery, an effect which may well have been produced by the drizzle itself. The drizzle continued for ten minutes, and during this period some cloud formed though it was not overhead and did not appear to be the source of the drizzle. Some idea of the intensity of the precipitation can be formed by the fact that after its cessation a paving stone in the ground appeared moist and the sloping glass roof of a verandah was thickly covered with water particles. . . . The sun shining on the drizzle formed a rainbow although not of any particular brilliance" (*Meteorological Magazine,* 70: 16, 1935).

On April 23, 1800, rain fell from a clear sky at Philadelphia, Pennsylvania. "Between 9 and 10 P.M., Philadelphia . . . was visited by a very curious phenomenon. A shower of rain of at least twenty minutes' continuance, and sufficiently plentiful to wet the clothes of those exposed to it, fell when the heavens immediately overhead were in a state of the most perfect serenity. Throughout the whole of it, the stars shone with undiminished luster. Not a cloud appeared, except one to the east and another to the west of the city, each about fifteen degrees distant from the zenith" (*American Journal of Science,* 2: 1: 178, 1839). Most such occurrences of cloudless rain are explained as due to high-altitude winds wafting rain horizontally over long distances.

An immense shower of meteors collided with the earth's atmosphere over the North American continent on November 13, 1833. One of the many diverse phenomena accompanying the abnormal influx of meteoric material was cloudless rain, presumably stimulated by the abundant dust nuclei. At Harvard, Massachusetts, "at about 8 o'clock on the morning of November 13, there was a slight shower of rain, when not a cloud was to be seen, the weather being what is called perfectly fair" (*American Journal of Science,* 1: 25: 398, 1834).

A report from T. H. Applegate tells of rain from a cloudless sky falling in an extremely limited area. It was July 18, 1925, near Cattewater, England. ". . . large drops of rain caused me to look up and observe that the sky was clear with the exception of cumulonimbus on the horizon and a small amount of altocumulus some distance ahead and receding toward the east. The latter was at a height of approximately 12,000 ft. Only about 20 yards of the ground, which was cemented concrete, showed the track of the shower. It was then a slight, very short, and very local fall of rain." Although the clouds were some distance away, horizontal winds might account for this shower (*Meteorological Magazine,* 60: 193–94, 1925).

POINT RAINFALL

The highly localized fall of rain observed by T. H. Applegate in the preceding item is termed "point rainfall"; but much more extreme cases have been observed. Indeed, tremendous quantities of rain may fall in extremely limited areas, leading to the popular description "It was a cloudburst!"

A modest case of point rainfall was observed by G. A. Hinkson in London on August 1, 1932. "It began to rain—heavily at first and then softly. Suddenly torrential rain fell only one hundred yards from where I was standing. The nearest trees in Kensington Gardens were almost hidden behind a milky mist of heavy rain. The rain-drops rebounding off the street created a layer of spray as high as the tops of the wheels of the taxis standing in the street. Where I was sheltering, hardly a drop of rain was falling. . . . Then the spray on the ground came nearer like a wave and receded. Suddenly it vanished completely" (*Meteorological Magazine*, 67: 159–60, 1932).

So-called cloudbursts can be very localized, as proven by poststorm observations. On May 3, 1849, ". . . during a storm of thunder, lightning, and hail, an enormous body of water rushed down a gully in Bredon Hill, North Gloucestershire, towards the village of Kemerton. The stream was broad and impetuous, carrying everything before it . . . The course of the torrent could easily be traced up the hill for more than a mile, to a barley field of five acres, the greater part of which was beaten down flat and hard, as if an enormous body of water had been suddenly poured upon it. Beyond this there were no signs of the fall of water to any great amount" (*Nature*, 125: 657, 1930).

Popular accounts of cloudbursts in the literature have been verified by modern meteorologists. Robert H. Stanley, a long-time weather observer living near Greenfield, New Hampshire, filed the following report for the storm of August 2, 1966:

"Rain began at about 1900 EST, or about an hour before the outbreak of more generalized showers in the region. It soon became a downpour, continuing until about 2300 EST, at which time Mr. Stanley went to bed. It was then still raining but had slackened noticeably. The rain may have stopped by midnight. A remarkable nonvariability of the intense rain was noted by Mr. Stanley. There was little slackening, even for brief intervals, during the period of heaviest fall, which was from about 1945 to 2215 EST. There was practically no wind. Neither thunder nor lightning was observed. The noise on the roof was terrific like that of a continuous waterfall. A plastic bird feeder mounted on the side of the house was broken by the impact of sheets of water from the eaves. Looking out the window, Mr. Stanley could see stones and gravel from the roadway, south of the house, being washed away by torrents of water.

"Upon rising in the morning, Mr. Stanley noted that the weather had cleared, with a brisk westerly wind. After finding the 5.75 in. of rain in the gage, he inquired from a neighbor 0.3 miles to the east. He found that the neighbor had but 0.50 in. in his gage. He thereupon examined the countryside for visible effects. The road washout extended for only a few hundred feet. Upon going one-half mile in either direction, no evidence of rain erosion of sand or gravel could be found. South of the house, beginning at the gage which was mounted on a pole, well distant from structures or trees, there stretches a 10-acre field. The knee-high grass therein was beaten down flat. By afternoon it began to revive. By the following noon it was erect. To the west of the house, a dry-wash brook running bankful at dawn was empty by 0800 EST.

"Drawing a line around the traces of erosion, one obtains an oval area about a mile north-south and about three-fourths of a mile east-west. Within this area, rain varied from the order of 1 in. on the limits to almost 6 in. in the center. Outside this limit, rain is believed to have fallen off sharply to less than one-fourth of an inch, generally within a few thousand feet" (*Monthly Weather Review*, 98: 164–68, 1970).

HAIL STRIPES AND MESHES

The internal dynamics of storms may generate geometrical patterns of precipitation, much like the points and stripes of heavy rainfall described above but two-dimensional. Hailstorms show this internal structure more frequently than ordinary rainstorms. Parallel streaks or swatches of heavy hail falling miles apart have long been recognized though not explained by meteorologists. Recently, parallel stripes on a much finer scale have been detected by analyzing crop damage. An Illinois hailstorm on June 29, 1976, produced an unusual pattern of damage in a cornfield. "The hailstripes were easily located in the fields. They were measured and varied considerably in size. Most extended across the field and had widths of < 15–25 meters. Several field inspections were made to determine, with standard crop-damage assessments, the nature of the stripes. The contrast in crop condition from the light (heavily damaged) to dark (less damaged) stripes was quite marked. As one walked from a less-damaged band into one of maximum damage, the visibility would change markedly—a companion who could not be seen more than a few meters away in the dark band could be seen 15 to 20

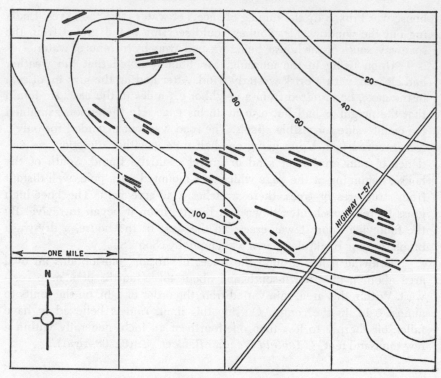

Map of hail stripes in an Illinois cornfield

meters away owing to the many broken cornstalks" (*American Meteo-rological Society, Bulletin*, 58: 588–91, 1977).

Once again old and modern observations agree, as exemplified by testimony from the hailstorm of July 3, 1863, in France. "About 6 P.M. a cloud approached rapidly from the west, at a height estimated as 5,000 feet. It resembled a huge net in form; the portion represented by the net-ting showed violent agitation, and soon after the arrival of the cloud there was a heavy hailstorm lasting about five minutes, the hailstones being as large as nuts. During the fall of the hail there was no wind. The hail caused considerable damage wherever it fell, and M. Lecoq, who saw the storm and described it in *Comptes Rendus*, stated that the dam-age was limited to small patches, which were surrounded by undamaged zones, forming a network the meshes of which were irregular but roughly 60–100 metres apart. The distribution of the hail corresponded with the form of the cloud" (*Nature*, 125: 994, 1930).

COLORED PRECIPITATION

Reports of rains of blood appear frequently in the ancient literature. Red precipitation was a bad omen; the local populace was always considerably agitated when the streets ran red. Red rains and red snows still occur today, but chemical analysis and studies of meteorological charts inevitably point to reddish dust blown in from desert areas. For Europe, the Sahara is the source of coloring matter. The red rains of Australia come from this continent's interior deserts. Black rains and snows are the next most common, thanks mostly to industrial smoke, although volcanic dust makes some contribution. Yellow rains are more rare and almost always are associated with an abundance of tree pollen. All in all, colored precipitation turns out to be simply unusual, not mysterious. A short excerpt describing an incident of each color will suffice.

January 1897, Australia: ". . . there was a heavy fall of rain, which was full of red dust, and the next morning the whole landscape was red. The 'rain of blood,' it was called, and really it looked like it. The funny thing was that it occurred on a public holiday and on a hot day, so that all the holiday-makers who were caught in it had their clothes stained a deep red; and as many people were dressed in white, you may guess what they looked like" (*Symons's Monthly Meteorological Magazine,* 32: 27, 1897).

April 28, 1884, England: "*Black Rain.* —Yesterday afternoon (April 28) a violent thunderstorm raged over the district between Church Stretton and Much Wenlock. Torrents of rain fell, seemingly a mixture of ink and water in equal proportions. One old man here says he never saw anything like it but once. I certainly never saw such a colored rain, and I intend to have a bottle of it analyzed. Even this afternoon the little brooks are quite black, and the ruts in the roads look as if ink and water had been poured into them.—Rev. R. I. Buddicombe, Ticklerton, Church Stretton" (*Nature,* 30: 32, 1884). Remember that in 1884 coal was burned in immense quantities in Europe.

March 12, 1867, Kentucky: "It seems that the days of miracles have not yet passed. On the night of the 12th inst. [March 12] we in this section had a copious fall of rain of about two and a half inches, and such vessels as were left standing out were found to contain water impregnated with a yellow substance such as is contained in the inclosed vial. We learn today from Bowling Green, fourteen miles distant, that it was the same there, and the inhabitants, believing it to be sulphur, are somewhat alarmed, not knowing but what it is the beginning of a preparation of that great fire in which sinners expect to find themselves ensconced in a coming day! Whatever it is, we are not chemists enough to make out. Clothes that were left lying out were made yellow with the substance. It seems to be odorless—has the resemblance of farina contained in the anthers of plants" (*Scientific American*, 16: 233, 1867).

SPARKLING RAIN

"Rain which on touching the ground crackles and emits electric sparks is a very uncommon but not unknown phenomenon. An instance of the kind was recently reported from Cordova, in Spain, by an electrical engineer who witnessed the occurrence. The weather had been warm and undisturbed by wind, and soon after dark the sky became overcast by clouds. At about 8 o'clock there came a flash of lightning, followed by great drops of electrical rain, each one of which, on touching the ground, walls, or trees, gave a faint crack, and emitted a spark of light. The phenomenon continued for several seconds, and apparently ceased as soon as the atmosphere was saturated with moisture" (*Symons's Monthly Meteorological Magazine*, 27: 171, 1892).

GIANT SNOWFLAKES

The so-called giant snowflakes recorded in the annals of meteorology are not single snowflakes but rather agglomerations of many individual flakes. How and why they unite in large collective disks is a puzzle.

On April 13, 1951, in Berkhamsted, England, "snowflakes of exceptional size, variously reported by postmen and other early risers to have been 'enormous,' 'as big as saucers,' and 'almost five inches across,' fell in Berkhamsted town and neighboring districts of the Chiltern Hills 400–600 ft. above sea level between 0430 and 0445 GMT on 13 April 1951" (*Weather*, 6: 254, 1951).

The size record for snowflakes seems to be held by the fluffy monsters that fell in Montana on January 28, 1887. "The great flakes were described as being 'larger than milk pans' and measuring 38 centimeters (15 inches) across by 20 centimeters (8 inches) thick. A mail carrier who was caught in the storm verified the occurrence. These tremendous flakes made patches all over the fields within an area of several square miles." Snowflakes of this size are usually agglomerations of many smaller flakes (*Monthly Weather Review*, 43: 73, 1915).

CONICAL SNOWFLAKES

The delicate lacey snowflakes of hexagonal symmetry so familiar to us all sometimes give way to hard cones of snow that seem halfway between normal snow and hail. On April 26, 1931, A. D. Moore, of the University of Michigan, observed three separate falls of conical snow at Ann Arbor. "The crystal formation was that of a solid cone with a round base. The side of the cone made an angle of about 30 degrees with the axis. The round base was part of a spherical surface. The shape was exactly like that of a conical section of a sphere. As nearly as the eye could see into the formation of a snowdrop, the whole structure seemed to be made up of conical needles, packed together, with the upper ends forming the pointed tip of the cone, and the larger lower ends forming the rounded base. The density was very high; a handful of snow, slightly compressed, immediately formed soft ice. . . . Hundreds if not thousands of individual snowdrops came under observation on a window sill; irrespective of size, from tiniest to largest, the crystals were of the same form" (*Science*, 73: 642, 1931).

Willis W. Wagener experienced a similar snowfall in September 1920, at an experimental station at 8,750-ft. elevation near Ephraim, Utah: "On one occasion, however, the precipitation, instead of being the usual form of rain or round hail, consisted of cones of hard compacted snow. The bases of the cones were hemispherical, giving the stones the general outline of an inverted parachute. In size they ranged larger than those observed by Professor Moore [see the preceding item], all being over one-quarter inch across the base and many of them reaching one-half inch" (*Science*, 74: 414, 1931).

UNUSUALLY SHAPED HAILSTONES

Hailstones come in many shapes, from quartzlike crystals to spheres with curious, geometrically arranged appendages. The urge to create variety seems not as strong as it is with snowflakes, but the weather watcher familiar only with the drab, spherical ice pellets that usually constitute hail will be surprised at the abbreviated collection of forms that follows.

Let us begin with relatively simple departures from spheres, such as saucer- and lens-shaped hailstones. James J. Bowrey saw some hail of this type fall on the island of Jamaica on May 2, 1887. "Shortly after midday on the 2nd inst. [May 2] a thunderstorm visited this city; the

Hat-shaped hailstones from Jamaica

rain began with the wind from the east, as is usual with our May seasons, but it speedily changed to the west, accompanied with much thunder and lightning. Immediately hailstones became mingled with the rain, attention being drawn to their advent by the sharpness with which they struck on the shingled roofs. . . . The hailstones were of clear ice, inclosing a few bubbles of air, varying from mere points to bubbles the size of a split pea. The shape of the stones was singular. Suppose a shallow and very thick saucer to have a shallow cup, without a handle inserted in it, and you will have a good idea of the form of the hailstones when unbroken. Many had more or less lost the 'saucer' [shape] by violence, while some were entirely without it, presenting the appearance of a double convex lens with faces of different curvature. By actual measurement the hailstones were found to vary from one-quarter to three-quarters of an inch in diameter, and from one-eighth to one-quarter of an inch in thickness at the thickest part" (*Nature,* 36: 153, 1887).

A resident of Guilford, England, submitted a sketch of Saturn-shaped hailstones that fell on June 25, 1888. "I have only time to send

Saturnlike hailstones

you the enclosed sketch of Ice Stones which fell here yesterday afternoon, during one of the heaviest thunderstorms we have had for many years" (*Symons's Monthly Meteorological Magazine,* 23: 89, 1888).

On February 8, 1954, the captain and chief officer of the S.S. *City of Lyons,* then in the Persian Gulf, reported hemispherical hail during a violent storm. "The stones fell with sufficient force that the brass binnacle cover of the standard compass was badly dented. The stones averaged about 1 1/2 in. diameter, and it was observed that many were perfectly hemispherical in shape, as though split in half, and showing ringed layers of ice on the flat surface" (*Marine Observer*, 25: 30, 1955).

Meteorologists have no difficulty in imagining how spherical hail might form inside a storm cloud, but there seems to be no natural mechanism that might manufacture near-perfect hemispheres. And hemispheres are scarcely as exotic as the remarkable forms that follow.

W. T. Black, of Leamington, England, sent G. J. Symons, the publisher of a monthly weather journal that was the forerunner of today's *Meteorological Magazine*, sketches and an account of pyramidal hail that fell on March 31, 1876. "Everybody ran into shelter, as well they might, considering the size of the stones, which were as big as pebbles, angular, and pointed. They appeared to be shaped like pyramids, with points, and convex bases, studded with tubercules, and had plain sides, either square, pentagonal, or hexagonal. They would probably have belonged to complete spheres, when their sides were adjusted together, and which

Pyramidal hailstones, Leamington, England

would have been about 1 1/4 in. in diameter, and these segments were, therefore, about 1/2 in. long. They were of crystalline ice, with concentric bands, and probably the perfect pyramids weighed from 10 to 20 grains, and, as 24 might be estimated to make up a sphere, this, at the least, might have been half an ounce in weight, and at the very most about one ounce" (*Symons's Monthly Meteorological Magazine*, 11: 55, 1876).

According to John C. Willis cubic hailstones are not unknown. "Another phenomenon I have observed here [England] some time ago. A fall of hail lasting a few minutes or so occurred, the hailstones being exact cubes, of size about 7 mm., and of consistence like lumps of salt" (*Nature*, 33: 319, 1886).

Looking more like geological specimens than products of the atmosphere, well-formed crystalline hail fell near Tiflis, Austria, on June 9, 1869. "The stones were not mere lumps, exhibiting indistinct crystalline forms, but spheroidal bodies of definite crystalline structure, overgrown along the plane of the major axis by a series of clear crystals exhibiting various combinations belonging to the hexagonal system. The commonest forms were those which occur in calcite and specular iron. Of the former type, by far the most abundant were combinations of the scalenohedron, with rhombohedral faces; crystals of fifteen to twenty millimetres (3/4 inch) in height, and corresponding thickness, prettily grouped with com-

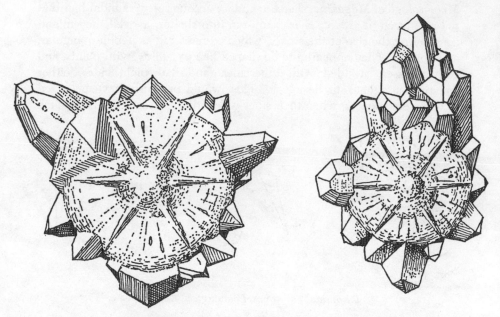

Crystalline hailstones that fell in Austria in 1869

binations of the prism and obtuse rhombohedra" (*Smithsonian Annual Report*, 1869, p. 420). Of course, ice comes in several crystalline forms, but large sharply defined crystals usually grow only under quiet conditions over long periods of time—hardly the situation inside a hailstorm.

The conical snow pellets mentioned a few pages back are matched geometrically by conical hail. In fact, hail and hard-packed snow pellets are probably closely related. Conical hail fell in Belfast on April 3, 1968. The fluted outer surface is a curious feature. "At about 1600 local time on Wednesday, 3 April 1968, there occurred a moderate shower of soft hail from cumulonimbus with a base [of] about 500 ft. Among the hailstones of normal character (i.e., roughly spherical) there occurred a fairly large proportion of stones which had the conical appearance shown in the diagram below. These stones had a distinctly fluted outer

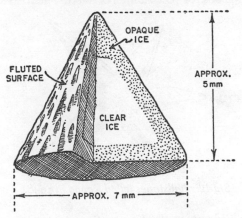

Detailed structure of a conical hailstone

surface with ridges running from base to apex. The stones were soft and easily sliced with a sharp penknife. The central core, shaped like a truncated cone, was of clear ice; the outer layer was opaque" (*Weather*, 23: 389, 1968).

E. J. Lowe, residing in Chepstow, England, wrote the editor of *Nature* about remarkable fibered hailstones that pelted his area on April 24, 1887, during a powerful storm. "The violent burst lasted about two minutes, in which time the ground was completely covered with large hailstones rather more than half an inch long. I say 'long' advisedly, for all the specimens I examined were conical and were all of them formed in the same way. The points all had the appearance of snow, being softer than the main bulk of the 'stones.' These snow portions occupied about one-third of the whole length, being white and non-transparent. The main portions of the hailstones were hard and icelike, stranded lengthwise with from forty to fifty fibres of ice—each fibre curved separately at the top—and together forming a curved surface, as of a sphere having the snow point for its centre. . . . On melting, the pointed part became translucent, while the other part became more opaque than at first, strands often remaining for a time, partially separated and curving outwards, as though they had been freed from compression in their lower extremities" (*Nature*, 36: 44, 1887).

Another strange class of hailstones includes those carrying spikes and protuberances around the body of the stone. It is difficult to conceive how these growths might form in the maelstrom of the storm cloud. The remarkable symmetry of some of the appendages seems to require the same quiescent conditions as crystal growth.

Star-shaped or spiked hail is the most common, as typified by that which fell in Kenya on August 6, 1948. "On Friday, August 6, on this Es-

Starlike hailstones fell in Kenya in 1948.

tate, 8 miles from Eldoret on the Kapsaret road, at 5 P.M., there occurred a rather singular fall of hail which I thought might be of interest to you, though it may be quite familiar to you. The sky became quite dark and large hailstones fell, but in the shape of stars similar to those of snow crystals in shape (when seen under the microscope). They all measured 1 1/2 in. in width. They consisted of large ice balls the size of a very large pea with fine radiating arms of ice" (*Meteorological Magazine,* 78: 55, 1949).

Perhaps the most remarkable hailstones of all were "tadpole-shaped" according to the witnesses. The beautiful symmetry reminds one of the drawings of molecules from a chemistry text. The fall occurred in Bavaria on August 21, 1881. "The hailstones fell at intervals and about six feet apart. There were very few of them, my family only picking up twenty in a space occupied by a full-sized lawn tennis court. . . . The great part were of the 'tadpole' shape and were as clear as glass, perfectly round, the five knobs being at equal distance from one an-

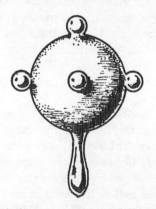

Spherical hail with odd projections

other. . . . My wife and three daughters, and two ladies staying with us, say that the stones looked just like a lady's looking-glass, with a knob at the top and on either side for ornament" (*Nature*, 23: 233, 1881).

Sketches provided by a Rev. J. M. Coates of hailstones that fell near Lincolnshire, England, on August 22, 1883, show forms that are grotesque in comparison with the Bavarian tadpoles. "At Hainton Hall gardens the ice was gathered up by the barrow load, pieces in some parts remaining unmelted until the next morning. The Rev. J. M. Coates made

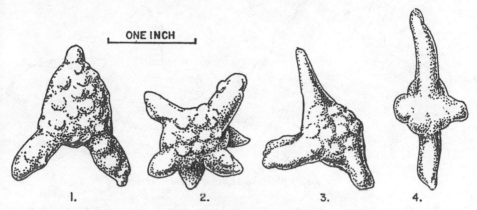

Odd-shaped agglomerations of hailstones

the accompanying sketches of some of the stones which fell at Welton-le-Wold at 4.30 P.M. [The first stone] weighed 90 grains 15 minutes after it fell. [The second] was drawn 42 minutes after it fell. [The fourth shown] measured 2 3/16 in. in length 50 minutes after it fell" (*Royal Meteorological Society, Quarterly Journal*, 20: 72, 1894).

The last class of anomalous hailstones consists of simple but large sheets of ice. Small, flat flakes of ice would occasion little comment, but here we have sheets several inches in breadth, resembling the thin sheets that form on ponds and puddles during an overnight freeze. How they are formed in the atmosphere is a mystery.

The sheets that fell at Manassas, Virginia, on August 10, 1897, are a bit on the small side. "There was some pretty severe thunder and lightning for half an hour or so, and then came a heavy shower of rain, during which there was the most remarkable fall of hail I have ever witnessed. I hurried out in the rain to examine the stones and picked up several. These were nearly square flattish blocks, say from 3/4 to 1 inch in length and breadth, and from 1/4 to 1/2 [of] an inch in thickness. They suggested, by both shape and size, the ordinary 'chocolate caramels' of the confectioner" (*Science*, 6: 448, 1897).

A tornado-spawning storm that swept eastern Oregon on June 3, 1894, dropped considerably larger ice sheets. "One correspondent states that the formation was more in the nature of sheets of ice than simple

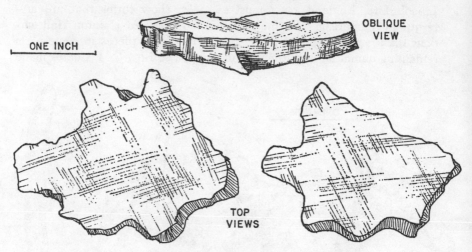

ONE INCH

OBLIQUE
VIEW

TOP
VIEWS

Ice sheets picked up after a storm in Oregon

hailstones. The sheets of ice averaged 3 to 4 in. square and from 3/4 in. to 1 1/2 in. in thickness. They had a smooth surface and in falling gave the impression of a vast field or sheet of ice suspended in the atmosphere that had suddenly broken into fragments about the size of the palm of the hand" (*Monthly Weather Review*, 22: 293, 1894).

SUPERHAILSTONES

Hailstone measurements are much like the tales of fishermen—almost a game of one-upmanship. Golf ball-sized hail is routine. Hail the size of hens' eggs is not too rare. When we get to reports of grapefruit-sized hail, most professional meteorologists become incredulous. Let us say that hail 4 in. in diameter is "recognized," and that's the upper limit of acceptance.

A modest superhailstone fell in Middlesex, England, on January 24, 1957. H. H. Annetts reports that "during a sudden storm beginning and ending with rain, with one clap of distant thunder, hailstones fell in High Street, Northwood, Middlesex. The sizes of the stones were variously of the pea, marble, and even golf ball order. But one which fell on the pavement close to a pedestrian was far larger. I saw it a quarter of an hour after its fall, it was 5 1/2 by four inches (140 × 100 mm.), more spherical than oblong. It had been taken to a nearby greengrocer, who had weighed it and found it to be 13 1/2 ounces" (*Weather*, 12: 167, 1957).

As hailstone size increases, the reports are older and from less reliable sources. For example, during the great storm of August 21, 1820, which slashed through England from London to the south coast, it was reported that "the hailstones were of immense size and [with] pieces of solid ice 18 in. by 6 in." (*English Mechanic*, 84: 18, 1906).

One wonders about the following item from Salina, Kansas, in 1882. Should it be classified with superhailstones or in the next chapter under ice falls—or was it a hoax? "Considerable excitement was caused in our city last Tuesday evening by the announcement that a hailstone weighing 80 lb. had fallen 6 miles west of Salina, near the railroad track. An inquiry into the matter revealed the following facts: A party of railroad section men were at work Tuesday afternoon, several miles west of town, when the hailstorm came upon them. Mr. Martin Ellwood, the foreman of the party, relates that nearly when they were at work hailstones of the weight of 4 or 5 lb. were falling and that returning toward Salina the stones increased in size, until his party discovered a huge mass of ice weighing, as near as he could judge, in the neighborhood of 80 lb. At this place the party found the ground covered with hail as if a wintry storm had passed over the land. Besides securing the mammoth chunk of ice, Mr. Ellwood secured a hailstone something over a foot long, 3 or 4 in. in diameter, and shaped like a cigar. These 'specimens' were placed upon a hand car and brought to Salina. Mr. W. J. Hagler, the North Santa Fe merchant, became the possessor of the larger piece, and saved it from dissolving by placing it in sawdust at his store. Crowds of people went down to see it Tuesday afternoon, and many were the theories concerning the mysterious visitor. At evening its dimensions were 29 by 16 by 2 in." (*Scientific American*, 47: 119, 1882).

Without question, the wildest stories of hail have come from India. Granted that the Indian subcontinent undergoes some fabulous hailstorms, can we believe the results of a survey made by Dr. George Buist, which was communicated to the British Association for the Advancement of Science in 1855? "There have been four occasions on which remarkable masses of ice, of many hundred pounds in weight, are believed to have fallen on India. One near Seringapatam, in the end of the last century, [was] said to have been the size of an elephant. It took three days to melt. We have no further particulars, but there is no reason whatever for our doubting the fact. In 1826, a mass of ice nearly a cubic yard in size fell in Khāndeish. In April 1838, a mass of hailstones, 20 feet in its larger diameter, fell at Dhārwār. On the 22nd of May, after a violent hailstorm, 80 miles south of Bangalore, an immense block of ice, consisting of hailstones cemented together, was found in a dry well" (*Report of the British Association, 1855,* p. 31).

EXPLOSIVE HAIL

The morning had been unseasonably warm at Columbia, Missouri, on November 11, 1911. W. G. Brown saw signs of an impending thunderstorm in the early afternoon. The storm broke about 2:30 with a few heavy raindrops. "Shortly afterwards there were two or three flashes of

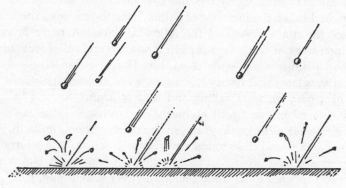

"Exploding" hail fell at Columbia, Missouri, in 1911.

lightning and thunder, followed by a fall of large hailstones, which on coming in contact with windows or walls or pavement in many instances exploded with a sharp report, so loud as to be mistaken for breaking window panes or a pistol shot. As the hail fell, the fragments sprang up from the ground and flew in all directions, looking like a mass of 'popping corn' on a large scale" (*Nature,* 88: 350, 1912). Possibly the hail was highly stressed, perhaps due to temperature changes, and the least mechanical shock was sufficient to cause it to shatter violently.

SLOWLY FALLING HAIL

Several careful observers of hail have remarked that the largest stones often do less damage than the smaller and, furthermore, that the large stones sometimes seem to fall very slowly. This latter situation prevailed during a hailstorm in Iraq on April 24, 1930. "The total diameter [of the average hailstone] was one and five-eighths inch, and in calm air the terminal velocity of hailstones of this size would be nearly 30 miles per hour. The descent of several specimens was actually timed against the wall of a building, and it was found that they fell 40 feet in about three seconds, giving a velocity of only 9 miles per hour." A strong updraft might have slowed the fall of the hailstones (*Meteorological Magazine*, 65: 143–44, 1930).

UNUSUAL INCLUSIONS IN HAILSTONES

Dust and wind-raised sand frequently serve as nuclei for both rain and hail. Even insects have been found in hailstones. A small chunk of alabaster (one-half to three-quarters of an inch in size) occupied the center of a large hailstone that was picked up near Vicksburg, Virginia, on May 11, 1894. The most frequently quoted example of an anomalous inclusion came from the same storm. "During the same storm at Bovina, 8 miles east of Vicksburg, a gopher turtle, 6 by 8 inches, and entirely

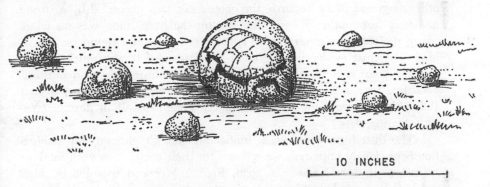

10 INCHES

Artist's sketch of the Bovina ice-encased turtle

cased in ice, fell with the hail" (*Monthly Weather Review*, 22: 215, 1894). The next chapter will cover many more "falls" of objects not normally found in the atmosphere.

Strange Fogs, Mists, and Hazes

Ordinary fogs are spooky enough. Murder mysteries are frequently set in fog-haunted mansions, and Jack the Ripper prowls London's pea-soupers (heavy fogs). In addition to hiding real and imagined hideous crimes, fogs have their own folklore. Some tales relate how "blasting fogs" rolled in over the countryside shriveling up vegetation and leaving behind a trail of death. Nevada has its *"pogonip,"* an ice fog; a similar phenomenon occurs in Spain. The onset of epidemics has sometimes been blamed on heavy, clammy fogs. The scientific literature has little to say about these lethal fogs; nevertheless a few curious items have accumulated.

Perhaps the most famous "fog" is actually not fog at all. The "dry" or "red" fogs near Cape Verde, off the Atlantic coast of Africa, have long been noted by sailors. When meteorological conditions are right, winds from the Sahara carry fine, red dust out over the Atlantic and frequently over much of Europe. A notable occurrence of the Cape Verde phenomenon lasted from February 16 through February 19, 1898. "A dense haze occurred over a large part of the eastern Atlantic off West Africa, extending for at least 1,500 miles north and south and a great but unknown distance east and west. The haze was caused by very fine red dust, so fine that it was impossible to sweep it up, and so dense that the sun and stars were completely obscured for two days. When visible, the sun was generally red, but one observer described it as 'a perfect blue ball' and another as greenish. At Tenerife the occurrence was preceded by a strong and very hot southerly wind, but during the haze there was no wind. Many insects were observed, of species not generally found on the island. The dust evidently originated in Africa, for it was much coarser near the coast and was thrown overboard from ships in large quantities" (Nature, 125: 256, 1930). Very similar dust fogs hover over the East Indies, being swept northward from the great Australian deserts (Nature, 94: 699, 1915).

The dust fogs would seem innocuous enough, though ship navigation is obviously impaired, were it not for their correlation with fatal air pollution. In late November 1930, French Morocco was hit by high winds that carried dust out into the Atlantic and over Europe. A mud rain fell over France soon afterward. "About the weekend of December 7, an extremely heavy fog prevailed in Belgium and England, and the daily press reported that in the neighborhood of Liege more than forty persons and a considerable number of cattle died, exhibiting symptoms of asphyxiation. . . . It seems probable that the more finely dispersed material carried by this storm reached considerable heights and settled down slowly over Belgium and England" (Science, 73: 96–97, 1931).

In the older literature, correlations between the appearance of a blue mist and cholera outbreaks was noted in England in 1832, 1848–49, and 1854. "When cholera broke out on board Her Majesty's ship Britannia in the Black Sea in 1854, several officers and men asserted positively that, immediately prior to the outbreak, a curious dark mist swept up from the sea and passed over the ship. The mist had barely cleared the vessel when the first case of disease was announced" (English Mechanic,

3: 474, 1866). The "blue mist" is a mystery, and the whole story is suspicious.

Before hurriedly relegating the foregoing observations to the realm of folklore, consider that a popular subject in today's scientific journals is the possible invasion of influenza viruses from outer space, perhaps carried in the dust of comets' tails!

In high, dry climates another curious type of fog appears suddenly on cold winter days. Doubtless, this account exaggerates the effects a bit. "A curious phenomenon is often witnessed in the mountainous districts of Nevada. Mountaineers call it *pogonip* and describe it as being a sort of frozen fog that appears sometimes in winter, even on the clearest and brightest of days. "In an instant the air is filled with floating needles of ice. To breathe the *pogonip* is death to the lungs. When it comes, people rush to cover. The Indians dread it as much as the whites. It appears to be caused by the sudden freezing in the air of the moisture which collects about the summits of the high peaks" (*American Meteorological Journal*, 4: 105, 1887).

The *pogonip* leads us logically to a rare account of a so-called "blasting" fog that visited Kensington, Connecticut, on April 3, 1758. "On the third instant, about sun-rise, at this place was a fog of so strange and extraordinary appearance, that it filled us all with amazement. It came in great bodies, like thick clouds, down to the earth, and in its way, striking against the houses, would break and fall down the sides in great bodies, rolling over and over. It resembled the thick steam rising from boiling wort and was attended with such heat that we could hardly breathe. When first I saw it, I really thought my house had been on fire and ran out to see if it was so; but many people thought the world was on fire and the last day come. One of our neighbours was then at Sutton, 100 miles to the eastward, and reports it was much the same there" (*Annual Register*, 1: 90–91, 1758).

Whirlwinds and Dust Devils

Whirlwinds and dust devils are rotary disturbances of the atmosphere like tornados and waterspouts, but they seem to be different phenomena altogether. The playful vortex that spins up a cloud of leaves on a sun-warmed hillside or tosses the farmer's hay up on the telephone wires is certainly different from the death-dealing tornados that can drive a piece of straw into a telephone pole like a nail. Size and strength are the obvious differences between these vortices. Whirlwinds and dust devils are in fact born on sunny days without menacing clouds overhead.

Their pranks are legendary, but they are not entirely harmless either. The larger whirlwinds may be violent enough to rip off roofs.

Whirlwinds are established by rising columns of warm air that are somehow invested with rotary motion. In the case of dust devils in particular, some electrical effects may be present. On rare occasions whirlwinds seem to be born violently with a sharp explosion, the nature of which is uncertain. Once in motion, they seem to have lives of their own and do not expire easily.

THE EXPLOSIVE ONSET OF SMALL VORTICES

The casual observer of nature would expect the sun's warmth to create languidly rising columns of warmer air that casually strengthen into weak whirlwinds. Rarely, however, whirlwinds form suddenly with a disconcerting rumble or even a sharp detonation. The reason for such unexpected violence is obscure, but clear-air turbulence (CAT) higher in the atmosphere may be powerful enough to tear an airplane apart. CAT is also invisible and there may be a link with violent whirlwinds. (Of course, one phenomenon is not really explained by associating it with another mysterious phenomenon.)

On October 20, 1949, Shoeburyness, England, was visited by a sudden whirlwind. "Mr. Whitaker, who happened to be outside his office at the time, said that while watching what appeared to be a frontal cloud he heard a muffled sound like distant thunder or an explosion, and on turning to the southwest saw that at a distance of about 1,000 yards the air was filled to a considerable height with leaves, twigs and similar light debris swirling violently as though after a large but smokeless explosion" (*Meteorological Magazine,* 79: 256–60, 1950).

Rumblings and thunderlike sounds seem to betoken whirlwinds of more than average strength. Conceivably, the more violent the vortex, the sharper and louder the sound, as in this report from East Kent, Ontario, in 1880. The phenomenon was described by David Muckle and W. R. McKay. "The gentlemen were in a field on a farm of the former, when they heard a sudden loud report, like that of a cannon. They turned just in time to see a cloud of stones flying upward from a spot in the field. Surprised beyond measure, they examined the spot, which was circular and about 16 feet across, but there was no sign of an eruption nor anything to indicate the fall of a heavy body there. The ground was simply swept clean. They are quite certain that it was not caused by a meteorite, an eruption of the earth, or a whirlwind" (*Scientific American,* 43: 25, 1880).

MINIATURE WHIRLWINDS

The energies of some whirlwinds may be concentrated into incredibly small volumes—and of course such concentration of energy should lead to the generation of sound. The following incident occurred in Surrey, England. "On 19th July, 1913, a narrow strip of wind, 1 1/2-ft. wide, drove through a hedge lifting newly cut hay 60 yards high, proceeded through a tree with great violence, blowing off the leaves of a hedge and tree, and upset a hay-cock in an adjoining field. It lasted some 10 minutes and was accompanied by great noise. I was informed by an old inhabitant [that] such occurrences were frequent at Coquet Head in the Cheviots. I doubt they are all as narrow as this was" (*Symons's Monthly Meteorological Magazine,* 49: 52, 1914).

If a powerful miniature whirlwind passes over water, a diminutive waterspout results. J. Gray observed a tiny spout on April 16, 1872, while fishing in the river Elwy, near St. Asaph, Great Britain. "My attention was suddenly called upstream by a remarkably strange hissing, bubbling sound, such as might be produced by plunging a mass of heated metal into water. On turning I beheld what I may call a diminutive waterspout in the centre of the stream, some forty paces from where I was standing. Its base, as well as I could observe, was a little more than two feet in diameter. The water curled up from the river in an unbroken cylindrical form to a height of about fifteen inches, rotating rapidly, then diverged as from a number of jets being thrown off with considerable force to an additional elevation of six or seven feet, the spray falling all round as from an elaborately arranged fountain, covering a large area. It remained apparently in the same position for about forty seconds, then moved slowly in the direction of the right bank of the river, and was again drawn towards the centre, where it remained stationary as before for a few seconds. Again it moved in the former direction, gradually diminishing and losing force as it neared the bank, and finally collapsed in the shallow water. Strange to say, its course was perpendicular to the bank and not with the current" (*Nature,* 5: 501, 1872).

WHIRLWIND MISCHIEF

Like ball lightning, whirlwinds have their enigmatic aspects. Usually erratic, often playful in action, they sometimes seem preternaturally curious and prankish. J. L. Capes, in relating his experiences with dust devils in Egypt, likens them to the desert "spirits" of legend. "The smallest of the type I have seen was only about 5 ft. high, that is, the visible column of sand, and less than a foot in diameter. It passed so close to me that it was easy to see its narrow cycloidal path marked on the sand, which was deposited and lifted as the eddy travelled on at not less than 15 miles an hour, although the wind was actually very light.

"I recently encountered a much more remarkable example while walking over a smooth surface of desert on a flat, calm day. Hearing a swishing sound behind me, I turned and observed a large revolving ring of sand less than a foot high approaching me slowly. It stopped a few feet away and the ring, containing sand and small pieces of vegetable debris in a sheet less than one inch thick, revolved rapidly around a circle of about 12 ft. diameter while the axis remained stationary. It then moved slowly around me after remaining in one spot for at least thirty seconds and slowly died down. It would be interesting to know if others acquainted with the desert have come across similar examples of a broad, flat eddy.

"The ancient superstition among desert tribes that these whirlwinds are spirits, called *afrit* or *ginni* (the 'genii' of the *Arabian Nights*), would seem to have a reasonable foundation in face of such an 'inquisitive' apparition" (*Nature*, 135: 511, 1935).

A much more energetic desert whirlwind or dust devil appeared in 1902 on the White Mountain Apache reservation in Arizona. Albert B. Reagan watched the whirlwind from a hill as it gathered strength while crossing a flat lava "lake." "As the twister was coming directly in my direction, I shifted southward over a gulch to another ridge to escape its fury. On it came. It entered the canyon in which I had been only a minute before. Here as the canyon both wedged-in and ascended toward the mountains in the direction it was going, the rushing whirl became 'angry,' as it were. The day had been perfectly clear. Yet in a moment there were chain lightning and ripping thunder on every side, while at the same time the whirler uprooted trees and tore large-sized boulders from their places on the canyon walls, finally destroying itself in that canyon. From my observations I am inclined to believe that the electrical display that accompanied this whirl was due to the friction caused by the whirling debris" (*Science*, 71: 506, 1930).

There is a logical progression here from the barely noticeable readings on instruments occasioned by the passage of a small dust devil, to the lightning of the Apache reservation whirlwind, to the hotly debated electrical phenomena associated with full-fledged tornados, as introduced in the next section.

A final whirlwind observation (assuming that it really was a whirlwind) suggests a comparison between energetic vortex phenomena and some of the fiery, low-level, supposedly meteoric phenomena of Chapter

1. Consider the following report: "In northern Kentucky, southern Ohio, and Indiana, violent wind and rainstorms causing great damage to crops and buildings were experienced on the 21st. [In] Americus, Ga., [on the] 18th, at some distance from the town a small whirlwind, about 5 feet in diameter and sometimes 100 feet high, formed over a corn-field where it tore up the stalks by the roots and carried them with sand and other loose materials high into the air. The body of the whirling mass was of vaporous formation and perfectly black, the centre apparently illuminated by fire and emitting a strange "sulphurous vapor" that could be distinguished [at] a distance of about 300 yards, burning and sickening all who approached close enough to breathe it. Occasionally the cloud would divide into three minor ones, and as they came together again there would be a loud crash, accompanied by cracking sounds, when the whole mass would shoot upwards into the heavens" (*Monthly Weather Review*, 9: 19, 1881).

On May 9, 1971, a small, sun-generated whirlwind only 15 ft. high, skittered through Lowell, Michigan, twisting TV antennas, ripping off a few shingles, and scattering debris as if it were Halloween. "A 3-year-old child weighing about 30 pounds was lifted 6–12 in. above the hood of a parked pickup truck upon which she was sitting and was carried slightly to one side before being caught by an older brother. The truck was parked between two buildings, and the Venturi effect may have produced accelerated forces. A small, healthy registered beagle puppy vomited after the whirlwind swept over him. He continued in convulsions for 5–10 minutes and was disposed of because the owners didn't feel he was going to recover" (*Monthly Weather Review*, 100: 317, 1972).

Another buoyant whirlwind was fatal to a girl in Bradford, England, in 1911 when it carried her to a height of 20 ft. before dropping her. Nearby onlookers who watched her flight helplessly were scarcely affected by the very narrow funnel (*Symons's Meteorological Magazine*, 46: 54, 1911).

ELECTRICAL CHARACTER OF DUST DEVILS

In Chapter 1, blowing snow and sand were found to induce electrical discharge phenomena. It should be no surprise then to find dust devils exhibiting strong electrical fields within their vortex structure. G. D. Freier obtained a record of this structure in an unexpected experiment. "At the time of obtaining measurements on the earth's electric field during an eclipse of the sun in the Sahara Desert at Kidal, French West Africa, an interesting record was obtained on the electric field associated with a large dust devil. This record is shown in [the illustration below], where positive values of the field imply positive charge above the earth. The dust devil was estimated to be between 100 and 200 meters high and about 8 meters in diameter, and its distance of closest approach to the electric field mill was about 30 meters. It was of sufficient strength to raise an army-type sleeping cot several meters into the air, and it was followed by truck for about 1 mile before it dissipated its energy. Its speed across country was about 4 meters per second.

"The two negative excursions with a tendency to go positive between them suggests a sort of dipole structure for the dust devil with a negative charge above (an inverted thunderstorm)" (*Journal of Geophysical Research*, 65: 3504, 1960). Here we have a purported whirlwind with luminous and acoustic phenomena, dividing and reuniting and leaving a trail of sulphurous odor—almost a meteor/tornado/ball lightning hybrid.

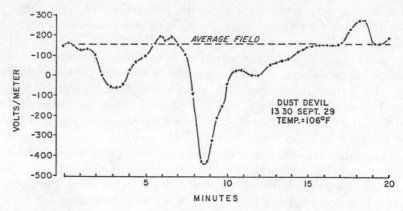

Electric field measurements made as a large dust devil passed within 30 meters

Idiosyncrasies of Tornados and Waterspouts

Ostensibly, tornados and waterspouts are the same species of rotary storm. The passage of a tornado from land to water converts it automatically to a waterspout, or so the prevailing theory goes.

A controversial hypothesis that unites the two phenomena is that of their purported electric origin. Both tornados and waterspouts are usually accompanied by severe lightning, but the hypothesis of electrical origin requires powerful earth-cloud currents to keep the storm's motor running. The effects of this large-scale flow of electricity should be observable. The "tornado lights" introduced in Chapter 1 may be considered evidence of strong electrical action. There are other effects mentioned below that are also confirmatory: large terrestrial current flows in the neighborhoods of tornados, the occasional smell of ozone and/or sulphur, and the burning and dehydrating effects sometimes noticed along the paths of tornados. The latter effects, however, are attributed more conventionally to the aerodynamic heat generated by tornados. Wherever the truth lies, the auxiliary phenomena accompanying tornados and waterspouts are most curious.

The physical mechanism of the waterspout is still a puzzle to some meteorologists who find the peculiar tubular vortex structure different from what theory would seem to require. Along this vein, conventional wisdom also has trouble dealing with forked waterspouts, waterspouts stretching between clouds, and waterspouts with two concentric tubes.

Both tornados and waterspouts are dangerous phenomena, the former being the more violent. Is there a continuous gradation of sizes from the small mischievous whirlwind to the tornado a mile wide that levels a whole town? Do all such rotary phenomena have the same cause? The answers are probably yes, but no one knows for sure. Meteorologists, in fact, do not really understand the genesis of atmospheric vortices. Something seems to trigger these atmospheric maelstroms, perhaps natural surface features or even automobile traffic!

THE SUPPOSED ELECTRICAL ASPECTS OF TORNADOS AND WATERSPOUTS

Since tornados and waterspouts are so much more powerful than whirlwinds and dust devils, even more intense electrical activity should be expected of them. Certainly, considerable electricity is observed in connection with tornados, but is it merely due to the thunderstorms that usually accompany tornados?

Geophysicist Bernard Vonnegut has been the primary champion of tornado electricity, not only as an associated phenomenon but as the possible instigator and power source of the funnel. Vonnegut points out that no other atmospheric phenomenon can generate wind velocities of several hundred miles per hour, suggesting that something besides aerodynamic forces is at work. A quotation from his 1960 paper on the subject summarizes the physical evidence for the "electrical tornado."

"Presence of Energetic Electrical Phenomena in Tornados. If the high velocity of the tornado is to be explained on the basis of thunderstorm electrical energy, one must first prove that intense electrical activity is closely associated with tornados. That this is the case is clearly evident from many different accounts that have been written about

tornados. *Flora* quotes Harrison's conclusion 'that lightning of a peculiar and intense character is an almost invariable accompaniment of tornados,' and that airplane pilots frequently so identify tornado clouds.

"The visual evidence of the close association between lightning and tornados is confirmed by the radio 'static' measurements made by *Jones*. He concluded from sferics measurements that in tornado-producing storms lightning discharges occur at the rate of 10 or 20 per second, which is about ten times the rate in ordinary storms.

"Further evidence of the close association between electricity and tornados is contained in reports of those who have looked up into the interior of a funnel and lived to tell about it. These observers report a variety of electrical phenomena, such as incessant lightning, a brilliant luminous cloud, a ball of fire, or a display 'like a Fourth of July pinwheel' in the tornado tube.

"Although no one has as yet photographed these striking displays, two different observers have made drawings of what they saw. *Hall* observed a tornado in Texas at close range and published a sketch . . . [of it]. *Montgomery* watched the devastating Blackwell, Oklahoma, tornado of 1955 from a distance of about half a mile and prepared the drawing shown on page 40. The approximate dimensions indicated were computed from angles subtended by the tornado relative to structures near the point of observation. There are other phenomena suggestive of electrical effects. Intense St. Elmo's fire is frequently observed near the funnel, and odors, probably of ozone and nitrogen oxides, have been described. Buzzing and hissing noises suggestive of electrical discharges have been reported near the funnel. After its passage, dehydration of vegetation and the surface soil has been noted along the path.

"In addition to the fairly well understood primary and secondary electrical effects discussed above, accounts of tornados rather frequently include mention of 'beaded lightning' and glowing or exploding fireballs. These phenomena are apparently the same as or are closely related to the controversial 'ball lightning' whose existence and nature are still debated. In view of our present almost complete ignorance, we shall make no attempt to discuss this class of observations. It is worth remarking, however, that an understanding of ball lightning may very well be necessary if the tornado puzzle is to be solved" (*Journal of Geophysical Research*, 65: 205–6, 1960).

Supplementing visual and radio observations, Marx Brook has found large electrical and magnetic effects in the neighborhood of tornados. "Measurements of the magnetic field and earth current in the vicinity of a tornado show large step-like deflections coincident with the touching down of the funnel. Calculations with a simple current model indicate that a minimum current of several hundred amperes must be postulated to account for the observed deflection in magnetic field. The existence of a steady current of 225 amperes for a period of about 10 minutes provides joule heat at the rate of approximately 10^{10} joules per second and involves a total charge transfer of 135,000 coulombs. The calculations imply that a tornado is electrically equivalent to several hundred isolated thunderstorm cells active simultaneously" (*Science*, 157: 1434–36, 1967).

What about those marine analogs of tornados, the waterspouts: do they manifest electrical symptoms? Not as frequently as tornados. There are a few old reports of sulphurous odors connected with waterspouts, plus the following account from the German bark *Ceylon*. While in the North Atlantic on April 10, 1885, the *Ceylon* was engulfed by a waterspout for two or three minutes. "During the time they were in the influence of the waterspout, there was a great deal of St. Elmo's fire on all the ironwork of the vessel" (*Science*, 5: 391, 1885). It is possible that the spout's tall column of electrically conducting salt water may effectively "short out" much of the activity.

BURNING AND DEHYDRATING EFFECTS OF TORNADOS

Several remarkable electrical storms cut parallel swaths across the French countryside on August 18 and 19, 1890. These storms seem to have been tornados of great strength. They were accompanied by extensive burning and dehydrating effects.

"At Pire the *trombe* [tornado] was investigated by M. G. Jeannel. There was an apparent whirlwind, transported parallel to itself, and turning counter-clockwise, as shown by the fallen trees. The first thrown down were from the south-east, the next from the east, and so on to the north-west. The greater damage was on the right hand of the track. The velocity of gyration was great and that of translation relatively much less.

"The roofs damaged were peculiar. On the right of the path, those facing north were carried away, while those facing south were unharmed; on the left of the track just the reverse was true. During the whole time the lightning was continuous. The odor of ozone was noted at different places. At Reinou a woman tending a cow, grazing in the meadow, saw her enveloped in violet flames. These were so intense that the woman, from fright, covered her face with her handkerchief. A moment later the wind struck down everything.

"[In] Domagne Dr. Pettier suddenly heard an extraordinary indefinite roaring. He rushed toward the garden, where the firs were being plucked up. At the gate, he felt a kind of pressure from above; he noticed an unusual smell of ozone; then he felt himself raised up, and this not by the wind, for it was calm, but as though by some invisible force. On many trees the foliage was scorched. About a mile west of Domagne, hail of the size of a walnut fell to a depth of over three inches, covering the ground.

"At Dreux the report was by M. Bort. At 10 P.M. a great cumulo-nimbus thundercloud was seen to the south-south-west of the town. On its upper part a very brilliant plume of sparks was directed toward heaven. In this cloud the lightning was incessant and the thunder loud. After some hail had fallen, at about 10.25 P.M., a loud roar was heard like that of a train entering a tunnel, and in less than a minute the storm reached the town. It blew off the tiles, plucked out the trees, and destroyed many houses. At the moment of the passage the sky was on fire, and some persons saw a cloud which reached the height of a house. Reaching the Blaise valley, it plucked up many poplars and left them lying generally from south-south-west to north-north-east. In the environs of Fontaine many trees were uprooted. At Brissard the hurricane made a passage through the western part of the village, destroying twenty houses. At another point most of the trees lay from south-west to north-east, but there were many, 220 yards from the first, that lay in an opposite direction.

"Lightning strokes were very rare, because no traces were found upon trees, and no houses were fired. There was a remarkable exception, however, in the Vivien house, built solidly of brick, which had traces of electric discharges. Some window-panes were pierced by circular holes, and those holes had a sharp edge on the outside. On the inside, the edge had suffered a beginning of fusion, which had rounded it off. The damage was reported at $300,000 in Dreux, and one person was killed. At the instant of the passage all the gas-lights were extinguished, and it is suggested that 'this indicated a rarefaction of the air near the centre of the whirl'" (*Science*, 17: 304–5, 1891).

Zurcher, in his description of the great tornado of Monville (France) noted several possible electrical effects. "The trees in the vicinity were flung down in every direction, riven and dried up for a length of from six to twenty feet or more. While clearing away the ruins, in the attempt to rescue the unfortunate people buried beneath them, it was noticed that the bricks were burning hot. Planks were found completely charred and cotton burned and scorched, and many pieces of iron and steel were magnetized" (Frederick Zurcher, *Meteors, Aerolites, Storms, and Atmospheric Phenomena*, New York: Scribner's, 1876, pp. 154–55).

It is peculiar that all our accounts of tornado burning and dehydration come from Europe where tornados are actually quite rare. Furthermore the reports are all old ones.

FREAKS OF THE TORNADO

No one has ventured to call tornados "inquisitive," and "prankish" seems too mild a term for such deadly storms. Yet the tales of tornado freaks are legion and devilishly hard to account for.

On May 18, 1883, a big tornado visited Sangamon County, Illinois. "The family of Mr. T_____, who had also sought shelter in a cellar from the same storm, were covered with a gummy substance, which would not wash off! This substance might have been formed from the sap of trees and juice of leaves, combined with the moist, heated atmosphere" (*Popular Science Monthly*, 23: 748–53, 1883).

In 1920, C. LeRoy Meisinger compiled a list of tornado freaks. A select few follow: "Half a dozen glass jars of fruit were carried 100 yards by the winds and not damaged. . . . There seemed to be two puffs of wind; one carried things toward the west. In about a quarter of a minute everything came back. I tried to keep my family down on the floor. One of my boys blew out of the house, then blew back. . . . a steel range from the Preston home was found 3 miles away in a wheat field; harrows, plows, and other agricultural implements were scattered over the fields for miles around" (*Science*, 52: 293–95, 1920).

CAN AUTOMOBILES CREATE TORNADOS?

Scientists have asked themselves this question in all seriousness. "The recorded annual incidence of tornados in the United States has increased steadily and dramatically in the past four decades, by at least a factor of six. We have examined the thesis that the development of widespread motor vehicle traffic in the United States over the last 40 years has perturbed atmospheric vorticity in such a way as to exacerbate the tornado incidence, principally by the introduction of cyclonic vorticity. Surprisingly, both the analysis and the evidence support the thesis." This study by John D. Isaacs et al. also noted that fewer tornados are reported on weekends, presumably because vehicular traffic is lower and more nearly unidirectional, as cities empty Saturday morning and refill Sunday night (*Nature*, 253: 254–55, 1975). Of course many scientists have objected to such a novel suggestion, citing many theoretical problems (*Nature*, 260: 457–61, 1976).

EMBRYONIC WATERSPOUTS

Turning again to the gentler phenomenon of waterspouts, one finds many reports of circular patches of agitated water that may or may not develop into full-fledged waterspouts. Unlike terrestrial whirlwinds, which form in fair weather, these embryonic waterspouts seem to require clouds overhead. If the spout approaches maturity, a curious thin funnel snakes down from the cloud and unites with the rising column of turbulent water.

An aborted attempt of nature to construct a spout was observed by the chief officer of the M.V. *Aldersgate* in the North Atlantic on September 28, 1962. "At 1815 GMT a wave breaking and giving off spray about 20 ft. from the vessel was observed to become agitated. The spray (which the observer thought at first was caused by a whale blowing) rose from the sea and began to revolve in a counter-clockwise direction, the time of rotation being 3–4 seconds. At first the diameter of the disturbed patch of water was about 8 ft., but it increased to about 15 ft.,

An incipient waterspout

which was also the height of the spray thrown up." The elevated patch of disturbed water subsided in about 10 minutes (*Marine Observer*, 33: 115–16, 1963).

The captain of the Norwegian ship *Majorka* saw a somewhat more successful attempt at spout formation on October 2, 1913, again in the North Atlantic:

"At 7:30 A.M. a whirlwind was seen about 1/8 mile to the leeward of the ship, which was headed north-west, and when it became apparent that it was an incipient waterspout, the wheel was put hard to starboard and the ship was gotten off toward the west-south-west, and immediately the whirlwind passed the ship's stern in a north-south direction at a distance of about 10 feet. It had taken the form of a thin spout, which increased in diameter and became denser. It was accompanied by a strong puff of wind, a heavy downpour of rain, and roaring sound.

"Within a circle of about 25 feet in circumference the water was in a violent uproar similar to a large waterfall. The spout grew until it was about 5 feet in diameter and had a lighter appearance in the centre about 3 feet in diameter, in which the water steamed up, and on each side of this a darker band about 1 foot in breadth, in which the water was descending. The motion in both the upward and downward currents was very rapid. The spout lifted and bent forward about halfway between the cloud at the top and the surface of the water. At that time it was about 1,500 feet from the ship. The duration of the spout from the beginning of the formation until it broke loose was about 10 minutes." After the spout had passed, the *Majorka*'s crew detected the odor of sulphur, indicating perhaps intense electrical activity (*Royal Meteorological Society, Quarterly Journal*, 40: 78, 1914).

DOUBLE-WALLED WATERSPOUTS

Waterspouts are generally not simple, solid columns of rotating water. Most seem to be hollow tubes, with water streaming up the inside and down the outside. The aerohydrodynamics of single-tube spouts are difficult to explain. To compound the quandary of the theorists, double-walled spouts are not especially rare. A good description of one comes from G. D. Hale Carpenter, who observed this phenomenon from near Entebbe, Uganda, while camped on the shores of Lake Victoria in 1922:

"I was in camp on the north end of Bagalla, the largest island of the Sese Archipelago. The camp lay about 300 yards from the shore of a small bay. At daybreak on June 30 there were very lowering black clouds and every indication of an immediate heavy storm. While looking out from the tent, I suddenly saw that a waterspout was travelling obliquely towards us, and as it eventually came to within about 100 yards of the shore a very good view was obtained for about five minutes before it came to an end.

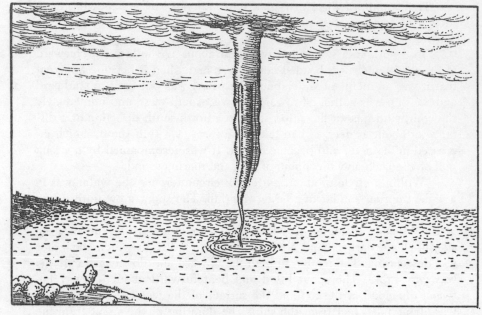

Waterspout with an incomplete second wall

"The pedicle arose from a well-marked circular area on the water, which was otherwise only faintly rippled by the preliminary puff of wind before the approaching storm.

"This circular area was evidently very violently disturbed as a cloud of vapour, greatly agitated, rose from it for a little distance.

"The pedicle was extremely narrow at its lower end, and not quite straight, being sinuous in outline. It broadened out gradually into a column which went up into the low cloud; the core of this column was much less dense than the periphery, and the violent upward spiral ascent of the water could be clearly seen.

"So far I have described nothing unusual, but the following was quite new to me and seemed of great interest.

"Surrounding the central core, but separated from it by a clear narrow space, was a sheath, the lower end of which faded away some distance above the water. The profile of this sheath was undulating, it being thicker in some places than others. A curious point is that this sheath *seemed* to pulsate rhythmically, but I could not say whether the appearance of pulsation might not have been an illusion caused by waves travelling up its outer surface.

"This pulsation gave an uncanny suggestion of a live thing, which was aided by the violent spiral movement upwards in the central core, the clouds of vapour boiling round its base, and the movement of the whole across the water—indeed, we watched it spellbound until the pedicle dissolved away at the bottom, and the ascent of the part above brought the phenomenon to an end" (*Nature*, 110: 414–15, 1922).

In recent years, the development of the laser has permitted meteorologists to probe waterspout structures and their motions from aircraft. Flights past double-walled spouts have proved that the two tubes are independent structures, each rotating at its own speed, but in the same direction. The laser data also revealed that waterspouts rotate both clockwise and counterclockwise in contrast to tornados, which are almost always counterclockwise. In this, waterspouts are more like whirlwinds and dust devils, which also seem to have no preferred direction of rotation (*Mariners' Weather Log*, 21: 387–88, 1977).

MAVERICK WATERSPOUTS

Not only are there spouts within spouts, but sometimes a single spout splits at its lower end creating a forked spout. Meteorologists tend to doubt the reports of forked spouts because such structures seem physically impossible. Nevertheless they do occur. P. M. Whitworth reported

A forked waterspout was spotted in the South China Sea.

one in the South China Sea on May 19, 1967. "A waterspout which divided into two branches about halfway between the cloud base and the sea, as shown in the sketch, was seen at 0715 LMT about 10 miles off. The parts joined together about 10 minutes later to form a single column, at the base of which great turbulence was observed" (*Marine Observer*, 36: 62–63, 1968).

Waterspouts are supposed to connect the sea surface and clouds, but on rare occasions they seem to connect clouds alone. Of course, tornado funnels often stop short of the earth's surface, but no reports of cloud-to-cloud tornados have yet been discovered. In several respects the spouts seen by G. Oldfield in the North Atlantic on June 14, 1928, seem akin to the cloud arches described earlier in this chapter. "At 1.55 P.M., a nimbus cloud bearing W.N.W. and moving in a N.N.E.'ly direction was observed to be connected to a bank of cumulus cloud by two waterspouts, which did not reach the sea, but merely stretched between the two cloud-banks" (*Marine Observer*, 6: 127, 1929).

Two clouds apparently connected by a double waterspout

On August 18, 1951, the S.S. *Pacific Nomad*, en route from Yokohama to Los Angeles, encountered a (seemingly) dynamically impossible waterspout. "It appeared to rotate rapidly, first clockwise, then anticlockwise, continually changing the direction of rotation" (*Marine Observer*, 22: 123, 1952). A given spout may rotate in either direction but should not change direction once formed. An optical illusion of some sort was suggested by meteorologists in this case.

LAND WATERSPOUTS

Seemingly a contradiction in terms, land waterspouts form over the land surface wherever there is ample sand and other loose materials to act as a "fluid." The hollow-tube structure between cloud and earth is typical of waterspouts, not of whirlwinds and dust devils, which are smaller, clear-weather phenomena. H. G. Busk saw one of these rare land-going spouts in Iran on December 27, 1915, 150 miles from the nearest sea. "Its distance from myself as observer was about two miles, and it was viewed through a pair of Zeiss glasses with a magnification of eight. As the pendant gradually dropped from the cloud, a hollow column of dust from the plain rose to meet it. The pendant and column eventually joined, the whole swaying about in a particularly beautiful manner. The height of column from the plain to the cloud was about 2,000 feet, and the motion of the column about fifteen miles per hour, but very irregular. I have no note on the direction of rotation of the column. The whole phenomenon lasted about fifteen minutes, and the pendant portion withdrew into the cloud first, leaving the lower portion rotating at the bottom. At the base of the column there was a fountain of large fragments thrown out, stones, sticks, and anything that was loose. The whole column appeared like a translucent glass tube, but flexible— that is, there was a dark edge and a brighter middle, just as I have drawn it. A solid column of mist would have given an exactly opposite effect, namely a dark middle and a bright edge. There is no doubt in my mind at any rate that the column was hollow, and that the lower part of it was composed of dust, which was of a browner colour than the cloud above it" (*Meteorological Magazine*, 61: 289–91, 1927).

Temperature Anomalies

Changing temperature is not unusual unless it rises or falls by many degrees in a few minutes. Such "temperature flashes" are usually associated with the sudden onset of hot, dry winds, like the Chinooks of the American West. But intense blasts of heat of unknown origin are reported elsewhere. Very localized hot-air blasts, for example, have been noted in the vicinities of thunderstorms. These may have an electrical origin, but no one really knows. The final variety of temperature anomaly presented here is regional in extent and seasonal in length, as exemplified by the famous "Year Without a Summer."

TEMPERATURE FLASHES

The Black Hills of South Dakota are often swept by the Chinook winds in winter months. Here are two "temperature flashes" recorded at Rapid City. "January 13, 1913—8 A.M. temperature: −17° F; 10 P.M. temperature: 47° F, an increase of 64° in 14 hours. January 22, 1943—beginning at 7:32 A.M., the temperature rose 49° in two minutes, from −4° to 45° F. Frost appeared almost instantaneously on car windshields" (*Monthly Weather Review*, 71: 29–32, 1943).

Rare and unexplained currents of intensely hot air appear during the summer in normally torrid climes. "In every quarter of the southwest, the heat of the present summer appears to have been unprecedented. In Montgomery, Ala., the thermometer stood for several days at 103° in the shade. In Mississippi, Louisiana, and Missouri, it has ranged from 95° to 105° in the shade, and the people call it 'the fiery term.'

"Several currents of intensely hot air have been experienced which appear to be similar to those which are common in Egypt, Persia, and some portions of India. A hot wind, extending about 100 yards in width, lately passed through middle Georgia and scorched up the cotton crops on a number of plantations. A hot wind also passed through a section of Kansas; it burned up the vegetation in its track, and several persons fell victims to its poisonous blast. It lasted for a very short period, during which the thermometer stood at 120°—far above blood heat" (*Scientific American*, 3: 106, 1860).

Temperature flashes have been observed in connection with thunderstorms for years. A hot gust arrives as if from the opening of an oven door and is gone in a few minutes. Much unstable air exists in the vicinity of a thunderstorm, but meteorologists have not been able to explain these pockets of very hot air. A typical example comes from Kimberley, South Africa. "It may interest you to know that at 9 P.M., on the 20th [of] September, a thunder cloud approached from the west, bringing with it a squall of wind that caused the temperature to rise in a few minutes to 110° F. By 9:45 P.M. it had fallen again to 67°, which I expect was about the temperature before the squall. I do not think my thermometer responded quick enough to register the highest point, but it is safe to say it rose 40° in five minutes" (*Symons's Meteorological Magazine*, 46: 201, 1911).

THE YEAR WITHOUT A SUMMER

"I well remember the seventh of June . . . dressed throughout with thick woolen clothes and an overcoat on. My hands got so cold that I was obliged to lay down my tools and put on a pair of mittens." So wrote Chauncey Jerome of Plymouth, Connecticut, of the year 1816. All over the northeastern United States, the weather was more than unseasonable. From June 6 to 9, severe frosts occurred every night, killing all crops. There were two snowfalls in June, heavy in northern New England, lighter in the south. The *North Star*, of Danville, Vermont, described it as "melancholy weather. . . . On the night of the 7th and morning of the 8th, a kind of sleet or exceedingly cold snow fell, attended by a high wind, and measured in places where it drifted 18 to 20 inches in depth."

After the middle of June, summer seemed to set in, but in July another freeze arrived, killing all the replanted crops. On August 20, yet another cold wave swept in, bringing frost as far south as East Windsor, Connecticut. Corn crops for 1816 were only about 10 percent of normal. Not surprisingly, the first general migration from New England to the Middle West began the following year.

Meteorology did not exist as a science in 1816, but in retrospect modern weathermen are inclined to blame volcanic dust for the Year Without a Summer. Three major volcanic eruptions between 1812 and 1817 injected vast quantities of dust into the atmosphere. In particular, Tambora, in Indonesia, seems to have blasted as much as 100 cubic miles of debris into the atmosphere. Indonesia is almost halfway around the world from New England, and it is difficult to understand how this distant volcano could have focused its effects on northeastern North America. Krakatoa's explosion in 1883, in the same area, created spectacular sunsets worldwide but no significant climatic anomalies (*Weatherwise*, 32: 108–11, 1979).

Weather and Astronomy

Folklore strongly suggests that the moon affects rainfall, and scientists have long suspected a solar influence on terrestrial weather. Neither effect is overwhelming, whatever the mechanisms may be, assuming that they really do exist. In fact, the effects are so small that most scientists have rejected both ideas for many years. Nevertheless an immense number of sources suggest that there are definite lunar and solar effects on terrestrial precipitation.

Recently, with spacecraft and rocket measurements, it has become apparent that solar activity does indeed affect the earth's atmosphere through sun-emitted streams of plasma. These atmospheric changes manifest themselves as weather modifications. This new creditability accorded to sun-weather relationships removes most of them from the "strange" category and thus outside the purview of this book.

The moon's influence on weather, however, is still highly controversial. Favorable and unfavorable data exist in quantity. Two kinds of effects are noted, each with a proposed physical mechanism: (1) lunar effects on rainfall through the gravitational modification of the influx of meteoric dust that serves as a source of condensation nuclei and (2) lunar effects on thunderstorms through the moon's interaction with the earth's magnetic tail that, in turn, modify the number of electrified particles entering the atmosphere and the planet's electrical energy balance.

Solar and lunar effects on the weather are so muted that other astronomical bodies would be expected to exert absolutely no influence at all. Correlations between the positions of the planets and radio transmissions were introduced in Chapter 2, and they are admittedly controversial. Now we must ask whether the planets can affect weather, too. Meteors must also come under scrutiny, for it is conceivable that sudden influxes of meteoric dust could trigger storms that would never otherwise have formed. In short, whatever orthodox science may say, we should not close our minds to the possibility of extraterrestrial influences on weather. Only 100 years ago, the foremost scientists declared with great certainty that the effects of the sun on weather were absolutely nil and that all who thought otherwise were fools!

SUNSPOTS AND THUNDERSTORMS

A century ago, "sunspottery" was the derogatory term applied to the urge to correlate just about all terrestrial phenomena to the sunspot cycle. Sunspottery was a joke to most serious scientists, and papers such as one by the German meteorologist Von Bezold were laughed off the scientific stage. The following description of Von Bezold's findings is from a digest in the *American Journal of Science:* "In years when the temperature is high and the sun's surface relatively free from spots, thunderstorms are abundant. Since, moreover, the maxima of the sunspots coincide with the greatest intensity of auroral displays, it follows that both groups of phenomena, thunderstorms and auroras, to a certain extent supplement each other so that years of frequent storms correspond to those of auroras and vice versa. He [Von Bezold] observes that such a connection between sunspots and storms does not by any means sanction the supposition of a direct electrical interaction between the earth and sun, but may be simply a consequence of a degree of insolation dependent upon sunspots" (*American Journal of Science,* 3: 9: 408–9, 1875).

It is most interesting that Von Bezold felt impelled to discount the possibility of a direct electrical connection between sun and earth and thus bowed at least in part to scientific dogma of the day. It was obvious to all that earth and sun were separated by 93,000,000 miles of near-perfect vacuum. Yet the correlations between solar activity, as measured by sunspot frequency, became more and more emphatic as scientific observation improved. In *Nature,* in 1974, M. F. Stringfellow published the accompanying correlation between sunspot numbers and lightning inci-

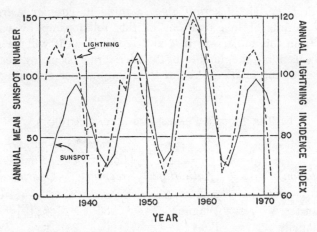

The frequency of lightning correlated with sunspot number

dence and began with this sentence. "The existence of a correlation between solar activity and meteorological or climatological parameters seems no longer in doubt." The mechanism that modern scientists believe ties sun and earth together is just that direct electrical connection that Von Bezold sought to avoid: the solar wind of electrons and protons that waxes and wanes with the solar cycle.

"Many atmospheric scientists believe that the earth's ambient field, usually about 100 to 200 volts per meter, plays a key role in creating more intense electric fields, which can build up to such proportions that huge discharges of electricity, [in the form of] lightning, are provoked. The researchers inferred the solar flare-related increase in thunderstorm activity from a threefold increase in recorded numbers of very low-frequency 'whistlers' during that time" (*Science News*, 111: 389, 1977). Whistlers are radio signals created by lightning discharges.

THE MOON'S EFFECT ON THUNDERSTORM FREQUENCY

When spacecraft discovered the solar wind impinging upon the earth's upper atmosphere, there was at last a physical link between earth and sun that could account for a solar effect on thunderstorms. But weather records kept over long periods of time also suggested a connection between thunderstorm frequency and lunar phases. The renowned American astronomer W. H. Pickering summarized some of these data in 1903.

"Evidence of a connection between the occurrence of thunderstorms and the moon's age has been referred to in *Nature* on several occasions. Prof. W. H. Pickering gives a table in *Popular Astronomy* to show the results of investigations of this relationship by various observers. From this table, which is abridged below, it will be seen that, with one exception, the number of thunderstorms occurring near the first two phases of the moon is greater than the number occurring near the last two.

THE MOON'S PHASES AND THUNDERSTORMS

Station	Authority	Years [Length of record]	New and First Quarter	Full and Last Quarter
Kremsmünster	Wagner	86	54 [%]	46 [%]
Aix-la-Chapelle	Pohs	60	54	46
Batavia, Java	Van d. Stok	9	52	48
Gotha [East Germany]	Lendicke	9	73	27
Germany	Koppen	5	56	44
Glatz County	Richter	8	62	38
North America	Hazen	1	57	43
Prague	Gruss	20	51	49
"	"	20	53	47
Göttingen	Meyer	24	54	46
Greenwich [England]	MacDowall	13	54	46
Madrid	Ventatasta	20	52	48
Providence, R.I.	Seagrave	6	49	51

"Prof. Pickering adds: 'The number of observations here collected seems to be large enough to enable us to draw definite conclusions, without fear that further records will revise or neutralise them. From these observations we conclude that there really is a greater number of thunderstorms during the first half of the lunar month than during the last half, also that the liability to storms is greatest between new moon and the first quarter, and least between full moon and last quarter. Also we may add that while theoretically very interesting, the difference is not large enough to be of any practical consequence. Thus it would seem that, besides the tides and certain magnetic disturbances, there is a third influence that we must in future attribute to the moon'" (*Nature*, 68: 232, 1903).

Like sunspottery, the notion of lunar influences on terrestrial activity was generally ridiculed. Pickering had suggested a *third* force beyond gravity and magnetism—but what could such a force be? Again, additional clues had to wait until spacecraft carried instruments beyond the earth's protective atmosphere. The moon, it seems, may interact with the earth's magnetic tail and thus modulate the solar wind, as postulated by Mae DeVoe Lethbridge in a more recent study of the lunar effect.

"*Abstract*. Using the superposed-epoch method, we statistically analyzed thunderstorm frequencies for 108 stations in the eastern and central United States in relation to lunar positions for the years 1930–33 and 1942–65. The results are as follows. With full moon as the key day, a peak in thunderstorm frequency occurs for 1953–63 two days after full moon, the mean being 2.7 above average level. This mean frequency is 4.8 above the mean when computed only for the full moons as key days that have a declination of 17° north or more. We suggest that these increases near full moon may be related to the earth's magnetic tail and the neutral sheet" (*Journal of Geophysical Research*, 75: 5149, 1970).

THE MOON AND WEATHER

> When the moon lies on her back
> Then the sou'-west wind will crack,
> When she rises up and nods
> Then north-easters dry the sods.

The literature of all nations abounds with references to the moon's influence upon general weather patterns, not merely the thunderstorms mentioned earlier. The scientific literature, too, delves into this purported correlation. Many studies were published toward the end of the last century; and then interest withered as the supposed lunar-terrestrial influences were lumped with astrology and pseudoscience. A century later, however, interest has revived. First, though, let us examine an overview of the moon-weather problem by a nineteenth-century scientist, John Allan Broun. Broun, like most scientists of his day was still fighting superstition, astrology, and established religious notions about the physical world.

"The popular beliefs in the moon's influence on the weather are first disposed of; they are conclusions from unrecorded observations where the coincidences are remembered and the oppositions are forgotten; and they are opposed to strict deductions when all the facts are employed.

"Agreeing, as all men of science do, with this decision, the question remains [as to] whether the moon may not have some slight effect in producing meteorological variations? She reflects, absorbs, and radiates the solar heat; may this heat, in accordance with the thesis, not produce some effect on our atmosphere?

"Sir John Herschel had observed the tendency to [the] disappearance of clouds under the full moon; this he considered a fact which might be explained by the absorption of the radiated lunar heat in the upper strata of our atmosphere. He cited Humboldt's statement as to the fact being well known to pilots and seamen of Spanish America. I may add the testimony of Bernardin de St. Pierre, who, in his 'Voyage à l' Île de Réunion,' says: 'I remarked constantly that the rising of the moon dissipated the clouds in a marked way. Two hours after rising, the sky is perfectly clear' ('Avril, 1768'). Herschel also cited in favour of his 'meteorological fact,' a result supported by the authority of Arago, that rather more rain falls near new than near full moon.

"Arago's conclusion that the phenomenon was 'incontestable of a connection existing between the number of rainy days and the phases of the moon' was founded on the observations of Schubler, of Bouvard and of Eisenlohr, three series which, on the whole, confirmed each other. Schubler also, as Arago showed, had found that the *quantity* of rain which fell was greater near new than near full moon. These results, accepted by Arago, have not been noticed by M. Faye when he cites Herschel only, as one of those 'men of science who interest themselves in popular prejudices, take bravely their defence in hand, and exert themselves to furnish not facts but arguments in their favour.' It seems, indeed, to have been forgotten that Herschel's argument was given to explain what he considered a meteorological fact.

"M. Faye founds his argument wholly on the conclusions of M. Schiaparelli from a weather register kept at Vigevano by Dr. Serafini during thirty-eight years (1827–64). The Italian physician entered the weather as clear, cloudy, or mixed (*misti*), or rainy from morning to evening. M. Schiaparelli finds from this register that the sky was clearest in the first quarter of the moon. It has not been remarked that if the moon's heat has any effect in dissipating clouds, as Herschel and others believed, this must be seen best when the moon is near full—that is to say, during the night hours, for which Dr. Serafini's register has nothing to say. In confirmation of the conclusion that the moon does not dissipate the clouds, another result from the Vigevano weather register is cited—namely, that the greatest number of rainy days happens near full moon. This result is opposed to that derived from the observations of Schubler, Bouvard, and Eisenlohr.

"The value to be given to observations of the number of rainy days must evidently depend on whether the observations include the rainy nights; and an investigation on this question, to have any considerable weight, should depend rather on the measured rainfall than on the term 'rainy day,' for which no distinct definition is given.

"The great objection to M. Faye's conclusions, as far as the facts go, is to be found in their entire dependence on the Vigevano weather register (*da máne à sera*). No notice is taken of other observations and results showing a lunar action on our atmosphere, such as those already mentioned, which Arago considered incontestable, those of Madler and Kreil, and the more recent investigations of Mr. Park Harrison and Prof. Balfour Stewart. All of these, and many others, must be carefully considered before we can accept the conclusion that the moon has no influence on our atmosphere. The subject is, however, too large to be entered into here at present, and it will be possible to study it better after other conclusions of the learned French Academician have been examined.

"There is, however, a part of the argument, whatever the results obtained may say, which merits particular consideration; and that is, that the moon's *heat* cannot produce the phenomena in question. M. Faye shows that if the moon's reflected heat is in the same proportion as the reflected light, such heat cannot produce a change of temperature of a thousandth of a degree Fahrenheit. I would remark that Lord Rosse's carefully-made experiments with the most delicate apparatus have shown for the total heat radiated and reflected, nearly ten times the proportion given by the reflected light; but, as M. Faye observes, if the proportion were increased a hundredfold the effect would still be insensible. 'How then,' it is added, 'can we expect such an action to dissipate the clouds when that of the sun does not always succeed?'

"If, however, we can establish that real lunar actions exist which cannot be explained by the moon's heat reflected or radiated, the only

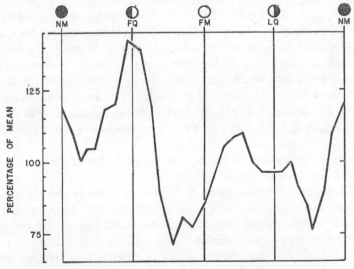

The frequency of depressions in the Indian Ocean seems related to lunar phase.

philosophical conclusion will be that the moon must act in some other way, which it will be in the interests of science to seek out" (*Nature*, 18: 126–27, 1878).

Modern analysis of weather records demonstrates very clearly the lunar effect on precipitation. The recent curves, in fact, are almost carbon copies of those drawn a century ago. Two such analyses are presented below; the second paper offers a possible physical mechanism to explain the effect.

Using data from the Indian Meteorological Department, T. R. Visvanathan demonstrated how depressions in the Indian Ocean are related to lunar phase. Visvanathan apparently did not know about the nineteenth-century studies.

"It was recently shown that the occurrence of heavy rainfall (10 in. and above in 24 h.) is related to lunar phase. It will be evident that such heavy falls are mostly associated with depressions, some of which intensify into [lesser] cyclones and severe cyclones. A study was therefore undertaken to examine the dates of formation of depressions in the Indian Seas *vis-à-vis* the lunar phase. This communication was prompted by Bradley's article 'Tidal Components in Hurricane Development' and is intended to provide some additional information to support his conclusions.

"The data for this investigation were taken from a publication issued by the Indian Meteorological Department which catalogues depressions formed in the Indian Seas, and gives the date on which the depression stage was reached and its corresponding position.

"The phase of the Moon for each day is given in terms of synodic decimals (hundredths of a synodic month) in the ephemeris by Carpenter. The synodic decimal corresponding to each date was taken from that source and the frequency of formation of depressions corresponding to each synodic decimal was found. Successive ten-unit moving totals of the frequencies were then made, and of the hundred such totals thirty were chosen to correspond to the thirty days of the lunar month. For purposes of comparison the frequencies were expressed as percentages of the mean" (*Nature*, 210: 406–7, 1966).

E. E. Adderley and E. G. Bowen found a similar lunar effect, but they published their finding with some hesitation.

"The influence of the moon in producing tides in the upper atmosphere and the appearance of a lunar component in daily temperature in certain parts of the world are comparatively well known, but the effects are extremely small and difficult to detect. The possibility of a large effect on rainfall first came to our notice in 1960 with the chance reading of a paper by Rodes. Rodes showed what appeared to be a connection between rainfall in the Spanish peninsula and both the declination and the position of apogee and perigee of lunar motion. An investigation was therefore made of the rainfall data in our possession, and it was apparent that it contained a strong lunar component. However, it was also clear that this was connected with the phase of the moon rather than with the parameters used by Rodes.

"At this point a decision was taken not to publish the data immediately but to reserve it for a later date. The reason for doing so was that our work on singularities in rainfall was still being treated with disbelief in meteorological circles, and to suggest a lunar effect on rainfall would simply not have met with the right response.

"We were not surprised, therefore, when we received a com-

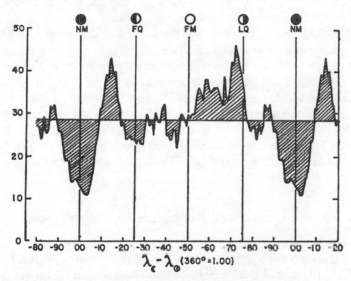

New Zealand rainfall plotted against lunar phase

munication from Bradley, Woodbury, and Brier indicating a pronounced lunar effect in U.S. rainfall. The effect is matched by similar effects in the Southern Hemisphere. A curve showing the heaviest falls of the month for 50 stations in New Zealand, plotted in the same way as the U.S. data are plotted, is given in [the accompanying illustration]. It shows variations of a magnitude comparable with those in the U.S. and closely related in phase.

"It should not be assumed from this that a lunar component will be found in all rainfall records. It is already apparent that there are distinct variations in harmonic content of the curves with geography and, in addition, some shifts of phase. But the effect is sufficiently widespread in the land masses of the Southern Hemisphere to warrant further investigation.

"It is not yet possible to advance a physical explanation of the phenomenon, but it is clearly not incompatible with the meteor hypothesis. Meteoritic dust reaching the earth is known to be distributed in orbits, the majority of which are in the plane of the ecliptic. The moon's orbit is also close to the ecliptic, and as the moon revolves around the earth, it could impose a lunar modulation on the amount of dust reaching the earth. However, a calculation of the magnitude of such an effect shows that it is unlikely that gravitational forces alone could produce a variation in rainfall as large as that shown by the accompanying curves. It may therefore be necessary to look for some other explanation for the phenomenon" (*Science*, 137: 749–50, 1962, copyright 1962 by the American Association for the Advancement of Science).

It should be emphasized that the two foregoing reports are selected from among dozens of recent analyses. Once again, spacecraft have been largely responsible for the renaissance of interest in lunar-terrestrial connections. They have shown that space is far from being a vacuum and that the electrically charged particles and meteorites (possibly electrically charged too) that course through the solar system are affecting solar activity, the earth's magnetic field, and the motion of the moon. The phenomenon of lunar modulation of terrestrial weather is not fully explained, but it is no longer relegated to the realm of pseudoscience.

OTHER SUPPOSED EXTRATERRESTRIAL INFLUENCES ON WEATHER

Meteor showers, comets, and the positions of the planets have also been connected with weather fluctuations. Is there any reason to believe that these purported extraterrestrial influences would be any more palatable to scientists? As a matter of fact, the micrometeoroids that float down through the atmosphere in immense numbers have long been considered as likely condensation nuclei. There was no uproar in 1956 when E. G. Bowen published a paper relating rainfall with meteor shower activity. Bowen made no claims smacking of astrology. The following quotation is from his abstract:

"Examination of rainfall figures for a large number of stations shows that there is a tendency for more rain to fall on certain calendar dates than on others. There is a close correspondence between the dates of the rainfall maxima in both the northern and southern hemispheres, and this is difficult to explain on a climatological basis. The effect might, however, be due to an extraterrestrial influence.

"The rainfall peaks occur approximately 30 days after prominent meteor showers, and it is suggested that they are due to the nucleating effect of meteoritic dust falling into cloud systems in the lower atmosphere, the time difference being accounted for by the rate of fall of the material through the atmosphere.

"The hypothesis is tested for a particular meteor stream, the Bielids, which is known to have a 6.5-year period. The rainfall 30 days after the meteor shower is found to have a similar period. Furthermore, the phase of the rainfall periodicity is almost identical with that of the meteor shower" (*Journal of Meteorology*, 13: 142–51, 1956).

Large influxes of cosmic dust might be associated with comets. If the earth happened to pass through the tail of a comet, one might not be unduly surprised to find an enhancement of rainfall. Only a few studies have been made along this line.

No one has claimed that the positions of the planets can actually affect the influx of meteors and thus modulate terrestrial weather, but some correlations between the two have been published. We know of no physical force that might encourage such a correlation; but then the solar wind was unsuspected a century ago—even 30 years ago. It is significant though that some scientists acknowledge the reality of the correlation between planetary positions and the sunspot cycle. The scientific literature contains dozens, perhaps a hundred, serious comparisons of planetary motions with the waxing and waning of solar activity. There seems to be a definite correlation, but no one can even guess at the physical reason for such a relationship, assuming it is real. Tidal forces due to gravity seem far too small to affect the sun. Electromagnetic forces seem to be ruled out too. Is there a third, undiscovered force? Strangely enough, this is the very same question that investigators asked themselves a hundred years ago when lunar phase and solar activity were first associated with weather. It is fitting that the question be posed again at this juncture because weather is now definitely known to be affected by solar activity; and if solar activity is in turn correlated with planetary positions, then weather is also related, at least statistically, with planetary positions. There may be no third force permeating the solar system, but it is also apparent that many subtle relationships exist among the members of the sun's family of planets.

4

FALLING MATERIAL

Anomalous rain, snow, and hail—colored and plain—are treated in Chapter 3. Beyond these nearly normal forms of precipitation are those falling materials that do not belong aloft at all: large ice chunks, living animals, nonmeteoric stones, and many other nominally terrestrial materials. Charles Fort made much of falling materials, even though most of them can be explained rationally by appealing to recognized meteorological mechanisms—i.e., waterspouts, whirlwinds, etc. Fort had a point; the minority of falling material not succumbing to conventional explanations requires truly revolutionary explanations. Such is the claim for residual anomalies in all areas of science—and this claim is perfectly valid in this chapter.

Where would anomalous falling material come from? Fort, in his customary tongue-in-cheek way, postulated that near space was full of debris that occasionally fell to earth and was replenished by unspecified levitating mechanisms. A half century later, we have found that space is not as empty as we had supposed. In addition, terrestrial catastrophes (meteor strikes, for example) are now recognized as possible ways in which terrestrial (and lunar) materials can be ejected into near space. Other mechanisms may exist. Perhaps violent storms create conduits between earth and space, transporting dust, lightweight debris, even bacteria and simple life forms. We do know that some violent thunderstorms and tornados reach far into the ionosphere. The atmosphere and magnetosphere, once believed to shield the earth's surface from space "weather," seem to have holes in them permitting a modicum of two-way traffic.

Falls of Living Animals

"Of course a waterspout or whirlwind deposited them," is the common response to news of a fish fall. No one can deny the possibility, even likelihood, of such a meteorological explanation after seeing the tornado of *The Wizard of Oz*. But the venerable waterspout and whirlwind must possess some unusual refinements if it is to account for all of the facts concerning animal falls.

To begin, there exist many well-documented fish, frog, and animal falls—no one seriously denies that they do take place. The stranger aspects of these falls appear only after reviewing many reports. First, the transporting mechanism (whatever it may be) tends to select only a single species of fish or frog, or whatever animal is on the menu for that day. Second, size selection is also carefully controlled in many instances. Third, no debris, such as sand or plant material, is dropped along with the animals. Fourth, even though saltwater species are dropped, there are no records of the accompanying rainfalls being salty. All in all, the mechanism involved is rather fastidious in what it transports. The waterspout or whirlwind theory is easiest to swallow when the fish that fall commonly shoal on the surface in large numbers in nearby waters. It is much harder to fit the facts when the fish are from deep waters, when the fish are dead and dry (sometimes headless), and when other animals fall in immense numbers.

A final feature of animal falls hints ever so slightly that some falls (certainly not *all*) may come from very high altitudes. This feature is the "footprint" or pattern of the fall, which is usually rather small (a few hundred feet long) and highly elliptical. Bunched objects in outer space or in the very high atmosphere that enter the lower atmosphere land in just this kind of pattern.

FISH

Over a span of several decades, E. W. Gudger, a scientist at the American Museum of Natural History, collected reports of fish falls. As of 1946, he had assembled 78 reports from all manner of observers, including many scientists. When Bergen Evans, a noted debunker of scientific anomalies, asserted that all fish falls were merely myths, Gudger responded vigorously with a formidable array of evidence supporting the reality of fish falls and the reliability of the observers.

"Most of the nonscientific observers and some of the scientists had no knowledge of what other men in their own lands and especially in foreign countries had seen and written about. Some of the observers had seen the fish while falling, some had been struck by the fishes, and some had eaten of the freshly fallen fishes. The mass of evidence is as prodigious in volume as it is widespread in time and space. To disregard all this evidence, ranging from hearsay to scientifically attested, and to brand as 'credulous' all those who, from personal observation or after much study of published accounts, accept much of it as credible, seems . . . to indicate a refusal to consider the evidence offered or an inability to evaluate it" (*Science*, 103: 693–94, 1946).

A representative report of a fish fall from the older literature is that of John Lewis, a sawyer:

"On Wednesday, February 9 [1859], I was getting out a piece of timber, for the purpose of setting it for the saw, when I was startled by something falling all over me—down my neck, on my head, and on my back. On putting my hand down my neck I was surprised to find they were little fish. By this time I saw the whole ground covered with them. I took off my hat, the brim of which was full of them. They were jumping all about. They covered the ground in a long strip of about 80 yards by 12, as we measured afterwards. That shed (pointing to a very large workshop) was covered with them, and the shoots were quite full of them. My mates and I might have gathered bucketsful of them, scraping with our hands. We did gather a great many, about a bucketful, and threw them into the rain pool, where some of them now are. There were two showers, with an interval of about 10 minutes, and each shower lasted about two minutes or thereabout. The time was 11 A.M. The morning up-train [northbound train] to Aberdare was just then passing. It was not blowing very hard, but uncommonly wet, just about the same wind as there is to-day (blowing rather stiff,) and it came from this quarter (pointing to the S. of W.). They came down with the rain in 'a body like'" (*Annual Register*, 101: 14–15, 1859). The oblong strip of fallen fish is typical.

On August 24, 1918, a brief rain shower left behind an extensive trail of fish at Hendon, near Sunderland, England. Note that the fish are all of the same species and evidently not fresh.

"In the rear of the storm the ground was 'strewn with thousands of little fishes.' The fall was apparently confined within a very circumscribed area just outside the town of Hendon and about one-quarter of a mile from the sea coast. The fish were of the variety known locally as 'sile,' eel-like things, two to three inches long, which are found in very considerable numbers at this time of the year, both in the river and the sea. The fish were quite stiff when found, and many of them were broken by striking the ground.

"Mr. T. W. Backhouse of West Hendon House has kindly supplied some further information bearing on this shower of fish. He was at his house at the time and did not remark anything unusual in the weather. The shower of fishes took place about three-quarters of a mile to E.S.E. At West Hendon there was a shower of a thundery nature, accompanied by considerable darkness, though thunder was not heard. The rainfall measured in the shower amounted to 0.04 inch, wind West to South-west, not strong. Mr. Backhouse has heard the fish described as sand-eels and that they exist in considerable numbers near the shore. Two men who were sheltering in their allotment huts at the time of the shower picked up handfuls of fish" (*Royal Meteorological Society, Quarterly Journal*, 44: 270, 1918).

An impressive, highly credible, relatively recent fish fall was observed by A. D. Bajkov on October 23, 1947, in Marksville, Louisiana.

"I was conducting biological investigations for the Department of Wild Life and Fisheries. In the morning of that day, between seven and eight o'clock, fish ranging from two to nine inches in length fell on the streets and in yards, mystifying the citizens of that southern town. I was in the restaurant with my wife having breakfast, when the waitress informed us that fish were falling from the sky. We went immediately to collect some of the fish. The people in town were excited. The director of the Marksville Bank, J. M. Barham, said he had discovered upon arising from bed that fish had fallen by hundreds in his yard, and in the adjacent yard of Mrs. J. W. Joffrion. The cashier of the same bank, J. E. Gremillion, and two merchants, E. A. Blanchard and J. M. Brouillette, were struck by falling fish as they walked toward their places of business about 7:45 A.M. There were spots on Main Street, in the vicinity of the bank (a half-block from the restaurant) averaging one fish per square yard. Automobiles and trucks were running over them. Fish also fell on the roofs of houses.

"They were freshwater fish native to local waters, and belonging to the following species: large-mouth black bass (*Micropterus salmoides*), goggle-eye (*Chaenobryttus coronarius*), two species of sunfish (*Lepomis*), several species of minnows, and hickory shad (*Pomolobus mediocris*). The latter species were the most common. I personally collected from Main Street and several yards on Monroe Street, a large jar of perfect specimens, and preserved them in Formalin, in order to distribute them among various museums. A local citizen who was struck by the fish told me that the fish were frozen; however, the specimens I collected, although cold, were not frozen. There is at least one record, in 1896 at Essen, Germany, of frozen fish falling from the sky. The largest fish in my collection was a large-mouth black bass 9 1/4 inches long. The largest falling fish on record was reported from India and weighed over six pounds.

"The fish that fell in Marksville were absolutely fresh, and were fit for human consumption. The area in which they fell was approximately 1,000 feet long and about 75 or 80 feet wide, extending in a north-southerly direction, and was covered unevenly by fish. The actual falling of the fish occurred in somewhat short intervals, during foggy and comparatively calm weather. The velocity of the wind on the ground did not exceed eight miles per hour. The New Orleans weather bureau had no report of any large tornado, or updrift, in the vicinity of Marksville at that time. However, James Nelson Gowanloen, chief biologist for the Louisiana Department of Wild Life and Fisheries, and I had noticed the presence of numerous small tornados, or 'devil dusters,' the day before the 'rain of fish' in Marksville. Fish rains have nearly always been described as being accompanied by violent thunderstorms and heavy rains. This, however, was not the case in Marksville" (*Science*, 109: 402, 1949).

Reading the above report by Bajkov, Major J. Hedgepath was inspired to submit the following note to the editor of *Science:* "While stationed on the island of Guam in September 1936, I witnessed a brief rainfall of fish, one of the specimens of which was identified as the tench (*Tinca tinca*) which, to my knowledge, is common only to the fresh waters of Europe. The presence of this species at a locale so remote from its normal habitat is worthy of note" (*Science*, 110: 482, 1949). *Note:* The tench is also known in freshwater habitats of western Asia.

In summary, fish do fall from the sky and sometimes under mysterious circumstances—i.e., the absence of vortex disturbances, the presence of far-from-home species, corpses in an unfresh condition, and so on. The whirlwind theory may be overly simplistic.

FROGS AND TOADS

Next to fish, amphibians are the most likely animals to fall from the sky. Heavy rain usually accompanies such falls, as in this report from W. Winter of Aldeby, England. It was July 1859. "I was out insect-catching by the side of the river Waveney, about a quarter-past 9 on Friday night, when a thunder-storm came on. I ran for shelter to the buildings at Aldeby Hall. The rain came down in torrents. Just before I was clear of the fens, I observed some small toads on my arms, and several fell in my net, and on the ground and paths there were thousands. I am quite sure there were none in my net before I started, as I took a *Leucania pudorina* out of it. I believe they fell with the rain out of the clouds. Can you enlighten me on the subject? Two other persons have told me that they met with the same occurrence some distance from the spot in which I was situated" (*Zoologist,* 18: 7146, 1859).

On the afternoon of June 16, 1939, large numbers of small frogs fell on Trowbridge, England. "Mr. E. Ettles, superintendent of the municipal swimming pool stated that about 4:30 P.M. he was caught in a heavy shower of rain and, while hurrying to shelter, heard behind him a sound as of the falling of lumps of mud. Turning, he was amazed to see hundreds of tiny frogs falling on the concrete path around the bath. Later, many more were found to have fallen on the grass nearby" (*Meteorological Magazine,* 74: 184–85, 1939). Even in the most likely marshy spots, one does not find such immense numbers of frogs—and what happened to the plant debris and other denizens of froggy places?

As if hundreds of frogs are not difficult enough to explain, millions were reported to have belched forth from a cloud near Gibraltar on May 25, 1915 (*Nature,* 95: 378, 1915).

A final amphibian observation brings home another peculiar feature of such falls: their selectivity. Joseph Fairhall, Jr., recalls a heavy rainstorm on a hot summer's day in 1890. "I was in the midst of this walking across a bare tract of land of about 160 acres, which was at least a mile from the nearest water; and I noticed as soon as the rain was over that the ground all around me for some distance was literally covered with small sun fish about 1 to 1 1/2 inches long and small frogs at 3/4 to 1 inch long and that these were as full of life as if they had just come out of the water" (*Scientific American,* 117: 271, 1917). How could a whirlwind or waterspout pluck just these two different species and nothing else from a body of water, especially when sun fish and frogs do not usually mingle in nature?

SNAILS AND SHELLFISH

Falls of snails have been reported several times in the older literature. However, scientific investigation of these claims has generally weakened them. Snails, it appears, may appear under perfectly normal circumstances in incredible numbers at certain times of the year. The representative report that follows, the reader will note, does not seem as airtight as the preceding "fish stories." A. H. Jenkin submitted this item to G. J. Symons. "Having heard that a fall of snail shells had taken place a few miles from here [somewhere in England], I visited the place and found from a man who lived on the spot that at about 9 P.M., just as it was nearly dark, what appeared to be a very black thundercloud rose from the west, and he went in for shelter. Next morning, on going to work, the roads, fields, and stone hedges were plentifully strewn with small living snail shells, the fall extending over about three acres of land, but beyond these limits no shells were to be found." Jenkin interviewed people and learned that the snails had never been seen in the locality before and that many believed they must have fallen from the sky during the storm (*Symons's Monthly Meteorological Magazine,* 21: 101–2, 1886). Manifestly, since no one saw the snails fall, they may have emerged *en masse* after the storm.

Less circumstantial is the following report reprinted from *Das Wetter.* On August 9, 1892, Paderhorn, in Germany, experienced a heavy thunderstorm, "in which a number of living pond mussels were mixed with rain. The observer who is in connection with the Berlin Meteorological Office sent a detailed account of the strange occurrence, and a specimen was forwarded to the Museum at Berlin, which stated that it was the *Anodonta anatina.* A yellowish cloud attracted the attention of several people, both from its colour and the rapidity of its motion, when suddenly it burst, a torrential rain fell with a rattling sound, and immediately afterward the pavement was found to be covered with hundreds of the mussels. Further details will be published in the reports of the Berlin Office, but the only possible explanation seems to be that the water of a river in the neighbourhood was drawn up by a passing tornado, and afterward deposited its living burden at the place in question" (*Nature,* 47: 278, 1893). No sand or other debris typical of the pond-mussel habitat were noted.

"Mr. John Ford exhibited to the Conchological Section, Academy of Natural Sciences, Philadelphia, specimens of *Gemma gemma,* remarkable as having fallen, accompanied by rain, in a storm which occurred at Chester, Pennsylvania, on the afternoon of June 6, 1869. The specimens were perfect, but very minute, measuring one-eighth inch in length by three-sixteenths of an inch in breadth. Though most of the specimens which fell were broken, yet many perfect ones were collected in various places, sheltered from the heavy rain which followed their descent. A witness of the storm, Mr. Y. S. Walter, editor of the Delaware County *Republican,* assured Mr. F. that he noticed the singular character of the storm at its very commencement, and, to use his own words, 'it seemed like a storm within a storm.' A very fine rain fell rapidly, veiled by the shells which fell slower and with a whirling motion" (*Scientific American,* 22: 386, 1870). In contrast with the preceding snail-fall account, this one has more substance.

WORMS AND CATERPILLARS

This charming report is from Riga, Latvia, dated June 14, 1819. "An event not unparalleled indeed, but very rare, has lately occurred here.

During a strong northwest wind, an immense quantity of young caterpillars fell upon the great meadows on the south bank of the Duna and
devoured the grass, with the roots, upon a very extensive tract. As soon
as this was perceived, the people employed all the means they could
think of to destroy them; they dug ditches, swept the insects together in
heaps, and crushed them, &c., but without much diminishing their numbers. On the fourth day they crept into the earth and changed into
chrysalisses, so that we have the bad prospect of seeing them return as
butterflies and propagate their species among us" (*Niles' Weekly Register*, 17: 15, September 4, 1819).

The account of a worm fall which follows also bears the marks of
age and the lack of scientific investigation. Who can attach the labels
"false" and "true" to such incomplete data?

"A letter from Bucharest, given in the Levant *Times*, reports a curious atmospheric phenomenon which occurred there on the 25th of July,
at a quarter past nine in the evening. During the day the heat was
stifling, and the sky cloudless. Towards nine o'clock a small cloud appeared on the horizon, and a quarter of an hour afterwards rain began to
fall, when, to the horror of everybody, it was found to consist of black
worms [each] of the size of an ordinary fly. All the streets were strewn
with these curious animals. It is to be hoped that some were preserved
and will be examined by a competent naturalist" (*Nature*, 6: 356, 1872).

SNAKES

On December 15, 1876, there was a report from Memphis, Tennessee, of a rain of live snakes. "Thousands of little reptiles, ranging from a
foot to eighteen inches in length, were distributed all over the southern
part of the city. They probably were carried aloft by a hurricane and
wafted through the atmosphere for a long distance; but in what locality
snakes exist in such abundance is yet a mystery" (*Scientific American*,
36: 86, 1877).

Supplementing the above note, we have the Memphis weather observer's report: "Morning opened with light rain; [at] 10:20 A.M. [it]
began to pour down in torrents, lasting fifteen minutes, wind SW.; immediately after, the reptiles were discovered crawling on the sidewalks, in
the road, gutters, and yards of Vance street, between Landerdale and
Goslee streets, two blocks; careful inquiry was made to ascertain if anyone had seen them descend, but without success; neither were they to be
found in the cisterns, on roofs, or any elevations above the ground. . . . I
have heard of none being found elsewhere; when first seen they were a
very dark brown, almost black; [they] were very thick in some places,

being tangled together like a mass of thread or yarn" (*Monthly Weather Review*, 5: 8, 1877).

Once more, the animals were not seen to fall, leaving open the likelihood that the heavy rain caused them to emerge from subterranean hiding places. The large numbers, however, are hard to explain with any theory.

BIRDS

Birds seem to have mastery of the air, so it is definitely unusual when they fall out of the sky. An Associated Press dispatch from Shreveport, Louisiana, on March 20, 1940, relates that "blackbirds by the hundreds dropped dead from the sky at Barksdale Field. They cluttered the army airbase so thickly that its police were called out to clear the ground. A soldier said large flocks of birds broke flight suddenly and plopped to the ground. Some of the dead birds were taken to the post hospital, where surgeons began autopsies."

A better-researched bird fall transpired on January 3, 1978, when 136 pink-footed geese fell dead out of the clouds in the county of Norfolk, England. The track of dead birds was 45 km. in length, oriented on a WNW.–ESE. line. It was reported that "105 of the pink-feet fell near Wicken Farm, Castleacre; two more fell into a garden at Meadowcroft, Washbridge, Dereham; fourteen were found alongside the post office at Wendling; another was found on the grounds of Gressenhall Museum; ten were found by Mr. Lesli Money on a meadow mid-way between Hethersett Lake and Thickthorn Lake (they lay in a line about 150 metres long); three were found at Carleton Forehoe; and one more at Swardeston. In addition, one bean goose [*Anser fabalis*] was picked up at Lodge Farm, Gressenhall." Several autopsies showed no signs of lightning or any shotgun pellets. The lungs of some, however, contained clotted blood and other signs of internal hemorrhaging. Livers were ruptured in some. At the time of the fall, a tornado-bearing cold front was advancing across the region. It was surmised that the storm carried a flock to such great heights that their lungs hemorrhaged, causing them to fall dead over a long strip of territory (*Journal of Meteorology, U.K.*, 4: 77–78, 1979).

Miscellaneous Organic Substances

Tornados and whirlwinds operate like vacuum cleaners. They suck up loose materials, carry them for miles, and then deposit them on amazed countryfolk. This method of transportation is analogous to that of fish by waterspouts. Very likely there is much truth in both hypotheses. However, the remarks made in the section on fish falls about peculiar patterns of object selection and dispersal also apply here.

Hay is probably the most common material transported by whirlwinds. Indeed, few farmers have not seen small whirlwinds capriciously depositing their cut hay on telephone wires on hot summer afternoons. With such a well-recognized method of levitation and deposition, the emphasis in this section must be on stranger materials and transporting mechanisms.

Ordinary wind is the transporting mechanism in the case of airborne cobwebs, which most investigations suggest are merely the products of bona fide spiders. The reason for introducing this seemingly tractable problem involves the question of "angel hair." Angel hair consists of wispy strands of material sometimes reported in the vicinities of UFO sightings. Scientific periodicals rarely deal with the angel-hair situation, but a few curious "cobweb" phenomena have been recorded. Particularly puzzling is the apparent disappearance of some cobwebs when held in the hand. This is reminiscent of angel-hair stories.

Finally, we have "manna from heaven." Like many tales of falling material, manna turns out to be a purely earthbound phenomenon. Humans, it seems, have a strong urge to assign the mysterious appearance of something to heavenly sources.

HAY FALLS

Since hay falls are so prosaic, two accounts will suffice. The first is what might be called a classic example of this engaging phenomenon. The place was Monkstown, near Dublin; the time, July 27, 1875; the reporter, J. Hawtrey Benson:

"About half-past nine o'clock this morning, as I was standing at a window facing the east, in Monkstown, my attention was called by the Rev. T. Power to a number of dark flocculent bodies floating slowly down through the air from a great height, appearing as if falling from a very heavy, dark cloud, which hung over the house. On going to the hall door, a vast number of these bodies were discerned falling on all sides, near and far, to as great a distance as their size permitted them to be seen—over an area whose radius was probably between a quarter and half a mile. Presently, several of these flocks fell close to my feet. On picking up one, it was found to be a small portion of new hay, of which I enclose a sample. When it fell it was as wet as if a very heavy dew had been deposited on it. The duration of this phenomenon, from the time my attention was first called to it till it had entirely ceased, was about 5 minutes, but how long it may have been proceeding before this I cannot tell.

"The flocks of hay, from their loose, open structure, made a large appearance for their weight, but the average weight of the larger flocks was probably not more than one or two ounces, and, from that, all sizes were perceptible down to a single blade. There was no rain from the dark cloud overhead, though it had a particularly threatening appearance at the moment of observation. The air was very calm, with a gentle under-current from S.E. The clouds were moving in an upper-current from S.S.W." (*Symons's Monthly Meteorological Magazine*, 10: 111–12, 1875).

The second instance is significant because of the highly localized nature of the transporting mechanism and the long period of time the hay was suspended in the atmosphere. How high was the hay carried, and what kept it from falling to the ground immediately? The report is by Francis Galton, a resident of Shropshire, England. "We had a curious sight from this house yesterday [July 26]. It was a dead calm, but in a field just below the garden, with only one hedge between us and it, the hay was whirled up high into the sky, a column connecting above and below, and in the course of the evening we found great patches of hay raining down all over the surrounding meadows and our garden. It kept falling quite four hours after the affair. There was not a breath of air stirring as far as we could see, except in that one spot" (*Nature*, 44: 294, 1881).

UNUSUAL FLIGHTS OF LEAVES

Surely wind-blown leaves cannot be unusual. They *can* if they have been carried many miles, in immense quantities, and especially if they are from the same species of tree. One of the strangest flights of leaves occurred in October 1889, in Dumfriesshire, Scotland, as reported by James Shaw. "I was struck by a strange appearance in the atmosphere, which I at first mistook for a flock of birds, but as I saw them falling to the earth my curiosity was quickened. Fixing my eyes on one of the larger of them, and running about 100 yards up the hill until directly underneath, I awaited its arrival, when I found it to be *an oak leaf*. Looking upwards the air was thick with them, and as they descended in an almost vertical direction, oscillating and glittering in the sunshine, the spectacle was as beautiful as rare. The wind was from the north, blowing a very gentle breeze, and there were occasional showers of rain.

"On examination of the hills after the leaves had fallen, it was found that they covered a tract of about a mile wide and two miles long. The leaves were wholly those of the oak. No oak trees grow in clumps together nearer than eight miles. The aged shepherd, who has been on the farm since 1826, never witnessed a similar occurrence" (*Nature*, 42: 637, 1890).

T. H. Astbury saw an even more widespread flight of beech leaves in 1900, in England. "At about four o'clock on the afternoon of Sunday last (April 1st), my attention was arrested by the fall of numbers of dried beech leaves. On looking up I found that the leaves were passing in large numbers from east to west, and as high as the limit of vision. Many appeared to be mere specks, whose height and motion promised them a journey of some miles at least. The shower continued for perhaps twenty minutes. The fall was noticed by many persons here, who were unable to account for it, as there are no beech trees within two miles at nearest." The same flight was observed three miles away (*Knowledge*, 23: 109–10, 1900).

SEAWEED FROM THE SKY

Seaweed, being a shallow-water plant, would seem less accessible to whirlwind levitation than hay and leaves. Nonetheless, seaweed falls are known, though rare. A notable example occurred in Fifeshire, Scotland, in 1879. "A discovery, startling and unusual, was made on Sunday in the Lomond Hills, near Falkland, which has since given rise to considerable speculation. The hills were found in several places to be covered with seaweed, or some substance as nearly resembling it as possible, and it was also seen hanging from the trees and shrubberies in the district. In some places the weed lay in a pretty thick coating, so that quantities of it could be collected from the grass. A heavy hailstorm, accompanied by T and L [thunder and lightning], passed over the district on Saturday evening (Aug. 30th), and it is thought that at a late hour a waterspout had burst over the hills. Many people have collected pieces of the weed for preservation" (*Symons's Monthly Meteorological Magazine*, 14: 136, 1879).

FEATHER FALLS

Feather falls seem unlikely to say the least. A single feather or even several would not stretch credibility, but when feathers fill the air like snow, one must look at the tale closely. In a report to the *Zoologist*, a Captain Blakiston recounted a strange story. "While we were in that land of water-fowl below Cumberland, I witnessed a shower of feathers; as we sailed up a reach of the river with a fresh breeze, without the knowledge of a human being within many miles of us, it appeared to be snowing; this was nothing more than small feathers, and we supposed that at some Indian camp in the swamps to windward the operation of goose-plucking must be going on; these feathers had likely travelled many miles, and would continue while the breeze lasts" (*Zoologist,* 17: 6442–43, 1859).

COBWEB STORMS

Naturalists have long recognized that some species of spiders migrate by casting a strand of cobweb into a breeze and hanging on while the wind carries it aloft. On occasion, floating cobwebs may descend in incredible quantities, as in the October 1881 "rain" at Milwaukee, Wisconsin. "The webs seemed to come from 'over the lake,' and appeared to fall from a great height. The strands were from two feet to several rods in length. At Green Bay the fall was the same, coming from the direction of the bay, only the webs varied from sixty feet in length to mere specks, and were seen as far up in the air as the power of the eye could reach. At Vesburg and Fort Howard, Sheboygan, and Ozaukee, the fall was similarly observed, in some places being so thick as to annoy the eye. In all instances the webs were strong in texture and very white.

"Curiously there is no mention, in any of the reports that we have seen, of the presence of spiders in this general shower of webs. It is to be hoped that some competent observer—that is, some one who has made a study of spiders and their habits—was at hand and will report more specifically the conditions of this interesting phenomenon.

"Quite a number of notable gossamer showers have been reported in different parts of the world. White describes several in his history of Selborne. In one of them the fall continued nearly a whole day, the webs coming from such a height that from the top of the highest hill nearby they were seen descending from a region still above the range of distinct vision.

"Darwin describes a similar shower observed by him from the deck of the *Beagle,* off the mouth of [the] La Plata River, when the vessel was sixty miles from land. He was probably the first to notice that each web of the gossamer carried a Lilliputian aeronaut. He watched the spiders on their arrival and saw many of them put forth a new web and float away" (*Scientific American,* 45: 337, 1881).

Under some conditions, the single strands of cobweb agglomerate to form wads and raglike patches of white material. With bright sunlight reflecting from these masses, one might suspect a flight of UFO's. P. Lewis reported a situation of this type from Port Hope, Ontario, on September 26, 1948. "This day was warm and the sky cloudless. We had had dinner in the garden and I was lying on my back on the lawn, my head just in the shade of the house, when I was startled to see an object resembling a star moving rapidly across the sky. The time was 2 o'clock Eastern Standard Time.

"At first it was easy to imagine that recent reports of 'flying saucers' had not been exaggerated.

"More of these objects came sailing into view over the ridge of house, only to disappear when nearly overhead. With field glasses I was able to see that each was approximately spherical, the centre being rather brighter than the edges. The glasses also showed quite a number at such heights that they were invisible to the naked eye.

"With only a gull flying in the sky for comparison, I should estimate the elevation of the lower objects to be about 300 ft. and the higher ones 2,000 ft.; the size was about one foot in diameter and the speed about 50 m.p.h., in a direction SW. to NE.

"Also visible every now and then were long threads, apparently from spiders. Some of these were seen to reflect the light over a length of three or four yards, but any one piece may of course have been longer. Each was more or less horizontal, moving at right angles to its length. In one case an elongated tangled mass of these gave the appearance of a frayed silken cord. These threads appeared only in the lower levels" (*Weather*, 4: 121–22, 1949).

The cobweb matter becomes more bizarre with the following datum from the M.V. *Roxburgh Castle*, moored at Montreal on October 10, 1962. "At 2000 GMT, while the Roxburgh Castle was moored to her berth (Section 24) in Montreal, I was walking round outside my accommodation and noticed fine white filaments of unknown kind hanging around stanchions and topping lift wires of derricks.

"Calling the attention of the Chief Officer, I pulled one of these strands from a stanchion and found it to be quite tough and resilient. I stretched it, but it would not break easily (as, for instance, a cobweb would have done), and after keeping it in my hand for 3 or 4 minutes it disappeared completely; in other words, it just vanished into nothing.

"Looking up, we could see small cocoons of the material floating down from the sky, but as far as we could ascertain there was nothing either above or at street level to account for this extraordinary occurrence.

"Unfortunately I could not manage to preserve samples of the filaments as the disappearance took place so quickly" (*Marine Observer*, 33: 187–88, 1963).

The peculiar features of the Montreal fall are the strength of the webs and their subsequent disappearance. Threadlike material termed "angel hair" has long been associated with UFO reports. Angel hair, it seems, has this same property of dissolving away before the eyes of the finder. So, too, does a gelatinous substance called *pwdre ser,* also associated with luminous phenomena and described later in this chapter. Another point of interest here is that folklore has it that silken threads fall from the sky when the aurora weaves its luminous magic.

MANNA FROM HEAVEN

The Biblical reference to manna falling from the skies to sustain the Israelites leaving Egypt has been explained in several ways—as a lichen, as a product of the tamarisk tree, and as the exudations of insects. Unlike many Biblical tales, the falls of manna persist, giving scientists a chance to confirm one theory over another. In 1890, for example, a heavy shower of manna fell in Turkey. "The rain which accompanied the substance fell over a surface of about ten kilometres in circumference. The inhabitants collected the 'manna' and made it into bread, which is said to have been very good and to have been easily digested. The specimen sent to *La Nature* is composed of small *spherules;* yellowish on the outside, it is white within. Botanists who have examined it say that it belongs to the family of lichens known as *Lecanora esculenta.* According to Decaisne, this lichen, which has been found in Algeria, is most frequently met with on the most arid mountains of Tartary, where it lies among pebbles from which it can be distinguished only by experienced observers. It is also found in the desert of the Kirghizes. The traveller Parrot brought to Europe specimens of a quantity which had fallen in several districts of Persia at the beginning of 1828. He was assured that the ground was covered with the substance to the height of two decimetres, that animals ate it eagerly, and that it was collected by the people. In such cases it was supposed to have been caught up by a waterspout and carried along by the wind" (*Nature,* 43: 255, 1891).

A substantially different picture of the phenomenon was presented in *Nature* in 1929: "There has always existed among scientific workers a wide divergence of opinion as to the true nature and origin of the manna, believed to have fallen from heaven to provide food for the Israelites in the Sinai desert during the Exodus from Egypt. Some authors considered the manna to be a desert lichen, *Lecanora esculenta Nees,* while others connected it with desert shrubs of the genus *Tamarix* and considered it to be either a physiological secretion of the plant or its sap flowing from the wounds caused by insects. In order to solve this problem, the Hebrew University in Jerusalem organised in 1927 a small expedition to the Sinai Peninsula, and the leaders of that expedition, Dr. F. S. Bodenheimer and Dr. O. Theodore, have just published a very interesting account of their investigations.

"The expedition visited some classical localities where manna was recorded. In the course of investigations, it was established beyond doubt that the appearance of manna is a phenomenon well known in other countries under the name of 'honey-dew,' which is a sweet excretion of plant-lice (*Aphidae*) and scale insects (*Coccidae*). Two scale insects mainly responsible for the production of manna were found, namely, *Trabutina mannipara*, occurring in the lowlands, and *Najacoccus serpentinus* . . . , which replaces the former in the mountains. Two other Hemipterous insects, *Escelis decoratus* . . . and *Opsius jucundus* . . . also produce manna, but to a lesser extent. All these insects live on *Tamarix nilotica* . . . ; no manna was observed on other species of *Tamarix*, a fact probably due to some physiological peculiarities of the former. The authors observed the actual excretion by the insects of drops of clear sweet fluid, and proved by experiments that the fluid is ingested by the insects from the vessels of the phloem. When in an experiment a twig bearing the insects was placed in water and the bark was cut below the insects, the production of manna continued in a normal manner, but it stopped as soon as the flow of carbohydrate solution from the leaves was interrupted by cutting off the bark above the insects. The dry desert climate of Sinai causes the syrup-like fluid excretion to crystallise, and the whitish grains thus produced, which cover the branches or fall to the ground underneath them, constitute the true manna of the Bible" (*Nature*, 124: 1003–4, 1929).

Apparently, manna has several sources; at least there is no unanimity in the scientific world concerning its formation. David Hooper added an interesting facet to the manna phenomenon in 1900, when he described the sudden appearance of bamboo manna in the Central Provinces of India. "This is said to be the first time in the history of these forests that a sweet and gummy substance has been known to exude from the trees. The gum has been exuding in some abundance, and it has been found very palatable to the natives in the neighborhood, who have been consuming it as a food. The occurrence of the manna at this season is all the more remarkable, since the greatest famine India has known is this year visiting the country, and the districts where the scarcity is most keenly felt are in the Central Provinces" (*Nature*, 62: 127–28, 1900).

SHOWERS OF SEEDS, NUTS, AND BERRIES

Other edible substances appear to fall from the heavens, such as seeds and nuts. Will the venerable whirlwind theory work here? Most scientists would reply that it must, for there are no alternatives. In the two examples that follow, the reader will again find that the objects reported falling seem to have been carefully segregated from other seeds as well as sticks, leaves, and similar debris that might be expected in field and forest.

First, two letters about a peculiar shower in Ireland. "Sir,—I enclose [for] you two extracts from one of our Dublin papers relative to some berries, which are reported to have fallen in large quantities in some parts of Dublin on the night of Thursday, 9th May. I have been given two of these berries; they are in the form of a very small orange, about half an inch in diameter, black in colour, and, when cut across, seem as if made of some hard dark brown wood. They also possess a slight aromatic odour.

"Various speculations have been given forth as to their origin, but none of them seem to be worth much. If you think the extracts herein worthy of a place in your magazine, you can insert them.—Yours very truly," (Arthur Pim).

"Sir,—I have daily [been] expecting to see some notice of the strange phenomenon which took place during the tremendous rain-fall of Thursday night. None have appeared in any of the journals; I hope [that] through your columns the public may learn to what cause we are to attribute the shower of aromatic smelling berries which fell over Dublin (and, possibly, other parts) on Thursday night.

"Both on the north and south sides of the river these berries fell in great quantities and with great force, some being larger than the ordinary Spanish nut.

"Numbers of these strange visitors were picked up in Capel-street, in Dame-street, and Bishop-street, and I am informed that so violent was the force with which they descended that even the police, protected by unusually strong head covering, were obliged to seek shelter from the aerial fusilade!—Yours truly," (*Resticus Expectans*) (*Symons's Monthly Meteorological Magazine*, 2: 59, 1867).

R. Hedger Wallace documented an even more extraordinary fall from Italy in 1897. "Some days ago the province of Macerata, in Italy, was the scene of an extraordinary phenomenon. Half an hour before sunset an immense number of small blood-coloured clouds covered the sky. About an hour later a cyclone storm burst, and immediately the air became filled with myriads of small seeds. The seeds fell over town and country, covering the ground to a depth of about half an inch. The next day the whole of the scientists of Macerata were abroad in order to find some explanation. Prof. Cardinali, a celebrated Italian naturalist, stated that the seeds were of the genus *Cercis*, commonly called the Judas Tree, and that they belonged to an order of *Leguminosae* found only in Central Africa or the Antilles. It was found, upon examination, that a great number of the seeds were actually in the first stage of germination" (*Notes and Queries*, 8: 12: 228, 1897).

Gelatinous Meteors or Pwdre Ser

Star jelly is still another name for *pwdre ser*, but nothing can be as descriptive as "rot of the stars," which is a tolerable translation of the Welsh *pwdre ser*. The basic phenomenon has been the same since written history began. A meteor is seen to land nearby; investigation reveals a jellylike mass in the approximate location—thus we have "star jelly" or, more scientifically, a "gelatinous meteor." The incongruity is that common meteorites are hard lumps of rock and metal well suited to surviving the fiery plunge through the earth's atmosphere from outer space. Gelatin would be consumed in a few seconds. Thus the simultaneous appearance of the meteor impact and gelatinous mass at one location must be coincidental.

Actually, several of the accounts that follow indicate that there is really little doubt that the observer did perceive gelatinous masses to fall and that there was also a luminous display of some kind. In addition, the testimony of legends and folklore is overwhelmingly in favor of the reality of gelatinous meteors. Obviously, this does not mean that all gelatinous masses found in meadow and field fell from the sky, but neither can we deny the possibility of gelatinous meteors just because terrestrial nature can produce lumps of gelatin.

Scientists who have tried to explain *pwdre ser* always opt for the terrestrial interpretation—that is, some form of plant or animal life or possibly some half-digested matter disgorged by an animal. It seems that a common characteristic of *pwdre ser* is its smell and general rottenness. But if rotten fish can fall from the sky, why not offensive gelatin? *Pwdre ser* often has one other interesting feature: it seems to evaporate away rapidly, removing all evidence of the unusual phenomenon. Genuine animal matter is not so fleeting and ephemeral.

Pwdre ser is one of the handful of phenomena reported in this book that is without question real but remains "damned," to use the terminology of Charles Fort. *Pwdre ser* cannot possibly exist. Yet the scientific literature yields several dozen consistent reports.

Let us begin with excerpts from the classic and most charming article by T. McKenny Hughes that nicely defines the dimensions of the problem.

"In my boyhood I often lived on the coast of Pembrokeshire. Wandering about with my gun, I was familiar with most natural objects which occurred there. One, however, which I often came across there, and have seen elsewhere since, greatly roused my curiosity, but I have not yet met with a satisfactory explanation of it.

"On the short, close grass of the hilly ground, I frequently saw a mass of white, translucent jelly lying on the turf, as if it had been dropped there. These masses were about as large as a man's fist. It was very like a mass of frog's spawn without the eggs in it. I thought it might have been the gelatinous portion of the food disgorged by the great fish-eating birds, of which there were plenty about, as kingfishers eject pellets made up of the bones of the fish they eat, or that possibly there might be some pathological explanation connecting it with the sheep, large flocks of which grazed the short herbage. But the shepherds and owners of the sheep would have known if such an explanation were admissible. They called it *pwdre ser,* the rot of the stars.

"Years afterwards I was in Westmoreland, on the Geological Survey, and again not unfrequently saw the *pwdre ser.* But I now got an addition to my story. Isaac Hindson, of Kirby Lonsdale, a man whose scientific knowledge and genial personality made him a welcome companion to those who had to carry on geological research in his district, told me that he had once seen a luminous body fall, and, on going up to the place, found only a mass of white jelly. He did not say that it was luminous. I have never seen it luminous, but that may be because when it was light enough to see the lump of jelly, it would probably be too light to detect luminosity in it.

"Then, in my novel reading, I found that the same thing was known in Scotland, and the same origin assigned to it, for Walter Scott, in *The Talisman,* puts these words in the mouth of the hermit: 'Seek a fallen star and thou shalt only light on some foul jelly, which in shooting through the horizon, has assumed for a moment an appearance of splendour.' I think that I remember seeing it used elsewhere as an illustration of disappointed hopes, which were 'as when a man seeing a meteor fall runs up and finds but a mass of putrid jelly,' but I have lost the reference to this passage.

"Thus it appeared that in Wales, in the Lake District, and in Scotland, there existed a belief that something which fell from the sky as a luminous body lay on the ground as a lump of white jelly.

"I asked Huxley what it could be, and he said that the only thing like it that he knew was a nostoc. I turned to Sachs for the description of a nostoc, and found that it 'consists, when mature, of a large number of moniliform threads interwoven of a specifically defined form. . . . The gelatinous envelope of the new filament is developed, and the originally microscopic substance attains or even exceeds the size of a walnut by continuous increase of the jelly and divisions of the cells.'

"All the nostocs, however, that I have had pointed out to me have been of a green or purplish or brown-green colour, whereas the *pwdre ser* was always white, translucent in the upper part, and transparent in the lower part, which appeared to occur among the roots of the grass, as if it grew there. Moreover, the mass was much larger than a walnut, in fact would generally about fill a half-pin mug. . . .

"Poets and divines carry the record of this curious belief far back into the seventeenth century.

"Suckling (1541) says:

> As he whose quicker eye doth trace
> A false star shot to a mark't place
> Do's run apace,
> And, thinking it to catch,
> A jelly up do snatch.

❊   ❊   ❊

"William Somerville (1740) says:

> Swift as the Shooting Star that gilds the night
> With rapid transient Blaze, she runs, she flies;
> Sudden she stops nor longer can endure
> The painful course, but drooping sinks away,
> And like that falling Meteor, there she lyes
> A jelly cold on earth.

❊   ❊   ❊

"I have found it commonly near the sea, but have never seen any trace of earthworms or other similar food in it.

"Here, then, we have a well-known substance which may be of different origin in different cases, respecting the general appearance of which, however, almost all accounts agree. The variety of names under which it is known point to its common and widespread occurrence—e.g., *pwdre ser*, star-slough, star shoot, star shot, stargelly or jelly, and star-fall'n.

"We have in every name, and in every notice in literature, a recognition of the universal belief that it has something to do with meteors, yet there does not appear to be any evidence that anybody ever saw any luminosity in the jelly. Nor has anybody seen it disgorged by birds, except in the case of those two wounded birds where some half-digested gelatinous mass was thrown up. Nor has anyone watched its growth like nostoc from the ground.

"In 1908 I was with my wife and one of my boys in Ingleborough, where we found the *pwdre ser* lying on the short grass, close to the stream a little way above Gaping Ghyl Hope. For the first time I felt grateful to the inconsiderate tourist who left broken bottles about, for I was able to pack the jelly in the bottom of one, tie a cover on, and carry it down from the fell. I sent it, with the sod on which it appeared to have grown, to my colleague, Mr. E. A. Newell Arber, with a brief sketch of my story and the reason why I thought it of interest. Mr. Arber reported that it was no nostoc, and said that he had sent it over to Mr. Brookes, in the Botany School, who reported that it was a mass of bacteria.

"That is the end of my story, but I confess I am not satisfied. The jelly seemed to me to grow out from among the roots of the grass, and the part still tangled in the grass was not only translucent but quite transparent.

"What is it, and what is the cause of its having a meteoric origin assigned to it? Has anyone ever seen it luminous?" (*Nature*, 83: 492–94, 1910).

Hughes's general introduction requires some specific observations to lend credibility. Typical of the older sightings is this from Loweville, New York, November 11, 1845. ". . . the most remarkable meteor ever seen in that section made its appearance from the west. It appeared larger than the sun [and] illumined the hemisphere nearly as light as day. It was in sight nearly five minutes and was witnessed by a great number of the inhabitants of that village, and finally fell in a field in the vicinity, and a large company of the citizens immediately repaired to the spot and found a body of fetid jelly, four feet in diameter" (*Scientific American*, 2: 79, 1846).

"[In] 1844, Oct. 8th, near Coblentz, a German gentleman (a friend of Mr. Greg's), accompanied by another person, late in the evening, after dark, walking in a dry ploughed field, saw a luminous body descend straight down close to them (not 20 yards off), and heard it distinctly strike the ground with a noise; they marked the spot, and returning early the next morning as nearly as possible where it seemed to fall, they found a gelatinous mass of a greyish colour so viscid as 'to tremble all over' when poked with a stick. It had no appearance of being organic. They, however, took no further care to preserve it" (*Reports of the British Association*, p. 94, 1855).

The following letter was submitted to *Nature* in response to the long article by Hughes on *pwdre ser*. The time and locality of the sighting were December 9, 1909, Allegheny, Pennsylvania. "Referring to the falling meteor of which my husband made mention at your lecture last evening, the facts are as follows. One evening some years since my father, Mr. Joel Powers, while walking on Lawrence St., Lowell, Massachusetts, saw a brilliant shooting star or meteor flash downward through the atmosphere, striking the earth quite near him. He found it upon investigation to be a jelly-like mass, and almost intolerably offensive in smell. I have often heard my father allude to this event, which greatly interested him, he being a close observer and an extensive reader. Respectfully yours, Ellen M. Adams" (*Nature*, 84: 105–6, 1910).

Gelatinous meteors have surprised scientists (who generally disbelieve them) in recent years, as in this letter from Mrs. M. Ephgrave of Cambridge, England. "I wonder if you could tell me what the substance was that alighted on my lawn during a very heavy rainstorm last Friday evening [June 23, 1978]. It glided down about the size of a football and settled like a jelly. It was white, and gloy-like [strawlike], but cellular. It did not appear to disintegrate, but had completely disappeared by the morning. It came down north-south. I showed it to several neighbors, but no one had seen anything similar." Further correspondence revealed that the jelly had the consistency of marshmallow and seemed to be odorless (*Journal of Meteorology, U.K.*, 3: 312–16, 1978).

In considering the actual origin of *pwdre ser*, one must ask whether gelatinous matter can actually exist in the near-vacuum of outer space for long periods. If it evaporates away so quickly on earth, its lifetime in space should be even shorter. The same thoughts will apply later to the discussion of the possible existence of ice in space in connection with the falls of large ice chunks. If gelatinous matter or ice were covered with dust or some other slowly evaporating, insulating layer, long space lifetimes might be possible—as in the case of cometary ices. But even if survival were possible, what is gelatin doing out there anyway? It seems as if *pwdre ser* must be terrestrial in origin! Such reasoning is dangerously restrictive, however. Who really has a complete and true manifest of space debris?

Pwdre ser may be connected in some way with the aerial bubbles mentioned in Chapter 1. A very old bubble report seems to indicate a gelatinous constitution. The time was 1808; the place, Biskopsberga, Sweden. "On the 16th of last May, being a very warm day, and during a gale of wind from south-west, and a cloudless sky, at about 4 o'clock, p.m., the sun became dim and lost his brightness to that degree, that he could be looked at without inconvenience to the naked eye, being of a dark-red, or almost bright colour, without brilliancy. At the same time there appeared at the western horizon, from where the wind blew, to arise gradually, and in quick succession, a great number of balls, or spherical bodies, to the naked eye of a size of the crown of a hat, and of a dark brown colour. The nearer these bodies, which occupied a considerable though irregular breadth of the visible heaven, approached towards the sun, the darker they appeared, and in the vicinity of the sun, became entirely black. At this elevation their course seemed to lessen,

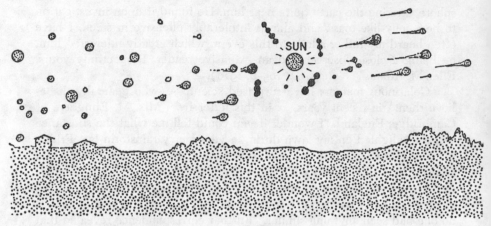

Immense number of aerial bubbles observed in Sweden

and a great many of them remained, as it were, stationary; but they soon resumed their former [course], and an accelerated motion, and passed in the same direction with great velocity and almost horizontally. During this course some disappeared, others fell down, but the most part of them continued their progress almost in a straight line, till they were lost sight of at the eastern horizon. The phenomenon lasted uninterruptedly, upwards of two hours, during which time millions of similar bodies continually rose in the west, one after the other irregularly, and continued their career exactly in the same manner. No report, noise, nor any whistling or buzzing in the air was perceived. As these balls slackened their course on passing by the sun, several were linked together, three, six, or eight of them in a line, joined like chain-shot by a thin and straight bar; but on continuing again a more rapid course, they separated, and each having a tail after it, apparently of three or four fathoms length, wider at its base where it adhered to the ball, and gradually decreasing, till it terminated in a fine point. During the course, these tails which had the same black colour as the balls, disappeared by degrees.

"It fortunately happened, that some of these balls fell at a short distance, or but a few feet from Mr. Secretary K. G. Wettermark, who had then for a long while been attentively looking at the phenomenon, in the aforesaid village. On the descent of these bodies, the black colour seemed gradually to disappear the nearer they approached the earth, and they vanished almost entirely till within a few fathoms distance from the ground, when they again were visible with several changing colours, and in this particular exactly resembling those air-bubbles which children used to produce from soapsuds by means of a reed. When the spot where such a ball had fallen was immediately after examined, nothing was to be seen, but a scarcely perceptible film or pellicle, as thin and fine as a cobweb, which was still changing colours, but soon entirely dried up and vanished. As somewhat singular, it may be observed, that the size of these balls, to the sight, underwent no particular change; for they appeared of the same dimension, at their rise from the western horizon, as well as on their passing by the sun, and during the whole of their course to the eastern part of the heavens, where they disappeared" (*North American Review*, 3: 320–22, 1816). Incidentally, the optical phenomena associated with the bubbles remind one of the kaleidoscopic sun effects from Chapter 2.

Ice Chunks (Hydrometeors)

Hail several inches in diameter, though unusual, has been recorded (see Chapter 3). Large, solitary chunks of ice weighing several pounds also fall from the sky. Unlike large hailstones, the solitary chunks cannot be explained away by extrapolating accepted modes of hail formation to larger sizes. A standard theory, however, does exist: the chunks simply fall from aircraft flying overhead. A corollary is that cases recorded before the Wright Brothers must be dismissed as old wives' tales.

Doubtless some ice chunks do fall from aircraft, but a second possibility exists—namely, that the chunks are truly meteoric (or cometary) and come from outer space, somehow surviving the searing descent through the atmosphere. In this radical context, it is curious that some hydrometeors fall during intense thunder and lightning, much like the legendary thunderstones. Thunderstones, as related in the next section, are strongly rejected by conventional scientists because there is no known connection between meteors and thunderstorms. Any meteor that reaches the earth during a thunderstorm does so by pure chance! The same reasoning could also be applied to thunderstorm hydrometeors except that intense thunderstorms are renowned fabricators of large hailstones.

ICE FALLS FROM A CLEAR SKY

The standard "aircraft theory" seems quite adequate to explain the following ice fall that was investigated by A. E. Carte from the National Physical Research Laboratory in Pretoria, South Africa. "A large lump of ice fell from a cloudless sky one morning in September 1964 and landed only ten yards from a farmer in the Brits district of the Transvaal,

South Africa. A whirring sound shortly before the impact alerted the farmer so that he saw the ice as it struck the ground.

"The lump was flattish-shaped and irregular, estimated at $11 \times 9 \times 6$ inches, and [it] gave off a peculiar odour. The farmer also observed that the ice was composed of numerous layers and that parts of its interior were brownish-coloured. He did not recall noticing aircraft in the vicinity at the time of the incident."

The ice chunk was preserved and taken to the National Physical Research Laboratory, where it was carefully analyzed. It contained traces of tea, coffee, and detergent. Furthermore, inquiry established that a commercial airliner had indeed passed over the farmer's field within 10 minutes of the incident on its descent to the Jan Smuts Airport (*Royal Aeronautical Society, Journal,* 69: 274-75, 1965).

Roger A. Pielke, at the University of Virginia, carried out a similar investigation of a larger chunk of ice that fell on the Cappar family's house at Fort Pierce, Florida, on December 13, 1973. Curiously, the fall was synchronous with the launch of a giant Titan 3C rocket from the Kennedy Space Center. Pielke's conclusion is that "the chemical and physical analyses of the ice pieces, although quantitatively describing the material, do not permit a definitive determination of the origin of the ice. The coincidence between a Kennedy Space Center rocket firing and the ice fall may suggest that the ice was dropped off during launch, but the trajectory of all rocket launches of which we are aware is to the southeast, away from the Cape and therefore well away from the Cappar home. A second, more plausible explanation may be that slush was collected off an airport runway and froze on an aircraft on take-off from a northern airport and then was dropped as the plane lowered to make a landing in south or central Florida. There was, in fact, a storm system producing snow on this date in the northern Midwest. Several airports in the immediate vicinity of Fort Pierce were contacted to determine if planes from northern airports were making landing approaches near the time of the ice fall, but none was reported.

"Since Fort Pierce is under a major air route of flights into the south Florida area, it is reasonable to suspect one of these aircraft dropped the ice. Unfortunately, it was impossible to check into all commercial, private, and military air traffic over the Fort Pierce area at the time of the ice fall.

"Our conclusion, therefore, is necessarily tentative and somewhat speculative. The physical appearance of the ice suggests it was frozen onto an aircraft during take-off, then dropped as the plane descended to land. The chemical composition of the ice, particularly the silver, selenium, gallium, germanium, and mercury, is somewhat unusual, and we have no explanation for this. The high sodium content could have resulted from salting of the runways from which the airplane would have taken off" (*Weatherwise*, 28: 156–60, 1975).

Regardless of the ease of explanation in the preceding two cases, many ice falls are difficult to account for with the aircraft hypothesis. To illustrate, three separate blocks of ice fell at Timberville, Virginia, on March 7, 1976, apparently simultaneously. The incident was reported by Robert J. M. Rickard, a well-known student of strange phenomena.

"That Sunday night, Wilbert W. Cullers (and two others) were watching television when at 8:45 P.M. they were startled by a loud crash which shook the house. A block of ice ('about the size of a basketball') smashed through a 2-ft.-square thin metal roofing tile, 'sheared' a 2 in. × 4 in. roofing strut to bounce off another and emerge into the Cullers' room through two holes in the plasterboard ceiling. Deputies from the Rockingham County Sheriff's Department arrived about an hour later and collected a 3-gallon bucket full of pieces of 'murky' ice. Sergeant C. R. Hottinger found the ice to be 'milky white, cold, and compressible in the hand.'

"A neighbor, John Branner, had been standing for about 3 minutes in his drive when he heard the impact ('like a muffled shotgun'). Then, about 20 seconds later, he saw an object hit the road outside their houses, about 50 yards away. He looked up but neither heard nor saw any sign of a plane. The object was found to be broken pieces of ice (Hottinger: 'like clear powder'). A girl living opposite the Cullers, Candy Lewis, 15, rushed out when she heard the first impact ('like a car crashed'), and then heard another noise. 'I looked up and heard this whizzing sound come flying.' She saw a chunk of ice hit the edge of the road. This was the event Branner observed, yet he said he heard no whizzing sound.

"I include the third incident because it is not without interest or possible connection with the previous two, although it was 'unwitnessed.' Laurence Cline, farming about a mile west of Timberville, found a block of ice on the ground when he fed his chickens early on Monday 8 March (i.e., the next day)."

The ice from the falls was analyzed at Eastern Mennonite College, where it was found to resemble local tapwater plus some bacteria and yeastlike organisms. One piece contained a piece of gravel. Meteorological conditions at the time of the fall were not conducive to aircraft icing, and it is doubtful that such large pieces could have accumulated anywhere on the aircraft—especially with enclosed gravel (*Journal of Meteorology, U.K.*, 2: 148–49, 1977).

G. T. Meaden, the editor of the *Journal of Meteorology, U.K.*, has collected an impressive list of recent falls of large ice chunks. One of the most amazing occurred at Long Beach, California, on June 4, 1953, when

50 ice lumps, some weighing 75 kg. each, fell. The total weight was about a ton—hardly something an airplane would be lugging about. Meaden compared the Long Beach fall with one at Shirley, Surrey, in England, on January 23, 1972, which measured 4-ft. square! Many other impressive chunks are on Meaden's list (*Journal of Meteorology, U.K.*, 2: 137–41, 1977). One wonders about the many more ice chunks that must statistically fall unwitnessed in unpopulated areas.

ICE FALLS DURING THUNDERSTORMS

Thunderstorms frequently generate very large hailstones as intense winds whip small hailstones around inside convection-cells. Each trip around the cell adds another layer to the hailstone. Finally, the weight of the hailstone is so great that it falls to the ground despite aerodynamic forces. The question meteorologists try to answer is how much weight can thunderstorm winds support?

A hydrometeor weighing between 2 and 4 lb. fell near R. F. Griffiths on April 2, 1973. Griffiths was a physicist at the University of Manchester (England) and was able to provide a thoughtful and competent assessment of the weather conditions at the time.

"At 1954 GMT a single flash of lightning occurred which extended over a very wide area of Manchester. This was noted by many people because of its severity, and because there were no further flashes. The Manchester Weather Centre recorded the lightning, which took a path at least 10 km. long from Cheadle in the south to the city centre, and may have gone farther. . . . At the time of the stroke, the author was walking along Burton Road, Manchester, near Withington Hospital, and, in his capacity as a lightning observer for the Electrical Research Association, he made a note of the time and nature of the flash as well as the prevailing weather. The estimated interval between the flash and the thunder was two to three seconds, which suggested a lightning channel about 800 metres away and, relative to the height of the cloud base, almost directly overhead. No precipitation was observed at this stage. As the author returned a few minutes later by the same route, a large object struck the roadway about three metres to his left front. . . . This object fell fast enough to be shattered into many pieces on impact with the ground; only one fragment of any appreciable size could be found, the rest being scattered in tiny pieces over an area of many square metres. On inspection, the fragments proved to be made of ice, and the large piece, when held up to the streetlight, showed rings of clear ice alternating with rings of bubbles trapped in the structure." The large fragment was preserved and analyzed. While the ice chunk seemed to be composed of cloud water, no mechanism could be proposed for the growth of such a large hydrometeor. Records of aircraft in the area indicated that it could not have fallen from them; in any case no aircraft reported icing problems at that time (*Meteorological Magazine*, 104: 253–60, 1975).

"A curious phenomenon occurred at the farm of Balvullich, on the estate of Ord, occupied by Mr. Moffat, on the evening of Monday last. Immediately after one of the loudest peals of thunder heard there, a large and irregular-shaped mass of ice, reckoned to be nearly 20 feet in circumference and of a proportionate thickness, fell near the farm-house. It had a beautiful crystalline appearance, being nearly all quite transparent, if we except a small portion of it which consisted of hailstones of uncommon size, fixed together. It was principally composed of small square, diamond-shaped [pieces] of from 1 to 3 inches in size, all firmly congealed together. The weight of this large piece of ice could not be ascertained; but it is a most fortunate circumstance that it did not fall on Mr. Moffat's house or it would have crushed it and undoubtedly have caused the death of some of the inmates. No appearance whatever of either hail or snow was discernible in the surrounding district" (*Edinburgh New Philosophical Journal*, 47: 371, 1849).

G. T. Meaden has noted that many superhailstones are composed of many smaller hailstones seemingly fused together. Perhaps, he suggests, thunderstorms may support vortices capable of drawing in, fusing, and levitating small hailstones in the neighborhood until an extremely large mass of ice builds up. A lightning stroke might then trigger the release of the mass, as in the preceding examples (*Journal of Meteorology, U.K.*, 2: 201–5, 1977).

Thunderstones

The thunderstone problem cannot be avoided. Many credible witnesses have reported the luminous descents of objects accompanied by claps of thunder. Upon retrieval the purported fallen objects turn out to be not meteorites (these also may fall with considerable noise) but ordinary terrestrial stones. Some of these events are ultimately identified as hoaxes or human errors. But, as with UFO's, some bona fide events seem to persist. If thunderstones truly exist, what are they? Can they be re-entering terrestrial material propelled long ago into orbit by meteorite impacts or some other catastrophes? An obvious parallel exists between thunderstones and the fall of large ice chunks. Are both phenomena real and, if so, do common terrestrial mechanisms provide adequate explanations for them?

A curious sidelight of the thunderstone problem concerns the extraordinary pains scientists and supporters of orthodox science have taken to debunk thunderstones. Possibly this intense dislike of a potentially fascinating natural phenomenon derives from the purported capabilities of various deities to hurl thunderbolts to strike down sinners. UFO's, ancient astronauts, and all phenomena hinting at superhuman agencies are given this debunking treatment.

Thunderstone data are difficult to find in modern literature because they are so unrespectable. C. Carus-Wilson, a wide-ranging English scientist of the last century, actually had in his possession a thunderstone that supposedly fell at Casterton, in Westmoreland, England. "It was seen to fall during a violent thunderstorm, and, killing a sheep *en route*, buried itself about six feet below the surface, and when dug out shortly after, it was still hot. In appearance it much resembles a volcanic bomb; it is about the size of a large cocoanut, weighs over 12 lb., and seems to be composed of a hard ferruginous [dark reddish-orange] quartzite. I have not yet submitted it to a technical analysis, but hope to do so shortly. There is an external shell of about an inch in thickness, and this contains a nucleus of the same shape and material as the shell but is quite independent of it, so that the one is easily separated from the other; I attribute this separation of the parts to an unequal cooling of the mass.

"I have often wondered from whence thunderbolts were derived and why they always fell as 'balls of fire' accompanied by flashes of lightning" (*Knowledge*, 8: 320, 1885).

Another secondhand account of a thunderstone was published by J. Rand Capron. It reminds one of *pwdre ser* reports in that a strange mass is associated with a natural phenomenon by virtue of proximity, although all the tenets of science resist the connection. "It is strange what vagaries lightning will sometimes play. I had recently brought to me a ball evidently largely composed of iron, spherical in shape, 14.38 oz. in weight, specific gravity 6.81. This had been found after a storm near the apparent place of fall of lightning, in a heap of refuse bark, thrown out from a barn door. In this heap was a round hole with charred sides, and at the bottom of this hole, 10 inches deep, was found the ball in question. As the finder was certain he had found a 'meteorite,' every means were taken by analysis, comparison, section, magnetic examination, etc., to ascertain its true character, and these proved it incontestably to be a charcoal smelted cast-iron ball, probably of considerable antiquity, as charcoal furnaces have long ceased. There yet remained the charred hole to be explained, and upon seeking advice from Mr. Preece, he came to the conclusion that an offshoot from a flash of lightning, falling near even so small a mass, may have penetrated to it, and thus led to its discovery and to the mistake about it" (*Symons's Monthly Meteorological Magazine,* 18: 57, 1883).

Yet, the eyewitness accounts are persistent. "Mr. H. Garrett, writing from Greensted Rectory by Ongar to the [London] *Times* (July 28), says: 'during the severe thunderstorm on the 13th inst. a meteoric stone fell in the stable yard here with a terrific explosion when within a few feet of the ground, embedding itself in the gravel about 8 inches, the ground around for several feet being perforated with small holes caused by the fragments. The main part and fragments which we could collect weighed 1 lb., 13 oz. The fall was witnessed by my daughters, who were sheltering about eight yards away'" (*Nature,* 81: 134, 1909).

The following thunderstone report is embellished with luminous and acoustic phenomena. "With pleasure I write all I remember of the incident referred to in Mr. Plenderleath's letter, and I will make it as clear as I can. In 1887 (I think early in August) there was a very heavy thunderstorm at Harrogate [England] and in the surrounding districts. We were then living at Starbeck, a hamlet between Harrogate and Knaresborough. I was watching the storm from the drawingroom window, when suddenly (simultaneously with a sharp, cracking clap of thunder, immediately overhead) I saw a bright white light fall, in a flash of lightning. As it touched the earth, I heard a loud fizz—like an enormous match being struck. When the rain ceased, I went to the spot where it fell, in a meadow, at the bottom of the garden, about 50 yards distant. I saw a disturbance in the ground, and on digging at a little below the surface I found a hard, heavy substance like slate. I collected it all and sent it to Professor Tyndal; by return of post I had a kind note from Mrs. Tyndal, saying that the Professor was [away] from home, but that she had notified him. In a few days I heard from Professor Tyndal, thanking me for the specimen and saying that it was 'ironstone,' and the fragments 'fusion of sand by the lightning'" (*Symons's Meteorological Magazine,* 38: 117–18, 1903). In this instance, the total phenomenon may provide a clue to the solution of some thunderstone reports—namely, that ball lightning is seen to fall and upon impact with the ground it fuses dirt, sand, and whatever else is about. Ordinary lightning creates long, branchlike fulgurites; ball lightning may produce thunderstones.

As if to confirm such a surmise, several reports exist of haystacks being hit by lightning, as in the following item: "In the summer of 1827, a rick of hay, in the parish of Dun near Montrose, was set on fire by lightning and partly consumed. When the fire was extinguished by the exertions of the farm-servants who were on the spot, there was observed in the middle of the stack a cylindrical passage, as if cut out by sharp instruments. This passage extended down the middle of the stack to the ground, and at the bottom of it there was found a quantity of vitrified matter, which, there is every reason to think, is the product of the silex contained in the hay which filled up the cylindrical passage. The existence of silex in the common grasses is well known, and the color of the porous and vesicular mass is very like that which is obtained from the combustion of siliceous plants" (*American Journal of Science*, 1: 19: 395, 1831).

A somewhat different aspect of the thunderstone problem appears when many stones fall along with heavy rain. In the report of Townshend M. Hall that follows, the fallen stones were called "meteoric." Of course, meteors often do disintegrate into many pieces during flight through the atmosphere, but this seems unlikely here. In addition, whirlwinds and waterspouts might conceivably pick up a few stones just as they vacuum up fish, hay, and sundry items. Hall writes: "With reference to the supposed shower of meteorites at Wolverhampton on Tuesday, May 25, it is perhaps worthy of notice that a precisely similar fall was recorded by Mr. Thomas Plant, F.M.S., as having taken place at Birmingham on Friday, May 29—only four days later. The following is an extract from Mr. Plant's letter, published in the Birmingham *Daily Post* for Saturday, May 30, 1869:

"'The thunderstorm this morning was remarkable for the immense quantity of rain which fell; also for the long duration of the tempest; likewise the strange shower of meteoric stones referred to at the close of this report. . . . There was an extraordinary phenemenon during the deluge of rain. From nine to ten [P.M.] meteoric stones fell in immense quantities in various parts of the town. The size of these stones varied from about one eighth of an inch to three eighths of an inch in length, and about half those dimensions in thickness. They resembled in shape broken pieces of Rowley ragstone. A similar phenomenon visited Birmingham ten years ago. On the 12th of June, 1858, during a severe thunderstorm, there fell a great quantity of meteoric stones, in every respect like those discharged this morning.'

"In a catalogue of all the known British meteoric descents, I find only twelve instances on record of the fall of meteorites in England, four in Scotland, and a like number in Ireland. But here we have not an isolated instance of this phenomenon, but two 'showers' in 'immense quantities'" (*Symons's Monthly Meteorological Magazine*, 4: 184, 1869).

Chemicals and Inorganic Materials

The winds of the high atmosphere can carry dust and sand for many hundreds of miles. Dust from the western states frequently falls in normal precipitation in states farther east. The famous "dry fogs" at sea off

Cape Verde and many European dust falls have their origins in the Sahara. Other dust falls are harder to explain for no handy nearby sources exist. Selected examples in all categories are recorded below.

The scientific and popular literature have noted many falls of yellowish substances. Investigations usually point to airborne pollen. Other reports insist that real sulphur has fallen from the skies. Sulphur is a common enough element, but it does not usually exist in elemental form where winds can pick it up and transport it elsewhere. "Sulphur rains," if true, have no conventional explanations. Salt and other "evaporates" are, on the other hand, much more common than sulphur. It is quite possible that wind action could sweep across alkali flats and desiccated seabeds and pick up enough material to cause salt falls and rains of other chemicals at great distances.

SAND, CINDERS, COAL, AND DUST FALLS

Despite what was just said about wind-carried sand, the most unusual sand fall discovered so far was associated with a meteor. It occurred on November 14, 1968, in Portugal. "It was nearly dark when a Portuguese man taking a walk heard a loud noise like a sonic boom. Suddenly [on November 14, 1968], an eerie glow lit up the landscape as though it were daytime. Seconds later, a 55-pound meteorite slammed into the ground about 100 feet away. The meteor had travelled from southwest to northeast across Portugal descending at a 50- to 60-degree angle. When it struck near the Portuguese village of Jurmenha, it caused a 'rain of sand.' It also formed a depression in the ground some three inches deep upon impact" (*The Pulse of the Planet*, p. 19, 1972).

Falling cinders are common—too common—in heavily industrialized areas, but the Ottawa, Illinois, cinder fall described below seems more likely associated with a meteor. The fall took place on June 17, 1857. "The cinders fell in a northeasterly direction in the shape of the letter V. The weather had been showery, but I heard no thunder and saw no lightning. There appeared to be a small, dense black cloud hanging over the garden in a westerly direction, or a little to the south of west. The cinders fell upon a slight angle within about three rods of where I was at work; there was no wind at the moment, or none perceptible. My attention was called first to the freak the wind had in the grass, and the next moment to a hissing noise caused by the cinders passing through the air. The longer ones were considerably imbedded in the earth, so much as only to show a small part of it, while the smaller ones were about one-half buried. I noticed at the time that the ground where I afterwards picked up the cinders showed signs of warmth, as there was quite a steam or fog at that particular point. I thought it singular, as the ground had been very cold previously."

"The scoria is in rounded inflated pieces, like what have been called volcanic bombs, the exterior being glassy, and the interior very cellular. They are little over an inch in the longest diameter. Color black" (*American Journal of Science*, 2: 24: 449, 1857).

On July 17, 1806, pieces of mica fell at Pimlico, England. From a letter to the editor of *Weather* from K. M. Glaister, we quote: "A friend of mine has in his possession an envelope containing what is labelled 'talc' but which appears to be a piece of mica about 5 cm. square with a note. 'The enclosed was picked up after a storm on 17 July 1806, the streets in Pimlico where this was found being covered with the same in the middle of the day.'" Glaister asked readers of *Weather* to help trace this fascinating tidbit (*Weather*, 8: 192, 1953).

Accounts of strange falls from the older literature are usually shrugged off—what did they know a century ago? The phenomena, however, persist throughout all of recorded time, as exemplified by the October 9, 1939, coal fall at Springfield, Missouri. Mothball-sized hail had just fallen in Springfield, when telephone calls to the weather bureau announced that pieces of coal had also come down with the hail. "Immediately after the hail storm, Mr. R. F. Buchanan of #868 S. Douglas Street in this city called the office and advised me that it had 'hailed coal in his part of town' and that he was bringing some of the hail stones to my office. He arrived shortly, but the hail had melted before he got here. He showed me his car which he had just finished washing previous to the storm. It was literally covered with small pieces of coal, varying from one sixteenth to one eighth of an inch cube size. Each little piece of coal was encased in a small muddy circle on his car where the hail had melted. There were thousands of them on the car top and surface. He said that each hail stone was black in the center before it had melted. His lawn, sidewalk and the street in his section was covered with bits of 'coal' while several blocks away others advised me that they had noticed the same thing only it was mostly a black dust deposit after the rain. In all other sections of the city the deposit was a yellow dust" (*American Meteorological Society, Bulletin*, 22: 122–23, 1941). Strip mines in extreme western Missouri and Oklahoma may have been the source of the coal and other material.

Ordinary terrestrial dust may be carried several hundred miles by the winds, eventually falling to the earth in the form of muddy rain, "blood" rain, black rain, etc. Such earthly dust is easily recognized and considered quite ordinary. A few very localized dust falls, however, seem to be comprised of true meteoric material. The immense numbers of small meteors that burn up high in the atmosphere cause a very slow, steady, planetwide rain of small particles. This gentle, widely dispersed influx of cosmic particles seems to be punctuated by anomalous, highly concentrated falls of the same meteoric matter. When these localized falls occur during thunderstorms, as in the case below, it is possible that the thunderstorm, reaching high into the upper atmosphere, somehow funnels incoming meteoric material into a small area.

"A metallic substance in powder or small granules has been sent to the *Science News* laboratory for examination. It proves to be meteoric dust, largely composed of iron, nickel, and silica. Dr. Batchelder, of Pelham, N.H., who sent the specimen, states that he collected the dust on the walk in front of his house after a smart thunder shower" (*Scientific American,* 52: 83, 1885).

SULPHUR SHOWERS

Virtually all sulphur falls turn out to be pollen falls when proper examinations are made. This account is typical. "The inhabitants of the village of Thames Ditton, Surrey, were, on Friday night, October 18th, 1867, a good deal startled at witnessing a very strange phenomenon, which had the appearance of a shower of fire. The shower lasted about ten minutes, and during its continuance afforded a brilliant light. Next morning it was found that the waterbutts and puddles in the upper part of the village were thickly covered with a deposit of sulphur. Some of the water has been preserved in bottles" (*Symons's Monthly Meteorological Magazine,* 2: 130, 1867).

On the other hand, lumps of sulphur have been reported to fall following meteor explosions, as in this item from Hungary on June 17, 1873. "It is remarkable that perfectly authentic statements were received of the deposition, soon after, or about the time of, the meteor's explosion over Zittau and its neighbourhood, of a mass of melted and burning sulphur the size of a man's fist, on the roadway of a village, Proschwitz, about 4 miles south of Reichenberg, where the meteor exploded nearly in the zenith. It was stamped out by a crowd of the villagers, who could give no other explanation of its appearance on the spot than that it had proceeded from the meteor; on examination at Breslau some remnants of the substance proved to be pure sulphur. With regard to the calculated course, the meteor must, however have passed quite 12 or 14 miles southwestwards from the place where this event is said to have occurred; and its questionable connexion with the fireball is accordingly rendered very doubtful from the great distance of the locality from immediately below the meteor's course. In Chladni's work on Fiery Meteors and Stonefalls, only one similar instance is recorded, from ancient chronicles, where burning sulphur fell at Magdeburg, of the size of a man's fist, on the castle-roof at Loburg, 18 miles from Magdeburg, in June of the year 1642" (*Report of the British Association,* p. 272, 1874). Manifestly the quality of the sulphur-fall reports is poor.

SALT STORMS

Apparently there are two varieties of salt storms. The first drops salt crystals swept up from surface deposits by high winds; the second type is a natural consequence of the evaporation of seawater blown inland.

An example of the first type occurred on August 20, 1872, in Switzerland. "Prof. Kenngott, of Zurich, states that in a hailstorm, lasting five minutes, on the 20th of last August, the stones, some of which weighed twelve grains consisted essentially of common salt, mainly in imperfect cubical crystals. He supposes that the salt had been taken up from the salt plains of Africa and brought over the Mediterranean.

"Hailstones containing each a small crystal of sulphide of iron are reported as having fallen recently, by Prof. Eversmann of Kasan. The crystals were probably weathered out of some rocks in the vicinity" (*American Journal of Science,* 3: 3: 239, 1872).

The only record found so far of the second type is this reference from *Science.* "Can any of your readers tell me the exact date of the so-called 'salt-storm' which came upon the coast of Massachusetts about 1815? As described by old inhabitants, there was a high wind and heavy rain, and the houses and all objects within a mile of the water were coated with salt. Are such storms of frequent occurrence, and what is their explanation?" (*Science,* 7: 440, 1886). No further information was forthcoming from *Science* readers.

5

THE STRANGE PHENOMENA
OF EARTHQUAKES

A sensation most humans find hard to ignore is that of physical motion; a category that includes shock, vibration, and gross physical movement. Short, sharp shocks are sensed kinesthetically like bumps on a highway. The frequent tilting effects of earthquakes, though, disturb one's sense of balance and induce disorientation. Whatever the mode of detection, the onset of physical motion of the earth's crust signals the existence of powerful local forces and thus the possibility of a variety of strange phenomena.

The physical motions of an earthquake need not occupy our attention here. Rather it is the remarkable spectrum of parallel events occurring before, during, and after the quake proper that command our curiosity. The phenomena fall into two major divisions: (1) concurrent effects, such as "earthquake weather," that have elusive and/or questionable origins; and (2) concurrent phenomena, such as solar activity, that seem to trigger seismic activity via unknown or hard-to-explain mechanisms. The mystery in this chapter, then, is not in the earthquake itself but in the curious effects and correlations that surround the event in time and space.

Unusual Phenomena Accompanying Earthquakes

A major earthquake disrupts the balance of terrestrial forces from deep in the rocky mantle to high in the ionosphere. As the earth's surface vibrates—not unlike the skin of a drum—great sea waves (*tsunamis*) and atmospheric pressure waves spread out rapidly from the epicenter. The sea waves may travel 10,000 miles, while the air waves may penetrate into the charged layers of the upper atmosphere, upsetting the electrical equilibrium. A truly great quake is felt globally.

Near the epicenters of big earthquakes, unusual phenomena abound —these are of course in addition to the physical motion of the earth itself. Loud groans, detonations, and grinding noises are emitted by the rent strata. Less common are flames issuing from the ground, moving lights, auroralike beams, and sky glows. Most of these luminous effects are documented in Chapter 1, but a few observations, especially those involving odd electrical effects, are retained in this chapter. Both earthquake lights and electrical effects are usually attributed to the piezoelectric effect stimulated by earthquake forces. These same pressures also force up geysers of water, sand, and even coal. The powerful quakes near New Madrid, in the Mississippi Valley, in 1811 and 1812, produced a wide spectrum of such phenomena, as the accounts that follow will prove.

The prediction of earthquakes is becoming more scientific. Scientists involved in these efforts have been intrigued by the ability of many animals to sense the coming of an earthquake long before humans hear the grating roars and feel the heaving ground. In Japan and China, fish, pheasants, and other animals have long been valued for their abilities to detect earthquake precursors. The ways in which animals sense the oncoming quake are not well understood and likely involve the detection of low-level sounds and slight tiltings of the ground.

Some people still swear that "earthquake weather" exists, even though some of the greatest quakes were not preceded by the hot, sultry, forboding calm that legend tells us presages a big convulsion. Still there are startling correlations between earthquakes, heavy rainfall, fog, and other weather events. It is understandable how the dust raised by an earthquake can trigger rainfall, and also how heavy rain can "lubricate" rock strata and help release seismic strains. Cause-and-effect relationships between quakes and other weather phenomena are harder to discern. In any case, big earthquakes release so much energy that almost all geophysical parameters are shaken a bit.

PECULIAR SOUNDS BEFORE, DURING, AND AFTER EARTHQUAKES

Rumbling and grating noises are to be expected during major quakes as subterranean rocks reposition themselves. Frequently, however, earthquakes generate various improbable noises: whizzes, detonations, screeches, the sound of breaking glass, etc. Furthermore, the noises sometimes seem to emanate from the sky above rather than below ground where the action should be centered. To enlarge upon the sampling presented below, the reader should refer to Chapter 7 on unusual natural sounds.

The great terrestrial convulsions we now call the New Madrid earthquakes devastated miles of countryside of Missouri and adjoining states in 1811 and 1812. Probably the most intense North American quakes in historical times, they struck with a rich repertoire of sounds, described by Myron L. Fuller in his detailed study of the event:

"The noises accompanying the more important shocks are among the most noticeable features of the earthquake. Bradbury tells of being 'awakened by a tremendous noise' at the time of the first shock and noted that 'the sound, which was heard at the time of every shock, always preceded it [by] at least a second and uniformly came from the same point and went off in the opposite direction.' Audubon, speaking of one of the more severe shocks, describes the sound as like 'the distant rumbling of a violent tornado.' Bringier does not mention the subterranean noise, but describes the 'roaring and whistling produced by the impetuosity of the air escaping from its confinement' in the alluvial materials. A similar roaring and hissing, like the escape of steam from a boiler, is also described by Hildreth. Eliza Bryan describes the sounds of the shock itself as 'an awful noise resembling loud and distant thunder but more hoarse and vibrating.' Flint compares the sound of the ordinary shocks to rumbling like distant thunder, but mentions the fact that the vertical shocks were accompanied by 'explosions and a terrible mixture of noises.' Linn describes the phenomena as beginning with 'distant rumbling sounds succeeded by discharges, as if a thousand pieces of artillery were suddenly exploded,' and notes the hissing sounds accompanying the extrusion of the water.

"In Tennessee, as described by Haywood, 'in the time of the earthquake a murmuring noise, like that of fire disturbed by the blowing of a bellows, issued from the pores of the earth. A distant rumbling was heard almost without intermission and sometimes seemed to be in the air.' Explosions like the discharge of a cannon a few miles distant were also recorded, and 'when the shocks came on, the stones on the surface of the earth were agitated by a tremulous motion like eggs in a frying pan, [which] altogether made a noise similar to that of the wheels of a wagon in a pebbly road.'

"In the more distant localities we must again rely on the compilation of Mitchill. At Herculaneum, Mo., the noise was described as a roaring or rumbling resembling a blaze of fire acted upon by wind; at St. Louis before the shocks, 'sounds were heard like wind rushing through the trees but not resembling thunder,' while more considerable noises accompanied the shocks. At Louisville the noise was likened to a carriage passing through the street; at Washington, D.C., the sound was very distinguishable, appearing to pass from southwest to northeast; at Richmond similar noises were heard, but they appeared to come from the east; at Charleston [S.C.] there was 'a rumbling like distant thunder which increased in violence of sound just before the shock was felt'; while at Savannah the noise was compared to a rattling noise like 'that of a carriage passing over a paved road.'

"From the above it would appear that earth noises were heard at most points where the earthquake was felt. In the region of marked disturbance there were the additional noises made by escaping air, water, crashing trees, and caving river banks. According to the best information, the sound in the Mississippi Valley was a somewhat dull roar rather than the rumbling sound of thunder with which it was compared at certain of the more remote localities. In reality, as has been stated to the writer in regard to the recent Jamaica earthquake, although suggesting many of the common noises, it was essentially unlike anything ever heard by the observers before" (*U.S. Geological Survey Bulletin* 494, 1912, 101–2).

One of the strangest earthquake sounds is that of a rushing noise in the sky. The origin of the windlike sound is hard to conceive given its unexpected location. It bears some resemblance to the Yellowstone Lake Whispers, described in Chapter 7, which may also have seismic origins.

The September 1812 quake in Los Angeles County, California, was marked by the precursory rushing noise. "The day was clear and uncommonly warm; it being Sunday, the people had assembled at San Juan Capistrano for evening service. About half an hour after the opening of service, an unusually loud, but distant rushing sound was heard in the atmosphere to the east and over the water, which resembled the noise of strong wind, but as the sound approached no perceptible breeze accompanied it. *The sea was smooth and the air calm.* So distant and loud was this atmospheric sound that several left the building on account of it.

"Immediately following the sound, the first and heaviest shock of the earthquake occurred, which was sufficiently severe to prostrate the Mission church almost in a body, burying in its ruins the most of those who remained behind, when the first indication of its approach was heard.

"The shock was very sudden and almost without warning, save from the rushing sound above noted, and to its occurrence at that moment is to be attributed the loss of life that followed" (*American Journal of Science*, 2: 22: 110, 1856).

The Assam, India, quake of August 15, 1950, was also accompanied by aerial sounds of uncertain origin. F. Kingdon-Ward provided a vivid eye- and earwitness account. "I find it very difficult to recollect my emotions during the four or five minutes the shock lasted; but the first feeling of bewilderment—an incredulous astonishment that these solid-looking hills were in the grip of a force which shook them as a terrier shakes a rat—soon gave place to stark terror. Yet my wife and I, lying side by side on the sandbank, spoke quite calmly together, and to our two Sherpa boys who, having already been thrown down twice, were lying close to us.

"The earthquake was now well under way, and it felt as though a powerful ram were hitting against the earth beneath us with the persistence of a kettledrum. I had exactly the sensation that a thin crust at the bottom of the basin, on which we lay, was breaking up like an ice floe, and that we were all going down together though an immense hole, into the interior of the earth. The din was terrible, but it was difficult to separate the noise made by the earthquake itself from the roar of the rock avalanches pouring down on all sides into the basin.

"Gradually the crash of falling rocks became more distinct, the frightful hammer blows weakened, the vibration grew less, and presently we knew that the main shock was over. The end of the earthquake was, however, very clearly marked by a noise, or series of noises, which had nothing to do with falling rocks. From high up in the sky to the northwest (as it seemed) came a quick succession of short, sharp explosions—five or six—clear and loud, each quite distinct, like 'ack-ack' shells bursting. It was the 'cease fire'" (*Nature*, 167: 130–31, 1951).

The Assam region of India has been famous for explosive sounds, and in the Ganges Delta, not too far away, are heard the famous Barisāl Guns. (See Chapter 7.) All of these sounds may stem from earthquake activity. The apparent aerial origin of the explosive sounds is mysterious, although the earthquake sounds may be bent by the atmosphere, creating in effect an acoustic mirage.

THE EARTH AS A DRUM

Really large earthquakes set the earth's lithosphere and hydrosphere into violent motion. The planet's solid crust may suddenly rise or sink by tens of feet; tidal waves (*tsunamis*) of even greater amplitude may be set in motion on the ocean's surface. The earth's surface appears to act like a drumhead. These rapid motions are communicated to the atmosphere, where they propagate as very long wavelength pressure waves—much like sound waves, only of very low frequency. Seismic air waves can travel long distances, even up into the ionosphere, where their passage can be detected through radio propagation anomalies.

The violent March 28, 1964, Alaskan earthquake disturbed both the atmosphere and ionosphere, to say nothing of the large-scale crustal distortions. Bruce A. Bolt recorded the air waves at Berkeley. "Exceptional atmospheric waves, resembling those from large nuclear explosions, have been recorded at Berkeley after the Alaskan earthquake of March 28, 1964. This severe earthquake occurred 3,130 km. away from Berkeley near the head of Prince William Sound. A preliminary determination made by the U.S. Coast and Geodetic Survey gives an origin time of 03 h. 36 min. 13 sec. GMT; the geographic latitude and longitude are 61.05° N., 147.50° W. Displacements of the adjacent seabed generated a damaging *tsunami* which was observed at numerous places around the Pacific. Changes in sea level indicate that the mainland in the disturbed region along the coast rose about 7 ft., while a portion of Kodiak Island subsided by about 5 ft.

* * *

"In addition to the seismic waves recorded by pendulum seismographs, two distinct wave trains were recorded by a microbarograph in the seismic vault. The instrument is a Davies Marion barovariograph designed to respond to pressure fluctuations with periods down to 10 seconds. An electric flow sensor is placed in an air-line between the atmosphere and a thermally insulated 40-liter flask. The sensor detects relative variations in the resistance of two thermistors placed symmetrically in the air-line about a heated thermistor. The signal is recorded continuously on a paper chart which moves at 6 mm. per minute. Sensitivity in March 1964 was set such that 1 mm. of pen deflexion corresponded to a pressure variation of 0.0048 millibars.

* * *

"The pressure pulse may be explained as a seismic air wave which was generated by sudden vertical displacement or tilting of the Earth's surface near the epicentre of the earthquake. Such movements account for the *tsunami* as well as the observed changes in sea-level. Computation shows that the approximate amplitude of the recorded atmospheric wave with [a] period [of] 3 minutes and velocity 317 metres per second is 0.75 metres. This is of the order of the noted changes in ground elevation. The seismic air wave would have a more extensive source than the corresponding waves from nuclear explosions. Although an extended source complicates the wave form, there is the possibility that correlation between similar recordings made at stations distributed around the epicentre may provide information on the direction of tilting of the displaced region.

"The *tsunami* arrived off San Francisco about 2.5 h. after the seismic air wave. A tide gauge operated by the U.S. Coast and Geodetic Survey near the entrance of San Francisco Bay responded to the first surge of the *tsunami* 5 hours, 9 minutes after the earthquake. (The mareogram shows a long train of oscillations of a predominantly 40-minute period. These are seismic seiches of the water of San Francisco Bay.)

"Pressure pulses propagating in the atmosphere after such natural events as the Krakatoa volcanic eruption and the Siberian meteoritic impact have been examined previously. A few observations of acoustic waves generated by displacement in the meizoseismal area of an earthquake have also been discussed. For example, Benioff and Gutenberg identified pressure variations with [a] period [of] 0.5–2 seconds on barographs written 670 km. from an earthquake epicentre. In 1926, Thomson reported sounds heard out to 270 km. from a New Zealand earthquake; F. J. Whipple remarked that he could find no earlier references to sounds at such great distances. An intense dispersive seismic air wave of the type generated by the Alaskan earthquake does not appear to have been previously reported. It is important to know how widely it was recorded by barographs.

"The present observation suggests the possibility of an additional method of prediction of a *tsunami*. After the detection of a large Pacific earthquake, the recording of a seismic air wave at a time appropriate to the epicentral distance would provide evidence that Earth movement favourable to seismic sea-wave generation may have occurred" (*Nature*, 202: 1095–96, 1964).

That the pressure waves launched by the Alaskan quake actually penetrated the ionosphere (over 50 miles up) was confirmed by ionosphere-measuring equipment in Alaska, Hawaii, and California (*Journal of Geophysical Research*, 70: 1250–51, 1965).

Such pressure waves are set in motion by the sudden ground and sea motions, just like sound waves from a drum. The wavelengths, of course, are thousands of times greater than for audible pressure waves (sound waves), but the principles of acoustics still apply. Pressure waves of this type may travel long distances horizontally as well as vertically. If the pressure changes are sufficiently sharp and strong, there is a possibility of creating secondary physical and physiological effects, such as luminous phenomena and, in humans, a kind of disorientation.

EARTHQUAKE FLAMES AND UNUSUAL LUMINOSITIES

In Chapter 1, several varieties of earthquake lights were described. The sky flashes, auroralike phenomena, ball lightning, and ordinary lightning were attributed to electrical forces built up between the earth and atmosphere due, in part at least, to the piezoelectric effect. Here, the category of earthquake-associated luminous phenomena is broadened to include flames, *ignis fatuus,* and similar effects caused by the actual release and burning of gases from the earth due to earthquake action. It is not always easy to distinguish between electrical action and the combustion of natural gases.

During their famous UFO study at the University of Colorado, Martin D. Altschuler, a member of E. U. Condon's group, prepared a concise summary of earthquake-associated sky luminescence. Several of these earthquake lights manifestly arise from the combustion of released gases.

"Intense electrical activity has often been reported prior to, during, and after earthquakes. Unusual luminescent phenomena seen in the sky have been classified into categories: (1) indefinite instantaneous illumination, [including] (a) lightning (and brightenings), (b) sparks or sprinkles of light, (c) thin luminous stripes or streamers; (2) well-defined and mobile luminous masses, [encompassing] (a) fireballs (ball lightning), (b) columns of fire (vertical), (c) beams of fire (presumably horizontal or oblique), (d) luminous funnels; (3) bright flames and emanations, [such as] (a) flames, (b) little flames, (c) many sparks, (d) luminous vapor; and (4) phosphorescence of sky and clouds. The classification is somewhat ambiguous but is rather descriptive of luminous events associated with earthquakes.

"The earliest description of such phenomena was given by Tacitus, who describes the earthquake of the Achaian cities in 373 B.C.E. Japanese records describe luminous effects during many severe earthquakes. In the Kamakura Earthquake of 1257 A.D., bluish flames were seen to emerge from fissures opened in the ground.

"Flying luminous objects are mentioned in connection with the earthquake at Yedo (Tokyo) during the winter of 1672. A fireball resembling a paper-lantern was seen flying through the sky toward the east. During the Tosa earthquake of 1698, a number of fireballs shaped like wheels were seen flying in different directions. In the case of the Great Genroku Earthquake of 31 December 1730, in Tokaido, luminous 'bodies' and luminous 'air' were reported during the nights preceding the day of the severest shock. Afterwards a kind of luminosity resembling sheet lightning was observed for about 20 days, even when there were clouds in the sky. One record of the Shinano Earthquake of 1847 states: 'Under the dark sky, a fiery cloud appeared in the direction of Mt. Izuna. It was seen to make a whirling motion and then disappeared. Immediately afterward, a roaring sound was heard, followed by severe earthquakes.' In Kyoto in August, 1830, it is reported that during the night preceding the earthquake luminous phenomena were seen in the whole sky; at times, illumination emitted from the ground was comparable in brightness to daylight. In the Kwanto Earthquake of 1 September 1923, a staff member of the Central Meteorological Observatory saw a kind of stationary fireball in the sky of Tokyo.

"The earthquake at Izu, 26 November 1930, was studied in detail for associated atmospheric luminescence. Many reports of sightings were obtained. The day prior to the quake, at 4 P.M., a number of fishermen observed a spherical luminous body to the west of Mt. Amagi, which moved northwest at considerable speed. Fireballs (ball lightning) and luminous clouds were repeatedly observed. A funnel-shaped light resembling a searchlight was also seen. Most witnesses reported pale blue or white illumination, but others reported reddish or orange colors" (*Scientific Study of Unidentified Flying Objects,* New York: Bantam Books, 1969, pp. 740–41).

Actual flames, seemingly due to combustion, were reported during the 1872 Cerro Gardo, California, quake. "Immediately following the great shock, men whose judgment and veracity are beyond question, while sitting on the ground near the Eclipse Mines, saw sheets of flame on the rocky sides of the Inyo Mountains, but half a mile distant. The flames, observed in several places, waved to and fro, apparently clear of the ground, like vast torches. They continued for only a few minutes" (*Nature,* 6: 89–90, 1872).

Professor Edgar L. Larkin of the Lowe Observatory solicited eyewitness accounts of luminous phenomena from the inhabitants of stricken San Francisco immediately after the 1906 convulsion. "'One of the most vivid, awe-inspiring, and impressive facts . . . is this: the people in this city did not hear subterranean sounds! But the awful reason why was because of the terrible roar roundabout, from seething flames, tumbling walls, the crashing of glass, and the hissing of sliding, rasping miles of wire. The literature of earthquakes does not present a more striking and startling fact, for the roaring of the city all aflame was louder than the thundering in the caves of gloom below.' Other observers failed to note that the city was already roaring with 'seething flames' in the forty-seven seconds through which the shock lasted.

* * *

"'The display of blue flames before the onslaught of the red ones, and their final yellow sequences, was very remarkable. The appearance of blue lights,' says Professor Larkin, 'was over a wider area than first thought. At Petaluma . . . blue flames eighteen inches in height played over a wide expanse of marsh land. . . . Blue flames were seen hovering over the bases of foothills in western San Francisco'" (*Science,* 24: 178–80, 1906).

The catastrophic 1976 Tangshan earthquake in China was noted for luminous effects. "Just before the earth began to shudder, residents were awakened by a brilliant incandescence that lit up the dark, early morning sky for hundreds of miles around. The glow was predominantly red and white. . . ." This glow may have been of electrical origin, but could electricity also be blamed for the following? "In the quake's aftermath, many bushes were scorched on only one side, much like snow accumulates preferentially on the windward side of a tree trunk during a driving blizzard" (*Science News,* 111: 388, 1977). The reader might note that similar scorching effects are associated with exceptionally powerful tornados.

DO EARTHQUAKES CAUSE MAGNETIC CHANGES?

For over 200 years, scientists have debated whether earthquakes alter the earth's magnetic field. Many reports in the older literature tell of suspended magnets suddenly oscillating at the onset of quake tremors. There are even cases of "keepers" falling off the ends of horseshoe magnets during an earthquake. In view of the purported electrical attributes of large earthquakes, it was reasonable to suppose that real magnetic charges were responsible for the observations. In any event, the flow of powerful electrical currents through the earth's crust in the neighborhood of a quake's focus would certainly disturb the ambient terrestrial magnetic field, just as an electrical current in a wire creates a magnetic field around the wire. Furthermore, a piezomagnetic effect also exists. The magnetic properties of rocks, principally those containing magnetite, can be changed by the application of pressure to the rocks. Thus basic physical laws do not rule out a seismomagnetic effect.

These old observations of seismomagnetic effects have been carefully studied in recent times and for the most part discarded. The mechanical effects of the earthquake shocks seem to be the real culprits. They were more than sufficient to account for all the quivering and jostled magnets. In effect the magnetic instruments were behaving as seismographs, registering ground motion rather than changes in the magnetic field. Today earthquake magnetism seems not only elusive but perhaps nonexistent.

Nevertheless seismogeologists have renewed their interest in earthquake magnetism because the strains building up in the earth's crust prior to a major quake might reveal themselves through the piezomagnetic effect. Quakes might be forecast through knowledge of these strains. In the United States and Japan, scientists have installed sensitive magnetometers in earthquake-prone regions, such as along the San Andreas fault. To be sure, there have been precursory magnetic fluctuations, but sometimes there are not. The whole business of earthquake magnetism is still poorly understood.

It also appears that earthquakes and geomagnetic changes may both be related to a third factor. Surendra Singh has recently studied the relationship between microearthquakes (tiny quakes detectable only through sensitive instrumentation) and equally small pulsations in the earth's magnetic field. Both types of phenomena seem closely linked to solar flare activity. A strong solar flare will substantially increase the force of the solar wind and other radiations hitting the earth's atmosphere, the effects being eventually communicated to the earth's crust through changes in barometric pressure and other factors. Microearthquakes are stimulated by such pressure changes, just as they are by the crustal strains produced by the gravitational effects of the moon passing overhead, also known as crustal tidal effects (*Seismological Society of America, Bulletin*, 68: 1533–35, 1978).

The question here is whether the magnetic pulsations are created by the microearthquakes through the piezomagnetic effect or whether they are simply due to the impact of solar radiations on the earth's magnetosphere. The two forces could be working simultaneously.

STRANGE EARTHQUAKE EFFECTS ON THE EARTH'S CRUST AND LIQUIDS

Cracks, gaping fissures, landslides, and similar distortions of the earth's crust are common during earthquakes. The intense pressures in the crustal rocks generate a curious class of phenomena with characteristics of both fluids and solids. Water geysers, sometimes hot and/or salty, occur frequently. Such squeezing or wringing out of crustal fluids is not surprising considering the intense pressures developed during quakes. More surprising are sand volcanos and the blowing out of coal and other solid sedimentary deposits. Such curiosities require the extreme forces produced by the greatest earthquakes.

In the United States, the colossal series of New Madrid, Missouri, quakes (1811–12) epitomize the intense forces that can be created in the crust. The following testimony on surface convulsions was taken from Godfrey Le Sieur: "The first shock came at 2 A.M., December 16, 1811, and was so severe that big houses and chimneys were shaken down, and at half-hour intervals light shocks were felt until 7 A.M., when a rumbling like distant thunder was heard, and in about an instant the earth began to totter and shake so that persons could neither stand nor walk. The earth was observed to roll in waves a few feet high, with visible depressions between. By and by these swells burst, throwing up large volumes of water, sand, and coal. Some was partly coated with what seemed to be sulphur. When the swells burst, fissures were left running in a northern and southern direction, and parallel for miles. Some were 5 miles long, 4 1/2 feet deep, and 10 feet wide. The rumbling appeared to come from the west and travel east. Similar shocks were heard at intervals until January 7, 1812, when another shock came, as severe as the first. Then all except two families left, leaving behind them all their property, which proved to be a total loss, as adventurers came and carried off their goods in flat boats to Natchez and New Orleans, as well as all their stock which

Curious craterlike vents made by a large earthquake

they could not slaughter. On February 17 there occurred another severe shock, having the same effect as the others and forming fissures and lakes. As the fissures varied in size, the water, coal, and sand were thrown out to different heights of from 5 to 10 feet. Besides long and narrow fissures, there were others of an oval or circular form, making long and deep basins some 100 yards wide and deep enough to retain water in dry seasons. The damaged and uptorn country embraced an area of 150 miles in circumference, including the old town of Little Prairie [now called Caruthersville] as the center, a large extent on each side of Whitewater, called Little River, [and] also both sides of the St. Francis in Missouri and Arkansas. Reelfoot Lake, in Tennessee, sank 10 feet" (*Journal of Geology*, 13: 46–47, 1905).

Even lesser quakes give rise to peculiar effects, such as the August 23, 1890, phenomena at Mono Lake, California. "The southern end of Mono Lake was considerably agitated last Sunday, and dwellers in that shaky locality were much perturbed. Steam was issuing from the lake as far as could be seen, in sudden puffs, and the water was boiling fiercely, while high waves rolled upon the beach and [in] receding left the sand smoking. In a moment the air was thick with blinding hot sulphurous vapor, and subterraneous moans and rumblings made the witnesses think that the devil was holding high carnival down below" (*Smithsonian Miscellaneous Collections*, 37: 153, 1898).

Kenneth Segerstrom has reported that a variety of unusual pressure effects occurred during the 1960 Chilean quake. "A side effect of the earthquake of May 21, 1960, near Concepción, Chile, was the eruption of water, sand, and clay from fissures, and circular or elliptical vents in a cultivated field and in tidal mud flats near the mouth of the Bío-Bío river. According to eye-witness accounts, muddy water continued to erupt for about 6 hours after the earthquake.

"Small ridges of sand along the fissures and cones of sand at the other vents were formed. Craterlike depressions in the center caused the cones to resemble volcanoes. Some of the miniature 'volcanoes' were double, others were breached on one side, still others had minute 'satellite' cones. 'Bombs' of clay and peat were ejected from the 'craters' and from fissures. Small cavities extended under the clayey topsoil.

"The accumulations of erupted sand ranged in width from 5 to 70 cm., and they attained a maximum height of about 10 cm. above the adjacent soil surface. Some of the fissures attained lengths of several tens of meters. Clay 'bombs' as much as 20 cm. across and 7–8 cm. thick were found as far away as 1.2 meters from the nearest fissure or 'crater'" (*Geological Society of America, Bulletin*, 71: 1972, 1960).

A DROLL PHENOMENON

The following item appeared under the above title in an old issue of *Scientific American*. "The Singapore Free Press, East Indies, of September 14, gives an account of a strange phenomena that occurred at Chantibun in the eastern part of the kingdom of Siam on the 13th of May last. First a violent shock of earthquake was felt, accompanied with tremendous noise and subterranean roaring. The doors and partitions of the houses were cracked and strained. But more extraordinary than all, it says: 'During the shock, there spontaneously came out of the ground a species of human hairs in almost every place—in the bazaars, in the roads, in the fields, and the most solid places. These hairs, which are pretty long, stand upright and adhere strongly to the ground. When they are burned, they twist like human hairs and have a burned smell which makes it to be believed that they are really hairs; they all appeared in the twinkling of an eye during the earthquake. The river of Chantibun was all rippling, and bubbles rose to the surface, so that the water was quite white. It is thought that these hairs may have been produced by electricity. The mountains of Chantibun run nearly from north to south and are united to the system which separates Camboja [Cambodia] from Siam.'

"The hairs were probably some interior bituminous substance melted and blown through the pores of the earth into fine strings and congealed, resembling hairs, as everyone knows is the case with rosin, &c." (*Scientific American*, 4: 139, 1848).

This irresistible item is not alone in the literature. Earthquake hairs made the pages of the prestigious *Nature*, but were quickly disposed of. A Mr. Furtune, who spent considerable time in China, had this to say about the "phenomenon": "Groups of Chinese were seen in the gardens, roadsides, and fields engaged in gathering hairs which are said to make their appearance on the surface of the ground after an earthquake takes place. This proceeding attracted a great deal of attention from some of the foreign residents in Shanghai, and the Chinese were closely examined upon the subject. Most of them fully believed that these hairs made their appearance only after an earthquake had occurred, but could give no satisfactory explanation of the phenomenon, while some, more wise than their neighbours, did not hesitate to affirm that they belonged to some huge subterraneous animal whose slightest shake was sufficient to move the world.

"I must confess, at the risk of being laughed at, that I was one of those who took an interest in this curious subject and that I joined several groups who were searching for these hairs. In the course of my travels I have ever found it unwise to laugh at what I conceived to be the prejudices of a people simply because I could not understand them. In this instance, however, I must confess the results were not worth the trouble I took. The hairs, such as I picked up, and such as were shown me by the Chinese, had certainly been produced above the earth and not below it. In some instances they might readily be traced to horses, dogs, and cats, while in others they were evidently of vegetable origin. The northeastern part of China produces a very valuable tree known by the name of the hemp-palm [*Chamaerops fortunei*, see Kew Report, 1880, p. 31] from the quantity of fibrous bracts it produces just under its blossoms. Many of these fibres were shown to me by the Chinese as a portion of the hairs in question; and when I pointed out the source from which such had come and which it was impossible to dispute, my friends laughed, and, with true Chinese politeness, acknowledged I was right, and yet I have no doubt they still held their former opinions concerning the origin of such hairs. The whole matter simply resolves itself into this: if the hairs pointed out to me were the *true* ones, then such things may be gathered not only after earthquakes, but at any other time. But if, after all, these were not the real things, and if some vegetable (I shall not say animal) production was formed, owing to the peculiar condition of the atmosphere and from other causes, I can only say that such production did not come under my observation" (*Nature*, 34: 56–57, 1886).

GROUND TREMORS UNRELATED TO EARTHQUAKES

Any city dweller can tell you that motor traffic shakes the ground. Those near airports will confirm that low-level jets do the same. Beyond legitimate earthquakes, man-made traffic noise and explosions, and natural volcanos and meteorite impacts, are there other sources of ground tremors—especially natural sources? There are, as the following accounts will prove.

Thunderstorms as atmospheric engines develop tremendous power levels. Some thunder is so strong that the ground seems to shake, although this may be illusory in some cases. If conditions are just right, some of the thunder's energy may be coupled to the earth's crust, much as one tuning fork can set another vibrating in sympathy. Such may have been the case of the storm that hit Alexandria Bay, New York, on October 27, 1917, as reported by Douglas F. Manning.

"Toward evening my aneroid [barometer] began to fall rapidly and the clouds increased, and by 8 o'clock a rain was falling. At about 10 [P.M.] I noticed a flash of lightning, and this was followed in a short interval by a deep, prolonged rumble, causing windows and doors to rattle, chinaware to jar, and a distinct earth tremor was felt; in fact many thought it was one. The lightning increased in intensity and frequency and the same marked earth tremors followed each flash at short intervals, and it seemed as if a series of earthquakes were taking place, so strong was the concussion produced. The storm gradually passed over, accompanied by a tremendous but brief downpour of rain mixed with small hail, and by 11 o'clock all was still again.

"To-day one hears many stories of the storm and its peculiar behavior, all making note of the trembling effect produced" (*Monthly Weather Review*, 45: 515, 1917).

The energy of the moving atmosphere can also set large ice sheets into vibration, like a reed in a musical woodwind instrument. This type of vibration is not at all like the strange rending squeaks and booming of lake ice in a strong wind. Rather these are true resonant vibrations, although they are at frequencies too low to hear. The 1933–34 polar expedition on the S.S. *Cheluskin* to the Chukchi Sea detected this type of ice-sheet vibration:

"The solid ice-cap of the sea, which represents as it were an immense elastic plate on a liquid foundation, is in a state of perpetual vibration. Though I had no special seismic apparatus at my disposal, I was nevertheless able, by means of very primitive hand-made instruments, to detect and roughly to measure these vibrations. They proved for the most part to be caused by the wind, and the direction of the greatest amplitudes tallied with the direction of the prevailing wind. A few cases of considerable vibrations running in a determined direction were observed on a windless day. Some hours later (up to eight hours), the wind blew in the same direction; evidently it did not keep pace with the sound oscillations it had created in the ice. We call those vibrations 'wind vibrations', but we admit that they may consist in a periodic warping of the ice-plate.

"Besides these strictly directed 'wind vibrations,' there may be observed 'disturbance vibrations' in the ice, spreading equally from the centre—the spot of the breaking up of the ice in different directions. A systematic investigation of the 'wind vibrations' would evidently greatly assist arctic synoptics. The study of the 'disturbance vibrations' will obviously permit periodicities in the dynamics of the ice-covered sea to be determined" (*Nature*, 134: 537–38, 1934).

A most interesting phenomenon occurs when water flows over a small dam possessing natural frequencies of vibration that can be excited by the flowing water. In a sense the phenomenon resembles the wind-created vibrations in large ice sheets, except that the water takes the place of the wind and the dam substitutes for the ice. The large concrete and earthen dams that are so common these days generally don't vibrate, but the old wooden mill-dams of bygone days could set the area around the dam to shaking and rouse the local citizenry. Elias Loomis made an extensive study of vibrating dams about 140 years ago, and here are some of his observations.

"Sometime in the winter of 1841–42, my opinion was asked respecting a remarkable phenomenon noticed at Cuyahoga Falls, a village on the Cuyahoga River about eight miles from [the] Hudson. The phenomenon consisted in the vibrations of the doors and windows and other movable objects belonging to the buildings in the village. They were noticed at certain stages of the water and at times ceased entirely. They were generally ascribed to a certain dam in the river, and various conjectures were formed as to the mode of their production. The subject was new to me, and I did not at first form any distinct idea of the phenomenon itself or its cause. Some weeks afterwards, I visited the locality, and although the water was at too low a stage to exhibit the phenomenon in question, I succeeded in obtaining a pretty good description of the facts and formed my opinion as to its cause. I published a notice of it in the

Ohio *Observer* which led to some discussion and brought to light several similar cases elsewhere. As I have not succeeded in finding any notice of this subject in such books as I have had the opportunity of consulting, I have thought it desirable that the facts should be placed on record. I propose therefore to communicate such information as I have been able to collect and shall conclude with some speculations as to the cause of the phenomena.

"*Dam at Cuyahoga Falls, Ohio.* This dam is a portion of an arc of a circle, the convexity of course being turned up stream. It is formed of hewn oak timbers one foot square, piled upon each other in tiers, all morticed firmly together, so as to form as it were one huge plank two feet thick; twelve and a half feet in breadth, and ninety feet in length, measured not between the banks but between the points of support. Its curvature is described with a radius of a hundred and twenty feet; that is, the arc is about one eighth of the circumference of a circle. There is an embankment of earth upon the upper side, which until recently was left in an unfinished state. The bank did not rise to the top of the dam and sloped off very abruptly. This dam was erected in the summer of 1840. During the winter of 1840–41 there was noticed considerable rattling of the windows of the neighboring houses, a phenomenon different from what had ever been noticed before; but during the winter of 1841–42, which was a very open and wet winter, the vibrations were more remarkable and became a matter of general complaint. The doors and windows of most of the houses in the village would shake for days together violently as with the ague, and to such a degree as seriously to disturb sleep. This phenomenon was apparently somewhat capricious. After continuing for a time, perhaps an hour or a day or longer, the vibrations would suddenly cease and after some interruption might be as suddenly resumed. The rattling of vibrating objects would frequently cease, while the vibrations could still be *felt*. A window, when *apparently* at rest, if put in motion by the hand, would continue to rattle. The buildings themselves (stone as well as wood) would vibrate with the doors and windows. This might be felt and also seen; as for example, a slender branch of a grapevine trained up against the side of a stone building, was seen to vibrate in exact time with the doors and windows.

"The vibrations ceased entirely when water ceased to pour over the dam; they were also inconsiderable when the depth of water was eighteen or twenty-four inches. A depth of five or six inches produced the greatest effect. The number of vibrations per second was thought to be about constant, but no accurate experiments on this point were ever made. From the best estimate I could obtain, they amounted to twelve or fifteen per second" (*American Journal of Science*, 1: 45: 363–65, 1843).

The analogy of the vibrating reed in a wind instrument seems to apply to the old vibrating wooden dams, but it cannot account for the low-frequency earth vibrations found in the vicinities of large natural waterfalls. In most instances, a single frequency of vibration predominates, and that frequency is inversely proportional to the height of the waterfall. The vibrations must result when the falling water hits the base of the fall, but if the water flow is more or less continuous, why should such steady flow set the ground into vibration? John S. Rinehart suggested one mechanism. "Water breaks up into discrete turbulent eddies as it falls, with the length of each eddy increasing with distance of fall. Such

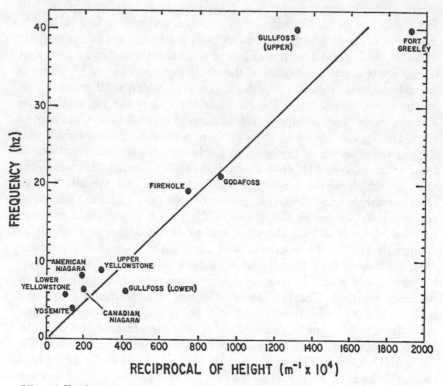

Waterfall vibration frequency is inversely proportional to waterfall height; the higher the fall, the lower the frequency.

separation, which would give intermittent impacts and lower frequency with greater heights, is clearly evident in most waterfalls. A small individual turbulent eddy usually does not maintain its identity the full length of the fall. It grows in length and then melds with others to form larger and longer eddies, each of which strikes the base of the fall, producing strong earth motion" (*Science*, 164: 1513–14, 1969).

DOES THE EARTH BREATHE BEFORE EARTHQUAKES?

If the earth spouts water, sand, and other substances during an earthquake, gases must certainly be expelled too. In fact, reports of sulphurous emanations are legion in the early earthquake literature. Is it possible that impending quakes may signal their arrival beforehand by squeezing the strata just enough to release small quantities of the contained gases? The evidence, as with seismomagnetic effects, is not clear-cut.

On one hand, we have many ancient accounts of sulphurous gas emission prior to quakes. "[On] November 1, 1835 in the Moluccas Islands. A violent and destructive earthquake. Preceded for three weeks by a heavy sulphurous fog" (*Report of the British Association,* 258, 1854).

Contemporary scientists place little value on these old "nosewitness" accounts, preferring to employ their instruments to detect emissions of radon, helium, and other distinctive gases contained in the earth's crust. The increased discharge of radon by hot springs and in mines has, for example, been linked to some earthquakes. We also have data such as the following reported by Hiroshi Wakita in a *Science* paper. "*Abstract.* 'Helium spots,' where a significant amount of helium is present in the soil . . . have been found along the fault zone formed by the 1966 Matsuhiro swarm earthquakes. The formation of the 'helium spots' and the occurrence of the earthquakes are interpreted as the results of a diapiric uprise of a magma approximately 1 km. in diameter" (*Science,* 200: 430–32, 1978). In simpler language, uprising molten rock (magma) releases helium that migrates upward through the solid crust. The molten rock also may initiate quake activity.

The time has come to unite two reasonably well-established precursory earthquake phenomena: the emission of crustal gases and electrification of the crust via the piezoelectric effect. Could the gases being squeezed out of the soil and rocks prior to a quake be electrically charged—that is, in the form of ion clouds?

Helmut Tributsch proposed that the answer is yes in a speculative paper published in *Nature* in 1978. Tributsch noted that a strong upward flow of ions from the surface before a big quake might account for many of the tales of animal agitation, human physiological effects, and strange atmospheric phenomena preceding major convulsions of the crust. Specifically he noted:

1. An increase in positive ion concentration increases human tension

and irritability, as it is observed to do during the well-known Alpine foehn winds.

2. Electrostatically charged aerosols can account for the peculiar fogs, clouds, and earthquake weather mentioned in earthquake literature.

3. Ion emission would encourage the production of earthquake lights—a well-established phenomenon (see Chapter 1).

4. Strange precursory animal behavior would be accounted for in the same manner as human prequake sensations.

5. There are several observations of electrometer discharge before earthquakes—i.e., actual ion flow is detected.

The evidence, as Tributsch readily admits, is all circumstantial; but his suggestion does provide a common cause for many of the elusive and controversial prequake phenomena (*Nature*, 276: 606–8, 1978).

THE CURIOUS SUPERSENSITIVITY OF ANIMALS TO IMPENDING QUAKES

Earthquake lore never fails to mention that many animals become agitated before a major earthquake. Long before humans hear, feel, or see anything, birds, fish, and mammals seem to know something unusual is imminent. For many years seismologists tended to ignore stories of precursory animal behavior as scientifically useless anecdotes, probably greatly exaggerated. Recently, large quakes in China were preceded by thousands of observations of anomalous animal behavior. The evidence was so strong that earthquake scientists are now taking a second look at the phenomenon.

What earthquake precursors could stimulate strange animal behavior? Subaudible sound, changing magnetic fields, modifications of the earth's electric field, and the release of subterranean gases are all possibilities. Instruments demonstrate that such changes often, but not always, precede seismic activity. Animals, of course, are much more sensitive than humans to some of these precursors, and this may account for the long history of anecdotal evidence. Much remains to be explained in this area, as the following data will prove.

First, we have two general descriptions of animal behavior during earthquakes. Both are rather old, but they are typical of dozens, perhaps hundreds, of similar observations.

"The records of most great earthquakes refer to the consternation of dogs, horses, cattle, and other domestic animals. Fish also are frequently affected. In the London earthquake of 1749, roach [*Rutilus rutilus*] and other fish in a canal showed evident signs of confusion and fright; and sometimes after an earthquake, fish rise to the surface dead and dying. During the Tokyo earthquake of 1880, cats inside a house ran about trying to escape, foxes barked, and horses tried to kick down the boards confining them to their stables. There can, therefore, be no doubt that animals know something unusual and terrifying is taking place. More interesting than these are the observations showing that animals are agitated just before an earthquake. Ponies have been known to prance about their stalls, pheasants to scream, and frogs to cease croaking suddenly a little time before a shock, as if aware of its coming. The Japanese say that moles show their agitation by burrowing. Geese, pigs, and dogs appear more sensitive in this respect than other animals. After the great Calabrian earthquake, it is said that the neighing of a horse, the braying of an ass, or the cackle of a goose was sufficient to cause the inhabitants to fly from their houses in expectation of a shock. Many birds are said to show their uneasiness before an earthquake by hiding their heads under their wings and behaving in an unusual manner. At the time of the Calabrian shock, little fish like sand-eels (*Cirricelli*), which are usually buried in the sand, came to the top and were caught in multitudes. In South America certain quadrupeds, such as dogs, cats, and jerboas [rats], are believed by the people to give warning of coming danger by their restlessness; sometime immense flocks of seabirds fly inland before an earthquake, as if alarmed by the commencement of some sub-oceanic disturbance. Before the shock of 1835 in Chile, all the dogs are said to have escaped from the city of Talcahuano. The explanation offered by Prof. Milne of this apparent prescience is that some animals are sensitive to the small tremors which precede nearly all earthquakes. He has himself felt them some seconds before the actual earthquake came. The alarm of intelligent animals would then be the result of their own experience, which has taught them that small tremors are premonitory of movements more alarming. Signs of alarm days before an earthquake are probably accidental; but sometimes in volcanic districts gases have emanated from the ground prior to earthquakes and have poisoned animals. In one case large numbers of fish were killed in this way in the Tiber, and at Follonica, on the morning of April 6, 1874, 'the streets and roads were covered with dead rats and mice. In fact, it seemed as if it had rained rats. The only explanation of the phenomenon was that these animals had been destroyed by emanations of carbon dioxide'" (*Nature*, 38: 500, 1888).

"In connection with the fearful catastrophes of recent date in Italy, California, and elsewhere, which, like so many others of like nature, will long retain a hold on human memory, attention has again been called to the fact that many animals give intimations of such great disturbances in advance by certain particular and often unusual conduct. It is particularly such animals as have their abode underground that often indicate, days before the event, that something unusual in nature is about to occur, by coming out of their hiding places underground into the open.

"Aelian mentions that, in the year 373 before Christ, five days before the destruction of Helike, all the mice, weasels, snakes, and many other like creatures, were observed going in great masses along the roads leading from that place. Something similar was noticed also, later, though not to so marked an extent as in the case mentioned by Aelian. This leaving of their subterranean abodes by underground creatures on such occasions might possibly be explained by the emission of various malodorous and noxious gases during these disturbances of the earth.

"But not only do animals living under ground furnish indications that something out of the ordinary is about to happen. The larger animals on the surface, such as cows, horses, asses, sheep, and many birds, even, seem to get premonitions of particular natural phenomena and events.

"Thus it is related that in 1805, during an earthquake, the cattle at Naples and its neighborhood set up a continuous bellowing some time before the event, at the same time trying to support themselves more firmly by planting the forefeet widely apart; the sheep kept up a continuous bleating, and hens and other fowl expressed their restlessness by making a terrible racket. Even the dogs gave many indications of uneasiness at the time. The actions of animals observed during the great earthquake of 1783 seem to have been most remarkable. Thus the howling of the dogs at Messina became so unendurable that men were sent out with cudgels to kill them. Their noise was most marked during the progress of the earthquake, while it was difficult to pacify the animals in the vicinity for some time even after the cessation of the shocks. Dogs and horses ran about meanwhile with hanging heads, or stood with outstretched legs, as if aware of the need of planting themselves firmly. Horses that were ridden at the time stopped and stood still without orders, trembling so at the same time that no rider could remain in the saddle. Scophus tells the story of a cat during an earthquake at Locris which set up a most dismal caterwauling at the approach of each new shock, meanwhile constantly jumping from one point to another. The roosters kept up a continual crowing, both before and during the earthquake. In the fields Scophus observed hares so under the influence of the terrestrial disturbance that they made no attempt to escape and seemed in no way disturbed by his presence. A flock of sheep could not be kept on the right road, notwithstanding the efforts of shepherd and dogs, but fled in affrightened haste to the mountains. During the same year of 1783, fear had taken such possession of the peasants of Calabria that they were seen to flee from their huts the moment dogs began to howl, asses to bray, or cows to bellow. Birds, also, seem to have premonitions of the coming of such catastrophes. During the earthquake at Quintero, in Chile, in November 1822, the gulls uttered all sorts of unusual cries during the whole of the preceding night and were in constant restless motion during the quake. On February 20, 1835, the day before the earthquake at Concepción, [also] in Chile, at ten in the morning, great flocks of seabirds, mostly gulls, were seen to pass over the city landward, a phenomenon not to be explained by any stormy condition of the weather. It was fully an hour and a half after their passage, at 11:40 of the forenoon, before the earthquake came, one so disastrous that nearly the entire city was reduced to ruins. Even the fish in the sea seem to be disturbed at the approach of an earthquake. Thus during the one of 1783, quantities of fish were caught at Messina, of a kind that usually keeps hidden in its secret abodes at the ocean's bottom. And Alexander von Humboldt, the famous traveler and naturalist, tells of having observed the crocodiles of the Orinoco leaving the water and fleeing to the forest during an earthquake" (*American Review of Reviews,* 37: 104, 1908).

Back in the 1930s, a few scientists wondered whether the growing mountain of anecdotal evidence on prequake animal behavior might be sufficiently valid to help predict impending earthquakes. Not surprisingly the quake-haunted Japanese performed the first experiments. "Two Japanese seismologists, Dr. Shinkishi Hatai and Dr. Noboru Abe, observed that catfish (*Siluroidea*) in natural conditions showed signs of restlessness about six hours before earthquake disturbances were registered on their recording apparatus. Since catfish are, ordinarily, placid unresponsive creatures, experiments were made to test the seeming responsiveness. Catfish placed in an aquarium were tested three times a day by tapping on the supporting table. When no earthquake was impending, the fish moved lazily or not at all; but about six hours before a shock the fish jumped when the table was tapped and sometimes swam about agitatedly for a time before settling down upon the bottom again. Several months' testing showed that in a period when 178 earthquakes of all degrees of severity had been recorded, the fish had correctly predicted 80 per cent of the shocks. They showed no discrimination in their movements between slight local shocks and more serious distant shocks. The experimenters think that the catfish are made sensitive through electrical changes in the earth, since it was only when the aquarium was electrically earthed, through the drainpipe, that they responded to a coming earthquake" (*Nature*, 132: 817, 1933).

In recent years, the Chinese have actively solicited testimony from their farmers concerning premonitory signs of earthquakes. In this they have had some success, perhaps because China is densely populated with hundreds of millions of people "close to the earth" who are alert to slight, subtle phenomena.

Shen Ling-huang, a Chinese writer, filed this report after the Tangshan quake. "A stock-breeder in northern China got up to feed his animals before dawn on July 28, 1976. He is a member of the Kaokechuang People's Commune which lies only 40 kilometers away from the city of Tangshan. When he went into the stable, he found that instead of eating his two horses and two mules were jumping and kicking until they finally broke loose and dashed outside. At that moment, a dazzling white flash illuminated the sky and huge rumbling noises were heard. The Tangshan earthquake (magnitude 7.8) had struck.

"This occurrence was reported to Chinese scientists during a survey of the earthquake-affected areas around Tangshan. Their mission was to find out about the feasibility of an earthquake prediction program that made use of observations of animal behavior. This survey, covering Tangshan and 400 communes in 48 counties around it, was conducted by Chinese biophysicists, biologists, geophysicists, chemists, and meteorologists shortly after the earthquake.

"Through interviews and discussions with local people, the scientists collected information on 2,093 cases of unusual animal behavior in the time shortly before the earthquake. Nearly all of the anecdotes were passed on to the scientists by survivors of the earthquake themselves; the majority of the reports involved domestic animals. Some examples included goats that refused to go into pens, cats and dogs that picked up their offspring and carried them outdoors, pigs that squealed strangely, startled chickens that dashed out of coops in the middle of the night, rats that left their nests, and fish that dashed about aimlessly" (*Earthquake Information Bulletin,* 10: 231–33, 1978).

HOW HUMANS REACT TO EARTHQUAKE TREMORS

Humans cannot match the sensitivity of animals to earthquake precursors. The subtle signs that set dogs to howling pass by humans undetected. Nevertheless, some people do report a certain tenseness and irritability prior to major quakes. As mentioned in the section on gaseous precursors, positive ions emitted from the crust may stimulate such feelings. A second class of physical reactions comes as the tremors sweep across the landscape. These induce sensations akin to seasickness. Of course any sizable earthquake will inspire strongly emotional reportage by onlookers, given man's innate fear of quakes.

In a lengthy study of earthquakes experienced in Great Britain over many years, David Milne summarized his physiological findings as follows: "In many of the reports which have been quoted, notice is taken of impressions still more peculiar, as connected with the earthquake shocks.

"A feeling of *nausea* was experienced by many individuals, and which is variously described as resembling 'sea-sickness,'—'sickness, like that felt before fainting'—'uneasy sensation, which I can compare only to the first disagreeable feelings which usually precede a fit of sea-sickness,' —'a most peculiar sickish sensation, such as I never felt before.'

"Headaches were produced, as attested by the Rev. Mr. Walker on the 12th [of] October, by Mr. Rutherfurd, W. S., on the 14th [of] October 1839, and by Mr. Young of Crieff, on the 23d [of] October 1839, all of whom ascribe these as the effects of shocks which occurred on these days.

Nervous sensations of a more indefinite kind are spoken of by various individuals. On the 14th October, 1839, at the moment that the shock occurred, an individual, though he was not aware of its occurrence, experienced 'an unusual feeling, which led him to suppose that some illness was impending.' Mr. Robertson, who felt the shock of 16th October at Glendevon, on the north side of the Ochils, says, 'I remember having just before felt as if some strange presence had been silently gathering round me and could not be shaken off.' Mr. Laurie, the parish schoolmaster of Monzie, says, 'the shock of the earthquake on 23d October, affected the nerves disagreeably and left a painful impression. It reminds me vividly of the shock from an electric machine.'

"The conviction of there having been an electrical discharge was decidedly entertained by a number of individuals. Thus, at Alva, near Tillicoultry, two clergymen felt as if electrified. Mr. Jeffrey, who felt the shock in the Carse of Falkirk, says, 'I may mention a circumstance which I have not seen taken notice of in any account of the late earthquake . . . I am convinced it was accompanied with an electric shock. I was perfectly calm and collected at the time when it came on and never had any doubt of what it was, nor was I at all alarmed for the consequences. But the feeling produced upon my body was exactly similar to what an electric shock has in other circumstances had upon me.' Mr. Stein, surgeon at Menstrie near Stirling (in a report not before quoted) says, 'I think the atmosphere (on the 23d October 1839) was highly charged with electricity, both before and at the time when the shock occurred.' He speaks of 'the slightly reddened or lurid appearance of the atmosphere towards the S. and SE., particularly observable for several evenings preceding the shock of the 23d'" (*Edinburgh New Philosophical Journal*, 35: 151–52, 1843). The sensation of electric shock is especially interesting in view of the controversy over the reality of earthquake electricity.

In early April of 1970, several strong quakes with many aftershocks hit Manila. According to J. P. Henderson, there were many minor physiological reactions. "The reactions of a large circle of acquaintances seem to have been remarkably similar, especially on the morning of 9 April before the second major tremor; not only were sleeplessness, headaches, and giddiness experienced . . . but, in some instances, nausea of the kind experienced in a cross-Channel steamer in an irregular sea. Like myself, many of my friends live in elevated apartments where earth movements are exaggerated, but some of the sufferers live in bungalows at ground level" (*New Scientist*, 46: 300, 1970). It seems unlikely that the emission of ionized gases from the earth's crust would have much effect on dwellers in elevated apartments.

EARTHQUAKE WEATHER

Earthquake weather seems much like tornado weather in the sense of uneasiness it creates in humans. The features of the phenomenon were presented in a charming way by Richard A. Proctor, an English popularizer of science of a century ago. "Anybody who has ever lived for any length of time at a stretch in a region where earthquakes are common objects of the country and the seaside knows perfectly well what earthquake weather in the colloquial sense is really like. You are sitting in the piazza, about afternoon teatime let us say, and talking about nothing in particular with the usual sticky, tropical languor, when gradually a sort of faintness comes over the air, the sky begins to assume a lurid look, the street dogs leave off howling hideously in concert for half a minute, and even the grim vultures perched upon the housetops forget their obtrusive personal differences in a common sense of general uneasiness. There is an ominous hush in the air, with a corresponding lull in the conversation for a few seconds, and then somebody says with a yawn, 'It feels to me very much like earthquake weather.' Next minute you notice the piazza gently raised from its underpropping woodwork by some unseen power, observe the teapot quietly deposited in the hostess's lap, and are conscious of a rapid but graceful oscillating movement, as though the ship of state were pitching bodily and quickly in a long Atlantic swell. Almost before you have had time to feel surprised at the suddenness of the interruption (for the earth never stops to apologize), it is all over; and you pick up the teapot with a smile, continuing the conversation with the greatest attainable politeness, as if nothing at all unusual had happened meanwhile. With earthquakes, as with most other things and persons, familiarity breeds contempt" (*Living Age*, 160: 307, 1884).

Beyond this appealing subjective account lies considerable testimony that the more cataclysmic quakes are presaged and accompanied by fogs, mists, darknesses, and general obscurations of the atmosphere.

The emission of gases from the ground and the raising of dust naturally contribute to these effects, but other unappreciated factors may be involved, too. Myron L. Fuller, who made a detailed study of the New Madrid quakes, included sections on both darkness and vapors in his extensive report, excerpts of which follow.

"*Darkness.* —As in most of the great earthquakes the atmosphere seems to have become darkened during the more severe shocks in the Mississippi Valley. Eliza Bryan notes that total darkness accompanied the first shock, while a similar 'awful darkness of the atmosphere' marked the severe shock of 4 P.M. on February 7. Godfrey Le Sieur also says a 'dense black cloud of vapor overshadowed the land' after the severe shocks. At Herculaneum the atmosphere, according to Col. Samuel Hammond, was filled with smoke or fog so that a boat could not be seen 20 paces, and houses were so shrouded as not to be visible 50 feet. The air did not clear until the middle of the day. A writer from New Madrid states that at the time of the shock the air was clear, but in five minutes it became very dark, and the darkness continued until nearly morning, during which period there were six shocks. At 6.30 the air cleared, but at the severe shock later in the morning the darkness returned.

"The darkness was probably due to a number of cooperating causes. In all probability the dust projected into the air by the agitation of the surface, the opening and closing of fissures in dry earth, landslides on dry hillsides, and possibly the falling of chimneys and buildings contributed to supply to the atmosphere the suspended particles which presumably produced the obscurity described. It is likely also that aqueous vapors, rising from fissures connecting with the warm ground waters (temperature 50° to 55° F.), or from the waters extruded from cracks and craterlets and condensed by the cold December air played a part. The extrusion of such vapors, usually more or less sulphurous, is described by many witnesses. It is not entirely impossible that conditions favoring condensation of atmospheric moisture either accompanied or resulted from the earthquake disturbance.

"Besides the darkness observed in the area of principal disturbance, similar manifestations were recorded in other localities. For instance, at Columbia, Tenn., a very large volume of something like smoke was declared to have risen in the southwest, from which direction the sound appeared to have come, and, proceeding northeastward, settled as a black cloud in the course of the 10 or 15 minutes the shock lasted.

"An unusual darkness during the earthquake was reported at a number of other points, but if it had any relation to the earth disturbances its nature is not known. It seems likely that in the outlying districts the darkness was due to ordinary clouds associated with storms then in progress across the country.

"*Odors and vapors.* —Sulphurous or otherwise obnoxious odors and vapors were an attendant feature of the earthquake at many points, as stated by nearly every writer. Bryan speaks of the complete saturation of the atmosphere with sulphurous vapor a few minutes after the first shock and of similar vapors after the shock of February 7. Hildreth speaks of the escape of sulphur gas through the cracks, tainting the air and impregnating the water for a distance of 150 miles so it was unfit to use. Another observer, writing to Mitchill from New Madrid, states that although the air was clear at the time of the shock, within five minutes a vapor with a disagreeable smell and producing a difficulty of breathing impregnated the atmosphere. At Jeffersonville, Ind., warmth and smokiness were noted for several days after the shock, while at Columbia, S.C., the air during the shock felt impregnated with vapor which lasted for some time.

"The source of the odors in the New Madrid region seems to have been the buried organic matter which here, as elsewhere in the Mississippi embayment, occurs in the alluvium and underlying Tertiary deposits, the emanations coming mainly from the carbonaceous material extruded from below through the fissures and craterlets, which were numerous in the region. In the more remote localities, the vapors probably represented normal atmospheric condensations which happened to be coincident with the earthquake disturbance" (*U.S. Geological Survey Bulletin* 494, 1912).

R. D. Oldham, an English earthquake authority, in commenting on the sudden fog that had settled on the Straits of Messina after the devastating quake of December 28, 1908, offered a different natural mechanism that might create earthquake weather. He noted first that in the Messina quake and many others, natural storm systems cannot be blamed for the mist, fogs, etc. "The earthquake in Mexico of January 24, 1898, was similarly followed by a heavy mist, at a time of year when mists are usually unknown, and rainfall is so frequently reported as the immediate successor of an earthquake that we can no longer reject the hypothesis of a real connection between the two. Earthquake weather is a common expression in earthquake countries, but is usually applied to a heavy and oppressive feeling in the air which is supposed to precede an earthquake. Mr. Maxwell Hall has attempted to find an explanation in alterations of the barometric gradient by rapid upheaval of the ground and has shown that uplifts, which are within the range of possibility, would produce the required effects, but whether there is or is not an earthquake weather, in the ordinary sense of the words, there seems reason for believing that in another sense they represent a reality, and that, as has been suggested by Prof. Milne, the disturbance of the ground, when transmitted to the overlying air, may determine precipitation and explain the apparent association of severe earthquakes with mist and rain. What may be the nature of the influence we know not, but if [it is] mechanical, it must be either the result of the vibratory motion of the ground or else of permanent changes of level, accompanied by the sudden upheaval or depression of the overlying column of air, and of this permanent change of level we are still without any satisfactory evidence" (*Nature*, 79: 368–69, 1909).

Heavy rains are frequently associated with major earthquakes. Precipitation falling during and after the quake can be blamed on the clouds of dust raised by the quake. The dust, in effect, seeds the clouds. But if long periods of heavy rain precede the seismic effects, there is always the possibility that the additional supply of water seeping into the ground may actually bring on the quake. To illustrate, scientists have known for many years that fluids pumped down deep wells will increase the frequency of earthquakes, though these are usually small in magnitude.

Earthquakes and Possible Triggering Forces

In the absence of triggering forces, earthquakes would presumably be distributed uniformly in time. However, lengthy records of earthquakes are emphatic that earthquakes occur more often during some time intervals than others. For over 200 years scientists have been correlating earthquakes with every imaginable natural phenomenon in hopes of discovering triggering forces. The search has been less than successful. In fact, in the case of earthquakes and the earth's wobble there seems to be doubt about which is cause and which is effect.

Earthquakes definitely seem associated with solar activity (sunspots and flares), the earth's wobble (measured by minute latitude variations), and geomagnetism. It is also known that the active sun projects solar plasma toward the earth and that the interaction of the plasma with the earth may affect the earth's rotation. Changes in the earth's rate of rotation, in turn, may give rise to earthquake-triggering forces in the mantle. Thus a cause-and-effect relationship does exist here. But is the earth's 14-month Chandler Wobble stimulated by solar activity or by earthquake activity?

It is also conceivable that tidal stresses created by the moon initiate quakes. (Seismometers left on the moon indicate that the earth may also trigger moonquakes, which is only fair.) But how could Uranus, at its great distance, or the even more remote pulsars stimulate earthquakes? Nevertheless such correlations seem to exist, although some scientists have rejected them for statistical reasons. It may be, though, that the enthusiasm of the detractors is inspired by the lack of known physical mechanisms that might reach from Uranus and pulsar to earth.

CORRELATIONS OF EARTHQUAKES WITH SOLAR ACTIVITY

As so often in preceding chapters, nonscientists and even some scientists have discovered that a terrestrial phenomenon is related to sunspot number, which in turn is a measure of overall solar activity. Earthquakes are not immune to solar influences. Before the advent of spacecraft and their discovery of the solar wind and energetic solar photons, there was no obvious physical connection between sun and earth beyond gravitation. Despite this total absence of scientific grounds for contemplating a connection between solar activity and earthquake frequency, the early accumulators of earthquake data were struck again and again by the clustering of quakes every 11 years—approximately the sunspot frequency. Charles Davison, a pioneer in earthquake research, provided a nice historical summary of thinking on the subject:

"Every few years we pass through a season of marked earthquake frequency, or, as Mallet called it, a 'period of paroxysmal energy.' In the mere fact of clustering, there is nothing remarkable; it is its intensity, rather than its existence, that is worthy of notice. In Italy, for example, as Marcalli pointed out, 209 destructive earthquakes occurred between the years 1601 and 1881, and 182 of them in 103 years. In other words, the average frequency of great earthquakes during one of the cluster-years was eleven times that during one of the remaining years.

"The first seismologist who examined the clustering of earthquakes, the first, indeed, who possessed the necessary materials, was Robert Mallet. In 1858 he drew curves representing the frequency of earthquakes in each year from 1500 to 1850. The intervals between successive maxima in these curves varied widely. Though he could trace no law in their variation—it should be remembered that he counted weak shocks as well as strong—their average duration was found to lie between five and ten years, the shorter intervals being those of fewer, and usually weaker, earthquakes.

"Fifty years later, John Milne went close to the heart of the problem by suggesting that variations of seismic activity in distant regions may be synchronous. Considering the earthquakes from 1899 to 1907, he noticed that, during the last six years, the annual numbers of 'large earthquakes' on the eastern and western sides of the Pacific rose and fell together. In the following year he found that the destructive earthquakes of Italy and Japan during the last three centuries occurred in periods of activity, the intervals between them ranging from five to twenty years, and that of the eighteen years of maximum frequency in Italy, fourteen agreed with years of similar activity in Japan. 'These coincidences suggest,' he says, 'that a relief of seismic strain in one part of the world either brings about a relief in some other part or that relief is governed by some general internal or external agency.'

"At this time, Milne's catalogue of more than 4,000 destructive earthquakes was still unpublished, though it must have been approaching completion. It is on the fuller portion of this great work—that relating to the northern hemisphere from 1750 (and for some purposes from 1701) to 1899—that the present inquiry is based. My object at first was merely to ascertain if the cluster years for different intensities were the same or in any way related, and this work led to the recognition of several periods in the recurrence of cluster years. I hope to give fuller details of these periods in a later paper.

"To each earthquake Milne assigned an intensity according to a scale of three degrees. Shocks of intensity 1 were strong enough to crack walls or chimneys or to shatter old buildings. By those of intensity 2, buildings were unroofed or shattered and some were thrown down. Earthquakes of intensity 3 destroyed towns and isolated districts. In order to smooth away minor inequalities, I have taken three-yearly means of the annual numbers of earthquakes of each intensity. The corresponding curves show definite years of clustering, which are given in the following table:

	Int. 3	Int. 2	Int. 1	Sunspot Minimum
A	1754–56	1755–56	1755–56	1755
B	1765–66	1767	1766–67	1766
			1771–73	1775
C	1785–90	1784–86	1785–86	1785
		1789–91	1791–92	1798
			1799–1800	
D	1810–11	1811	1811–13	1810
E	1822–23	1818–20	1821–22	1823
F	1828–29	1827	1827–29	–
	1834–36	1832	–	1833
G	1840–41	1840–42	1840–42	1843
H	1845–47	1846–48	1846–47	–
J	1852–57	1852–56	1852–57	1856
		1859–60	1861–63	–

	Int. 3	Int. 2	Int. 1	Sunspot Minimum
K	1868–72	1869–72	1867	1867
			1873–74	
			1880–81	1878
L	1884–86	1884	1885–86	
M	1892–93	1893–94	1895	1889

"It will be seen that, in all three classes, there are twelve clusters at approximately the same times. They are denoted by the letters A–M. There are also six other clusters, two common to two classes, and four of earthquakes of intensity 1 only. Of the latter, two may not be real exceptions, for in the other classes there are traces, too slight to be otherwise noticed, of clusters about the years 1773 and 1798. In any case, the existence of at least four of these additional clusters seems to imply that they are not consequences of the great shocks of intensity 3, but rather that the clusters of all classes are the effects of some common cause or causes.

"More important, however, than the coincidences of the clusters are the intervals between the years of maximum frequency. Some of the intervals are so suggestive of an eleven-year period that it was only natural that the cluster years should be compared with the turning epochs of sunspot frequency. The last column of the table shows that eight clusters in all three classes (A–E, G–K) agree closely with the years of low sunspot frequency and that this correspondence also holds for three other clusters (1771–73, 1799–1800, and 1832 or 1834–36) which appear in only one or two classes. The only divergences are for the last two years of sunspot minima.

"In order to test more closely the existence of an eleven-year periodicity, I counted the numbers of earthquakes of each intensity in the years 1755, 1766, . . . , 1887; 1756, 1767, . . . , 1888; and so on, and took five-yearly means of these eleven sums, with the following results, the first subsequent year of least sunspot frequency being 1765:

Intensity	First Maximum Epoch	Amplitude
3	1764	0.16
2	1762–63	0.12
1	1763–64	0.09

"Thus in destructive earthquakes of every intensity, the maximum-epoch of the eleven-year period occurs shortly before the epoch of least sunspot frequency, and the amplitude increases with the intensity of the shock. It may be added that the epochs are almost exactly the same for the same three classes for the separate intervals 1701–99 and 1801–99, and for all three intensities together for the interval 1501–1698, and for each season of the interval 1701–1898.

"It is interesting to notice that the same periodicity holds in widely separated regions. Taking the three intensities together, the maximum occurs in 1764 in Europe, in 1763–64 in Asia, in 1764 in Italy, in 1764–65 in China, and in 1763–64 in the island groups of the western Pacific. Even in the slight earthquakes of Great Britain, the same period is present with its maximum in 1763–64. Thus by a somewhat different line of evidence, Milne's remarkable generalization seems to be confirmed" (*Nature*, 120: 587–88, 1927).

Forty years after Davison's study, John F. Simpson confirmed the solar connection with modern data: "*Abstract*. Solar activity as indicated by sunspots, radio noise, and geomagnetic indices, plays a significant but by no means exclusive role in the triggering of earthquakes. Maximum quake frequency occurs at times of moderately high and fluctuating solar activity. Terrestrial solar flare effects, which are the actual coupling mechanisms which trigger quakes, appear to be either abrupt accelerations in the earth's angular velocity or surges of telluric currents in the earth's crust. The graphs presented in this paper permit probabilistic forecasting of earthquakes, and when used in conjunction with local indicators may provide a significant tool for specific earthquake prediction" (*Earth and Planetary Science Letters*, 3: 417, 1967).

Given this seemingly incontrovertible evidence for solar-stimulated earthquakes, just how might the two phenomena be connected across 93 million miles? Once again, the solar wind and solar radiation seem to be the ties that bind. In 1971 R. A. Challinor presented strong evidence that large solar flares very slightly but abruptly changed the earth's rate of rotation. The impact of a burst of solar energy upon the earth's upper atmosphere changes its speed of rotation. The impulse is next communicated down through the atmosphere to the crust itself (*Science*, 172: 1022, 1971).

John Gribbin quickly pointed out that sudden changes in our planet's rate of rotation, no matter that they are slight, could trigger earthquakes in areas where strains in the crust had built up to just short of the earthquake threshold. Thus a real physical link could really be established between solar flares and the earth's slight hesitation or acceleration to the release of pent-up strains in the crust (*Science*, 173: 558, 1971).

Gribbin's suggestion connecting earthquake-triggering forces with the earth's motion in space leads directly to a closely related phenomenon: wobble-induced earthquakes.

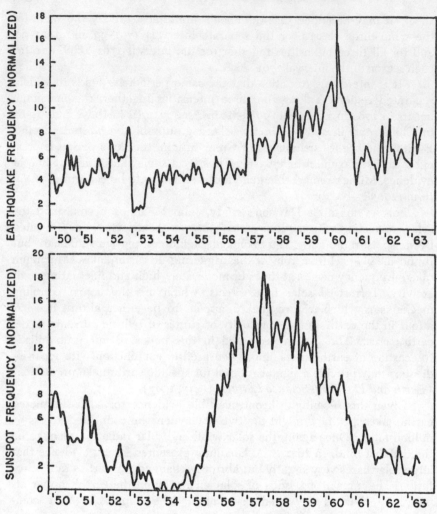

Earthquake frequency seems weakly related to sunspot frequency.

THE RELATION BETWEEN EARTHQUAKES AND THE EARTH'S WOBBLE

As the earth's axis of rotation proceeds through the signs of the zodiac in its 26,000-year cycle, it also wobbles (nutates). The wobble is slight, about 0.5 seconds of arc maximum, and has a period of about 14 months. Called the Chandler Wobble, after S. C. Chandler, who discovered it in 1891, this minuscule nodding motion should die out quickly according to geophysicists. But it doesn't, and no one knows why. Something must add energy to the wobble motion to keep it going. In 1967 and 1968, L. Mansinha and D. E. Smylie of the University of Western Ontario claimed that large earthquakes fed energy to the wobble. The sudden off-axis shifts of mass during quakes in effect made the planet

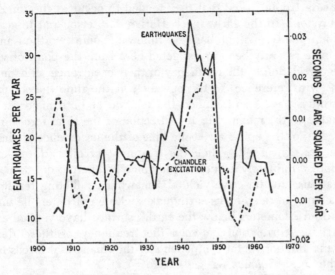

Earthquake frequency peaks when the Chandler Wobble is greatest.

lurch. The Canadian scientists pointed out that the frequency of large earthquakes was correlated with the magnitude of the Chandler Wobble (*New Scientist*, 49: 105, 1971).

Other geophysicists suggested that the reverse might be true; that is, the wobble might excite quakes rather than vice versa. Still others opined that an unrecognized third factor might cause *both* quakes and wobble. Basically, the wobble-earthquake connection remains a mystery. They may be connected through a transfer of mechanical energy, but one cannot rule out that both phenomena are tied to something else, such as motions of the earth's liquid core through an electromagnetic link.

EARTHQUAKES AND THE MOON'S PHASES

In Chapter 3, precipitation was tentatively linked to the phases of the moon through that orb's effect on micrometeoroids reaching the earth's upper atmosphere. Surely this mechanism cannot affect earthquake frequency. Even so, the moon's gravitation is strong enough to create a tidal bulge in the solid crust of the earth. To be sure, the bulge is thousands of times smaller than the 50-ft. tide pushing up the Bay of Fundy, but the minute flexure of the crust is sufficient to trigger microearthquakes and possibly some larger ones too.

Myron L. Fuller, in his analysis of some 178 aftershocks of the New Madrid catastrophe noted that they tended to occur at the times of new and full moons. In the early 1930s, Harlan T. Stetson put lunar-induced quakes on a more scientific basis, as follows: "Some two thousand earthquakes have recently been investigated here from the point of view of a possible correlation of the frequency of their occurrence with the moon's position [with reference] to the epicenter at the time the shocks occur. These studies have also included the relation of both major and minor earthquakes to the magnitude and direction of the tidal forces operating in the region of the epicenter at the time of the occurrence of the seismic disturbances concerned. While the treatment of all earthquake disturbances indiscriminately in such a study may be open to question, and the investigations thus far have yielded somewhat conflicting results, nevertheless a study of deep-focus earthquakes whose epicenters lie more than one hundred kilometers below the earth's surface have yielded a surprisingly striking correlation between the frequency of these deep-focus quakes and the horizontal components of the lunar tidal forces in operation at the time" (*Science*, 82: 523–24, 1935).

That lunar tidal forces produce a general "wringing out" of the earth's crust was discovered by Frank Perret on the island of Montserrat.

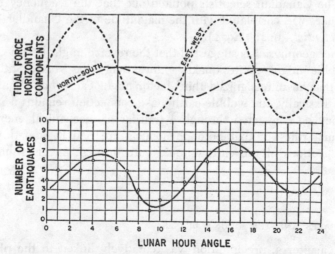

The incidence of deep-focus earthquakes varies with moon-caused tidal forces.

Not only were earthquakes related to tidal stresses but also to the frequency of gas eruptions from the crust. "Studied intensively for four years by Dr. Perret, this small volcanic island in the British West Indies showed a high degree of correlation between the occurrence of local earthquakes and gas eruptions and the positions of the moon and sun. Earthquakes came most frequently and abnormal gas eruptions were most likely to occur near the times when sun and moon were in opposition (on opposite sides of the earth) or in conjunctions (in line on the same side of the earth). Dr. Perret does not believe that these are direct effects of the gravitational pull of sun and moon on the earth, setting up tidal strains in the solid rocks of its crust, but that these strains, added to strains already accumulated through volcanic forces at work below, finally play 'last-straw' roles and release the pent-up geophysical energies" (*Science News Letter*, 37: 233, 1940).

As a matter of fact, modern analysis of microearthquake frequencies near an Alaskan volcano demonstrate that not only do earth tides trigger microearthquakes, but the crustal pressures caused by somewhat later oceanic tides initiate a second group of tiny quakes (*Science*, 182: 386–89, 1973).

The reality of earthquake triggering by very small tidal forces, the changing pressures of oceanic tides, and minute changes in the earth's spin encourage one to ask whether there may not be even weaker forces capable of pulling the earthquake triggers.

BEWARE NIGHTS AND SUMMERS

Old-time collectors of earthquake data never failed to notice that quakes seemed more common at night. Summer is also the season of highest earthquake frequency. Why? Earthquake expert Charles Davison gave his theory in the following paper:

"*Abstract.* Though noninstrumental records of earthquakes give an apparent nocturnal maximum, it is shown that, for several regions in which earthquakes are weak or moderately strong, there is a real diurnal period, with its maximum about midnight. The instrumental records obtained in Japan and Italy and at various seismological observatories [have been] examined, and it is shown that the maximum epoch of the diurnal period usually falls about noon or midnight and that the noon maximum of the diurnal period is associated, as a rule, with a summer maximum of the annual period, and the midnight maximum of the former with a winter maximum of the latter. It is suggested that the noon and summer maxima occur in earthquakes caused by an elevation of the crust, and the midnight and winter maxima in those caused by a depression of the crust. It is noticed that the midnight and winter maxima prevail in regions in which the earthquakes are of slight or moderate intensity, and the noon and summer maxima in those visited by the most destructive shocks. In the aftershocks of great earthquakes, the maxima epochs are suddenly reversed, usually from near noon to near midnight, and the duration of the reversal varies from about a week to a year or more" (*Journal of Geology*, 42: 449–68, 1934).

Despite the stature of Davison in the geophysical community, the reality of a preponderance of nocturnal quakes was strongly questioned. The whole subject is still controversial, as demonstrated by the following review from *Nature:*

"The suggestion that seismic activity fluctuates with the seasons or the time of day has been made on numerous occasions in the past; but as Bullen (*Introduction to the Theory of Seismology*, Cambridge University Press, 1963) pointed out some years ago, claims for such periodicities have never been substantiated. Not, that is, until last year when Shimshoni (*Geophysical Journal*, 24: 97, 1971) produced evidence which seemed to show that seismic activity is significantly higher during the night than during the day. At first sight such a correlation appears inherently unlikely, except that it is never possible to ignore completely the idea of trigger forces. In other words, although there can be no suggestion that minor forces, such as, for example, temperature effects, tidal effects, and abnormal changes in barometric pressure, produce the elastic strain which is ultimately released in earthquakes, it is just conceivable that minor forces act as the 'last straw' (Bullen) leading to the actual release of strain.

"But whatever the cause may be, a correlation is a correlation; and that is just what Shimshoni seemed to have from a statistical analysis of the 15,325 seismic events reported by the U.S. National Oceanic and Atmospheric Administration for 1968 to 1970. If seismic events occur randomly with local time throughout the twenty-four–hour period, the number of events within each hourly period over the three years should be 638.5 (that is, 15,325/24). In practice, however, x^2 for the randomness hypothesis turned out to be 80.1137, the probability of obtaining a figure as high as this for a truly random process being less than 10^{-7}. Shimshoni thus concluded that seismic events do not occur randomly throughout the twenty-four hours and went on to show that within the daily cycle there is a peak of seismic activity around midnight and a minimum around noon.

"Three authors or groups of authors have now descended upon Shimshoni to point out that although there may indeed be a correlation of the sort he demonstrates, it represents a data deficiency rather than a real variation in seismicity. Davies (*Geophysical Journal*, 28: 305, 1972), for example, notes that the number of earthquakes recorded over any given period of time will reflect not only the number of earthquakes actually occurring over that period, but also the detection capability of the recording network, and that it is the latter which varies between night and day.

"To see how this effect works, he considers an earthquake occurring on the equator at the equinox. The location of such an event will be determined from observations made within epicentral distances of 100°; and so if the shock occurs at midday it will be observed (P waves) at most of the relevant stations in daylight, and if it occurs at midnight, it will mostly be observed in darkness. Seismic background noise—most of it probably local cultural noise—correlates strongly with light and dark, however, the detection threshold at many stations being significantly higher during the day. According to Davies, it is possible to observe at many stations a dawn noise level rise of 10 to 20 dB.

"The result of all this is that more of the earthquakes occurring at night will actually be detected—a circumstance which is bound to bias the data in any published list of earthquakes. On the other hand, this situation will not obtain for events occurring far from the equator. At high latitudes, P waves from midnight earthquakes will be observed at many stations during daylight. Under these circumstances no day-night correlation would be expected, nor is it found. Events occurring at middle and lower latitude will, however, be sufficient to give an overall bias" (*Nature*, 239: 131, 1972). No one yet knows whether the so-called biases in quake detection can account for the long-believed, data-supported claim that nocturnal quakes are more frequent.

The summertime effect on earthquake frequency seems fairly well established. Few realize that Charleston, South Carolina, is one of the most likely places to experience an earthquake in the United States. The historic Charleston quake of August 31, 1886, was followed by a multitude of aftershocks. The frequency of these aftershocks was unquestionably highest in the late summer. Davison's theory that the accumulating summer heat makes the crust thermally expand and thus triggers quakes might apply here (*Seismological Society of America, Bulletin*, 4: 108–60, 1914).

QUAKES AND PLANETS

Even more elusive and certainly more controversial are the occasional claims that earthquake frequency correlates with planetary positions. This concept harks back to Chapter 2 with its discussion of a radio

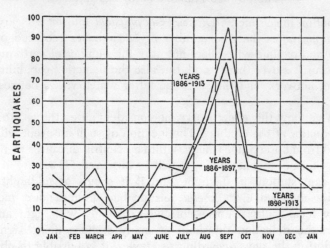

Aftershocks of the Charleston earthquake were maximum in the summer months.

engineer who insisted that radio transmission quality varied significantly with the positions of planets in the sky. Current wisdom insists that the only way a planet can influence terrestrial phenomena is through gravitation, and a planet's gravitational force weakens so much over the tens of millions of miles that palpable terrestrial effects are unthinkable. Despite these appeals to logic and reason, the actual data must be examined.

Notwithstanding the astrological overtones, the best planet-quake correlations seem to come from our more enlightened present-day science. R. Tomaschek's startling correlation between great earthquakes and the astronomical position of Uranus is typical of the genre.

"Thanks to the excellent collection of uniform data of earthquakes given by Gutenberg and Richter, it is now easily possible to study statistically the influence of different factors on earthquakes. In the course of a study of tidal effects on earthquakes, the astronomical positions of the planets have also been taken into account and a remarkable correlation between the positions of Uranus and the moment of great earthquakes has been established for a certain period. Gutenberg and Richter's data of all earthquakes equal or greater than magnitude 7 3/4 have been used. The investigations will be published in detail later, but here attention is directed to the results concerning the position of Uranus.

"A total of 134 earthquakes has been investigated. In this a fairly significant amount of cases has been found, where Uranus was very near its upper or lower transit of the meridian of the epicentre in the time of great earthquakes. Closer investigation showed that this occurred especially during the years 1904, where Gutenberg-Richter's data start, and also 1905 and 1906.

*   *   *

"The correlation cannot be explained by a tidal effect, since the statistical investigation for all the great earthquakes ($M > 7\ 3/4$) during 1904–50 in regard to the absolute and relative positions of the Sun and the Moon give no indication of a significant deviation from chance distribution. The tidal forces of the planets are extremely small compared with those of the Sun and the Moon. That the accumulated stresses within the Earth's crust are released at times which, at least for a period of several years, are strongly correlated with certain positions of Uranus may, therefore, not be a relationship of cause and effect in the usual mechanical sense" (*Nature*, 184: 177–78, 1959).

Protest against Tomaschek's correlation appeared quickly, for how could one of the most distant planets—and one not nearly as large as the closer Jupiter or Saturn—possibly influence earthly events? The attack of E. J. Burr was entitled "Earthquakes and Uranus: Misuse of a Statistical Test of Significance," a title that pinpoints the character of the criticism. Burr's paper was immediately followed by a reply from Tomaschek, who was obviously undeterred by the attack. "To state the plain facts: One is led to the conclusion that the position of Uranus within $x \pm 15°$ of the meridian at the moment of great earthquakes can be regarded as significant and that there exist times of longer period (several years) when it is very highly significant. It is quite obvious that the strains and stresses in the earth's crust are the primary cause of earthquakes, but it has been shown, given the presence of these factors of sufficient magnitude, that the timing of the event in a significant number of cases can be described by the position of Uranus" (*Nature*, 186: 337–38, 1960).

The possible effect of the planets on the sun was popularized by John Gribbin and Stephen Plagemann in their 1974 book *The Jupiter Effect*. Their idea, which had been proposed earlier by K. D. Wood, was that planet-caused tides on the sun modulate the sun's cosmic-ray flux reaching the earth. The movements of terrestrial air masses are, in turn, affected and subsequently coupled to the earth's period of rotation. These slight changes of spin rate, as discussed earlier, might stimulate earthquakes. Gribbin and Plagemann predicted that in 1982, when Jupiter, Saturn, Uranus, and Neptune all line up, conditions will be ripe for a spate of major earthquakes.

The Jupiter Effect was condemned vigorously. The similarity between the length of the 11.1-year sunspot cycle and the 11.86 orbital period of Jupiter was labeled as only fortuitous. To show how far Gribbin and Plagemann had wandered from the path of reason, W. -H. Ip examined the long record of Chinese earthquakes. He found that an ominous alignment of planets which occurs about every 178.73 years, did not seem to appear in the Chinese records in terms of peaks of earthquake activity. The well-publicized 1982 occurrence of this alignment produced no exceptional increase in earthquake activity (*Nature*, 265: 12, 1977).

QUAKES AND STARS

Ever since Einstein's Theory of General Relativity predicted their existence, scientists have been trying to detect gravitational waves. As these waves sweep over the earth, large objects vibrate in tune ever so slightly. In fact, gravitational wave detectors are unusually huge masses of metal with attached motion detectors. The earth itself is obviously a large mass—a perfect detector of those gravitational waves rolling in from the cosmic sea. When the waves pass, the whole earth flexes and earthquakes are more frequent. So the theory goes, but no one has yet convincingly demonstrated the existence of gravitational waves with laboratory detectors. Not knowing the frequency, direction, or even the very reality of gravitational waves, we cannot tell whether sudden spurts in earthquake frequency are correlated with the passage of these hypothetical waves.

Dror Sadeh and Meir Meidav claimed in 1972 that terrestrial seismicity was enhanced in step with the frequency of Pulsar CP 1133 (*Nature*, 240: 136–38, 1972). Their data, however, were criticized, and this type of earthquake trigger remains in limbo.

AMAZING CORRELATIONS BETWEEN EARTHQUAKES AND MISCELLANEOUS PHENOMENA

This whole business of correlating waxing and waning natural phenomena is fraught with difficulties. How far afield should a scientist search for earthquake trigger forces or for other phenomena that seem to respond to the same trigger forces? It is a fact that nature, perhaps with a mischievous smile, serves up some very unlikely correlations. "Prof. T. Terada has shown that there exists a curious relation between the numbers of earthquakes in the Idu peninsula and the numbers of fishes caught near the northern end of Sagami Bay (*Proceedings of the Imperial Academy, Tokyo*, 8: 83–86, 1932). During the spring of 1930, swarms of earthquakes occurred in the neighborhood of Ito on the east coast of the peninsula (*Nature*, 126: 326, 1971). It was found that the epochs of abundant catches of horse mackerel (*Caranx*) at the Sigedera fishing ground coincided very nearly with those of the earthquakes. This result led Prof. Terada to compare the numbers of fishes caught in the six years 1924–29 with the numbers of felt and unfelt earthquakes in and near the Idu peninsula. For the year 1928, the parallelism of the two curves was very close, though in other years it was less conspicuous. During 1928 the curve representing the numbers of immature tunny (*Thynnus*) [tuna] caught shows a remarkable similarity with the horse mackerel and earthquake curves. In another paper (*Earthquake Research Institute Bulletin,* 10: 29–35, 1932) Prof. Terada points out that, though the daily numbers fluctuate, the time-distribution curve of the Ito earthquakes resembles on the whole the probability curve, and he shows that the daily number of falls of camelia flowers follows a similar statistical distribution" (*Nature,* 130: 28, 1932).

Are there wafting through the universe, the solar system, and the web of humanity undreamed-of forces that make completely unrelated phenomena march in step?

6

PHENOMENA OF
THE HYDROSPHERE

Weather is a phenomenon of the atmosphere, but seven-tenths of the earth is covered by a thin coating of water possessing "weather" of an entirely different sort. The most accessible of these oceanic phenomena occur on the ocean surfaces: the waves, the more ponderous water movements called tides, and various localized disturbances. What transpires below the surface is still largely a mystery. We can conjecture from surface clues and a few subsurface measurements that the subsurface movements of water are very complicated.

Lack of knowledge of the subsurface realm focuses our attention on events occurring in the interface between ocean and atmosphere. Centuries of sea lore, plus data from a fleet of research vessels and thousands of shore instruments, have discerned tidal regularities (and irregularities) and charted wave patterns on many seas. It is, however, an empirical business, with exceptions frequently sending scientists back to their computers to modify general laws for local conditions. When such situations prevail, as they do for both atmospheric and oceanic phenomena, we must conclude that we do not yet understand all of the nuances of these two fluid media.

Solitary Waves and Small Groups of Waves

Many mariners tell of "waves from nowhere" that suddenly broke over their ships, sweeping men and equipment into the sea. Great solitary waves are rare, and they pose problems of explanation. If a solitary wave is merely a bit larger than the general run of waves, it can be written off as a chance addition of two smaller waves. Single, giant waves preceded and followed by relatively calm water are not explained so readily. Distant storms and submarine disturbances are, of course, possible progenitors. Such sources, though, habitually generate wave trains with very long wavelengths. *Tsunamis* or earthquake-generated waves, for example, are barely noticed in the deep ocean and rise to catastrophic heights only as they approach shallow waters. Solitary waves in constricted areas such as the English Channel may be the piling up of a storm surge, but a single giant wave in the open, otherwise calm ocean is harder to comprehend.

Small groups of waves come and go as mysteriously as the solitary giants. We may suppose that like ripples in a pond they are caused by some distant disturbance possibly thousands of miles away. Again, this is a surmise, perhaps not a reasonable one at that, but there are no reasonable alternatives.

GIANT SOLITARY WAVES

L. Draper provided this nice introduction to the problem of freak solitary waves. "Stories abound of monstrous waves; every sailor has his tale of how a great wave arose from nowhere and hit his ship, leaving a trail of damaged lifeboats and shattered crockery. Estimates of the heights of the highest waves which can be encountered at sea vary widely. Cornish reported a freak wave, 70 ft. from crest to trough, seen in the North Pacific in 1921. More recently, Captain Grant of the cargo vessel *Junior* reported a wave estimated to be 100 ft. high, about 100 miles off Cape Hatteras. There must be many more reports of similar waves in the history of the seas. As early as 1826, Captain Dumont d'Urville, a French scientist and naval officer in command of an expedition, reported encountering waves 80 to 100 ft. high. The poor fellow was openly ridiculed for making such an outrageous report, even though three of his colleagues supported his estimate. Perhaps the most famous reliable report was that of the wave encountered by the U.S.S. *Ramapo* in the North Pacific in 1933; that wave was estimated to be 112 ft. high, a monster indeed" (*Weather*, 21: 2–4, 1966).

The literature is full of other well-verified giant solitaries. "Admiral FitzRoy, the first Director of the Meteorological Office, has left on record that he personally measured seas that were 60 feet in height. Waves exceeding this height are exceptional, but there are a few cases on record of which the following are instances:

"The highest seas yet recorded, reaching to a height of 80 feet, were measured by Sir Bertram Hayes and his officers in the R.M.S. *Majestic* during a North-Westerly gale of hurricane force [*sic*], in Latitude

48° 30' N., Longitude 21° 50' W., on December 29th, 1922. Dr. Vaughan Cornish, the British authority on water waves, in a letter to the Editor of *Lloyd's List* remarked that he had never met with any other account of waves of such a great height taken under conditions so favourable for observation.

"The R.M.S. *Olympic,* when bound from Southampton to New York on February 27th, 1925, was struck by a 70-foot wave, during a heavy gale, which badly damaged her navigation bridge, 75 feet above sea level. The R.M.S. *Aquitania* bound from New York to Southampton encountered the same gale during which a heavy sea swept her bridge, carrying away a locker and smashing a chronometer and three sextants. *Aquitania's* bridge is 70 feet above sea level.

"In 1875 the late Captain Kiddle of the R.M.S. *Celtic* from reliable measurements determined a height of 70 feet for several waves in mid-Atlantic.

"Solitary waves of an exceptional height have been met with unexpectedly in mid-ocean which cannot be accounted for by the wind then blowing. These waves are commonly referred to as tidal waves but this is a misnomer: they are in all probability due to submarine seismic disturbances.

"In 1881 a solitary wave struck the barque *Rosina* in the North Atlantic sweeping overboard all hands then on deck. In the same year this unfortunate ship encountered another such wave while both watches were engaged shortening sail. On this occasion the whole crew were carried away with the exception of a sick seaman lying in his bunk. He was eventually rescued by a passing steamer.

"In 1882 the well-known four-masted barque *Loch Torridon,* when off the Cape of Good Hope, encountered an unexpected solitary wave which washed overboard the Captain, Second Mate, and the whole watch on deck.

"In 1893 the barque *Johann Wilhelm,* when 300 miles east of Charleston, S.C., had a similar experience to the *Rosina.* A solitary wave struck the vessel and, throwing her on her beam ends, washed overboard all hands with the exception of one man who was later rescued by the S.S. *Electrician.*

"The S.S. *Rheinland* was nearly lost some years ago in the North Atlantic when a solitary wave submerged the vessel for a short interval. Her commander, Captain Randle, stated that only the funnel and masts were distinguishable. Every boat was washed away, one man lost overboard, and several of the officers and crew received broken limbs" (*Marine Observer,* 10: 17, 1933).

With the reality of giant solitaries thus confirmed, what shapes these watery mountains? Powerful storms naturally generate large waves, and occasionally these waves will reinforce one another to give birth to a giant wave. Richard W. James used this approach in explaining the wall of water that smashed into the Italian vessel *Michelangelo* in 1966.

"On April 12, 1966, the Italian liner *Michelangelo* was steaming westward at 16 knots, some 600 miles southeast of Newfoundland. Generated by whole gale winds, waves of 25 to 30 ft. in height pounded the ship as she headed for New York. Suddenly a huge wave towered high above the others, smashed into the *Michelangelo*, inundating the forward

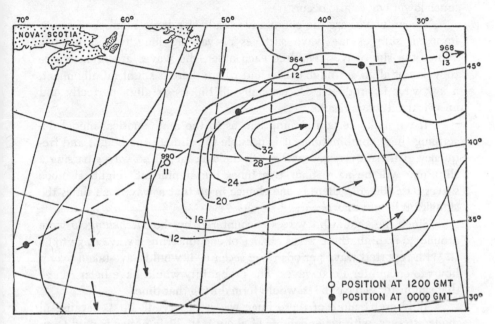

Wave-height map of the North Atlantic, showing the path of the Michelangelo

half of the ship. Steel superstructure gave way, bridge windows 31 ft. above the waterline were crushed in, furniture in the public lounge flew through the air, heavy steel flaring on the bow was torn off, and the bulkhead under the bridge was bent back at least 10 ft. Three people were killed and 12 were injured.

"What causes these monster waves that occasionally strike ships? How do they form, and when can you expect them? Can they be predicted?

"Unfortunately, although something *is* known of the nature and behavior of these oversized waves, the answer to the last question is 'no.' The exact time and place an oversized wave will develop cannot be forecast. The probability that one will occur . . . and its approximate height can be calculated.

"Under the influence of a strong wind, the ocean surface becomes complex, with mounds and hollows of water in chaotic motion. Careful observation of a number of waves passing a ship will disclose a variety of wave heights, and high waves followed by lower waves—or the reverse— in a random fashion. The average of such visually observed waves, called the significant wave height, occurs most frequently, but much higher and much lower waves also occur.

"Ocean waves are the cumulative result of a large number of super-imposed, simple sine wave surfaces of varying lengths and heights. Where the sine waves reinforce each other, the waves are high; where they do not align, a trough exists; and where there is slight misalignment, a low wave is produced. Occasionally all the crests align perfectly and an oversized wave results.

"If we make certain assumptions as to the mathematical model de-scribing these combinations, it is possible to estimate the height and fre-quency of these oversized waves. On the average, of 20 waves passing a ship, one will be more than 1.73 times the significant height. If 1,000 waves pass the ship there is one chance in 20 that a wave 2.22 times the significant height may occur.

"Since the significant waves encountered by the *Michelangelo* were around 30 ft. high, there was a chance of encountering a wave of 52 to 66 ft. With reported wave periods of 12 seconds, it would have taken over 3 hours to encounter 1,000 waves. The probability would have been 1 in 20 that a monster wave of 66 ft. would form during that time.

"Why aren't more of these huge waves observed? First, because in moderate seas, with wave heights of about 5 ft., little notice is paid to an occasional 8- to 10-ft. wave. It is only when the seas are high that over-sized waves attract attention. Secondly, these waves are generally unsta-ble, peaking and breaking before traveling any distance; nevertheless many ships have encountered such waves, usually with disastrous results. It should be noted that during any heavy weather the possibility exists of running into a giant wave" (*Mariners Weather Log*, 10: 115–17, 1966).

A second possible source would be shallows or reefs that magnify the sizes of already large storm waves. In 1887, several ships in the mid-Atlantic were hit by monster waves. C. E. Stromeyer collected these data and pointed out that the waves could all have originated at Faraday Reef. A portion of his report follows:

". . . the exact positions of the vessels, and the directions from which these solitary waves seemed to come, being also marked on the chart. In the case of H.M.S. *Orontes* the ship's course was not stated, and on account of darkness and other causes the directions from which some of the other waves came are not to be depended upon. None of these encounters would have been reported had they not caused much damage—masts and funnels going by the board, and bulwarks, deckhouses, and lifeboats being smashed; but many seafaring men can recall solitary and abnormally high waves having struck their vessels, although the sea was otherwise quiet. Amongst the strange results which these blows have produced may be mentioned that the magnetism of the steamship *Energia* was thus suddenly altered sufficiently to introduce an error of 18° into the compass readings. The full details about this and a few other vessels have not been obtained.

"The following are short summaries of each case:

"S.S. *Faraday.* —The wave was visible like a line of high land on the horizon about five minutes before it struck the vessel.

"S.S. *Westernland.* —A huge wave rose to a great height just in advance of the ship. No other similar waves were met with. About noon the wind had changed from S.W. to W.N.W.

"S.S. *Germanic.* —Wind W.N.W. with terrific squalls. Shipped a tremendous sea over bow.

"S.S. *Umbria.* —The disturbance came from N.W. and consisted of two waves. The first one was broken, the second one green. The wind had previously changed from S.W. to N.W.

"H.M.S. *Orontes.* —While steaming in smooth water, a huge wave broke over the vessel forward.

"S.S. *Festina Lente.* —A steep sea fell on board from both sides.

"S.S. *Manhattan.* —The sea was high, but fairly true until a mountainous wave broke on board from N.W.

"S.S. *Diamond.* —Lying to, awaiting daylight to enter port. The wave was heard some time before it was seen, and then seemed to be about 40 feet high. The vessel never rose to it, but was literally submerged for a time. An examination of the chart will show that, with the exception of the *Westernland,* each wave may have originated at a common center, and might therefore be due to subaqueous volcanic activity. However, as the solitary waves which strike the west coast of South America and the so-called Death Waves on the west coast of Ireland are said to be regarded as precursors of storms, it is possible that these solitary Atlantic waves may be due to a similar cause; but even then it is inexplicable how a number of comparatively small and regular waves can be converted into one abnormal one, or how the reported changes of wind and consequent confused sea could produce such a wave. It will be noticed that the dates for the *Festina Lente, Manhattan,* and *Diamond* are very close together, and therefore there is a possibility that they were struck by the same wave" (*Nature,* 51: 437–38, 1895).

The "superwaves" off southeast Africa are notorious. In 1972 alone, over 160 lives were lost in this area. Two factors seem to contribute to the high frequency of giant solitaries in this area: First, strong south-westerly winds traveling over a long distance (the "fetch" of the waves) pile up big waves as the shallow African continental shelf is approached; second, the swift Agulhas Current sweeping down the eastern coast of Africa runs counter to the waves. The big wave fronts seem to be steepened as the current flows under them, creating cavernous troughs from which some ships cannot escape without severe damage. The biggest troughs, of course, appear when smaller waves reinforce one another. On May 17, 1974, the Norwegian supertanker *Wilstar* was severely damaged by one of these African superwaves. "The skipper of *Wilstar*, Captain Janiszewski, said the tanker was fully loaded and running southward in a gale below Durban. 'Waves were coming in sequences of seven, but the seventh wave in one sequence did not hit us. Instead it drew back all of a sudden. There was no sea in front of us—just a big hole. The bow fell into this hole, and then the seventh wave crashed onto us. It was higher than the bow, and I felt the ship shudder beneath my feet'" (*Sea Frontiers*, 22: 106–16, 1976).

Trains of storm-generated waves, when funneled into a narrow strait, will sometimes build up to fearful heights, as in this report from

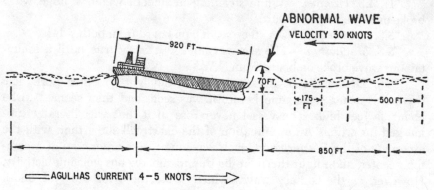

Superwaves off southeast Africa have exceptionally steep fronts.

the English Channel. "The Weymouth and Channel Islands Steam Packet Company's mail steamer *Aquila* left Weymouth at midnight on Friday for Guernsey and Jersey [islands]. On her passage across [the] Channel, the weather was calm and clear, and the sea was smooth. When about one hour out, [at] 1 A.M., 31st March, 1883, the steamer was struck violently by mountainous seas which sent her on her beam ends and swept her decks from stem to stern. The water immediately flooded the cabins and engine room, entering through the skylights, the thick glass of which was smashed. As the decks became clear of water, the bulwarks were found to be broken in several places, one of the paddle boxes was considerably damaged, the iron rail on the bridge was completely twisted, the pump was broken and rendered useless, the skylight of the ladies' cabin was completely gone, and the saloon skylight was smashed to atoms. The cabins were baled out with buckets, while tarpaulins were placed over the skylights for protection. Five minutes after the waves had struck the steamer, the sea became perfectly calm. Several of the crew were knocked about, but no one was seriously injured" (*Symons's Monthly Meteorological Magazine,* 18: 42, 1883).

ABNORMAL GROUPS OF WAVES

The giant solitaries usually, though not always, appear in seas that are already fairly heavy. Spookier are those small packets of waves that suddenly appear on otherwise calm seas, buffet the observer's ship for a brief period, and are gone. Explanations of these isolated wave packets are not too convincing. A typical instance was observed from the R.R.S. *Discovery* in the Indian Ocean on March 28, 1964. "Bands of breaking

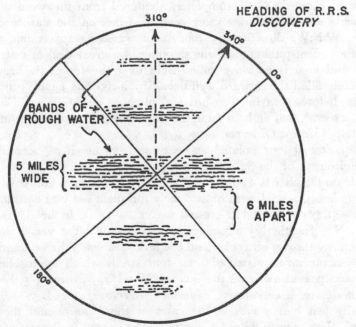

Anomalous groups of waves pass the R.R.S. Discovery in the Indian Ocean.

waves of height 2 ft. and period 1 second, about 1/2 mile in width and 6 miles apart were observed by radar, heading in a 310° direction. When the bands passed the ship, which was hove-to, the wind did not change in direction or increase in force. The swell died down completely. There were five bands in all, the first and last being comparatively weak while the middle one was the strongest. They had the appearance of waves breaking on a flat sandy shore. Wind ENE., force 3. Sea temperature, 85° F.

"Position of ship: 11° 30′ S., 58° 00′ E.

"29th March. Similar waves, moving from 300°, were observed 0530–0620 GMT. Wind NW., force 3. Sea temperature, 84.9° F.

"Position of ship: 11° 30′ S., 58° 00′ E.

"*Note*. This phenomenon appears to be a resonance between wind and current. The sea surface temperature was extremely high (85° F.) and probably only a very shallow layer of the sea was involved in the waves" (*Marine Observer*, 35: 60, 1965).

A packet of four isolated waves hit the S.S. *Madura* on February 28, 1936, en route from Marseilles to Gibraltar. "0240 G.M.T., proceeding down the Spanish coast, from Marseilles towards the Gibraltar Straits, seven miles from the coast. Prevailing weather, strong west winds, moderate sea, moderate short swell, fine and clear. The vessel, whilst under the lee of Cape de Gata, completely sheltered from the wind and experiencing only a moderate short swell, was met on the starboard bow from a W.N.W. direction by four large waves in succession, which caused a violent pitching and the shipping of a great deal of water; the fourth and final large wave rolled right over the forecastle head and completely filled the forward well deck. Upon righting again, conditions were as before, spraying forward and pitching easily. When Cape de Gata bore 270°, half an hour later, the full force of the westerly wind was again felt" (*Marine Observer*, 14: 7, 1937).

A packet of four isolated waves came from nowhere, according to the chief officer of the S.S. *Grelmarion*, when the ship was in the North Atlantic on October 8, 1956. "At 1235 G.M.T. while on a course of 043°, speed 12 knots, a small area of extremely turbulent sea was encountered, with steep swell and white-crested waves 12–15 ft. in height running from a N'ly [northerly] direction. As waves struck the vessel she was momentarily thrown off course and one large sea was shipped amidships. The phenomenon consisted of some four swells which approached the vessel and passed away on the quarter. Wind 045°, force 4–5. Sea and swell moderate, direction 045°" (*Marine Observer*, 27: 203, 1957).

Why just four waves in the cases of the *Madura* and the *Grelmarion?* Wave-counting has an aura of mystery about it. Packets of seven and nine waves are not uncommon. The interference of intersecting wave trains is usually responsible for the formation of repetitive packets, in analogy to the beat frequency of two tuning forks vibrating at slightly different frequencies. The numerology of wave packets, however, is not as mysterious as the sudden appearance of isolated packets on placid seas.

The complex character of wave packets is seen in the experience of the S.S. *City of Lucknow* in the Red Sea. It was July 27, 1961. "At 1930 GMT the wind veered from 330° to 060° and increased to force 4; the air temperature dropped from 89° F. to 86°, and a shower was seen near the ship. A sudden swell, 5 ft. in height, came in from 300° with a period of 5 seconds. It arrived in four or five lines at a time, then died down for about 30 seconds to 1 minute, after which interval it again moved in. This cycle kept repeating, though with decreasing height of waves, until 2120. Throughout the day the wind had been light and variable.

"Position of ship: 18° 25′ N., 39° 58′ E.

"*Note.* We are advised by the National Institute of Oceanography that there is no standard explanation for this phenomenon. From a meteorological point of view, it was associated with the atmospheric division between dry northern hemisphere air and the more humid southern hemisphere air" (*Marine Observer*, 32: 116–17, 1962).

SEA SURGES

Most of us observe waves from the safety of the beaches, but even here the surf may suddenly rise to damaging and dangerous heights. Earthquake-generated waves, called tidal waves by many but *tsunamis* by the scientists, are the most feared. They are also fairly well understood and have unmysterious origins, so we pass along to the so-called sea surges that challenge oceanographers more severely.

The real puzzles among the sea surges are those that cannot be associated with either distant storms or seismic activity. The perplexing Valparaiso sea surge of 1968 falls in this category. "Suddenly and without warning, tidal waves 15 to 18 feet tall rolled into the Chilean coastline near the capital city of Valparaiso on July 25 and 26. The huge waves were apparently caused by a sea surge far offshore. Although much coastal property and many ships were damaged, there were no personal injuries reported.

"The question that needed answering, however, was what caused the sea surge? Some reports indicated the waves were associated with seismic phenomena; other theories attributed the waves to a storm far out at sea. Today, however, their origin remains a mystery" (*The Pulse of the Planet*, New York, 1972, p. 11).

Barbados, Ascension, St. Helena, and other islands are occasionally beset by unexpected, monstrous waves. The Dutch Captain F. Fokkens described the St. Helena phenomenon in 1852 vividly (even through translation). "The atmosphere is bright and clear, the barometer remains as ordinarily and the sea smooth in the distance. . . . In an instant, all is confusion around, from a sudden, upheaving wave rolling onwards and breaking in the outer shallows with tremendous force. Instantly the surf follows, one wave succeeded by another with redoubled force towards the shore breaking up on the rocks. . . . The rollers or extraordinarily high swells, first appear in the form of a high, steep, long mountainous ridge and gather fresh strength as they approach, astonishing the beholder; water mountains seem to follow each other with redoubled violence until they reach the receding waters from the shore, meeting them as walls, and with irresistible fury dash over the beach. The shore is a mass of foam, while the houses in the town are shaken almost to their foundations" (*Royal Meteorological Society, Quarterly Journal*, 103: 655–75, 1977).

Grand as the spectacle of the St. Helena sea surges may be, modern investigations of sudden onsets of heavy swell are conclusive that most come from powerful storms churning hundreds, perhaps thousands, of miles away. Nevertheless, there are still unaccountable sea surges, such as that at Valparaiso.

SEICHES AND LAKE SURGES

To a lesser degree, sea surges have their counterparts on bodies of fresh water. The well-known seiches are really sloshings of lake waters in their basins. Usually set into motion by earthquakes, these water oscillations have a period dictated by the dimensions of the basin. On the other hand, lake surges generally precede storms and are thus completely analogous to the sudden onsets of oceanic swell described above.

Charles Stewart provided the following account of a seiche in one of the Scottish Lochs. "Upon the 12th of September, 1784, a very extraordinary phenomenon was observed at Loch Tay. The air was perfectly calm, not a breath of wind stirring. About six o'clock in the morning, the water at the east end of the loch ebbed about 300 feet and left the channel dry. It gradually accumulated and rolled on about 300 feet further to the westward, when it met a similar wave rolling in a contrary direction. When the waves met, they rose to a perpendicular height of five or six feet, producing a white foam upon the top. The water then took a lateral direction southward, rushing to the shore, and rising upon it four feet beyond the highest watermark. It then returned and continued to ebb and flow every seven minutes for two hours, the waves gradually diminishing every time they reached the shore, until the whole was quiescent. During the whole of that week, at a later hour in the morning, there was the same appearance, but not with such violence" (*Knowledge*, 4: 395, 1883).

Energetic quakes in Italy commonly set lakes all over Europe to vibrating. But even oceanic inlets and bays may be affected by large earthquakes for, like lakes, they are more or less isolated from the sea and have their own natural frequencies of sloshing. Geophysicist William L. Donn found that the great 1964 Alaskan quake set coastal waters around the Gulf of Mexico into oscillation. "After the intense Alaskan earthquake of 27 March, 1964, unusual waves up to 6 feet (about 2 meters) in height occurred at about the time of arrival of seismic waves at many localities along the coasts of Louisiana and Texas. The parameters of local channels at the tide gauge in Freeport, Texas . . . yield seiche periods close to those of the seismic surface waves suggesting that the water waves were generated by wind in resonance with the seismic waters" (*Science*, 145: 261–62, 1964).

The American Great Lakes often exhibit abnormal waves and surges in response to storms still far out over the lake. The abrupt rises of lake level are unexpected and frequently do great damage as well as drown animals and humans. The Lake Erie surge of July 19, 1895, was observed by R. J. Moorehead off North East, Pennsylvania. "Between eight and nine o'clock, while we were sitting near the shore of the lake, the water rose sudden about six feet, vertically, running back on the beach about sixty feet. But for the sharply shelving beach just at the water's edge, many would undoubtedly been drowned. . . . When the water subsided, it receded to a distance of fifty-six feet out beyond its normal margin. I paced it during the comparative repose following the recession of the flood, though in a very few minutes it began to assume its normal condition. The flood and outflow did not occupy over a very few minutes, I should say not over five minutes. This was followed by calm (no wind during this time) for about ten minutes, when we heard a low ominous roar, gradually increasing in volume, which we knew was the wind coming down the lake. . . ." (*American Naturalist*, 33: 653–60, 1899).

On June 26, 1954, a disastrous wave smashed into the Lake Michigan shore near Chicago. Driven by an atmospheric disturbance traveling at the unusually high velocity of 66 miles per hour, the storm energy was resonantly coupled to the surface waves, pushing up a mountain of water. "On the morning of 26 June about 9:30 CDT, an abrupt increase in the level of Lake Michigan occurred along the waterfront in the vicinity of Chicago, at the southwestern corner of the lake. At least seven lives were lost in the Chicago area as a result of the first unexpected increase, which reached 8 ft. at Montrose Harbor, Chicago, and 10 ft. at North Avenue" (*Science,* 120: 684–86, 1954).

Curious Phenomena of Natural Water Surfaces

If wind-generated waves could be subtracted, the surfaces of the oceans would still be marked by curious rips, rollings, slicks, calms, and sundry disturbances. Many of these phenomena are probably manifestations of subsurface movements of water. Internal ocean waves that intersect the surface and submarine upwellings can turn a calm surface into patches and long patterns of choppy sea that contrast in color and temperature with the surrounding "normal" ocean. Submarine volcanos and quakes can spew forth mud, bubbles, geysers, and dead fish. Huge shoals of fish and mile-long windrows of floating plants also festoon the ocean surfaces. This section presents a unique group of phenomena that are not so much unexplained as they are strange and unexpected (at least to "landlubbers").

FOAM STRIPS ON INLAND SEAS

Strange bands of foam often stretch all the way across the Dead Sea. The number of explanations seems proportional to the number of students of the phenomenon. Here is one impression and a subsequent interpretation.

"The Dead Sea seen from the air during a gale on February 7th, 1932, presented a striking appearance. The height of the aircraft was about 4,000 feet, and at this height the wind was south-westerly 65–70 m.p.h. The wind in the deep depression near the Dead Sea was therefore probably S.–SSW., force 6–8. The surface of the sea was 'moderate' on the sea disturbance scale, but the striking feature was the parallel bands of white foam which ran the whole length of the sea. These bands were orientated roughly south by west to north by east—i.e., slightly across the sea's major axis. The impression was that the lines of foam were interference bands due to two sets of waves or to one set of waves and their reflections from one shore.

"As the sea was obscured at times by cloud and rain, it was not possible to count the number of bands accurately, but it is estimated that there were about 20 between the east and the west shore (J. Durward).

"[The Dead Sea has a length of 47 miles and is 9 1/2 miles across at its widest part, so that the bands of foam referred to would be somewhat less than a half mile apart. According to the Encyclopaedia Britannica a

line of white foam extends along the axis of the lake almost every morning. This was supposed by Blanckenhorn to mark the line of a fissure
under the bed of the lake (which lies along the line of a great geological
fault) but has also been explained as a consequence of the current of the
Jordan—Ed. M.M.]" (*Meteorological Magazine,* 67: 41, 1932).

Additional description and, naturally, more explanations are provided in this item from *Nature.* "A peculiar phenomenon often to be
seen on the northern waters of the Dead Sea is that of arcs of foam, more
or less semicircular, spreading out fanwise from certain points of the
west and east shores. The arcs seem to spread from the shores in early
morning and often meet and even cross during the forenoon. These lines
of foam often bear reeds and other vegetation debris that have reached
the Dead Sea by inflowing rivers, and, at the seasons of migration, the
foam may attract flocks of birds searching for food. Dr. D. Ashbel has
recorded some of his observations on this phenomenon and offers an explanation (*Geographical Review,* January 1938). The arcs originate from
springs on the two shores, and they make discontinuities between bodies
of water of different salinity and density. When the outflow of the
springs is strong, the arc is frequently not smooth but zig-zag. This explanation contradicts the earlier one of Blanckenhorn that the lines of
foam originate from warm water arising along lines of fault on the sea
floor. The suggestion does not explain lack of replacement of the lines as
each moves forward, which Dr. Ashbel thinks is due to the gentle winds
that frequently blow from the land onto the sea during the night and
early morning. These winds do not ruffle the water, and so mixing does
not occur. Gusty west winds such as often occur in the afternoon cause
mixing, and so the lines of discontinuity disappear" (*Nature,* 143: 468,
1939).

STREAKS, SLICKS, AND CALMS

A panoramic view of any expanse of water often reveals alternating
lanes and patches of rough and smooth water. These "slicks" and patches
are irregular in shape and change very slowly. One would expect that
waves from a wind-roughened area of water would invade adjacent calm
patches, but this doesn't happen. Some force suppresses wave action in
the slicks. As geophysicist H. Stommel suggests in the following survey
of the problem, there may be more than one answer.

"Most natural bodies of water have a streaky appearance which results from a natural process, although artificial streaks (due to the passage of a ship, for example) are also frequently observed. There has been
quite a difference of opinion in the literature as to the nature of the pro-

cess which produces streaks. I am personally inclined to admit that under certain circumstances any one of the processes suggested may account for them; to attribute all streaks to the same mechanism would be a great mistake. I should like, therefore, to review briefly what little material there is in the literature about these streaks on the surface of natural bodies of water.

"The streaks themselves may consist of accumulations of floating objects, such as Gulf-weed, pine needles, or bubbles of foam, all of which are visible because of their colour. Others are local concentrations of an oil film (presumably of planktonic origin) which damp the tiny wind-raised capillary waves. These are visible because of the marked difference in reflectivity of sky light between ruffled and slick areas.

"*Single Streaks.* Single long streaks are often observed in harbours. They may stream out from a single continuous source of contamination and run downwind with the surface water, or follow tidal or other currents. For convenience they may be called 'trail-streaks.' Single long streaks may also develop from an initially localized concentration of surface contamination in regions of strong horizontal shear by a simple stretching of elements of water in the shear zone. These 'shear-streaks' occur on the edges of strong tidal currents and in rivers. A third kind of commonly observed single streak is seen to remain parallel to a coast-line a hundred feet or so offshore, most frequently with an onshore wind. The cause of these 'shore-streaks' is not known, but I venture to suggest that they are due to the horizontal convergence and sinking of surface water which is driven toward the shore by the wind, sinking somewhere offshore, where the water is reasonably deep, rather than at the vanishingly small depths at the very water's edge.

"The kinds of single streaks mentioned above are described in order to avoid confusion with other kinds which are really more interesting. I am referring to the large numbers of streaks often arranged in geometric patterns over large areas of a lake or ocean. Although it may be dangerous to draw a sharp distinction, these multiple streaks usually appear either in long parallel lines or with a vein-like pattern. I find it convenient to call them 'parallel' and 'venous' streaks respectively.

"Parallel and venous streaks are plentiful in nature. Windrows of Gulf-weed in the deep ocean are conspicuous examples of parallel streaks. Unfortunately there are no good photographs of these lines of weed. I have tried to photograph them on several occasions, as have others at this institution, and so far we have had no success. Similar streaks are observed on lakes and have been carefully studied.

"*Air- and Water-Cell Theories.* A large proportion of the parallel and venous streaks are aligned up- and down-wind. Two possible mechanisms have been suggested. One is the air-cell theory, which maintains that there is a cellular structure of the wind, which sweeps the surface water into lines. Langmuir on the other hand has reported that cellular motions exist in the water and that the streaks are located along lines of surface convergence and sinking water, a mechanism which may be called the water-cell theory. He has suggested that the cellular motion extends down to the thermocline, and indeed that it plays an important role in the formation of the thermocline. If this idea be true, it certainly deserves further investigation, because the lack of an adequate theory of the thermocline is one of the most glaring lacunae in oceanography and limnology. Langmuir believes the water-cells are mechanically driven by the wind, although in just what manner is obscure. Woodcock indicated the presence of films of colder water on the surfaces of lakes and ocean waters and suggested that the water-cells are thermally driven convection-cells similar to those observed in the laboratory. I do not think the results of these laboratory studies are directly applicable to lake and ocean processes without further investigation.

"Ewing has observed other parallel streaks whose orientation bears no obvious relation to the direction of the wind. He attributes them to alternate contractions and dilations of the surface film due to progressive internal waves travelling along at some distance beneath the surface.

"*Cinematographic Studies.* During June and July of last year, I made a number of cinematographic studies of streaks on small ponds on Cape Cod, Massachusetts. They were of the venous and parallel types and consisted of oil-slicks and lines of foam. The steadier the wind direction, the more nearly parallel they seemed. Upon showing the pictures at some 80 times their normal speed, interesting features, which otherwise escaped the eye, were visible: the structure of the wind was so gusty and turbulent that it was obvious that no permanent structure in the air maintained the streaks; these were so quickly reoriented after a shift of wind (only 1 or 2 minutes was necessary) that deep motions such as those reported by Langmuir did not seem likely. Thermal convection seemed also unlikely because the streaks occurred at times of intense heating of the ponds and with a very stable *epilimnion* ($0.1°$ C. m^{-1}). Although surface convergence into the lines was confirmed, using Woodcock's ballasted-bottle technique, cellular motions were not observed at depths of one foot or deeper. The indications were that these streaks were due to a process confined to the top few inches at most and did not play a role in the formation of the deep thermocline, which in this instance was at a depth of about thirty feet. It seems, therefore, that they were due to yet another process, perhaps associated with differences of wind-stress in and out of streaks, but which I must admit I do not understand. It would be misleading to conclude that this classification of various types of surface marking is complete. For example, Woodcock and

Wyman have published photographs of mysterious bands on the surface of the ocean which may be due to some still undiscovered process" (*Weather*, 6: 72–74, 1951).

Small, isolated patches of calm water on the open sea are anomalous; the prevailing and not unreasonable explanation is that water of different temperature, density, and color is upwelling in the area. Whatever the explanation, these oases of peace and quiet surrounded by restless seas are striking and unexpected. On October 2, 1963, the M.V. *Mahout* passed through such a patch in the western Mediterranean. "At 0700 GMT the vessel passed through a patch of calm water approx. 2,000 yd. wide and several miles long, extending in a line lying 350°–170°. The wind at the time was force 5, and all the surrounding sea was covered with breaking wave crests. There was no sign of oil on the surface of the water. Sea temperature, 68° F." (*Marine Observer*, 34: 174–75, 1964).

A remarkable patch of blue water was observed by the crew of the S.S. *Pacific Envoy* in the Atlantic on December 23, 1960. "At 1815 GMT a patch of brilliant blue water was observed some 50 by 100 yd. in extent and oval in shape. The surrounding sea was dark grey in colour and had been so, for the past 24 hours. Sea temperature, 82° F. Wind E.' N., force 5. Rough sea and short E'ly [easterly] swell.

"Position of ship: 20° 40′ N., 64° 51′ W.

"*Note.* Dr. T. J. Hart, of the National Institute of Oceanography, comments: 'Blue is the desert colour of the sea, and unless we are to assume that the surrounding dark grey sea was uniformly rich in plankton, and the blue patch barren, it is hard to see how it could have any biological explanation.

"'The trade-wind weather is usually fine, and plankton scanty in the Caribbean, except in winter close in to the Venezuelan coast, so far as we know'" (*Marine Observer*, 31: 181, 1961).

An anomalous oceanic slick 30 miles long was encountered off Portugal in 1958. Edward H. Batt relates this strange discovery. "An extraordinary experience happened to me during a passage from Gibraltar to the United Kingdom, and I should be grateful for an explanation. I am a master of a small motor yacht of a little over 60 tons, and on September 16, 1958, I was on passage from Gibraltar to England. I rounded Cape St. Vincent at about 0830 and ran into a pretty stiff north-west wind about Force 4; course was set, 310°, for Cape Espichel with the intention of putting in to Lisbon, but after steaming for about four hours the wind from the north-west began to increase and a bad sea was now running with much salt water on board, and I was thinking of running all the way back to the shelter of Cape St. Vincent if the bad weather continued to increase.

"However, by reducing speed from 10 knots to about 6, the going was made more comfortable, and I kept on course until we were abeam Sines, which was 12 miles distant. We were still having a pretty horrible time when there appeared ahead quite a calm patch with no broken water and a little more than half an hour's steaming brought us up to it.

"I was quite dumbfounded at what I was about to experience. This calm patch was at least a cable wide and stretched away in a north-easterly direction for about 30 miles. I was able to steam along it for three hours in almost a complete calm at full speed, while on either side of me was a steep sea [see the accompanying illustration]. The lane was abso-

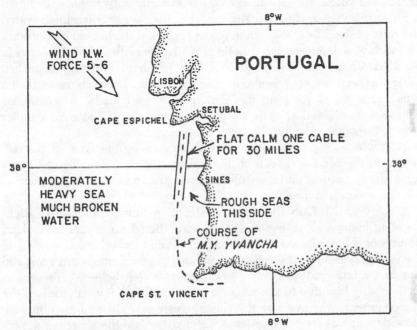

Thirty-mile-long lane of calm water off Portugal

lutely dead straight, and the demarcation line of where the broken water flattened itself out into this marine *autobahn* had to be seen to be believed. Needless to say, I kept in it and steamed right into Setúbal without even any spray on deck.

"The points to remember are: (1) the wind was north-west and blowing [at force] 5 to 6 on land, (2) we were in deep water, (3) we were 12 miles from the nearest point of land when we came upon the entrance (12 miles off Cape Sines).

"I have spent over 30 years at sea and have made the passage to the Mediterranean on many occasions, but I have never experienced such a phenomenon as this before. It was most definitely not an oil slick; there was no sign of any oil, and the lane was dead straight for 30 miles with clearly defined sides on both port and starboard sides. Had it come from an oil leakage, I am sure it would have been curved from the source as it was blown away by the wind" (*Weather*, 16: 86–87, 1961).

STRANGE SURFACE DISTURBANCES

Modern oceanography has demonstrated that the sea floor is strewn with active volcanos, hot springs, and seismically active zones. It comes as no surprise when ship captains report boiling water, discolored water, and rafts of dead fish. Still, some of the surface disturbances are curious. One such was described by Captain H. C. Large of the M.V. *Eumaeus* in the East China Sea. "At 0650 G.M.T. a patch of violently disturbed water was seen, which was about 40 sq. ft. in area. It closely resembled a squall or shoal of jumping fish, but no fish were to be seen. Similar patches were sighted at 0710, all about the same size. The echo sounder gave 54 fathoms" (*Marine Observer*, 28: 69, 1958).

No whale ever made spouts like those seen by the crew of the S.S. *Malmö* in the Mediterranean on December 4, 1960. It is difficult to conceive of any natural undersea phenomenon that would create geysers of this size and persistence.

"At 0830 GMT, as the ship was steaming through a calm to slight sea at 12 knots on a course of 124° towards Benghazi, a strange-looking column of what seemed to be white Cu [cumulus] cloud appeared to rise vertically from near the horizon, about 45° on the starboard bow, and vanished a few seconds later. The officer on watch believed his eyes to be deceiving him due to the sun's glare, but within a few minutes all the observers named above saw the column reappear. On examination with binoculars, it was seen to be a jet of water rising into the air at regular intervals of about 2 minutes, 20 seconds. Each spurt lasted for about 7 seconds and then disappeared. They were visible until the vessel left them far astern. The radar was switched on, but no echo appeared on the screen; however, by sextant altitude and calculation the jets were found to be 494 ft. high; they resembled an underwater explosion, but no such noise was heard" (*Marine Observer*, 31: 183, 1961).

Where oceanic currents meet or upwellings reach the surface, ships find long streaks of disturbed water, often called rips. The M.V. *St. John* crossed a long, well-defined rip in the equatorial Atlantic on August 29, 1963. "At 1630 GMT, the vessel passed across a 500-ft. wide band of agitated water which was darker than the smooth surrounding sea. It stretched from E. to W. as far as the eye could see. There were white breaking waves all along both edges of the band of disturbed water"

(*Marine Observer,* 34: 118–19, 1964). It is quite possible that the long, stationary bands of luminescence mentioned in Chapter 1 may be coincident with rips of this type, with the boiling waters stimulating bioluminescence.

A moving rip, termed a "bore" by the commander of the steamship *Bulgarian,* was observed from this vessel on December 29, 1884. "The water boiled and seethed. The surface of the bore was about two feet above the general level of the ocean, and its extent about six miles long and from three to five miles wide, moving to the northeast" (*Science,* 5: 61, 1885). Note that this phenomenon was probably due to a subsurface wave intersecting the surface rather than the tidal action associated with the usual bore found in estuaries.

On March 13, 1891, the Swedish *Eleanora* was plying a calm sea near St. Paul's Rocks when it encountered a typical example of a surface disturbance caused by an undersea volcanic eruption. ". . . a noise was heard on the port side, like a heavy surf, and almost immediately the sea began to bubble and boil like a huge kettle, the broken water reaching as high as the poop deck. No distinct shock was felt, but after the disturbance struck the ship, she continued to tremble as long as it lasted. After about an hour it ceased for an hour and then was followed by another similar disturbance. A bubbling sound was all that could be heard, and the water appeared foamy, but it was impossible, on account of the darkness, to say whether it was muddy" (*Nature,* 44: 41, 1891).

A curious, wind-sculpted wave was seen from the M.V. *Tancred* while it was riding out a typhoon in early October 1954 in Kōbe Bay, Japan. "The vessel was hove-to with two anchors down facing the incoming gale (133 km./hr.) and the waves with crests up to 10 and 15 ft. were passing neatly along her side. From the rail we were struck by the peculiar appearance of the wave-slopes facing the wind.

"On many of these there were a number of well-defined steps, carved so to stay into the water just like the steps of a ladder, starting from the trough of the wave up to about half its height. Although the waves were moving quickly, the steps remained, steadily extending parallel to each other for one or two metres in length. There were at times as many as twenty of these nicely successive steps cut into the body of the wave. We tried to photograph them, but the very poor visibility and the fast motion of the waves resulted only in a blurred print.

"Were these steps carved in the wave slopes by high harmonics of the period of the typhoon squalls? These higher harmonics have been registered by sensitive modern microbarographs, and they might have something to do with the quite peculiar screaming of the wind, often reported by seamen during the squalls of tropical storms. Strangely

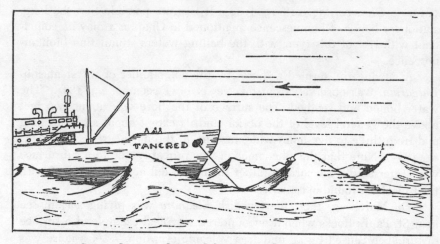

Stepped waves observed during a typhoon in Kōbe Bay

enough, the peculiar whistling has never been noticed in the squall line of extratropical storms" (*Nature,* 175: 310, 1955).

Vague references in ancient literature, including the Bible, suggest that the Dead Sea on rare occasions turns completely white. This is not to be confused with the spectacular bands of foam that form fairly regularly. The Dead Sea is usually perfectly clear in August, but on August 25, 1943, it turned completely white, verifying the ancient observations. "The same observation was made on the same morning at the northern and southern ends, which are 70 km. apart, and it was further ascertained that during the night the whole Dead Sea had turned white. During winter storms a seam of some 100 metres occurs frequently along the shores, turbid and yellowish, but it was never observed that the whole Dead Sea surface had turned white. The turbidity gradually disappeared, and in December 1943 the water became almost clear again." Analysis revealed the whiteness was due to calcium carbonate (*Nature,* 154: 402–3, 1944). A later paper in *Nature* suggested that an earthquake had stirred up chalk from strata under the lake surface.

Far away from the restless ocean, J. Shaw once noticed a peculiar honeycomb appearance of the water in a mountain stream. "This afternoon, [in Tynron, England] while ascending a mountain pathway adown which water was trickling, after the torrents of rain that fell in the morning had ceased, I observed an appearance of the surface of running water so exactly like the hexagons of the bees' cells that I looked at it carefully for some time. Little air-bells of water seemed to issue from under the withered leaves lying in the tract, which rushed towards the hexagons, occupying an irregular space about four inches by five. As soon as these air-bells arrived at the hexagons, they arranged themselves into new cells, making up, apparently, for the loss occasioned by the continual bursting here and there of the cell-walls. No sooner had these cell-walls burst, than others closed in and took their places. The worst-formed hexagons were those at the under or lower side of the surface —the part of the surface farthest down the hill; here they were larger and more like circles. By an ingenious mechanical theory, Darwin accounts for the hexagonal structures of the cells of the hive-bee so as to supersede the necessity of supposing that the hive-bee constructed its comb as if it were a mathematician. But here the blind forces of Nature, under peculiar conditions, had presented an appearance, on running water less than half an inch in depth, so entirely like the surface of a honeycomb, that it would be a startling result could it be reproduced in a laboratory" (*Nature*, 43: 30, 1890).

The Bewildering Variety of Tides

For most people living on the sea coast, tides come and go with clockwork regularity twice a day. Some places, though, experience only one tide per day; in others, the tides follow the sun rather than the moon. Elsewhere the situation becomes even more complex.

Basically, tides are the sloshings of the oceans in their relatively shallow basins (2 miles deep on the average, but thousands of miles across) under the combined influences of the moon and sun. Obviously, the shape and bottom contour of the coastline have strong effects, too. Geophysicists are generally satisfied that tides, regardless of their idiosyncrasies, can be explained by appealing to the fluctuating attractions of the moon and sun and the natural frequencies of oscillation of the various ocean basins. Despite this assurance, the reader will probably agree that some of the tidal phenomena described below are very strange.

Tidal bores, too, can be described in terms of the onrushing tide and the constricting influences of river estuaries. This explanation cannot detract from the eeriness of the foaming walls of advancing water seen on the Amazon and other properly configured rivers around the world.

GENERAL TIDAL PROBLEMS

The German scientist Krummel, in an address in 1897 at the University of Kiel, outlined some of the tidal anomalies still perplexing oceanographers. Here are a few excerpts from his talk as summarized in *Science*. "The tide wave advances progressively from south to north on the west coast of Europe but arrives simultaneously along a great stretch of eastern North America. It advances northward along the east coast and southward on the west coast of New Zealand but arrives all at once on the eastern coast of Australia over a belt covering 26° of latitude. Spring tide is delayed from 1/2 day to 2 1/2 days after new moon at most Atlantic stations, but at Toulon, on the Mediterranean, it occurs 4 3/4 hours before the syzygies [moon, earth, and sun in alignment]. The diurnal inequality, which should reach its maximum with the greatest declination of the moon, is belated on the European coast by from four to seven days, while at one point in the Gulf of Mexico it is accelerated by 17 hours. Much consideration is given to Boergen's discussion of interfering waves, whereby the notable differences between the tides of oceanic islands may perhaps be accounted for. The once-a-day tides on lunar time in the Gulf of Mexico and on solar time at Tahiti and elsewhere are thus to be explained. The studies of George Darwin and Lord Kelvin on the modifications suffered by the tide waves when running ashore have shown that 'overtides,' having shorter periods than normal tides, may thus be produced, and these are compared with the overtones of musical sounds, as explained by Helmholtz. The three tides in a day in the Tay at Stirling, Scotland, and in the harbors back of the Isle of Wight are thought to be of this nature. The continuous records of tide gauges reveal an increasing number of stations at which waves of short periods, from 5 to 90 minutes, are found, the shortest of these being much longer than the longest period of wind-made swells (12–15 seconds). Some of these oscillations, as in various arms of the Mediterranean, are probably to be compared with the seiches of lakes" (*Science*, 7: 705–6, 1898).

TIDES OUT OF THE MOON'S CONTROL

I quote next from H. A. Marmer's classic survey of tidal variations. Marmer demonstrates the wide range of tides observed around the world. Of course, all these deviations from the norm may, as Krummel ventured above, be explained by appealing to the effects of land masses and tidal wave interference.

"The usual explanation of the tide in textbooks of physical geography or astronomy makes of it a simple phenomenon. It is shown that the gravitational attraction of sun and moon on the earth gives rise to forces which move the waters of the sea relative to the solid earth. It is further shown that these forces have different periods, but that the predominant ones have a period of about half a day; therefore there are two high waters and two low waters in a day. And finally it is shown that the moon plays the leading role in bringing about the tide, for the tide-producing power of a heavenly body varies directly as its mass and inversely as the cube of its distance from the earth.

"On the basis of these general considerations, numerous features of the tide can be explained. Thus, at the times of new and full moon, when the tide-producing forces of sun and moon are in the same phase, the tides are greater than usual, while at the times of the moon's quadratures the tides are less than usual. In the same way, when the moon is in perigee, or nearest the earth, greater tides result than when the moon is in apogee or farthest from the earth. To be sure, it is known that the tides at different places vary in time, in range, and in other features. But these differences are ascribed to modifications brought about by local hydrographic features. And thus the whole phenomenon is seemingly reduced to simple terms.

"To the navigator who is familiar with the Seven Seas, however, this very much oversimplifies the subject. For he finds that the tides at different places vary not only in time and in range, but also in character of rise and fall. Quite apart from differences in time and in range, which may be regarded as merely differences in degree, it is found that tides present striking differences in kind. There is, in fact, an almost bewildering variety in tides.

"Take for example the actual records of the rise and fall of the tide at three such well-known places as Norfolk, Va., Pensacola, Fla., and San Francisco, Calif., for the last 4 days of May 1931. These are [illustrated here], the horizontal line associated with each tide curve representing

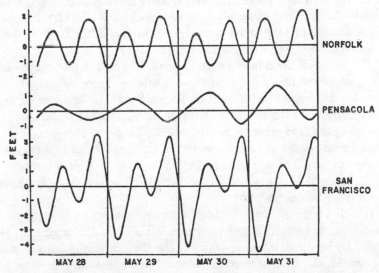

Different kinds of tides around the continental United States

the undisturbed or mean level of the sea. At Norfolk, it is seen, there are two high and two low waters in a day, morning and afternoon tides differing but little, and the high waters rising approximately the same distance above sea level as the low waters fall below it. At Pensacola, on the same days, there were but one high and one low water each day. And at San Francisco, while there were two high and two low waters each day, the morning tides differed very considerably from the afternoon tides.

* * *

"Throughout the world, with but rare exception, the sovereignty of the moon over the tide is clearly exhibited by the retardation in the times of high and low water by about 50 minutes each day. Thus in [the illustration] it is seen that the first high water of May 28 at Norfolk occurred at 6 o'clock and that each day thereafter it came about an hour later. The other high water and also the low waters are seen to have occurred approximately an hour later each day. And at Seattle, with a totally different kind of tide, a similar retardation in the times of high and low water is seen to have occurred. This merely confirms the old adage that 'the tide follows the moon.' For the transit of the moon over any place occurs each day later by 50 minutes, on the average.

"There are some places, however, where the tide appears to follow the sun rather than the moon. That is, instead of coming later each day by about 50 minutes, the tide comes to high and low water at about the same time day after day. Thus at Tahiti in the Society Islands, it has been known for many years that high water generally comes about noon and midnight and low water about 6 A.M. and 6 P.M. In fact, it appears that the natives use the same word for midnight as for high water. At Tahiti, therefore, the tide is solar rather than lunar.

"The range of the tide at Tahiti is small, less than a foot on the average. A better example of the solar type of tide has recently come to light at Tuesday Island, a small island in Torres Strait, lying about 15 miles northwesterly from the northern point of the Australian mainland. Here the range of the tide averages nearly 5 feet. The peculiar behavior of the tide here with regard to time is clearly brought out if the tide curves for a number of days are arranged in [a] column, as in [the accompanying illustration], which represents the tide curves for each day of the week beginning September 10, 1925.

"It will be noted that the high and low waters in this figure fall practically in a vertical line—which means that instead of coming later each day by about 50 minutes, which is the state of affairs at most places in the world, the tide here comes about the same time day after day. That this is not a general feature of the tides in the South Pacific Ocean is evident from a comparison with the tide curves for Apia, [Western]

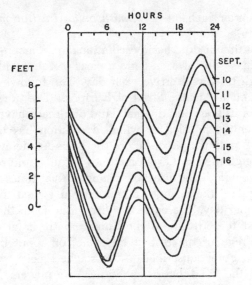

The sun-dominated tides at Tuesday Island, in the Pacific

Samoa, for the same week. . . . It will be noted that here there is a distinct shift to the right in regard to the times of high and low water in following down the curves.

"The mathematical process of harmonic analysis permits the tide at any place to be resolved into its simple constituent tides. At Apia the principal lunar constituent has a range of 2.5 feet, while the principal solar constituent has a range of 0.6 feet. Hence the tide here follows the moon. At Tuesday Island, the principal lunar and solar constituents both have the same range of 3.1 feet. Hence here the tide is no longer predominantly lunar but as much solar as lunar.

"The answer to the question as to why the tide at some places is governed by the sun rather than the moon is again found in the physical characteristics of the various oceanic basins and seas. Where the conditions are such as to restrict the response to the lunar tide-producing forces but not the response to the solar tide-producing forces, the latter become the more prominent and give rise to solar tides.

"An interesting form of tide is found at Jolo, in the Sulu Archipelago [Philippines]. Here the high waters follow the moon, but the low waters appear to follow the sun. The tide curves for the week beginning September 10, 1925, at Jolo . . . [show that] the tide here is complicated by the fact that for part of the month there are two high and two low waters in a day, while at other times there is but one high and one low water. It is seen, however, that the high waters exhibit the distinct shift to the right characteristic of lunar tides, while the low waters lie almost perpendicularly under each other" (*Smithsonian Institution Annual Report*, 1934, 181–91).

The superposition of tidal basin oscillations upon moon-created tides may completely mask the latter in certain parts of the world. Where this occurs, many high tides will arrive each day. The following note deals with the tidal anomalies in the Strait of Euripos. "The tides in this narrow strait between Euboea and the mainland of Greece have from classic times been a scientific puzzle, for which a solution has been recently suggested by M. Forel, in a paper before the Paris Academy of Sciences. The currents through the strait are sometimes 'regular' and sometimes 'irregular.' When 'regular,' the direction changes *four* times in the lunar day. When 'irregular,' the changes number from *eleven* to *fourteen* or even more in a lunar day. The current is 'irregular' from the 7th to 13th and from the 21st to 26th day of the lunar month, or at the times of *quadrature*, and 'regular' the rest of the time, or about the syzygies." François Alphonse Forel subscribed to the seiche theory, whereby resonant sloshing in the tidal basin sometimes overpowers lunar effects (*American Journal of Science*, 3: 163, 1880).

Replying to a discussion in *Nature* of extralunar fluctuations of the water levels in Sydney harbor, Australia, Anthony S. Thomson noted that "it is a matter of common knowledge to naval officers and others concerned, that the irregular variations of sea level in the Maltese inlets are at times sufficiently great to completely mask the slight lunar tide; and that the Port Officials are in the habit of insisting on a considerable margin of depth before permitting vessels to pass over the sills of the dry docks. . . . My observations showed conclusively that there is at certain times in Malta Grand Harbour a perfectly regular ebb and flow with a period of twenty-three minutes; about the same period obtaining in Sydney Harbour, which Mr. Russell gives as twenty-six minutes" (*Nature*, 59: 1251–56, 1898).

SPECTACULAR TIDAL BORES

Tidal bores cannot fail to impress the onlooker as they advance irresistibly up a river channel, boiling and hissing, sweeping all before them. When the volume of water attracted by the moon into a narrow estuary is very large in relation to the capacity of the channel, the onrushing water piles up into a steep wave, which may be 30 ft. high in the Hangchow River, and traveling as fast as 15 miles per hour.

Since the tidal bores are more spectacular than strange, one account will suffice. This is John C. Branner's description of the *pororoca*, the great tidal bore of the Amazon River.

"While travelling upon the Amazon in 1881, I was fortunate in having an opportunity to observe some of the effects of a remarkable phenomenon which occurs at the northern *embouchure* of that river, in connection with the spring tides. It is known to the Indians and Brazilians as the *pororoca*, and is, I believe, generally supposed to be identical with the 'bore' of the Hugli branch of the Ganges, of the Brahmaputra, and of the Indus. I regret very much that like [La] Condamine, who passed through this part of the country about 1740, I could not observe this phenomenon in actual operation; but the gentleman whose guest I was at the time, and upon whose boat I was a passenger, was fairly horrified at my suggesting such a thing, while his boatmen united in a fervent 'God forbid that we should ever see the *pororoca!*' and ever afterwards doubted my sanity. I venture, however, to give some of the results of my own observations, in order that those who in the future visit this region, concerning which so little is known, may be able to see and establish as far as possible the rate of destruction and building-up here being carried on.

*　*　*

"As I shortly afterwards met and conversed with a man who had seen the *pororoca,* I shall first give his description of it and then speak of its effects as observed by myself. This man was a soldier in the Brazilian army and, on the occasion referred to, was going with a few other soldiers from the colony to Macapá in a small open boat. Arriving at the mouth of the Araguari, they went down with the tide, and anchored just inside the bar which crosses the mouth of this stream, to await the turning of the tide, which would enable them to pass the shallows and then carry them up the Amazon. Shortly after the tide had stopped running out, they saw something coming toward them from the ocean in a long white line, which grew bigger and whiter as it approached. Then there was a sound like the rumbling of distant thunder, which grew louder and louder as the white line came nearer, until it seemed as if the whole ocean had risen up, and was coming, charging and thundering down on them, boiling over the edge of this pile of water like an endless cataract, from four to seven metres high, that spread out across the whole eastern horizon. This was the *pororoca!* When they saw it coming, the crew became utterly demoralized and fell to crying and praying in the bottom of the boat, expecting that it would certainly be dashed to pieces and they themselves drowned. The pilot, however, had the presence of mind to heave anchor before the wall of waters struck them; and, when it did strike, they were first pitched violently forward, and then lifted and left rolling and tossing like a cork on the sea it left behind, the boat nearly filled with water. But their trouble was not yet ended; for before they had emptied the boat, two other such seas came down on them at short intervals, tossing them in the same manner and finally leaving them within a stone's throw of the river-bank, where another such wave would have dashed them upon the shore. They had been anchored near the middle of the stream before the waves struck them, and the stream at this place is several miles wide.

"But no description of this disturbance of the water can impress one so vividly as the signs of devastation seen upon the land. The silent story of the uprooted trees that lie matted and tangled and twisted together upon the shore, sometimes half-buried in the sand as if they had been nothing more than so many strings or bits of paper, is deeply impressive. Forests so dense that I do not know how to convey an adequate idea of their density and gloom, are uprooted, torn, and swept away like chaff; and, after the full force of the waves is broken, they sweep on inland, leaving the *debris* with which they are loaded, heaped, and strewn through the forests. The most powerful roots of the largest trees cannot withstand the *pororoca,* for the ground itself is torn up to great depths in many places and carried away by the flood to make bars, add to old islands, or build up new ones. Before seeing these evidences of its devastation, I had heard what I considered very extravagant stories of the destructive power of the *pororoca;* but, after seeing them, doubt was no longer possible. The lower or northern ends of the islands of Bailique and Porquinhos seemed to feel the force of the waves at the time of my visit more than any of the other islands on the south-east side of the river, while on the northern side the forest was wrecked and the banks washed out far above Ilha Nova.

"The explanation of this phenomenon, as given by [La] Condamine, appears to be the correct one; that is, that it is due to the incoming tides meeting resistance, in the form of immense sand-bars in some places and narrow channels in others" (*Science,* 4: 488–90, 1884).

A Peek Below the Surface

Subsurface "weather," as we have seen, frequently betrays itself on the surface in the guise of slicks, calms, boiling waters, rafts of dead fish, rips, and even geysers. Oceanographers are just beginning to appreciate the complexity of the fine structure of oceanic circulation and the local storms that rage unseen below. Since the oceans cover seven-tenths of the earth's surface, there is more weather beneath the waves than above the land.

UNDERWATER CYCLONIC STRUCTURES

The presence of many huge current rings in all oceans has recently startled oceanographers, who considered them great rarities just a few years ago. North Atlantic rings have been studied the most intensively. At any time, more than a dozen rings, 150 to 300 km. across may be drifting about the North Atlantic. Reaching down 2,500 to 3,500 meters (more

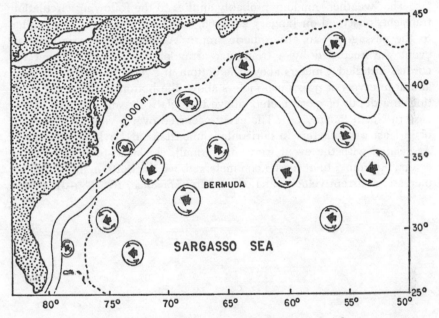

Large, stable current rings drift around the North Atlantic.

than 2 miles), almost to the bottom, the rings consist of circulating currents with speeds up to 4 km. per hour. Rings are apparently formed when currents meander to form loops that eventually close and detach themselves from the main currents. Both cold-core and warm-core rings are known. They tend to drift a few kilometers per day and have lifetimes of 2 or 3 years (*Science*, 198: 387–89, 1977).

VERTICAL SPIRES AND WALLS OF PARTICULATES

Peculiar humps or hills of particulate material, thousands of feet long and hundreds high, have been detected in the Florida Current using ultrasensitive, 20-kHz. sonar. The humps extend from the bottom of the so-called mixed layer almost to the surface. Sediment and plankton probably make up the humps, but the actual constitution and origin of these undersea clouds are unknown. The ever-present interplay of oceanic currents might concentrate the particulate matter; so could some sort of coordinated biological activity (*Nature*, 276: 360–62, 1978).

DEEP-OCEAN TRANSIENT EVENTS

The "weather" analogy probably applies to the following circulation transients observed on January 24, 1968, which were surprisingly similar to the passage of an atmospheric front: "A transient deep-circulation event was recorded by a triangular array of autonomous current recorders installed 3 meters above the bottom at two of the three positions and at intervals of 3 to 1,000 meters above the bottom at the third position in a depth of 3,950 meters above the relatively smooth floor of the eastern North Pacific. . . . The event occurred over a volume of the sea of at least 2 kilometers in horizontal dimensions and 1 kilometer thick. Associated with the event were many small, clockwise-rotating features extending from 3 to at least 1,000 meters above the bottom and a rapidly increasing current velocity at 1,000 meters" (*Science*, 165: 889–91, 1969).

7

UNUSUAL NATURAL SOUNDS

When the research work for this book began, the number and variety of mysterious natural sounds was not foreseen. Strange lights, mirages, and weather oddities were believed to constitute the majority of strange phenomena. The famous Barisāl Guns were recognized, of course, due to the publicity given them by Sir George Darwin. Additional curious sounds have been discovered in our foray through the literature at a modest but surprising rate. Even now, after years of search, this chapter cannot be considered close to completion, for how many individuals take the time to write to scientific journals about ephemeral, elusive sounds? For that matter, who, in these noisy latter days, can separate natural and man-made sounds? Almost all strange sounds reported below have been heard either in remote spots of the globe, where almost all sounds heard are natural, or in earlier and quieter days.

Modern technology for all of its masking of natural sounds has also led us to the knowledge of infrasound—that is, pressure waves at very low frequencies. As infrasound observations accumulate, puzzling data will doubtless be found. Much infrasound seems to originate with the auroras, with weather systems, and with seismic activity—just those phenomena that give rise to many of the curious observations reported here involving all sensory channels.

Extraordinary Detonations

In this day of sonic booms and frequent blasting, detonations heard afar are written off as man-made with good reason. Eighty years ago the world was quieter and people tried to track down the causes of strange sounds. For example, E. Van den Broeck compiled several hundred pages of testimony on *mistpouffers* in the French scientific journal *Ciel et Terre* (Sky and Earth) in 1895 and 1896. *Mistpouffers* are dull, distant explosive sounds heard around the coast of Europe all the way to Iceland. Every European country has its own name for them, and it turns out that they are also heard on North American and Asian coasts too. Despite the universality of unexplained detonations and despite ample proof of their existence, they are a dead issue in the scientific world.

The most famous unexplained detonations are the Barisāl Guns heard in the vicinity of the Ganges delta. Such "waterguns," however, are not confined to salt water. Some of New York's finger lakes have their own private waterguns; so do lakes in Europe. Doubtless, many reports of waterguns have never seen print in scientific journals and are thus excluded from this collection. We have to assume that they are as common on freshwater shores as on saltwater shores.

"Landguns" are also ubiquitous. Residents in dozens of localities all over the world hear strange detonations year after year, often emanating from beneath their feet, sometimes apparently from the atmosphere overhead. Scientists ascribe these noises to seismic hot spots, where subterranean forces are slowly cracking rocks below the surface. Some but not all of these explosive sounds can be correlated with earth tremors, lending credence to the seismic explanation.

Those elusive detonations accompanied by "swishes" and sounds like escaping steam may tentatively be assigned to meteors. Here we include only cases where there are no visible manifestations of meteors. Presumably clouds and distance may conceal some of the meteoric sound-producing events. There is always the possibility, though, that some of the detonations blamed on meteors, especially those in the interior of Australia, may actually be seismic.

MISTPOUFFERS OR "FOG GUNS"

Mistpouffers (fog dissipators) are dull, explosive sounds heard all over the world, but especially near the sea coasts. The Italians call them *marina* or *brontidi;* the Japanese, *uminari;* each locality has its own name for them. Their origin is still mysterious. We only know that somehow they are probably connected with the sea. Modern investigations of mysterious explosive sounds heard along the sea coasts of North America and Europe have generally written such phenomena off as sonic booms. The difficulty with this theory is that *mistpouffers* have been heard and recorded for well over a century. Another modern hypothesis attributes the *mistpouffers* to eruptions of natural gas from the ocean-covered continental shelves. The recent discovery of abundant pockmarks on many continental shelves supports this idea of frequent releases of large volumes of natural gas. Some of the "lake guns" introduced later in this section may be natural gas explosions too.

A quick tour of the globe will sketch out the magnitude of the *mistpouffer* phenomenon. We begin with Samuel W. Kain's short description of the detonations heard for many years along the eastern coast of Canada. "Everybody who has been much upon our Charlotte County coast must remember that upon the still summer days, when the heat hovers upon the ocean, what seem to be gun or even cannon reports are heard at intervals coming from seaward. The residents always say, in answer to one's question: 'Indians shooting porpoise off Grand Manan.' This explanation I never believed; the sound of a gun report could not come so far, and, besides, the noise is of too deep and booming a character. I have often puzzled over the matter, and it is consequently with great pleasure that I find in *Nature* for October 31, 1895, a short article of Prof. G. H. Darwin, in which he calls attention to the occurrence of what is obviously the same phenomenon in the delta of the Ganges, upon the coast of Belgium, and in parts of Scotland, and in which he asks for experiences from other parts of the world. Two explanations are suggested by his correspondent, M. Van den Broeck, of Belgium, who called his attention to the phenomenon, one that the reports are of atmospheric origin, due to peculiar electrical discharges; the other that they are internal in the earth, due, perhaps, to shock of the internal liquid mass against the solid crust. The following number of *Nature* contains notes which suggest that the reports may accompany the formation of faults or may result from earthquakes too slight to be otherwise perceived, and later numbers of that journal contain numerous letters upon strange sounds heard in different parts of the world, with various explanations.

"The discussion upon the subject by this society on December 3, 1895, has called out further information showing that others besides myself have noticed these or similar sounds in New Brunswick. The late Edward Jack, a keen observer of things in nature, wrote me under date December 13, 1895, 'I have often noticed in Passamaquoddy Bay, when I was duck-shooting in the early spring mornings, the noises of which you speak; they always seemed to come from the south side of the bay. They resembled more the resonance from the falling of some heavy body into the water than that of the firing of a gun, such as is produced by a cake of ice breaking away from a large sheet of it and toppling over into the sea. These noises were heard by me only in very calm spring mornings when there was no breath of air . . . there was nothing subterranean in them.' Capt. Charles Bishop, of the schooner *Susie Prescott*, has told Mr. S. W. Kain that he has heard these sounds 40 miles from land between

Grand Manan, the Georges Banks, and Mount Desert Rock. They are reported also from the Kennebecasis. Mr. Keith A. Barber, of Torryburn Cove, wrote [on] December 26, 1895, to this society: 'I have heard sounds similar to those on the Kennebecasis [Bay] in the warm days of summer. They seemed to come from a southeasterly direction.' Mr. Arthur Lordly, a member of this society who resides in the summer at Riverside, has also told Mr. Kain that he has heard similar sounds, on clear warm days, on the Kennebecasis, from a southwest direction. No other reports of this occurrence in New Brunswick have reached me" (*Monthly Weather Review*, 26: 153, 1898).

A stop in the Philippines reveals that the same acoustic phenomenon is heard there. "The Rev. M. Saderra Maso, who has for many years studied the earthquakes of the Philippine Islands, is now turning his attention to the subterranean noises known in other countries under various names, such as *mistpouffers*, *marinas*, *brontidi*, *retumbos*, &c. In the Philippines many terms are used, generally signifying merely rumbling or noise, while a few indicate that the noises are supposed to proceed from the sea or from mountains or clouds. Most of the places where they were observed lie along the coasts of inter-island seas or in enclosed bays; very few are situated on the open coast. The noises are heard most frequently at nightfall, during the night, and in the early morning, especially in the hot months of March, April, and May, though in the towns of the Pangasinan province they are confined almost entirely to the rainy season. They are compared in 70 per cent of the records to thunder. With rare exceptions, they seem to come from the mountains inland. The instances in which the noises show any connection with earthquakes are few, and observers usually distinguish between them and the low rumblings which occasionally precede earthquakes. It is a common opinion among the Filipinos that the noises are the effect of waves breaking on the beach or into caverns and that they are intimately connected with changes in the weather, generally with impending typhoons. Father Saderra Maso is inclined to agree with this view in certain cases. The typhoons in the Philippines sometimes cause very heavy swells, which are propagated more than a thousand kilometres, and hence arrive days before the wind acquires any appreciable force. He suggests that special atmospheric conditions may be responsible for the great distances to which the sounds are heard, and that their apparent inland origin may be due to reflection, possibly from the cumulus clouds which crown the neighbouring mountains, while the direct sound waves are shut off by walls of vegetation or inequalities in the ground" (*Nature*, 85: 451, 1911).

The floor of the Gulf of Mexico certainly covers many deposits of natural gas; therefore it is not surprising to discover *mistpouffers* in this area, assuming that gas eruptions are involved. W. S. Cooper relates his experience. "On the evening of December 28, 1885, I was with a companion in a sailboat on the Gulf of Mexico about 20 miles southeast of Cedar Keys, Florida. We were becalmed. The next morning the sky was cloudless. There was a light fog and no breeze. The atmosphere was bracing but not frosty. We were about 10 miles out but in shallow water. Shortly after sunrise we heard reports as of a gun or distant cannon. They came at intervals of about 5 minutes. We were not certain as to the direction. My companion, who lived several miles further down the coast, said he had often heard the reports on still mornings" (*Scientific American,* 75: 123, 1896).

The *Monthly Weather Review* summarized a paper presented by A. Cancani in 1898, which gave a vivid account of the Italian version of the *mistpouffers* (called *marinas* and *brontidi* in that region). "The observations on which his discussion is founded are collected from places in or near the inland province of Umbria, where the noises are known as *marina,* it being the popular belief that they come from the sea. The sound is quite distinct and easily recognized; it is longer than that of a cannon shot, and though more prolonged and dull, it is not unlike distant thunder. It invariably seems to come from a distance, and from the neighborhood of the horizon, sometimes apparently from the ground, but generally through the air. The weather, when the *marina* is heard, is calm as a rule, but that it often precedes bad weather is shown by the common saying, '*Cuando tuona la marina o acqualo vento o strina*' ('when the ocean thunders, expect rain or wind or heat'). The interval between successive detonations is very variable, sometimes being only a few minutes or even seconds. They appear to be heard at all times of the day and year, the experience of observers differing widely as to the epochs when they are heard most frequently. With regard to the origin of the *marina,* Dr. Cancani concludes that they can not be due to a stormy sea, because *mistpouffers* are frequently observed when the sea is calm; not to gusts of wind in mountain gorges, for they are heard on mountain summits and in open plains. If their origin were atmospheric, they would not be confined to special regions. Nor can they be connected with artificial noises, for they are heard by night as well as by day and in countries where the use of explosives is unknown. There remains thus the hypothesis which Dr. Cancani considers the most probable, that of an endogenous origin. To the obvious objections that there should always be a center of maximum intensity, which is never to be found, and that they are so rarely accompanied by any perceptible tremor, he replies that, in a seismic series, noises are frequently heard without any shock being felt, and of which we are unable to determine the center" (*Monthly Weather Review,* 26: 216, 1898).

Finally, an example from the East Indies completes this quick survey. Bear in mind that there are many, many more reports of *mistpouffers* in the scientific literature. "Capt. P. Jansen, St. Helens Court, London, E.C. 3, has sent us an interesting account of sounds heard by him near the mouths of rivers in the Dutch East Indies. Except in their higher pitch, they seem to resemble the Barisāl Guns of the Ganges delta and the brontides [*brontidi*] of certain districts in Italy. On the roads of Sourabaya in Java, he says, two or three noises, as of foghorns of different notes, were heard at irregular intervals of a few seconds, each lasting for one or two seconds. In the hold of an empty ship, the noise was deafening. After continuing for one or two hours, the noises ceased as suddenly as they began. Capt. Jansen has heard the same noises, but less frequently, at the mouth of the Palembang River in Sumatra. At the mouths of some of the rivers of the Malay Peninsula, other noises were heard, like that of plucking the strings of a musical instrument all on the same note and at irregular intervals. Although Barisāl Guns and brontides have for a long time been carefully studied, their origin is still obscure. They are heard frequently in seismic districts and also in countries free from earthquakes. Possibly they have more than one origin, but their frequent occurrence near the mouths of great rivers seems to connect them with the settling of the delta or of the underlying crust" (*Nature*, 134: 769, 1934).

THE BARISĀL GUNS

Now we come to the most famous of all natural detonations, the Barisāl Guns. Since their habitat in the Ganges delta geologically resembles the locations of almost all other *mistpouffers*, it is likely that the Barisāl Guns are also *mistpouffers*, but better known. The two descriptions below are selected from among a dozen covering about a century of observations. The descriptions of the Barisāl Guns vary a bit from report to report, but in general these detonations seem to be sharper, more like a true explosion than the *mistpouffers*. For this reason, some investigators have supposed that the Barisāl Guns have a seismic origin.

G. B. Scott's "earwitness" account is thorough and straightforward. "I first heard the Barisāl Guns in December 1871, on my way to Assam from Calcutta through the Sundarbans. The weather was clear and calm, no sign of any storms. All day the noises on board the steamer prevented other sounds from being heard; but when all was silent at night, and we were moored in one or other of the narrow channels in the neighbourhood of Barisāl, Morelgunge, and upwards, far from any villages or other habitations, with miles and miles of long grass jungle on every side, the only sounds the lap of the water or the splash of earth, falling into the water along the banks, then at intervals, irregularly, would be heard the dull muffled boom as of distant cannon. Sometimes a single report, at others two, three, or more in succession; never near, always distant, but not always equally distant. Sometimes the reports would resemble cannon from two rather widely separated opposing forces, at others from different directions but apparently always from the southward, that is seaward. We were not very far from the sea when I first heard them, and on mentioning to an old lady on board that I heard distant cannon, she first told me of the mysterious sounds known as the 'Barisāl Guns.' For the next two years I was in Upper Assam, above Goālpāra, and do not remember ever hearing them there; but in 1874 I was working in the Goālpāra district in the tract south of Dhubri, between the Brahmaputra and the Garo Hills; sometimes near the river, sometimes near the foot of the hills, at others between the two. I gradually worked down as far as Chilmari Chat (I think it is called), the landing-place for Tura, the headquarters of the Garo Hills district, and distant quite 300 miles from the mouths of the Brahmaputra and Ganges. The villages are few and far between and very small, firearms were scarce, and certainly there were no cannon in the neighbourhood, and fireworks were not known to the people. I think I am right in saying I heard the reports every night while south of Dhubri and often during the day. The weather on the whole was fine. Short, sharp, 'nor'westers' occasionally burst on us of an evening, with much thunder and lightning; but the days were clear, and, as a rule, the sounds were heard more distinctly on clear days and nights.

"I specially remember spending a quiet Sunday, in the month of May, with a friend at Chilmari, near the river-bank. We had both remarked the reports the night before and when near the hills previously. About 10 A.M. in the day, weather clear and calm, we were walking quietly up and down near the river-bank, discussing the sounds, when we heard the booming distinctly, about as loud as heavy cannon would sound on a quiet day about ten miles off, down the river. Shortly after, we heard a heavy boom very much nearer, still south. Suddenly we heard two quick successive reports, more like horse pistol or musket (not rifle) shots close by. I thought they sounded in the air about 150 yards due west of us over the water. My friend thought they sounded north of us. We ran to the bank and asked our boatmen, moored below, if they heard them and if so in what direction. They pointed south!" (*Nature*, 53: 197, 1896).

The next description by Henry S. Schurr is more colorful, with local background added. His assertion that the Guns are always heard as triplets does not agree with all other reports.

"Barisāl Guns are heard over a wide range extending from the

Twenty-four Pergunnahs through Khulna, Backergunge and Noākhāli, and along the banks of the Megna to Naraingunge and Dacca. They are heard most clearly and frequently in the Backergunge district, from whose headquarters they take their name.

"These Guns are heard most frequently from February to October, and seldom in November, December, or January. One very noticeable feature is their absence during fine weather, and they are only heard just before, during, or immediately after heavy rain.

"The direction from which they are heard is constant, and that is the south or south-east. I have heard them west of me when down in the extreme south of the district, but never north of me. On the other hand, I have been told by captains of river-going steamers that they have heard these reports to their north. These gentlemen, however, ply along waters outside the range of my observations, which lie on the mainland and its adjacent waters.

"These Guns are always heard in triplets, i.e., three guns are always heard, one after the other, at regular intervals, and though several guns may be heard, the number is always three or a multiple of three. Then the interval between the three is always constant—i.e., the interval between the first and the second is the same as the interval between the second and the third, and this interval is usually three seconds, though I have timed it up to ten seconds. The interval, however, between the triplets varies, and varies largely, from a few seconds up to hours and days. Sometimes only one series of triplets is heard in a day; at others, the triplets follow with great regularity, and I have counted as many as forty-five of them, one after the other, without a pause.

"The report is exactly like the firing of big guns heard from a distance with this peculiar difference, that the report is always double—i.e., the report has (as it were) an echo. This echo is so immediate that I can best describe its interval by an illustration. Suppose a person standing near the Eden Gardens heard the 9 o'clock gun fired from Fort William, he would first hear the report of the gun and its immediate echo from the walls of the High Court. The Barisāl Guns sound exactly like this, only as if heard from a distance of several miles, very much the same as the sound of the Fort gun heard at Barrackpore on a clear night in the cold weather.

"The report varies little in intensity, and I cannot recollect that there was much difference in the sound, whether heard at Barisāl itself or some 70 or 80 miles to the south at the extreme end of the district. The state of the atmosphere may affect it, but to no appreciable extent.

"The Backergonian peasant is celebrated for the bombs he is in the habit of fireing at his weddings and festivals, and many residents have asserted they can distinguish no difference between the reports of these festive bombs and the so-called 'guns'; but to anyone with a fairly acute sense of hearing, who listens attentively, the difference is very marked, and their assertions are completely refuted by the facts: (1) that wedding bombs vary very noticeably in the intensity of their sound; (2) are wanting in the very marked feature of the triplets; and (3) are naturally confined to the wedding season, a very short season in each year, whilst the Barisāl Guns are heard almost through the year, and very noticeably during the annual fast—the *Rosa*—when, of course, there can be no festivals of any kind" (*Nature,* 61: 127–28, 1899).

LAKE GUNS

Mysterious "guns" also boom forth from several large lakes. In the United States, the Seneca Guns, heard in the environs of Lake Seneca, New York, seem to have been firing ever since history has been recorded in that region. Even the local Indians had their legends about these booming sounds. The few scientists who have deigned to notice the Seneca Guns claim they come from natural gas eruptions. Since natural gas is known to occur around the lake, this seems the most reasonable explanation. The general character of the Seneca Guns resembles that of the typical *mistpouffer:* a distant, muffled explosion.

During the 1930s, *Science* published several letters on the Seneca Guns and their possible relation to the escape of natural gas. Herewith is the contribution of Albert G. Ingalls to this exchange, submitted in reply to an earlier *Science* paper entitled "Silencing the 'Guns' of Seneca Lake":

"Professor Fairchild offered an explanation of a mystery of sound which, as he states, 'has hovered over Seneca Lake, in central New York, for more than a century.' This is what is known by the local residents as the 'lake guns,' an occasional low, dull boom suggesting a distant muffled explosion.

"The explanation offered in Professor Fairchild's communication was that Seneca Lake occupies the upper part of a glacially deepened valley which cuts the Oriskany Sandstone at a depth of about 1,450 feet below the surface of the lake, and that the 'lake guns' are caused by volumes of natural gas which escape from that porous gas-bearing stratum, find their way upward through the 450 feet of superincumbent glacial drift, and ascend rapidly through the 600 feet of lake water above it, exploding at the surface. He states that these 'guns' have now suddenly ceased, 'with no sound reported for the last summer,' and that they are probably silenced forever. The interpretation given is that the many gas wells which have recently been drilled in the Wayne-Dundee field not far from Seneca Lake have diminished the gas pressure in the Oriskany, so that the gas no longer escapes into the lake.

"This hypothesis is ingenious and at least plausible on the evidence presented, but the purpose of the present communication is to state that Professor Fairchild's obituary of the 'guns' comes before their demise, for the writer heard these sounds as recently as last October.

"During many years the lake 'guns' were heard on innumerable occasions when the writer lived adjacent to Seneca Lake and, as a youth, spent month in and month out on it and in it, camping, swimming, sailing, boating, and fishing. Each autumn at the present time he returns to the same scene for a vacation, and this is spent in a way which should bring to notice most of the audible lake sounds; that is, in working alone from morning till night laying stone masonry on a rock cabin situated actually on the lake waters, at the base of a cliff (which may incidentally be instrumental in concentrating sounds which proceed across the lake). This is at Glenora, close to the Dundee gas field, and it was from there that the 'guns' were heard last October. The previous absence of reported observations of lake 'guns' in 1934 may have been due to the fact that it is the fishermen who most frequently report them and that last autumn the bass fishing was so poor that relatively few fished.

"In itself the hypothesis of escaping gas bubbles is not new, having been commonly current among the native residents of Seneca's shores for many decades, but its association with the depletion of the nearby gas fields, credited by Professor Fairchild to Mr. A. M. Beebee, geologist of the Rochester Gas and Electric Corporation is a new and ingenious hypothesis which probably will acquire standing if the lake 'guns' actually become silent later on.

"Interested readers will find in Davison's *Manual of Seismology* a discussion of phenomena of a similar description, under the section 'brontides.' 'Guns' are evidently heard in several localities—Italy, the Philippines, Africa, Haiti, Belgium—though their cause is unknown. Those heard at Seneca Lake seem to be most frequent in the autumn and in the daytime—in fact, the writer has never heard them after dark. Their direction is vague, and like the foot of a rainbow, they are always 'somewhere else' when the observer moves to the locality from which they first seemed to come. No large bubbles or volumes of gas have actually been observed broaching on the surface of the lake, but is it not probable that a large single volume of gas, starting from the bottom of the waters 600 feet below, would be broken up into very many small bubbles during its upward passage through that amount of water? Theoretically, this should not occur, but actually, due to some form of instability, it possibly would" (*Science*, 79: 479–80, 1934).

In Northern Ireland, Lough Neagh generates cannonlike sounds that compare favorably with the Seneca Guns. Rev. W. S. Smith sent the editor of *Nature* a fine description of these sounds in 1896.

"Lough Neagh is a sheet of water covering an area of upwards of 150 square miles, with very gradually receding shores, excepting at one or two spots. For many years after my settlement as minister here from England, I heard at intervals, when near the lake, cannon-like sounds; but not being acquainted with the geography of the distant shores, or the location of towns, or possible employments carried on, I passively concluded that the reports proceeded from quarrying operations, or, on fine summer days, from festive gatherings in [County] Derry, or [County] Tyrone. In time I came to understand that it was not from the opposite shores, but from the lake itself that the sounds proceeded. After questioning many of the local residents, I extended my inquiries to the fishermen, but they could assign no cause. A strange thing about the matter is that the people generally knew nothing of the phenomenon and that it is shrouded in mystery. I have heard the sounds during the whole year. . . . I have heard the reports probably twenty times during the present year, the last being on a Sunday afternoon a month since, when I heard two explosions; but with two exceptions they have all seemed to come from many miles away, from different directions at different times. They have come apparently from Toome Bay, from the middle of the lake, and from Langford Lodge Point, about nine miles distant. A fisherman thought they must be the result of confined air that reached the lake by means of springs that are believed to rise here and there in the bottom. But the lake is shallow, seldom more than 45 feet deep. The depression now covered by the lake having been caused, it is believed, by volcanic action when the trap-rock of [County] Antrim was erupted, there may possibly be subterranean passages, though I confess their occurrence does not seem very probable; while the sounds emanate, as stated, from various parts of the lake. I have as yet spoken to no one who observed any movement of the waters when explosions took place, nor have I spoken to any one who was close to the spot at the time. Rather every one seems to have heard them only in the distance, which is strange, as fishermen are on the lake during many months of the year, at all hours of the day and night.

"Last winter the whole of the lake was frozen over, for the first time since 1814. One fine afternoon, when the air was still, I was skating in the neighbourhood of Shande's Castle, when these mystical guns boomed forth their reports every five or six minutes. On the last day of the skating, when thousands of people from Belfast and elsewhere were assembled in Antrim Bay, there were two fearful boomings that startled every one near me. They seemed to think some dreadful catastrophe had occurred, as the sounds appeared to proceed from not more than half a mile away. I never before heard them so near. The ice in Antrim Bay remained as it was, but I afterwards learned that it was then breaking up six miles away, but with no alarming sounds" (*Nature*, 53: 197–98, 1896). Lough Neagh, of course, is not far from the North Sea, which is a prime habitat of the *mistpouffers*.

AERIAL DETONATIONS, POSSIBLY METEORIC IN ORIGIN

Explosive noises appearing to emanate from the sky above are most likely due to an exploding meteor or a supersonic jet. However, if no planes are known to be in the affected area and no visual phenomena, such as a bright flash, accompany the sound, other sources must be considered. Since sounds may be transmitted for long distances in high atmospheric channels, distant terrestrial earthquakes or human-ignited explosions may cause aerial explosions when the sounds are bent back towards the earth. One might term these sounds "acoustic mirages," as noted in Chapter 4 in connection with earthquake noises that seem to come from above. When planes, quakes, visible meteors, and human agencies are ruled out, a real mystery remains.

On June 14, 1903, H. Bourhill, living in the Transvaal, South Africa, experienced what may have been the low-level explosion of a meteor. "I was awakened by a report like the firing of a cannon, followed by a more or less long whizzing noise, with a second report a second or two after the first one. At first I thought a cannon must have been fired somewhere not very far off, only the sound seemed to be up in the air. Making up my mind to try and find out in the morning what caused the noise, I tried to go to sleep again. I had hardly turned over when a terrific explosion took place, as it appeared to me, just over the house I am living in. It was a sudden, terrifying report followed by a tearing, rending noise, giving one the idea that some large wooden structure was being torn asunder by some great force and ending with a peculiar crackling sound.

"My first idea was that the dynamite magazine here had exploded, and I jumped out of bed immediately to look around outside. I saw at once, by former experience, that the magazine had not exploded. My next idea was that it must have been a meteor, more especially as both I and another member of my family were sure that we had heard some hard particles falling on the iron roof of the house. But on examination in the morning, just after sunrise, all round the house and on the roof, no meteoric particles were to be found. I then came to the conclusion that the explosion must have been caused by some electrical disturbance or phenomenon; and on discussing the matter with the electrical engineer on this mine, he agreed there was no other way of accounting for it, stating at the same time that the electrical conditions of the atmosphere here were most unusual. As far as I have been able to ascertain at present, the explosion was heard at places 10 or 12 miles apart and was noticed by about twenty people. There are miles of country here without a house, so that, taking that into consideration, it was heard by quite a number of persons. The night was perfectly calm and clear without a cloud in the sky, and there was brilliant moonlight. I served through the siege of Kimberley, and so heard many 100-pounder shells explode, but the noise they made was small compared to the explosion I have been writing about" (*Royal Meteorological Society, Quarterly Journal,* 30: 55–56, 1904).

The desolate interior of Australia is noted for unexplained detonations. They are usually ascribed to seismic sources, but the following observation of February 1829 by Captain Sturt seems definitely to be aerial in nature. "About 3 P.M. on the 7th Mr. Hume and I were occupied tracing the chart upon the ground. The day had been remarkably fine; not a cloud was there in the heavens, nor a breath of air to be felt. On a sudden we heard what seemed to be the report of a gun fired at the distance of between five and six miles. It was not the hollow sound of an earthly explosion, or the sharp cracking noise of falling timber, but in every way resembled a discharge of a heavy piece of ordnance. On this all were agreed, but no one was certain whence the sound proceeded. Both Mr. Hume and myself had been too attentive to our occupation to form a satisfactory opinion; but we both thought it came from the N.W. I sent one of the men immediately up a tree, but he could observe nothing unusual. The country around him appeared to be equally flat on all sides and to be thickly wooded: whatever occasioned the report, it made a strong impression on all of us; and to this day, the singularity of such a sound, in such a situation, is a matter of mystery to me" (*Nature,* 81: 127, 1909).

Again from Australia, a triplet of detonations (possibly like the Barisāl Guns, but with an accompanying hissing sound) was the subject of a letter submitted to *Nature* by W. E. Cooke. "I have just received the following note from Mr. H. L. Richardson, Hillspring Station, 100 miles northeast of Carnarvon, on our west coast: 'A peculiar incident happened here last evening (June 26) about an hour after sunset. In a south-easterly direction from here, three reports took place high up in the air, and then a rushing noise like steam escaping, lasting for a few seconds, and gradually dying away. Mr. Loeffler, one of the owners of the station, was standing outside with me at the time. It was a beautifully clear evening, and there was nothing visible at all in that direction. The reports sounded like explosions of some combustible to which there was no resistance" (*Nature,* 78: 390, 1908).

UNEXPLAINED DETONATIONS: POSSIBLY SEISMIC

In many regions of the world, booms, cracks, and breaking noises erupt from the ground. Since their place of origin is well-determined, such sounds must be considered seismic. Subterranean rocks readjusting themselves and grinding into new positions account for many long series of acoustic events. Although these seismic sounds often closely resemble *mistpouffers*, there may be some overlap in these two classes of phenomena.

Seismic detonations are most frequent in mountainous areas (*mistpouffers* are seacoast phenomena). Lewis and Clark noted unexplainable detonations as they were crossing the Rockies. For the date July 4, 1808, we have this entry from their journal. "Since our arrival at the Falls, we have repeatedly heard a strange noise coming from the mountains in a direction a little to the north of west. It is heard at different periods of the day and night, sometimes when the air is perfectly still and without a cloud, and consists of one stroke only, or five or six discharges in quick succession. It is loud and resembles precisely the sound of a six-pound piece of ordnance at the distance of three miles. The Minnatarees frequently mentioned this noise like thunder, which they said the mountains made, but we paid no attention to it, believing it to be some superstition or falsehood perhaps. The watermen . . . of the party [also] say that the Pawnees and Recaras give the same account of a noise heard in the Black Mountains [Black Hills] to the west of them." Similar sounds have been heard since then, emanating from the main range of the Rockies (*Nature*, 53: 487, 1896).

"At the village of Babino-poglie [Babino Polje] in the centre of a valley in the Island of Meleda [Mljet], in the Adriatic Sea, remarkable sounds were heard for the first time on the 20th March, 1822. They resembled the reports of cannon, and were loud enough to produce a shaking in the doors and windows of the village. They were at first attributed to the guns of some ships of war, at a distance, in the open sea, and then to the exercise of Turkish artillery, on the Ottoman frontiers. These discharges were repeated four, ten, and even a hundred times in a day, at all hours and in all weathers, and continued to prevail until the month of February, 1824, from which time there was an intermission of seven months. In September of the same year, the detonations recommenced and continued, but more feeble and rare, to the middle of March, 1825, when they again ceased.

"These noises have been accompanied by no luminous phenomena or meteors of any kind. Dr. Stulli, who furnishes the statement, conjectures that these remarkable detonations arise from sudden emissions of gas, elaborated in cavities beneath the islands, and which [when] issuing through subterranean passages strike the air with such force as to produce loud detonations" (*American Journal of Science*, 1: 10: 377, 1826).

An outbreak of typical seismic sounds began on October 10, 1896, near Franklinville, New York. "These sounds succeeded each other at intervals of about five minutes. They closely resembled the sounds produced by coarse black powder used in blasting rocks in the construction of tunnels. The same sounds were heard at the same time by Mr. McStay at his residence. . . . McStay attributed the sounds to the firing of cannon at Cuba, but there was no cannon at Cuba, 13 miles distant. East Hill lies between McStay's and Cuba. . . . This hill is about 500 feet high—i.e., using the valley at Franklinville as a base. This region is covered with deep drift. The valley at Franklinville is filled with 'till' 100 to 150 feet deep. The underlying rocks belong to the Chemung group, dip to the southwest, and are formed of thin lamellae of sandy shale and thick beds of sandstone. The surface of the soil is strewn with quartz and limestone pebbles, sandstone, and granite boulders. Many moraines extend along the hillsides, showing that this section was once covered with glaciers. On the summit of East Hill is a large sandstone boulder in which is a depression—a mortar—said to have been formerly used by the Indians for grinding corn. Single sounds, like those described, are heard in the hills about here, but so far as the writer knows, no series of sounds have been so closely located as those of October 10, 1896, in East Hill; they appear to be due to breaking of the strata of underlying rocks" (*Monthly Weather Review*, 25: 393, 1897).

Portions of the Blue Ridge Mountains are seismically active. Stimulated by the wide discussion of Barisāl Guns in the 1890s, Barry C. Hawkins provided a colorful description of similar phenomena in the Blue Ridge region.

"In northern Georgia, in the extreme north of Rabun County, close to the North Carolina state line and [the] thirty-fifth parallel of latitude, is Rabun Bald Mountain, forming one of the highest peaks on the very crest of the Blue Ridge. This mountain has the same bulky shape and long rambling ridges running for miles in all directions as are spoken of by Hugh Miller as characterising the gneissic mountains of Scotland. On the east side there is a small cliff over which a small stream falls in wet weather, and from the ranges to the east the peak appears in form exactly like a brace—viz., ⌒⌒ . The entire mountain is of gneiss.

"Now, on this mountain are heard mysterious sounds resembling distant cannon firing, and these sounds have been heard for many years, probably at least fifty; they have been heard in all kinds of weather and at various points on the mountain.

"Numerous observers have noted the sounds, and two reliable gentlemen once spent a night on the summit. About 10 o'clock P.M., sounds were heard which were supposed to be cannon firing at Walhalla, S.C., in celebration of the presidential election, this being in November 1884; but soon the sounds were found to issue *from the ground* and from a ridge to the southwest of the mountain. The explosive sounds continued till late in the night. At times they seemed to proceed from the ground immediately under the observers. In early days when bears were plentiful, the pioneers said the sounds were caused by these animals rolling small boulders off the mountain sides in search of worms, snails, etc., but the bears have passed and the sounds still continue. Later the sounds were ascribed to 'harnts' (haunts or ghosts); two men were murdered in 'the sixties' and buried at some unknown point on the 'Bald.' Some have heard these sounds so near them in the woods that the sound was like that of a falling tree. But ordinarily the sound is like distant firing, as noted above. They are not heard at all times, people having spent the night on the peak and not heard them" (*Monthly Weather Review*, 25: 393–94, 1897).

Hanley's Guns are an Australian phenomenon. They have been heard between Daylesford and Maryborough, Victoria. "It was originally thought in Daylesford that the noises were merely those ordinarily caused by people shooting rabbits on an estate owned by Mr. Hanley, which lay eight miles to the north-west of the town; but this explanation was shown to be wrong when it was discovered that people living far to the northwest of Hanley's property also heard the noises in a north-westerly direction. Neither were the noises due to blasting in the mines of Moolort, for they did not cease when the mines were eventually closed down.

"During the years 1912–14, Mr. Ebury listened for the noises at Sandon South, recording the time of occurrence and the direction from which the sound appeared to come, and he collected similar observations from residents of the Kooroocheang district. The Weather Bureau of Melbourne also gathered information from various localities and placed it at Mr. Ebury's disposal. It appears that the noises could be heard at any hour of the day or night, but that they were most frequent in the forenoon, the average time of occurrence during 1913 and 1914 being about 11 A.M. The chart which accompanied Ebury's article shows the direction from which the explosive sounds appeared to come in various parts of the area. It is seen that the majority of the observations indicate an origin of the sounds in the district known as Stony Rises, lying two miles to the north-west of Mount Kooroocheang" (*Weather*, 5: 293, 1950).

Comrie, Scotland, is famous for seismic activity that produces a wide variety of sounds. Some of the nonexplosive noises resemble those buzzes and swishing sounds emanating from meteors. The Comrie noises were reported in many English journals during the nineteenth century. A few typical observations follow:

"About 3 P.M., I was walking, when I heard a sound somewhat resembling a peal of thunder at a great distance—or rather the echo which succeeds a louder thunder peal passing along through the clouds. I would have believed it *was* from thunder, had I not felt the motion of the ground under me, as if a heavy carriage had passed over it rapidly at a short distance from me. The sound preceded the movement of the ground about 3″ or 4″.

". . . The shocks of [the] twelfth at 1 and 4 P.M. (which were very similar and which were attended with a considerable tremor of the earth) were accompanied with a noise resembling a mixture produced by the rush of the strong wind and the peal of distant thunder. It was different from any noise which I ever heard before. The shock of 3 P.M. (which was far more severe than any that had preceded it and which was attended with greater tremor or heaving of the earth) was accompanied by a noise which at first resembled the murmurings of distant waters. This continued, increasing in intensity for about 2″, and then followed a very loud and terrific sound resembling that of a double shot for blasting rock immensely charged.

"There was a very loud noise, like the emptying of a cart of stones. At *Ardvoirlich*, the first of these shocks is [described] by those who heard it 'as particularly severe,' and the noise was described as having a sort of hissing sound and was compared to a large steam-vessel letting off steam.

"In the great shock of the 23rd there were two reports, with an interval of 4″ or 5″ between the first report and the commencement of the second, before any sensible vibration or concussion ensued. The nature of the noise usually resembles the report of a gun discharged among rocks, when the sound produced is deep and hollow. This marks the first explosion. Then follows the sharp rumble, as if through a cavity in the earth, and in the sharper shocks [it] produces a jingle like the jarring of some metallic body in the earth" (*Edinburgh New Philosophical Journal*, 31: 119, 1841).

The *gouffre*, as they are called, sound forth from the West Indies. Most are thunderlike, but some have been likened to breaking glass. Maxwell Hall, the government meteorologist at Jamaica, related a few observations of the *gouffre*, which are manifestly seismic. "In 1835, at the time of the eruption of Coseguina (a volcano on the west coast of Nicaragua), noises like those of a cannonade were heard at Jamaica, 700 English miles away.

"At the beginning of January 1907, before the great earthquake of January 14th of that year, similar noises were heard at Mandeville and in other parts of the parish of Manchester, and at certain places in the parish of St. Elizabeth. They were heard several times at the same places and were mistaken for noises of distant thundering or of the firing of large caliber cannon.

"At 8:30 A.M., December 3, 1907, distinct rumblings were heard at Kings-Valley, Westmoreland. They seemed to come from a chain of high mountains to the north. No shock was felt.

"Noises like the sound of enormous waves on the shore were heard at Kings-Valley, Westmoreland, at 10 P.M., January 15, 1908. They came from the north, and lasted thirty or forty minutes" (Seismological Society of America, Bulletin, 5: 171–73, 1915).

Although the offshore booms that startled residents of the United States East Coast in 1978 and 1979 were reported in the media to have been sonic booms, some were probably mistpouffers (especially those off eastern Canada) and still others were seismic. The North Carolina coast was plagued by booms long before the 1978 series began. "For at least a decade, audible seismic disturbances have been reported in the Cape Fear, N.C., area. Reports include booming noises, falling plaster, and rattling doors. There are some colorful folk names for the noises, and one common folk theory is [that] 'the continental shelf is falling off.' Manmade origins seem to have been ruled out. David M. Stewart and Kenneth B. Taylor of the University of North Carolina present five sets of facts for a natural origin and conclude: 'Our tentative hypothesis is that they are shallow submarine earthquakes'" (Science News, 110: 346, 1976).

THE MOODUS NOISES

The most thoroughly investigated of the seismic sounds are the renowned Moodus noises, known from pre-Pilgrim times and sounding forth from the heart of densely populated Connecticut. As early as 1840 a Reverend Chapman wrote a rather sensationalized paper on these curious sounds that even today occasionally startle the residents of the East Haddam area near the Connecticut River.

"In attempting to give an account of the circumstances attendant on subterranean noises, so frequently heard at East Haddam, perhaps it may be proper to mention the common opinion respecting them.

"East Haddam was called by the natives *Morehemoodus,* or the places of noises, and a numerous tribe of cannibals [was said to have] resided there. They were famous for worshipping the evil spirit, to appease his wrath. Their account of the occasion of the noises is 'that the Indian god was angry because the English god intruded upon him, and those were the expressions of his displeasure'; hence it has been imagined that they originated after the arrival of the English in this country.

"About fifty years ago, a European by the name of Steele came into the place and boarded in the family of a Mr. Knowlton for a short period. He was a man of intelligence and supposed to be in disguise. He told Mr. Knowlton in confidence that he had discovered the place of a fossil which he called a carbuncle and that he should be able to procure it in a few days. Accordingly, he soon after brought home a white round substance resembling a stone in the light, but became remarkably luminous in the dark. It was his practice to labor after his mineral in the night season. The night on which he procured it he secreted it in Mr. K.'s cellar, which was without windows, yet its illuminating power was so great that the house appeared to be on fire and was seen at a great distance. The next morning he enclosed it in sheet lead and departed for Europe, and [he] has never since been heard of. It is rumored that he was murdered on his way by the ship's crew. He said that this substance was the cause of the noises—that a change of temperature collects the moistness of the atmosphere, which causes an explosion.

"These shocks are generally perceived in the neighboring towns and sometimes at a great distance. They begin with a trembling of the earth, and a rumbling noise nearly resembling the discharge of very heavy cannon at a distance. Sometimes three or four follow each other in quick succession, and in this case the first is generally the most powerful.

"The particular place where these explosions originate has not been ascertained. It appears to be near the northwest corner of the town. It was near this place that Steele found his fossil. The place where the ground was broken when the first one occurred which I mentioned above was about three and a half miles from this place. There was no appearance of a deposit near where the ground was broken, but it has been observed that this place has been repeatedly struck with lightning.

*   *   *

"The awful noises, of which Mr. Hosmer gave an account in his historical minutes and concerning which you desire further information, continue to the present time [1729]. The effects they produce are [as] various as the intermediate degrees between the roar of a cannon and the noise of a pistol. The concussions of the earth, made at the same time, are as much diversified as the sounds in the air. The shock they give to a dwelling house is the same as the falling of logs on the floor. The smaller shocks produced no emotions of terror or fear in the minds of the inhabitants. They are spoken of as usual occurrences and are called Moodus noises. But when they are so violent as to be heard in the adjacent towns, they are called earthquakes" (*American Journal of Science*, 1: 39: 335–42, 1840).

THE EAST COAST MYSTERY BOOMS

Were they supersonic jet planes, earthquake sounds, or igniting bubbles of natural gas rising from the sea floor? Several theories have been proposed for the 1978–79 spate of detonations heard along the East Coast of the United States. Although attention was focused in this region, similar booms were heard in the same time period from England, California, Canada, and elsewhere.

"The affair started on 2 December, when two loud booms were heard and felt in the coastal town of Charleston [S.C.]. Residents of the New Jersey coast heard their own boom later that afternoon. Thirteen days later Charleston was rocked by five more booms, and explosions were also heard off the coast of Nova Scotia. On 20 December, Charleston had two more explosions and New Jersey, one. More followed in the different locations on 22 and 30 December and [on] 5, 12, and 18 January" (*New Scientist*, 77: 341, 1978). Luminous phenomena accompanied a few of the explosions.

A typical newspaper account of the period follows: "Newark, N.J. (AP)—Residents in northern and central New Jersey lit up police switchboards last night with reports of loud booms and shaking homes. Parsippany Police Lt. James Moore said, 'The switchboard lit up like crazy for about 10 minutes.' . . . One caller described the mysterious noise as 'like wind shaking the house but there was no wind'" (Baltimore *Sun*, February 11, 1979, p. A-10). There are literally hundreds of such reports from the newspapers.

When federal agencies and atmospheric scientists looked at the data, opinion was divided, with most suggesting that the Concorde supersonic transatlantic flights should take the blame. William Donn, a geophysicist at the Lamont-Doherty Observatory, had several pressure-recording instruments in place along the East Coast. He was emphatic that the booms were not Concorde-produced. "They are either 'direct booms from close-in planes in a series of exercises' or 'something entirely different.' Donn has several reasons for his strong statements. Foremost, he says, is that the sounds detected by the Lamont, Charleston, and Wilmington [N.C.] stations all originate in the south. And they are different from SST signals the station has picked up since the start of the flights, he says" (*Science News,* 113: 181, 1978).

Today the East Coast booms (and those occurring elsewhere) have still not been explained to everyone's satisfaction.

Hisses and Hums

Detonations intrude upon our sensory apparatus more readily than hums and hisses. Civilization's background of traffic noise, aircraft, and air-conditioners conceals natural hums and hisses very effectively. Yet nature generates a variety of curious murmurs, sighs, swishes, and buzzes. Most of these sounds are readily attributed to insects, wind in the trees, and so on. Happily for this book, not all hums and hisses can be explained away so readily.

Swishes, hums, hisses, and cracklings have long been associated with auroras and meteors. In both cases, these sounds have been synchronous with the motions of the phenomena. The phenomena, however, are too far away (typically 50–100 miles) for the sounds to reach the observer instantaneously. Scientists regarded such observations as auditory illusions or the consequence of inexperience for many years, mainly because no acceptable physical mechanisms were available to explain the observations. Nevertheless, high-quality observations kept accumulating. Many investigators now accept the reality of these sounds and ascribe them to: (1) electromagnetic radiation perceived as sound—some people can hear radar!—or (2) electrical discharge (brush discharge) arising from electrical effects created by the phenomena.

More mysterious are the hums and hisses not associated with any obvious physical event. Blowing sand, running water, seismic activity, insects, and other agents are blamed for sounds that seem to come from nowhere. Hums and hisses of this kind are generally perceived only where man-made noise is far-removed. A famous example in this category are the Yellowstone Lake Whispers that have been heard in Wyoming for generations.

Geophysical disturbances, such as storms and earth tremors, are known to generate very long wavelength sound (infrasound) that propagates hundreds of miles. Auroras, meteors, and winds gusting over mountain ridges create infrasound, although the frequencies are too low to be detected by the ear. It is possible, though, that these sources of infrasound may, on occasion, produce higher frequencies that we perceive as hums and hisses that seem to come out of thin air.

THE SUPPOSED SOUND OF THE AURORA

When auroras dip low near to the ground, some but not all observers claim to hear swishing and rustling sounds. Indeed, the scientific literature brims with testimony from hundreds of reliable observers who do and do not hear the aurora. The phenomenon is in doubt on two counts: first, auroras are never supposed to descend close enough to the earth's surface so that they could be heard; and second, there is apparently no physical reason why the auroras should make any sound at all.

That auroras do sometimes dip down almost to the surface was demonstrated by the evidence in Chapter 1. As for a physical mechanism to generate auroral noise, we are at a loss and must fall back on the reality of testimony that it does occur.

Antoine Henri Becquerel, the discoverer of radioactivity, was one of the few scientists supporting the reality of low, sound-producing auroras. In a paper before the Academy of Sciences of Paris in 1871, he presented the experience of Paul Rollier from Mount Ide in Norway at an elevation of 4,000 feet. "I saw through the thinner fog the moving of the brilliant rays of an aurora borealis, spreading all over its strange light. Soon after, an incomprehensible and loud roaring was heard, which, when it ceased completely, was followed by a strong smell of sulphur, almost suffocating" (*Scientific American*, 25: 208, 1871).

Rollier's description contains three questionable elements: low altitude, sound, and smell. Nevertheless, C. S. Beals, a Canadian geophysicist, collected many similar accounts from individuals living in the auroral zone of North America. For example, S. G. Squires, of Valparaiso, Saskatchewan, sent Beals this engaging description of his experience on August 8, 1924: "I saw the northern lights, as we call it, waving close to the ground and among the poplar trees, with clear sky above. I went out into a field of wheat close to the house, and the light played around me and among the wheat like whirlwings [a type of insect], with a sound like silk rustling or tissue paper" (*Royal Astronomical Society of Canada*, 27: 184–200, 1933).

Scientists working in the arctic are not immune to the sibilant aurora. Hans S. Jelstrup and his assistant noticed the sound in 1926. "Some curious phenomena accompanying the splendid aurora of October 15, 1926, were observed by me. On the night in question, I was working as observer of international determinations of longitude at the top of a hill named Voxenaasen in the neighbourhood of Oslo (approximate altitude, 470 metres). I was at work in a field observatory with a transit in-

strument registering star transits and chronometer beats for time determinations, when an initial aurora attracted my attention. My assistant
was Mr. G. Jelstrup, electrotechnical student.

"I was able, during intervals between my observations of time and
polar stars, to observe the aurora, which was certainly one of the most
splendid I had ever seen. But what is of preponderant interest is the following fact: When, with my assistant, at 19 h. 15 m. Greenwich Civil
Time, I went out of the observatory to observe the aurora, the latter
seemed to be at its maximum; yellow-green and fan-shaped, it undulated
above, from zenith downwards—and at the same time both of us noticed
a very curious faint whistling sound distinctly undulatory, which seemed
to follow exactly the vibrations of the aurora.

"The sound was first noticed by me, and upon asking my assistant if
he could hear anything, he answered that he noticed a curious increasing
and decreasing whistling sound. We heard the sound during the ten minutes we were able to stay outside the observatory, before continuing our
observations" (*Nature,* 119: 45, 1927).

The year 1933 was a banner year for pro–auroral-sound articles in
the scientific journals. While the following two rather lengthy reports are
not especially rigorous scientifically, they are rich in background, particularly in describing the glorious spectacles the auroras paint on the polar
skies and the attitudes of those who live in this frigid clime toward them.

"An extensive inquiry among traders, policemen, missionaries, and
Eskimos concerning the audibility of the aurora was made by members
of the Canadian Polar party stationed near Chesterfield Inlet on the west
coast of Hudson Bay. The majority of the white people who were questioned had more than twenty years' experience in the eastern Canadian
Arctic. The Eskimos were questioned only after we found that they were
calling us 'foolish white men,' because we had said that the aurora was
inaudible. Natives living in the region extending from Repulse Bay in the
north to Eskimo Point in the south, and from Baker Lake in the west to
Southampton Island in the east were included in the inquiry.

"All the white people insisted that they had heard rustling or swishing sounds accompanying brilliant auroral displays. These sounds were
heard more frequently by them at Burrel-on-Hudson Straits, at Harrison
on the east coast of Hudson Bay, and in the region between Chesterfield
Inlet and the Churchill River than farther north. Bishop Turquetil, who
has had more than twelve years' experience at both Reindeer Lake in
northern Saskatchewan and Chesterfield Inlet, stated that sounds with
aurora were more frequent at the former place. Nothing in their description of aurora at such times would suggest unusually low aurora, because
forms common to normal displays were always mentioned.

"The natives in this region call the aurora, *akshanik,* meaning that which moves rapidly. The same expression is used also by them for Chesterfield Inlet, because of the rapid flow of the tides in the Inlet. Stories involving the audibility of the aurora have been handed down from one to another for many generations. One that is repeated frequently explains that the sounds are made by spirits playing a game. A small group of the natives have also a story of the aurora coming low enough to kill some of their people. In this particular case the story may have originated from the effects of a destructive lightning flash, although lightning is so rare in this region that the natives often seek shelter with white men during even the mildest storms.

"Very few natives from Baker Lake, Chesterfield Inlet, and north of these places, had heard the aurora, although all knew people who had heard it. Natives from Southampton Island knew of no one who had heard it there. Practically all natives from south of Chesterfield Inlet had heard the aurora and described the sounds by blowing through rounded lips. According to them, the aurora was heard more frequently during some winters than others. None had heard it during the winter of 1932–33. Nothing of a definite nature concerning low aurora could be found from them.

"The collected testimony of both whites and natives indicates that the region of maximum audibility lies in the region of maximum auroral frequency. Unfortunately, this does not distinguish between an objective or a subjective explanation of the sounds, since the greater the number of aurora seen, the more likely it is that conditions favourable to either effect may occur.

"The extent to which the testimony of natives can be relied upon is debatable. As observers of unusual occurrences in their native habitat, they are superior to the average white man. However, traditional accounts of the sounds may be faulty and have induced a greater susceptibility to a subjective effect.

"The members of the party listened occasionally for auroral sounds during brilliant displays, but were unsuccessful except on the night of March 20, when J. Rea, assistant observer, heard sounds with a brilliant display. We were occupied with double-station photographs at the time and listened carefully but unsuccessfully for the sounds. Our failure to hear the sounds may have been due to less sensitive hearing since conditions for detecting objective sounds were extremely good. During the day, a pilot balloon had been followed for 138 minutes, and the same clear, calm conditions prevailed during the night with a minimum temperature of −17° F. During the interval in which the sounds were heard, brilliant greenish-white flashes were darting overhead from south to north, and some of these may have come momentarily lower than usual. Height determinations have yet to be made from the double-station photographs taken at this time, but the plates show no unusual displacements. Rea is of the opinion that the sounds did not occur simultaneously with the flashes.

"One account which we heard of audible aurora indicates a subjective origin for the sound. In this case the aurora was heard in central Saskatchewan from the observation platform of a moving train. Here the noise of the train would have drowned all sounds coming from the aurora and having the low intensity commonly reported.

"On at least three occasions at Chesterfield, an auroral condition prevailed which may explain the reports of individuals who claim that they have walked in the aurora. Following the active display with ray structures predominating, a continuous auroral glow covered the whole sky except for a small area in the north. The light from this glow, together with the light reflected from the snow, made it difficult not to feel that one was in an auroral mist or fog" (*Nature*, 132: 855–56, 1933).

"The proposition of the audibility of the aurora borealis has been the subject of considerable speculation and much doubt. Some scientists have claimed with much positiveness that the aurora emits no audible sounds and that the beams of light or electrical waves, such as they may choose to call them, do not come close enough to the earth's surface to be audible, even if any sound were emitted. In my own mind there can be no doubt left as to the audibility of certain types of aurora, for I have heard them under conditions when no other sound could have been interpreted as such, for no other sounds were present.

"From the Eskimos I first learned that the aurora could be heard and, like most people, was rather skeptical about it, believing that their statements were based to a great extent on their superstitions. I was told by some of the older Eskimos that when the aurora displays become audible, they are able to imitate the sound by whistling in such manner that the beams of light will be attracted or drawn down to them. This, of course, is purely superstition. However, it does bring out the fact that the Eskimos were frequently able to hear the aurora.

"The following is my own personal experience which convinced me that the aurora borealis was actually audible. In the winter of 1925–1926 I was engaged in making a drive of reindeer across the mountain range bordering the Arctic coast north of Cape Prince of Wales on Bering Strait. One night during this drive found me traveling by starlight across the divide at the head of Nuluk River. This divide has an elevation of approximately two thousand feet. It was two o'clock in the morning when my native driver and I broke camp in order to overtake the reindeer herd ahead of us. As we climbed with our dog team to the summit of the divide, we were both spellbound and astounded by the magnificent display of aurora, the most wonderful display I have ever witnessed during my eight years of life among the Eskimos.

"Great beams of light shot up from the northern horizon as if a battery of gigantic searchlights were searching the arctic landscape. In front of these beams and throughout the whole length of the northern horizon, great waves of iridescent light traveled from west to east like gigantic draperies before the stage of nature's amphitheater. Great folds or waves, ever changing in color, traveled one after another across the horizon, and from behind them streamed the powerful beams of white light. These beams of light could be seen passing directly over our heads, and when one chanced to come over the divide, it appeared to be not more than a hundred feet above the surface. The spectacle was so awe-inspiring that the dog team was stopped, and I sat upon the sled for more than an hour absorbing the marvelous beauty of this most unusual display. As we sat upon the sled and the great beams passed directly over our heads, they emitted a distinctly audible sound which resembled the crackling of steam escaping from a small jet. Possibly the sound would bear a closer resemblance to the crackling sound produced by spraying fine jets of water on a very hot surface of metal. Each streamer or beam of light passed overhead with a rather accurate uniformity of duration. By count it was estimated to require six to eight seconds for a projected beam to pass, while the continuous beam would often emit the sound for a minute or more. This particular display was so brilliant that traces could easily be seen long after daylight" (*Science*, 78: 213–14, 1933).

METEOR HISSES, HUMS, AND WHIRS

Meteors streak into the earth's atmosphere at velocities several times those of supersonic aircraft. Sonic booms are common from those meteors that penetrate into the palpable atmosphere. Uusually, one boom completes the audible repertoire, but more rarely there are repeated booms from the various pieces of the disintegrating object. If the meteor fragments into many pieces, a machine gun–like popping is heard. Thunderlike noises occur too. Whirring noises may emanate from those bits of spinning stone and metal that survive the fiery plunge and hit the ground. All of the preceding sounds are completely understandable in terms of current meteor science. It is the sibilant sound heard from high-altitude meteors, often before and simultaneous with the visual sighting, that perplexes scientists. The nature of the anomaly is explained well in M. A. R. Khan's letter to *Nature* in 1945.

"Many responsible eye-witnesses, in their descriptions of fireballs, have emphatically stated that they have occasionally heard a peculiar hissing sound simultaneously with the flight of a meteor. From personal observation, I can also testify to the validity of these statements. Fireball literature is full of such accounts. Three recent cases (connected with fireballs seen by a number of competent observers at Hyderabad, on October 13, 1936, on March 25, 1944, and on August 6, 1944, respectively) have placed the matter beyond any doubt whatever.

"The obvious difficulty is about the simultaneity of the light and sound phenomena noticed by observers fifty to a hundred miles distant from the meteor. But it must be remembered that the fireball rushes through the upper atmosphere with parabolic speed (about 26 miles per second); its duration of visible flight is generally 6–8 seconds. Assuming its height to be roughly 75 miles, *matter* from a *friable aerolite* can issue in a regular stream along its entire path, into the lower atmosphere, with velocity large enough to bring it in the vicinity of an observer while the meteor is still in sight. For the height assumed, four or five seconds may suffice (even allowing for air resistance) for the *matter* from the meteor to reach the air in the neighbourhood of the observer and thus give rise to sounds variously described as like the swish of a whip, the hissing noticed while a cutler sharpens a knife on a grindstone, or a hot iron being plunged into cold water.

"A shower of fine sand beating against the leaves of trees was noticed immediately after the apparition of the fireball of October 13, 1936, described in detail in *Science and Culture* (Calcutta), 2: 5: 273, 1936" (*Nature*, 155: 53, 1945).

To amplify on the character of the reports asserting the near-instantaneous transmission of meteor sounds, I present a small sampling from a very large file. "Between half-past ten and a quarter to eleven on the night of August 7th last, I was riding home on my bicycle, when I distinctly heard a faint but clear sound above my head like that made by a rocket as it passes through the air at a considerable distance. On looking up I saw a shooting-star still on the move, but leaving a streak of light behind it. It is difficult to describe, but when I first looked up there was a streak of light which got increasingly longer from one end until after quite an appreciable time the moving end suddenly stopped. The streak seemed to remain still for a while, and then quite gradually ceased to exist, the light diminishing from both ends and then going out" (*Symons's Meteorological Magazine*, 41: 190–91, 1906).

The Athens meteor fell on July 11, 1933. "Mr. Hardiman is a farmer living about six miles west of Athens, Alabama. He and his son were working in the field that forenoon when their attention was attracted by a peculiar humming or singing noise, like an airplane flying high. This noise grew louder, in their opinion for five minutes. It changed to a whizzing noise and ended with a swish and a thud. The object making the thud struck within 30 feet of the son. He walked over, expecting to find an object weighing 100 pounds, but found a small hole perhaps five inches across and five inches deep, with a small dark stone in it. . . . The little stone, weighing about nine ounces, was then removed and found to be noticeably warm, but not hot" (*Popular Astronomy*, 41: 468–70, 1933). Here the sound preceded the meteor by minutes, and the meteor was not observed as a fireball at all.

One observer of the Texas meteor of June 23, 1928, heard the meteor before he saw it. "An observer at Leakey, twenty-five miles northeast of Laguna, states that at the time of the appearance of the meteor he was repairing a wire fence and was stooping over close to the ground fastening the lower wires of the fence. In this position he heard distinctly a whizzing sound which he at first supposed to be made by an aeroplane with the engine shut off preparatory to lighting in an aeroplane field nearby. Upon looking up, however, he saw the flash of the meteor" (*Science*, 69: 297–98, 1929).

W. F. Denning, a British meteor expert of some years ago, assembled numerous accounts like those above and was driven to accepting the phenomenon by virtue of the sheer quantity and quality of the data. Nevertheless his scientific colleagues rejected such data as strictly imaginary or perhaps psychological. H. H. Nininger, an American who studied meteors most of his life, was, like Denning, forced to accept the reality of some unknown type of sound or possibly radiation that the human sensory apparatus converted into sound.

PSEUDOSOUND FROM ELECTRICAL APPARATUS

The crackling of the aurora and swish of high meteors are no longer rejected out of hand by science. Evidence is accumulating that some people—not all by any means—hear radars and other high-power electromagnetic transmitters. "This idea, which was first proposed by H. H. Nininger in the 1930s, is not as strange as it first seems. After all, fireballs evidently convert much kinetic energy into visible light, and this occupies only a small portion of the electromagnetic spectrum. If some of this radiation were in the far infrared or at radio frequencies, a possible explanation for the sounds might emerge from some recent experiments on electrophonic hearing carried out by A. H. Frey.

"He found that some human subjects exposed to beams of low-power radar sets perceived sensations of sound described as buzzing, clicking, hissing, or knocking, depending on the transmitter characteristics. Care was taken to exclude possible rectification (by loose tooth fillings and the like) of the pulse-modulated signal. A peak electromagnetic power density of as low as 400 microwatts per square centimeter at the observer could be perceived as sound.

"The effects occurred only in those subjects whose audible hearing by air or bone conduction was good above 5,000 cycles per second. If the background noise level was higher than 90 decibels, the radio-frequency sound was somewhat masked (wearing earplugs improved the reception). We shall not discuss here the possible mechanisms for electrophonic hearing, but perhaps the electromagnetic waves act directly on the brain. It is apparent that there are similarities between these sounds and the anomalous sounds associated with fireballs, and the power levels are not prohibitively large" (*Sky and Telescope,* 28: 214–15, 1964).

A somewhat different situation exists with those few who claim to be plagued by humming noises. "In 1977 the English *Sunday Mirror* ran a story about someone who claimed to hear a steady and very annoying humming noise. To everyone's surprise, the article elicited some 800 letters from others who heard hums. Amazed by the magnitude of the problem, doctors began examining some of the afflicted. In a few cases, the hum seemed internally generated—something akin to tinnitus, which causes one to hear a high-pitched whine. Many others, however, heard a 40 Hz. hum modulated at 1.6 kHz., and apparently of external origin. The hum sufferers were inclined to blame industrial noise, but no obvious sources could be uncovered. The hum investigators have considered sea noise, jet-stream noise, and other natural sources. Whatever the source, most people do not hear it at all. It is possible that a small percentage of the population is abnormally sensitive to sound at 40 Hz." (*New Scientist,* 84: 868–70, 1979).

THE YELLOWSTONE LAKE WHISPERS

From high in the sky over Yellowstone Park comes a strange ethereal sound that has invariably intrigued all those lucky enough to hear it. What could cause it? Could it be a seismic sound emitted from the surrounding mountains as they groan and strain under the influence of the upwelling hot magma that underlies this region? Another guess is that the wind blowing across the peaks somehow causes the hum, perhaps establishing standing sound waves as one does when blowing into an empty bottle (i.e., a valley). This phenomenon is so rich and curious, revealing nature in one of her playful but beautiful moods, that I quote at length from two scientists who have written about these mysterious whispers.

The first is Edwin Linton who collected some otherwise obscure reports in a *Science* article.

"While engaged in making certain investigations for the United States Fish Commission in the summer of 1890, my attention was called to an interesting phenomenon in the vicinity of Yellowstone Lake, of which I am pleasantly reminded by the following brief but vivid description in a recent report by Prof. S. A. Forbes.

"Under his description of Shoshone Lake, Professor Forbes, in a foot note, thus alludes to this phenomenon:

" 'Here we first heard, while out on the lake in the bright still morning, the mysterious aerial sound for which this region is noted. It put me in mind of the vibrating clang of a harp lightly and rapidly touched high up above the tree tops, or the sound of many telegraph wires swinging regularly and rapidly in the wind, or, more rarely, of faintly heard voices answering each other overhead. It begins softly in the remote distance, draws rapidly near with louder and louder throbs of sound, and dies away in the opposite distance; or it may seem to wander irregularly about, the whole passage lasting from a few seconds to half a minute or more. We heard it repeatedly and very distinctly here and at Yellowstone Lake, most frequently at the latter place. It is usually noticed on still bright mornings not long after sunrise, and it is louder at this time of day; but I heard it clearly, though faintly, once at noon when a stiff breeze was blowing. No scientific explanation of this really bewitching phenomenon has ever been published, although it has been several times referred to by travellers, who have ventured various crude guesses at its cause, varying from that commonest catch-all of the ignorant, 'electricity,' to the whistling of the wings of ducks and the noise of the 'steamboat geyser.' It seems to me to belong to the class of aerial echoes, but even on that supposition I cannot account for the origin of the sound' ("A Preliminary Report on the Aquatic Invertebrate Fauna of the Yellowstone National Park, etc." *Bulletin of the United States Fish Commission for 1891*, April 29, 1893, p. 215).

"In a paper which was read before the Academy of Science and Art of Pittsburgh, Pa., March 18, 1892, entitled 'Mount Sheridan and the Continental Divide,' I recorded my recollections of this phenomenon and reproduce them here with no alteration. Although the style is, perhaps, somewhat lacking in seriousness, the descriptions were made from notes taken at the time and written out while the memory of the facts was still fresh. Indeed, even now, after a lapse of three years, I have a very distinct recollection of the sound, vivid enough at least to teach me how imperfect my description of it is. Words describe an echo very inadequately when one is in ignorance of the original sound, and especially so when he is in doubt as to whether the sound is the echo of a noise or the noise itself.

"Following is the account of these overhead noises given in the paper alluded to above and published soon after by the academy:

"Overhead Noises. —The last topic which I shall discuss in this somewhat desultory paper is what I shall call overhead voices.

"Lest I be thought to be indulging in some ill-advised or disordered fancy, I shall first quote from Hayden's *Report for 1872, on Montana, Idaho, Wyoming, and Utah.* Mr. F. H. Bradley, p. 234, in that part of his narrative which relates their visit to Yellowstone Lake, says: 'While getting breakfast [this was near the outlet of the lake], we heard every few moments a curious sound, between a whistle and a hoarse whine, whose locality and character we could not at first determine, though we were inclined to refer it to water-fowl on the other side of the lake. As the sun got higher, the sound increased in force, and it now became evident that gusts of wind were passing through the air above us, though the pines did not as yet indicate the least motion in the lower atmosphere. We started before the almost daily western winds, of which these gusts were evidently the forerunners, had begun to ruffle the lake.'

"With this warrant I shall proceed to describe as well as I can my impressions of these overhead noises, which appear to belong exclusively to the lake region of the Park.

"The first time I heard them, or it, was on the 22d of July, about 8 A.M., on Shoshone Lake. Elwood Hofer, our guide, and I had started in our boat for the west end of the Lake. While engaged in making ready for a sounding on the northern shore, near where the lake grows narrow, I heard a strange echoing sound in the sky, dying away to the southward, which appeared to me to be like a sound that had already been echoing some seconds before it had aroused my attention so that I had missed the initial sound and heard only the echo. I looked at Hofer curiously for an explanation. He asked me what I thought the sound was; I immediately gave it up and waited for him to tell me, never doubting that a satisfactory explanation would be forthcoming. For once this encyclopedia of mountain lore failed to come up to date. His reply was that it was the most mysterious sound heard among the mountains. From the first this sound did not appear to me to be caused by wind blowing. Its velocity was rather that of sound. It had all the characters of an echo, but of what I am not even yet prepared to give an altogether satisfactory answer. I am afraid that my conclusions are about as satisfactory as those of the Irishman, who having been sent out from camp in the night to investigate a strange noise believed to be made by some wild beast, returned with the announcement that 'it was nothing at all, only a noise just.' Upon our return to camp, I questioned both our guides and one of the packers, who had had much experience in the mountains. They agreed substantially in what they had to say about it. They had never heard it farther west than Shoshone Lake, nor farther east than Yellowstone Lake, and not at all north of these lakes. Hofer thought he had heard it once about 30 miles south of Yellowstone Lake. Dave Rhodes had heard it usually shortly after sunrise and up to perhaps half-past eight or nine o'clock. Hofer said that he had heard it in the middle of the day but usually not later than ten o'clock A.M. Neither of them remembered to have heard it before sunrise.

"On the following morning we heard the sound very plainly. It appeared to begin directly overhead and to pass off across the sky, growing fainter and fainter towards the southwest. It appeared to be a rather indefinite, reverberating sound, characterized by a slight metallic resonance. It begins or is first perceived overhead; at least, nearly every one, in attempting to fix its location, turns his head to one side and glances upward. Each time that I heard the sound on Shoshone, it appeared to begin overhead, or as one of the men in the party expressed it 'all over,' and to move off to the southwest. We did not hear the sound while on Lewis or Heart Lake. The next time I heard the sound was on August 4th, when we were camped on the 'Thumb' of Yellowstone Lake. Professor Forbes and I were out on the lake making soundings about 8 A.M. The sky was clear and the lake was quiet. The sun was beginning to shine with considerable power. The sound seemed loudest when overhead and apparently passed off to the southward or a little east of south. It had the same peculiar quality as that heard on Shoshone Lake and is just as difficult to describe. There was the same slight hint of metallic resonance and what one of the party called a kind of twisting sort of yow-yow vibration. There was a faint resemblance to the humming of telegraph wires, but the volume was not steady nor uniform. The time occupied by the sound was not noted, but [was] estimated shortly afterward to be probably a half a minute. As I heard it at this time, it seemed to begin at a distance [and] grow louder overhead where it filled the upper air, and suggested a medley of wind in the tops of pine trees and in telegraph wires, the echo of bells after being repeated several times, the humming of a swarm of bees, and two or three other less definite sources of sound, making in all a composite which was not loud but easily recognized and not at all likely to be mistaken for any other sound in these mountain solitudes, but which might easily escape notice if one were surrounded by noises. On August 8th, at 10.15 A.M., Professor Forbes and I heard the sound again while we were collecting in Bridge Bay at the northern end of the lake.

"While on Shoshone Lake, I ventured the suggestion that the sound might be produced beyond the divide east of us and be reflected from some upper stratum of air of different density from that below. Hofer evidently considered himself responsible for an explanation of the origin of the sound and frequently remarked that it reminded him of the noise made by the escaping steam of the so-called Steamboat Geyser, on the eastern shore of Yellowstone Lake, about 6 miles from the outlet. I passed between Steamboat Point and Stevenson's Island twice but was not near enough either time to hear the escaping steam. Moreover, on each occasion the wind was blowing a lively breeze in the direction of Steamboat Point. On the afternoon of August 9th, at 3.20 P.M. while in a row-boat on the southeastern arm of Yellowstone Lake, near the entrance of the upper Yellowstone River, I heard a sound overhead, like rushing wind or like some invisible but comparatively dense body moving very rapidly through the air and not very far above our heads. It appeared to be travelling from east to west. It did not have the semi-metallic, vibrating, sky-filling, echoing resonance of the overhead noises that I had heard before and was of rather shorter duration. It had, however, the same sound-like rapidity of the other. The sky was clear except for a few light fleecy and feathery clouds, and there was just enough wind blowing to ruffle the surface of the water. If this sound was produced by a current of air in motion overhead, it is difficult to understand why it did not give some account of itself, either in the clouds that were floating at different levels in the upper air or among the pines which covered the slope that rose more than 1,000 feet above our heads, or on the waters of the lake itself.

"I am inclined to attribute the typical echoing noise to some initial sound, like that of escaping steam, for example, from some place like Steamboat Geyser, and which is reflected by some upper stratum of air that is differently heated from that below by the rays of the sun as they come over the high mountain ridges to the east of the lake. The sound may thus be reflected over the low divides west to Shoshone and south to Heart Lake, or even farther in the direction of Jackson's Lake. I am not strenuous for this theory and will be glad to hear a better explanation of this phenomenon. I have a dim recollection of some legend of phantom huntsmen and a pack of ghostly but vocal hounds which haunt the sky of the Hartz Mountains. Can any one tell whether there is any natural phenomenon belonging to mountains or mountain lakes, which could give foundation to such legend?

"The phenomenon has not yet been successfully explained, and I do not know that any similar phenomenon has been observed elsewhere.

"It is to be hoped that some one will investigate the matter soon and give a scientific explanation of its cause" (*Science*, 22: 245–46, 1893).

The next important communication to *Science* on the subject had to wait until 1926, when Hugh M. Smith added further background to the acoustic environment of Yellowstone National Park.

"It is highly gratifying that the American people are making yearly increasing use of the Yellowstone National Park and that each season many thousands become for the first time acquainted with its beauties and wonders. Among future visitors there will be some who will experience the strange and bewildering musical sounds that for many years have been noted in certain parts of the park. As a partial contribution to the solution of the mystery, a personal observation on one manifestation of the weird phenomena may be of interest.

"This subject has received scant mention in various published reports and articles, and by some people has been relegated to the category of yarns and myths which helped to make Jim Bridger famous. The best account seems to be that contained in the best work on the park, that of General Chittenden, from which the following quotation is taken (pp. 288–89):

"'A most singular and interesting acoustic phenomenon of this region, although rarely noticed by tourists, is the occurrence of strange and indefinable overhead sounds. They have long been noted by explorers, but only in the vicinity of Shoshone and Yellowstone Lakes. They seem to occur in the morning and to last only for a moment. They have an apparent motion through the air, the general direction noted by writers being from north to south. They resemble the ringing of telegraph wires or the humming of a swarm of bees, beginning softly in the distance, growing rapidly plainer until directly overhead, and then fading as rapidly in the opposite direction. Although this phenomenon has been made the subject of scientific study, no rational explanation of it has ever been advanced. Its weird character is in keeping with its strange surroundings. In other lands and times it would have been an object of superstitious reverence or dread and would have found a permanent place in the traditions of the people.'

"In the summer of 1919, during a visit to the park in connection with governmental fish-cultural and fish-planting work therein, the present writer, in company with Mr. A. H. Dinsmore, of St. Johnsbury, Vermont (a former superintendent of fish hatcheries in the park), made a camping trip to Lewis and Shoshone Lakes, employing pack horses, with helper, and having as a part of the equipment an Oldtown canoe transported by motor truck from Yellowstone Lake to Lewis Lake.

"About eight o'clock on the morning of July 30, after having camped for two days and two nights on the shore of Shoshone Lake at its outlet at the southern end, we entered the canoe and pushed off from the shingly beach, headed for the northern end of the lake. The surface of the lake was glassy, the air was still, a faint haze overhung the water, the sky was cloudless, and the lake for a considerable distance out was in the shadow of heavily timbered hills. The canoe had barely gotten under way and was not more than twenty meters from the shore when there suddenly arose a musical sound of rare sweetness, rich *timbre,* and full volume, whose effect was increased by the noiseless surroundings. The sound appeared to come from directly overhead, and both of us at the same moment instinctively glanced upward; each afterward asserted that so great was his astonishment that he was almost prepared to see a pipe organ suspended in midair. The sound, by the most perfect gradation, increased in volume and pitch, reaching its climax a few seconds after the paddling of the canoe was involuntarily suspended; and then, rapidly growing fainter and diminishing in pitch, it seemed to pass away toward the south. The sound lasted ten to fifteen seconds and was subsequently adjudged to range in pitch approximately from a little below center C to a little above tenor C of the piano-forte, the tones blending in the most perfect chromatic scale.

"It was at once realized that this was probably a manifestation of the strange phenomena referred to by General Chittenden, whose book had been read in camp, and that an opportunity was presented to investigate and perhaps elucidate the mystery. So favorable was the opportunity that in a short time we were reproducing the sound at will.

"Following the dying away of the music and the short period in which we were held spellbound, paddling was resumed and, as the canoe gained sufficient headway, the music recurred in practically the same form as at first, and, as the paddling ceased and the momentum of the canoe fell off, the sound died away. It was then perceived that the sound was coincident with the motion of the canoe: when a certain speed was reached and maintained, the sound was produced and maintained; before that speed was attained there was no sound, and after that speed was lost the sound ceased.

"A search for the cause of the sound disclosed the following situation: A jointed bamboo salmon rod with its butt-end touching the side of the canoe was projecting backward about half a meter beyond the gunwale; the waxed silk line was reeled in, but about a meter of line with the lure at the end was wrapped several times around the terminal joint; a lead sinker weighing one hundred grams, that had been attached in order to carry the lure into deep water frequented by the large trout with which the lake had been stocked, was dangling from the end of the rod about five centimeters below the surface of the water. As the canoe moved through the water, the short length of free line, held taut by the sinker, rapidly vibrated in conformity with the speed of the boat; the vibrations were transmitted through the bamboo rod to the canoe, whose thin, curved, rigid sides and bottom acted as a sounding board and gave out an augmented volume of sound that seemed to be concentrated or focused overhead. The combination of essential factors present in this case seems to have been a smooth water surface, a vibrating cord, a resonant body to which the vibrations were transferred, and still air, with perhaps other favorable atmospheric conditions. Later, in other parts of the lake, where the surface was disturbed by ripples or waves and there was slight to moderate movement of the air, attempts to reproduce the sound were futile, although the other factors were as in the original manifestation.

"It is not to be inferred that the conditions and explanation herein given are held to account for all the mysterious musical sounds that have been heard in the park. On the contrary, owing to the rarity of the occasions when canoes had been used in park waters, it seems likely that the exact combination of factors noted must have been exceptional. All that is claimed for this manifestation is that it fulfilled the requirements of the mystery as described by the best observers and that its cause was ascertained. An account of the occurrence was promptly given to the superintendent of the park.

"That acoustic conditions on Shoshone Lake that morning may have been peculiar is suggested by another observation as the canoe was skirting the eastern shore of the lake and the Shoshone Geyser Basin came within visual range. During several of the eruptions of the principal geyser, the splashing of the geyser water on the hard siliceous platform was distinctly heard. The distance in an air line, according to the official Geological Survey map, was approximately 9 km." (*Science*, 63: 586–87, 1926).

In 1930, 37 years after his first paper in *Science* on the curious overhead sounds at Yellowstone, Edwin Linton expanded on his experiences of 1890. "Following are all of the references to overhead sounds which I find in the diary which I kept during the six weeks of our stay in the park. I copy from the diary without making any changes in the text, such comments as seem to be called for being enclosed in parentheses.

"(1) July 23 (1890). Yesterday, when (Elwood) Hofer and I were on our way to the upper (western) end of the lake (Shoshone), I heard a strange noise, which I supposed was off to the southward and echoing among the mountains. (At the time, about 8 A.M., I was seated in our Osgood canvas boat, with the oars in my hands, but not rowing. I was probably ten or twelve feet from the shore, where Hofer was seated measuring off our dredge rope, which we were going to use for a sounding line. As I remember the situation, we were from twenty to thirty feet apart.) Hofer asked me what I thought it was and where it seemed to be. I told him the apparent direction and asked him what it was. He replied that it was the most mysterious sound that was heard in the mountains. Since then we have talked about the sound a good deal in camp, and this morning [we] heard it again very plainly. (My recollection of this event is that it occurred just after we had had breakfast and before we had separated for the day's work.) This time it appeared to be directly overhead and to pass off across the sky, growing fainter and fainter toward the southwest. Hofer and Dave Rhodes, both of whom have had wide experience in the mountains, agree in their testimony in regard to it. They say they have never heard it anywhere out of the park, except to the south, about the forty-fourth parallel, some thirty miles south of here. He (Hofer) does not remember to have heard it farther west than Shoshone Lake or east than Yellowstone Lake—not to the north of these points. It is heard mostly in the morning, shortly after sunrise, and up to, perhaps, half past eight, or nine o'clock. Hofer says he has heard it in the middle of the day, but usually not later than 10 o'clock A.M.; [he] doesn't remember to have heard it before sunrise. The description[s] given of the sound, before I heard it and since, agree with my observations with regard to it. (The meaning of this somewhat obscure sentence is that the descriptions which Hofer and Rhodes give of the sound as they have heard it on previous occasions and their description of the sound as they have heard it here on Shoshone Lake agree with my own observations.) When heard best, it appears to be a rather indefinite, reverberating sound in the sky, with a slight metallic resonance, which begins, or at least is at first perceived, overhead; at least, nearly every one in attempting to locate it turns his head to one side and glances upward. (I remember that while I was having my first experience with this sound in the sky I noticed that Hofer was watching me very closely. Later I found that he had been observing my reactions. He told me that people invariably behaved that way when they were trying to locate the source of the sound. I had at first looked up and then had tried to follow the diminishing sound toward the southwest.) The sound is as difficult to describe as an echo, which has been repeated several times in quick succession. Each time I have heard (it) here on Lake Shoshone, it appeared to begin to the southward, or, when first noticed, beginning overhead, or, as some one (Dave Rhodes) expressed it, 'all over,' and moving off toward the south.

"(2) Camp on the 'Thumb,' Yellowstone Lake, August 4. While out on the lake this morning, Professor Forbes and I heard again the strange noise which we heard several times on Shoshone Lake. It was about 8 A.M., morning still and clear, lake quiet, sun beginning to shine with considerable power (this mention of overhead sounds was preceded by an entry, which may, of course, have nothing to do with this phenomenon: 'minimum temperature last night 33.5° F.'), sound loudest almost overhead—seemed to pass to the southeast (so it stands in my diary). Since my other entries, where the apparent direction of these elusive sounds is recorded, indicate a direction west of south, which is in accord with my recollection of these events, I am inclined to think that this may be an example of those slips which Oliver Wendell Holmes cites in 'Over the Teacups,' where one writes north when he means south, and the like; sound of same nature as that heard on Shoshone (Lake)—very hard to describe—a certain metallic resonance—Professor Forbes calls it a kind of twisting, yow-yow vibration, resemblance to sound made by telegraph wires, but not a steady, uniform volume. The sound lasted probably half a minute, time not noted. As I have heard the sound here, it seemed to begin at a distance, something like a mixture of wind in pine tops, in telegraph wires, the echo of bells, after being repeated several times, the humming of a swarm of bees and two or three other sources of sound—all making a not loud, but easily recognized sound, not at all likely to be mistaken for any other sound, but easily overlooked if one is surrounded by noises. The party on shore heard the same sound at the same time that we heard it on the lake. (On this occasion Professor Forbes and I were in our canvas boat, one hundred yards, more or less, from shore. Hofer was on the beach at the water's edge. The others were at the camp, which was some fifty feet or more back from the edge of the lake terrace, in a grove of pine-trees. I have a Kodak picture of the scene which was taken from our boat as we were nearing shore on our return from this trip.) Hofer says he doesn't remember to have heard it when the sky was cloudy, has heard it when 'quite considerable breeze' was blowing. Remembers that it was usually heard when the sky is clear, or with few clouds, and the morning calm; as a rule in the morning, but has heard it as late as noon. Dave Rhodes thinks he has heard it only in the mornings, and when the sky is clear, or with light, fleecy clouds.

"(3) August 8. Professor Forbes and I rowed up to Bridge Bay (northwest end of Yellowstone Lake), where we collected—back (to hotel) about 12:30 (P.M.). . . . We heard our mysterious sound again this morning, at 10 and 10:15, while out (on the lake) collecting. There is reason to believe that it is caused by the steamboat *Geyser* (on [the] east shore of the lake) and heard through some peculiar condition of the atmosphere at distances of several, perhaps thirty to fifty, miles away. (Here I seem to have arrived at that state of mind where consolation is derived from belief in a theory.)

"(4) August 9, 2:20 P.M., at head of southeast arm of (Yellowstone) lake. While in boat heard sound overhead, like rushing wind traveling very rapidly or like something rushing through the air, did not have the semimetallic sound, or like echo; seemed to travel from east to west; clear, except light, fleecy and feathery clouds, enough wind to ruffle the surface of the water. (On this occasion I was one of a party of five which had left the Lake Hotel on the afternoon of the eighth in two rowboats, with tent and camp outfit. My companions, who were engaged on the construction of a new building, were Mr. L. D. Boothe and Messrs.

Couglin, Curl, and Thomson. Mr. Curl and I were in one boat, and three others in the other. We were making our way from the east to the west side of the east arm of the lake and were rowing slowly in the very shallow water of this part of the lake when the sound attracted our attention)" (*Science*, 71: 97–99, 1930).

OTHER NATURAL HUMS AND ETHEREAL SOUNDS

Granted that the Yellowstone Whispers are perhaps the most famous of the ethereal aerial sounds, several other hums have also crept into the scientific literature. Most of them occur in quiet places well away from civilization so that any electromagnetic effects on human sensory apparatus, assuming that they exist, are unlikely.

The "wind-in-the-mountains" phenomenon described below by L. G. Grubb is vaguely akin to the Yellowstone Whispers and may actually result from winds blowing across mountain peaks.

"A sound locally known as 'wind in the mountains' was heard here all day. When first noticed before 8 h., it sounded like the noise of a motor running and distinct from the noise of the wind. It was persistent, unvarying except in the degree of loudness, and without anything like throbbing. In the afternoon its volume of sound was like that of the rush of a heavy train through a tunnel nearby. (There is no railway tunnel within about twenty miles. It seemed to come from the Comeragh mountains, a few miles to the south-west. One man who has lived in the district all his life had thought it was the noise of the Millvale stream, but as that is a slow-flowing, shallow stream more than a mile away, such an explanation does not seem likely.

"Locally it is considered a presage of storm and rain. It was heard also about a fortnight ago for a short time, we understand.

"About 16 1/2 h. the SSW. wind here was very light, the trees not moving, but the sound was as described above; then suddenly a strong wind sprang up here which within two hours had reached force 8 or 9. The gale continued until after midnight but had lessened by 3 h. Only 3.1 mm. of rain fell during the night. At 18 1/2 h. and possibly later the sound from the direction of the mountains could be heard apart from the noise of the gale" (*Meteorological Magazine*, 63: 66–67, 1928).

The deserts of the world produce in some unknown way a spectrum of thin, sometimes musical, sounds. The desert hums are often ascribed to blowing sand, but no one really knows. "The following account of a strange phenomenon occurring in the South American Desert, as told [to] the writer by Mr. Travers Ewell, a consulting engineer who has made frequent and extended trips into the desert regions of northern Chile and Peru.

" 'Shortly after darkness sets in, the mysterious sound begins. At first it is a sort of hum, fairly high pitched, but weird, eerie, and almost beautiful. Soon, mingled with the hum at regular intervals, there is a deep bass boom, like the far-off beating of a great drum. Sometimes the sound lasts for an hour or two, sometimes all night. I have heard it as often as three or four times a month. I have been told that the phenomenon is brought about by the movement of the sand under certain conditions of wind, temperature, and humidity producing the proper vibrations. I know that on the nights when the sound occurs there is a moderate southwest wind blowing, sufficient to move a film of sand along the surface. But whatever the cause, the phenomenon is certainly very real and very astonishing' " (*American Meteorological Society, Bulletin,* 12: 40, 1931).

Reginald G. Durrant and his companions heard a curious pulsating sound in Africa that they attributed to a distant waterfall. The same rhythmic beat seems a hallmark of natural hums.

"In June 1903, I was trekking towards the Victoria Falls. On the night before arrival, we 'outspanned' some twelve miles to the south, and on retiring to rest on the bare ground I became aware of a curious, rhythmic sound, quite distinct when my ear was pressed against the soil. I told my two brothers, who found they also could hear the pulsation, and one of them suggested that it must be due to the booming of the distant cataract.

"To me the most interesting point is not that the sound was transmitted by the earth, but that it was transformed into rhythmic vibration —very different from the constant roar one hears when close to the Falls. Some process of interference would seem to occur and give rise to this result" (*Nature,* 107: 140, 1921).

When general hums are heard in a verdant countryside in the summer, one naturally thinks of insects. Immense hordes of midges and other small insects sometimes assemble over tree tops, producing thin wirey hums. But in the following item, C. Tomlinson objects to the insect hypothesis in some situations.

"In a book that was popular about fifty years ago, entitled *Journal of a Naturalist,* the author says that the purely rural, little noticed, and indeed local occurrence, called by the country people 'hummings in the air,' was annually to be heard in fields near his dwelling. 'About the middle of the day, perhaps from twelve o'clock till two, on a few calm sultry days in July, we occasionally hear, when in particular places, the humming of apparently a large swarm of bees. It is generally in some spacious open spot that this murmuring first attracts our attention. As we move onwards the sound becomes fainter, and by degrees is no longer audible.' The sound is attributed to insects, although they are invisible.

"A writer in the *Edinburgh Philosophical Journal* objects to this sound being attributed to insects, first because the fact is stated as being local and partial, heard only in one or two fields, at particular times of the year when the air is calm and sultry. He has often heard a similar humming in a thick wood, when the air is calm, and has diligently searched for insects, but in no case was able to detect them in numbers sufficient to account for the sound.

"The same writer refers to remarkable sounds heard in a range of hills in Cheshire. When the wind is easterly, and nearly calm on the flats, a hollow moaning sound is heard, popularly termed the 'soughing of the wind,' which Sir Walter Scott, in his glossary to *Guy Mannering*, interprets as a hollow blast or whisper. The explanation seems to be that a breeze, not perceptible in the flat country, sweeps from the summit of the hills and acts the part of a blower on the sinuosities or hollows, which thus respond to the draught of air like enormous organpipes, and become for the time wind instruments on a gigantic scale" (*Nature*, 53: 78, 1895).

The few scientists who have thought and written about mysterious hums (mostly in the last century) have almost invariably mentioned Rev. Gilbert White's note on the hums he heard at Selborne. In his short letter to *Nature* in 1886, W. Harcourt Bath was no exception.

"In a letter to the Hon. Daines Barrington (letter *lxxx*) the Rev. Gilbert White, the well-known author of the *Natural History of Selborne*, mentions a strange humming sound in the air. He writes: 'There is a natural occurrence to be met with upon the highest parts of our downs in hot summer days which always amuses me much without giving me any satisfaction with respect to the cause of it; and that is a loud audible humming as of bees in the air, though not one insect is to be seen. This sound is to be heard distinctly the whole common through, from the Honey Dells to my avenue gate. Any person would suppose that a large swarm of bees was in motion and playing about over his head. This noise was heard last week on June 28.'

"It is singular that no explanation has been offered by anyone of such a common phenomenon. I am convinced that the humming sound mentioned by Gilbert White was nothing more than the noise occasioned by the vibrations of millions of insects' wings in the air. In hot summer evenings in particular, I have heard these peculiar humming sounds and know them to be caused by immense hordes of gnats and midges which fill the air with their numbers" (*Nature*, 34: 547, 1886).

Bath was obviously satisfied that the hums heard by White and others in England were insect-generated. Of course, the hums presently disturbing residents of England cannot be from insects, for they are heard in all seasons.

Looking back over the hum phenomena, they occur in several locales under different conditions. It seems probable that there are more sources than insects, waterfalls, and wind. It is a pity that such fascinating phenomena should attract so little scientific attention.

Natural Bells, Musical Notes, and Melody

A patient observer of nature soon discovers many sources of musical tones and bell-like notes—all above and beyond the common sounds of birds, trees creaking in the wind, and the like. A frozen lake, for example, is a whole orchestra of squeaks and throbbing notes. But here we include only those musical sounds that are difficult to identify or are strange due to their mode of production. Also excluded are "ringing rocks," which have been included in the companion handbook on geology, *Unknown Earth,* 1980.

Mysterious sounds near water are often created by fish and other animals, which possess a surprising repertoire of vocal talents. Unlike bird songs, fish calls are not well-identified in the field guides. In view of this ignorance, some of the oceanic sounds reported below are likely the products of aquatic life. As for the rest, who knows? The wind, moving ice, electrical discharges, and other natural agents may be at work.

SOUNDS FROM THE GREENLAND INTERIOR

In Chapter 6, I noted that the arctic wind blowing across shelf ice caused distinct vibrations. If the vibration frequency is high enough, sound may be emitted. This wind-driven mechanism, or perhaps just the rhythmic groaning of ice, may be responsible for the following sounds reported by A. Dauvillier.

"During the month of August 1932, when setting up the French Expedition of the International Polar Year in Scoresby Sound, on the East Greenland coast, some of my colleagues and I heard four times the mysterious sound called by the late Prof. A. Wegener the *'Ton der Dov-Bai.'* The sound was heard in the morning, generally at 11 A.M. (G.M.T.), and also during the afternoon. It was a powerful and deep musical note coming far from the south, lasting a few seconds. It resembled the roaring of a fog-horn. After that it was not heard during the course of the Polar Year.

"A. Wegener and five of his companions heard it eight times in five different neighbouring places, both during the day and the polar night. It lasted sometimes a few minutes, and Wegener ascribed it to the movements of inland ice. In fact, it seemed, in Scoresby Sound, to come from beyond Cape Brewster, precisely from the part of the coast where the inland ice flows into the sea from the large glaciers.

"Is this vibrating sound really caused by the detachment of icebergs or is it similar to the 'desert song,' that strange musical note produced by the sand? In fact, there is a close analogy between the fields of powdery dry snow of the inland ice and the fields of sand of the Arabian desert" (*Nature*, 133: 836, 1934).

MUSICAL SANDS

Along sea coasts and in deserts, wherever sands occur, strange sounds are sometimes heard—hums, bell-like tones, startling roars, even barking sounds. The cause is not hard to find; it is a peculiar variety of sand. Musical sand, sonorous sand—or whatever the local populace terms it—emits a surprising variety of sounds when disturbed by man or nature. Some beach sand merely squeaks like snow when trod upon. A booming dune, on the other hand, may be heard a mile away when a small cascade of sand slides down its slope.

No deep dark secrets of nature are implied here, although musical sands have led to numerous intriguing local legends. The notorious Bell of Nakous, in the Sinai and the legendary "morning cry of the Sphinx" may originate in the action of musical sand. They may also create the strange hums sometimes heard in deserts. No one with a modicum of curiosity can ignore such tantalizing phenomena.

Although the mystery of musical sands is hardly profound, no one really understands how the great variety of sounds is made. Can the same physical mechanism produce a deafening roar in one location and a pure, delicate Aeolian-like tone in another? And just why are musical sands so localized; what special geological conditions are conducive to their formation? On the same beach, the line of demarcation between musical and nonmusical sands is generally sharp but indistinguishable to the eye and even to the microscope. Musical sands represent a curious, relatively unexplored byway of geology.

Most famous are the musical sands of Jebel Nagus (spellings vary) in the Sinai. Of the many reports available, there are few more interesting than this old summary by H. S. Palmer.

"Jebel Nagus is the name given to a high sand-slope in the western-coast range of the peninsula of Sinai, about five miles north of the port of Tor. The sand of this slope possesses the peculiar property of giving forth loud musical sounds when set in motion by design or by natural causes. According to a quaint native legend, founded on the former monastic occupation of this part of the peninsula, the sounds are said to proceed from the *nagus*, or 'wooden gong,' of a monastery buried beneath the sand. Hence the application of the name Nagus to the slope in question.

"The sand-slope is about 200 feet high, and 80 yards wide at its base, narrowing toward the top; it faces west-south-west. Sandstone cliffs overhang it and bound it on either side, and an open sandy plain stretches from the foot of the slope to the sea-shore, about three-quarters of a mile distant. The sand of the slope appears to be that from the neighbouring desert plain, derived in the first place from the waste of the sandstone rocks and then conveyed to its position on the hill-side by the drifting action of high winds; its grains are large and consist entirely of quartz. The rock *in situ* is a soft friable quartzose sandstone, of a pale brown inside and weathered externally to a dull dark brown. The sand of the slope is so clean, and in its usual condition so extremely dry, and inclined at so steep an angle (about 29 1/2°) to the horizon, that it may be easily set in motion by such causes as the passage of men or animals across it, falling *debris* from the cliffs above, or disturbance by the wind. Sometimes also, movement on a smaller scale may arise from an abnormal excess of heat and drought, or from the separation of the surface-particles, after their consolidation by rain or dew, on the return of heat and the sun's burning rays. When any considerable quantity of the sand is in movement, rolling gradually down over the surface of the slope in thin waves an inch or two deep, just as oil or any thick liquid might roll over an inclined sheet of glass, and in similar festoons or curves, then is heard the singular acoustic phenomenon from which the hill derives its name, at first a deep, swelling, vibratory moan, rising gradually to a dull roar, loud enough, when at its height, to be almost startling, and then as gradually dying away, till the sand ceases to roll. The sound is difficult to describe exactly; it is not metallic, not like that of a bell, nor yet that of a *nagus*. Perhaps the very hoarsest note of an Aeolian harp or the sound produced by drawing the finger round the wet rim of a deep-toned finger-glass, most clearly resembles it, though there is less music in the sound of the rolling sand; it may also be likened to the noise produced by air rushing into the mouth of an empty metal flask; sometimes it almost approaches to the roar of very distant thunder, and sometimes it resembles the deeper notes of a violoncello or the hum of a humming-top. The author found by experiment that hot surface-sand was more sonorous than the cooler layers beneath; it also seemed to run more quickly; the first experiments on any one part of the slope produced louder effects than subsequent ones. Surface-sand, at a temperature of

103° F., exposed to the sun's full glare, produced the grandest effect observed, while sand in shade, at 62°, was almost mute. By day the heat on the slide is generally very great. Movement of the sand when moist is not accompanied by unusual sounds. Excavation was impossible on account of the continuous flow of the sand when disturbed; in some places nothing solid could be reached by probing; in others, rock was felt a few inches below the surface, but whether *in situ* or not could not be ascertained. When sand is rolling down and producing sound, there is a distinct vibration on the slide, increasing with the intensity of the sounds. Throughout Capt. Palmer's stay, the wind blew from [the] N.W.; the effects produced on the slide by winds from other quarters have yet to be observed. Experiments on two other sand-slides, a little to the south of Jebel Nagus and resembling it in many particulars, did not result in producing any similar sounds. But phenomena of a kindred character had been noticed in other parts of the world, as for instance at Reg-Ravan forty miles north of Cabul [Kābul, Afghanistan], and on the sandy plains of Arequipa in Peru" (*Report of the British Association, 1871*, pp. 188–89).

There are dozens, perhaps hundreds, of localities around the world where musical sands startle the passerby. Most are not very musical, emitting instead roars, booming noises, and, when stepped upon, unappealing squeaks. The subject is so large that it needs an entire book in its own right.

One more item will have to suffice for musical sands. It describes "a remarkable hill of moving sand in the eastern part of Churchill County, Nevada, about sixty miles from Land Springs Station. It is about four miles long and about 1 mile wide. In the whole dune, which is from 100 to 400 feet in height and contains millions of tons of sand, it is impossible to find a particle larger than a pinhead. It is so fine that if an ordinary barley sack [were] filled and placed in a moving waggon, the jolting of the vehicle would empty the sack, and yet it has no form of dust in it and is as clean as any sea-beach sand. The mountain is so solid as to give it a musical sound when trod upon, and oftentimes a bird lighting on it, or a large lizard running across the bottom, would start a large quantity of the sand to sliding, which makes a noise resembling the vibration of telephone wires with a hard wind blowing, but so much louder that it is often heard at a distance of six or seven miles, and it is deafening to a person standing within a short distance of the sliding sand" (*Knowledge, 3*: 63–64, 1883).

NATURAL MELODY

Sir Richard Paget once recalled how "on the evening of October 8, I was at Angmering-on-Sea, and my host, Mr. Kenneth Barnes, called me to listen to the wind playing, and took me to the bathroom, which faced down wind. The wind was blowing hard and gustily and was producing a most amazing effect—exactly as though a flageolet were being played by a human performer.

"The melody was in E major, with A♯ substituted for A♮, and it ranged over five semitones, of approximate frequency 1290, 1448, 1625, 1824, 1932. The melody did not slur up and down, as when the wind whistles through a cranny, but changed by sharply defined steps from note to note. The melody included runs, slow trills, turns and grace notes, and sounded so artificial that I felt bound to open the window and make sure that the tune was not being played by a human performer out of doors.

"The sounds were traced to the overflow pipe of the bath, through which air was rushing in at the rosette (of six holes, each 9 mm. diameter, set in a circle) covering the inner end of the pipe where it joined the bath.

"Next morning I examined the pipe. It was about 3 cm. in diameter, and about 3 ft. 5 in. long, in the form of an S-bend, of which the lower portion passed through the outer wall and ended in an open mouth. The natural frequency of the pipe when blown into by mouth was about 161—that is, three octaves below the keynote of the scale previously indicated. Evidently the wind was playing on the 7th, 8th, 9th, 10th, and 11th overtones of the pipe, and the melody was being produced by the rapid fluctuations of wind-pressure.

"I wonder whether such an effect can ever have occurred in Nature —a broken bamboo stem, for example, partially obstructed at its windward end and so 'shielded' by vegetation, soil, etc., as to produce a pressure difference between its open ends?

"The effect of elaborate melodies thus produced without human intervention would be highly magical and suggestive" (*Nature*, 130: 701, 1932).

Paget's question regarding the possibility of nature playing such tunes was answered by J. B. Scrivenor, who pointed out that bamboo stems do indeed create strange sounds in the wind though they are speechlike rather than musical. His reference was Godinho de Eredia's *Report on the Golden Chersonese, circa* 1600.

"To conclude entirely with the Peninsula, I will relate a curious

phenomenon which occurs at the mouth and entrance of the River Panagim [now called the River Linggi—J. B. S.]. Here there are dense
thickets of Bamboos, and among them are two very tall stout Bamboos
which are set in such a manner that one of them towers over the other;
now it is an actual fact that by day and by night human voices are heard
proceeding from these Bamboos; one of them says, '*Suda*'—that is to say,
'Enough'—and the other replies, '*Bolon*,' which is as much as to say, 'Not
yet.'

"I always regarded this as a worthless fairy tale, until Alfonso Vi-
cente, Ambassador to Achem, assured me that he personally heard these
voices saying '*Suda*' [and] '*Bolon*' when he went to this place on the
Panagim for the sole purpose of observing this most curious occurrence
in the year 1595" (*Nature*, 130: 778, 1932).

Rupert T. Gould was a collector of oddities. One of his most delightful accounts describes the "cry of Memnon." This strange sound, emanating from this ancient Egyptian statue on the desert's edge, was recorded
by dozens of visitors between 20 B.C. and 196 A.D. It has since become
enshrined in poetry by Oscar Wilde.

"'Still from his chair of porphyry gaunt Memnon strains his lidless eyes
Across the empty land, and cries each yellow morning unto thee.'

"If Tennyson, as seems likely, excelled Wilde as a poet, he nevertheless showed himself inferior to the author of *The Sphinx* when he
wrote: '. . . from her lips, as morn from Memnon, drew Rivers of melodies.'

"The sounds which are recorded as having been emitted by the famous 'vocal statue of Memnon' were neither many nor melodious. Infrequently, but always at sunrise, those who stood near it long ago might
hear a thin, strident sound, like the breaking of a harp string. That was
all—an aimless cry heard at rare intervals during a relatively short period
of two hundred years, a period preceded and followed by many centuries of silence. Yet it was a phenomenon of which hardly any similar
case is on record—and it was not, it should seem, a deception. The statue,
which had been silent so long and again has sunk into silence, did once
acquire the exercise [of] some strange inherent power of saluting the
sun" (*Enigmas*, University Books, New Hyde Park, 1965, p. 26).

Nature's musical talents sometimes manifest themselves in otherwise
heavy-handed thunderstorms, as reported by G. H. Martyn for a storm
on June 24, 1906, at Tottenham, England. "Early this morning a storm
broke in this neighbourhood accompanied by heavy thunder. During the
storm I noticed that two of the peals began with a musical note of distinct and definite pitch. The 'musical' portion of the peal lasted for about

two seconds in each case, and the frequency of the note was both times about 400 per second.

"This sound closely resembled a foot-fall in a narrow alley between high walls and was only heard in two consecutive peals, separated by an interval of about a minute, the first being much more definitely musical than the second. In each case the interval between the flash and the first sound of thunder was about five seconds.

"As is well known, a peal of thunder from lightning near at hand frequently sounds like a quick succession of raps or a volley of guns. Can the successive raps have followed one another so rapidly in this case that they combined to form a note?

"If so, and if this note was due to a special configuration of reflecting surfaces in the clouds, possibly to others in slightly different positions, considerably different frequencies may have been observed.

"The fact that two peals only sounded in this manner, separated by the short interval of about one minute, and that the second was not so decidedly musical as the first, seems to indicate that they were due to some rapidly changing source such as one might expect the reflecting surfaces of a cloud to be. I listened carefully to determine that the note had its origin outside and was not due to resonance within the room, and in the second peal it was certainly outside, and probably had the first had its origin within the room I should have observed it" (*Nature*, 74: 200, 1906).

When one delves farther back into history, romantic tales and curious myths tell of strange natural music. "Of this nature were the oracular voices of the oaks at Dordona, a rustling of the trees around the temple of Zeus, which, with the accompanying murmur of the sacred fountain, was held to be prophetic. . . . The filao [*Casuarina equisetifolia*], a tree of the island of Bourbon, emits soft, melancholy tones when its slender boughs are shaken by the wind. An avenue of such trees is the source of wonderfully touching harmonies. The reeds and rushes of the island of Sylt, with their supple stems and interlaced roots, give forth, whenever the slightest wind is blowing, tones which are at times like whispers, like a subdued singing, or like a loud whistle" (*Popular Science Monthly*, 17: 772–76, 1880).

Of course, no modern scientist would deign to study such magical acoustic phenomena, and what government agency would provide a grant to support such an effort?

OCEANIC MUSIC

In the tropical forests, one is treated to all manner of musical notes—screams, songs, chirps, howls, and other animal noises. Birds emulate bells and organs, and howler monkeys deafen the ear. Such sounds are expected in these environments. But when music seems to well up from the ocean, we must take a closer look (or rather, a closer listen). Whales and porpoises are well-known singers, and the various species of drumfish (family *Sciaenidae*) are aptly named for their sound-making abilities. With this brief background, consider first the famous Grey Town oceanic noises. Two letters to *Nature*, by Charles Dennehy and C. Kingsley, respectively, outline the phenomenon.

Dennehy writes: "I must premise that this phenomenon only takes place with iron vessels, and then only when at anchor off the port of Grey Town. At least, I have never heard of its occurring elsewhere, and I have made many inquiries.

"Grey Town is a small place, containing but few inhabitants, situated at the mouth of the river St. Juan, which separates Nicaragua from Costa Rica, and empties itself into the Atlantic, latitude 10° 54′ N. and longitude 83° 41′ W. In this town there are no belfries or factories of any kind.

"Owing to a shallow bar, vessels cannot enter the harbour or river and are therefore obliged to anchor in from seven to eight fathoms of water, about two miles from the beach, the bottom consisting of a heavy dark sand and mud containing much vegetable matter brought down by the river. Now, while at anchor in this situation, we hear, commencing with a marvellous punctuality at about midnight, a peculiar metallic vibratory sound, of sufficient loudness to awaken a great majority of the ship's crew, however tired they may be after a hard day's work. This sound continued for about two hours with but one or two very short intervals. It was first noticed some few years ago in the iron-built vessels *Wye, Tyne, Eider,* and *Danube.* It has never been heard on board the coppered-wooden vessels *Trent, Thames, Tamar,* or *Solent.* These were steamers formerly employed on the branch of the Company's Intercolonial service, and when any of their officers or crew told of the wonderful music heard on board at Grey Town, it was generally treated as 'a yarn' or hoax. Well, for the last two years the company's large transatlantic ships have called at Grey Town and remained there on such occasions for from five to six days. We have thus all had ample opportunity of hearing for ourselves. When first heard by the negro sailors, they [*sic*] were more frightened than astonished, and they at once gave way to superstitious fears of ghosts and Obeihism. By English sailors it was considered to be caused by the trumpet fish, or [whatever] they called such (certainly not the *Centriscus scolopax,* which does not even exist here). They invented a fish to account for it. But if caused by any kind of fish, why only at one place, and why only at certain hours of the night? Everything on board is as still from two to four, as from twelve to two o'clock, yet the sound is heard between twelve and two, but not between two and four. The ship is undoubtedly one of the principal instruments in its production. She is in fact for the time being converted into a great musical sounding board.

"It is by no means easy to describe this sound, and each listener gives a somewhat different account of it.

"It is musical, metallic, with a certain cadence, and a one-two-three time tendency of beat. It is heard most distinctly over open hatchways, over the engineroom, through the coal-shoots, and close round the outside of the ship. It cannot be fixed at any one place, always appearing to recede from the observer. On applying the ear to the side of an open bunker, one fancies that it is proceeding from the very bottom of the hold.

"Very different were the comparisons made by the different listeners. The blowing of a conch shell by fishermen at a distance, a shell held to the ear, an Aeolian harp, the whirr or buzzing sound of wheel machinery in rapid motion, the vibration of a large bell when the first and louder part of the sound has ceased, the echo of chimes in the belfry, the ricocheting of a stone on ice, the wind blowing over telegraph wires, have all been assigned as bearing a more or less close resemblance; it is louder on the second [night] than the first and reaches its acme on the third night; calm weather and smooth water favour its development. The rippling of the water alongside and the breaking of the surf on the shore are heard quite distinct from it.

"What is, then, this nocturnal music? Is it the result of a molecular change or vibration in the iron acted on by some galvanic agent peculiar to Grey Town? [And] bear in mind that it is heard nowhere else, not at Colón [Canal Zone], some 250 miles distant on the same coast, not at Portobelo [Panama], Cartagena, or Santa Marta [Colombia]. The inhabitants on shore know nothing of it" (*Nature*, 2: 25–26, 1870).

Kingsley's letter expands the fishly repertoire considerably.

"I am glad to see that the vexed question of the noise heard from under the sea in various parts of the Atlantic and Pacific has been reopened by a gentleman so accurate and so little disposed to credulity as Mr. Dennehy. The fact that this noise has been heard at Grey Town only on board the iron steamers, not on board the wooden ones, is striking. Doubtless if any musical vibration was communicated to the water from below, such vibration would be passed on more freely to an iron ship than to a wooden one. But I can bring instances of a noise which seems identical with that heard at Grey Town being heard not only on board wooden ships, but from the shore.

"I myself heard it from the shore, in the island of Monos, in the Northern Bocas of Trinidad. I heard it first about midnight, and then again in the morning about sunrise. In both cases the sea was calm. It was not to be explained by wind, surf, or caves. The different descriptions of the Grey Town noise which Mr. Dennehy gives, will each and all of them suit it tolerably. I likened it to a locomotive in the distance rattling as it blows off its steam. The natives told me that the noise was made by a fish, and a specimen of the fish was given me, which is not *Centriscus scolopax,* the snipe-fish, but the trumpet-fish, or *Fistularia.* I no more believe that it can make the noise than Mr. Dennehy believes (and he is quite right) that the *Centriscus* can make it.

"This noise is said to be frequently heard at the Bocas, and at Point à Pierre, some twenty-five miles south; also outside the Gulf along the Spanish main as far as Barcelona. It was heard at Chagreasancas (just inside the Bocas) by M. Joseph, author of a clever little account of Trinidad, on board a schooner which was, of course, a wooden one, at anchor. 'Immediately under the vessel,' he says, 'I heard a deep and not unpleasing sound, similar to those one might imagine to proceed from a thousand Aeolian harps; this ceased, and deep and varying notes succeeded; these gradually swelled into an uninterrupted stream of singular sounds, like the booming of a number of Chinese gongs under water; to these sounds succeeded notes that had a faint resemblance to a wild chorus of a hundred human voices singing out of time in deep bass.'

"He had, he says, three specimens of the trumpet-fish, said to make the noise, either by 'fastening the trumpet to the bottom of a vessel or a rock,' or without adhering to any object. The whip-like appendage to the tail, which he describes, marks his specimens at once as *Fistularias.*

❊   ❊   ❊

"Another instance of this sound being heard on board a wooden ship (and this time again in the Pacific) is given (in p. 304 of Mr. Griffith and Colonel Hamilton Smith's edition of *Cuvier's Fishes*) on no less an authority than that of Humboldt who (say the editors and authors of the Appendix) did not suspect the cause. 'On the 20th of February, 1803, toward seven in the evening, the whole crew were astounded by an extraordinary noise, which resembled that of drums beating in the air. It was at first attributed to the breakers. Speedily it was heard in the vessel and especially toward the poop. It was like a boiling, the noise of the air which escapes from fluid in a state of ebullition. They then began to fear that there was some leak in the vessel. It was heard unceasingly in all parts of the vessel, and finally, about nine o'clock, it ceased altogether. From the narration (says Cuvier) which we have extracted, and from what so many observers have reported touching various Sciaenoids, we may believe that it was a troop of some of these species which occasioned the noise in question.'

"For there is, without doubt, a great deal of evidence to show that certain Sciaenoids make some noise of this kind. The *Umbrinas,* or 'maigres' of the Mediterranean and Atlantic are said to be audible at a depth of twenty fathoms, and to guide the fishermen to their whereabouts by their drumming. The fishermen of [La] Rochelle [in France] are said to give the noise a peculiar term, *seiller,* to hiss; and say that the males alone make it in spawning time; and that it is possible, by imitating it, to take them without bait. The 'weak-fish' of New York (*Labrus squetaquee* of Dr. Mitchell) is said to make a drumming noise. But the best known drum-fishes are of the genus *Pogonias,* distinguished from *Umbrina* by numerous barbules under the lower jaw instead of a single one at the symphysis. M. Cuvier names them *Pogonias fusca,* and mentions that 'it emits a sound still more remarkable than that of the other Sciaenoids and has been compared to the noise of several drums.' The author of the Appendix states that these 'drumfish' swim in troops in the shallow bays of Long Island; and according to Schoepf (who calls them *Labrus chromis*) assemble round the keels of ships at anchor, and then their noise is most sensible and continuous. Dr. Mitchell, however, only speaks of their drumming when taken out of the water. Species of the same genus, if not identical, are found as far south as the coast of Brazil; and it is to them, probably, that that noise is to be attributed which made the old Spanish discoverers report that at certain seasons the nymphs and Tritons assembled in the Gulf of Paria, and made the 'Golfo Triste glad with nightly music!'" (*Nature,* 2: 46, 1870).

From the Gulf of Mexico comes still another example of oceanic music. "The mystic music sometimes heard at the mouth of the Pascagoula River, on a still night, is one of the wonders of our coast. It is not confined, however, to the Pascagoula River but has often been heard at other places. At the mouth of the Bayou Coq del Inde and other inlets opening into the Gulf along the coast of our own country, the curious listener, lying idle in his boat, with lifted oars, when every other sound is hushed, may sometimes hear its strains coming apparently from beneath the waters, like the soft notes of distant Aeolian harps. We have always supposed that this phenomenon, whatever its origin might be, natural or supernatural, was peculiar to our own coast. It appears, however, from Sir Emerson Tenant's recent work on Ceylon, that something very like it is known at Batticaloa, in that island, and it is attributed to a rather less poetical and mysterious origin—that it is a peculiar species of shellfish. They are said to be heard at night, and most distinctly when the moon is nearest the full" (*Scientific American,* 3: 51, 1860).

MUSICAL ECHOES

Untold numbers of fascinating natural phenomena remain to be revealed. It is only when someone jogs our collective memory that the strange tales come pouring forth. This evoking of anecdotes has occurred several times with the phenomena of this book. The long spate of letters and articles on natural detonations that began this chapter were inspired by George Darwin's request for reports relating to *mistpouffers* and the Barisāl Guns. A similar situation prevailed when Alexander Forbes wrote a short article for *Science* on "analyzed sounds" in 1924. The responses to the article revealed a rich lode of unpublished experiences with what we term "musical echoes." (There must be much more data on similar strange phenomena still untapped in the collective memory of our species.)

Forbes first related the experience of Dr. Charles Thomas Jackson. "While engaged in the geological survey of Maine, I had occasion to make a trip through the forests from Farmington to Saddleback Mountain—and, after passing over a hill, we suddenly came in view of Saddleback between which and our party lay a large dismal swamp with a lake in the midst of it. The huge mountain range covered with snow stretched away for a great distance and presented so magnificent a sight as to call forth a shout from my party. The echo, after some moments, came back in musical tones, though the shout was anything but musical.

"A fierce Indian war whoop was returned to us in the softest musical tones, not one of the discords being heard.

"A gun was fired and the report came back in a *feu de joie* of long continuance and decidedly musical in its effect. Very discordant yells were made to try the effect, but only musical tones were returned" (*Science*, 60: 5–7, 1924).

H. A. Allard responded to the little collection of musical echoes reproduced by Forbes with his experience on August 11, 1892, at Oxford, Massachusetts. "As an early train passed by this morning, I noted a most remarkable echo every time it whistled. The first echo was immediate, sharp and distinct, appearing to rebound from a neighbor's buildings nearby. Some seconds after, all was quiet, another faint, faraway musical echo came stealing up the valley, apparently emanating from a wooded hillside far away. The echo ever increased in intensity until it seemed to pervade every corner of the landscape, filling it with a wonderful harmony of sound that beat upon the air in ever fainter waves, becoming farther away, until the sounds could no longer be heard. At no time were the sounds loud but seemed to fall upon the ear in infinite waves, as if thrown back from some invisible dome overhead. . . . I think some obscure atmospheric condition overhead was responsible for this remarkable echo, the most exquisite, the most sweetly celestial sound I have ever heard in the skies" (*Science*, 60: 245, 1924). Allard seems to have been caught up in Emerson's love of nature, but forests and mountains actually do seem to recycle coarse human emanations into music.

In 1925, C. Macfie Campbell passed on an observation from *Blackwood's Magazine*, in an article entitled "In Lapland," by Jan Gordon and Cora J. Gordon. "'Under the high and purplish cliffs of the other side of the lake, we had a peculiar experience in acoustics; the clatter of the motor was gathered up and reflected back by these scarped rocks in a hundred echoes, but by some strange trick blended in so peculiar a fashion that the vulgar rattle and roar came to us sweetened into the chiming of cathedral bells, pastoral England's Sunday morning unbelievably imitated, now surging louder, now drifting fainter, as one would hear the bells themselves in a shifting breeze'" (*Science*, 61: 540–41, 1925).

Infrasound

Infrasound consists of pressure waves beating below about 15 cycles per second, the lower frequency limit of the human ear. This does not mean that humans are unaffected by infrasound. Indeed there is a growing body of evidence suggesting that infrasound makes people jumpy and edgy—just the "feelings" that are so common during earthquake and tornado weather.

It is, in fact, surprising to discover that many of the natural phenomena described earlier in this book are accompanied by infrasound, although we usually detect the events visually or through other senses. Being of very low frequency, infrasound may travel hundreds of miles with little attenuation. An incomplete list of known sources of natural infrasound follows:

> Storms and other severe weather
> Auroras
> Meteors
> Volcanos
> Terrain-induced wind disturbances
> Earthquakes
> Ocean waves and surf

One might generalize and say that any phenomenon that creates audible sounds very probably emits infrasound as well. There may also be a connection between infrasound and the elusive sounds supposedly heard by some people during low-level auroras and meteor flights.

For infrasound to be of more than theoretical importance to an observer of nature, it must be detectable to human observers unaided by instruments. The senses that tell us that we are being bathed in infrasound are subtle and not yet clearly delineated by science. R. W. B. Stephens listed a few human reactions to infrasound in 1969. "Physiological effects include nausea, disequilibrium, disorientation, blurring of vision, lassitude. Internal damage may occur due to the fact that infrasonic waves easily penetrate deeply and may induce resonant effects on organs. . . . Accidents, absenteeism, and other factors indicating degradation of human performance can be correlated with infrasonic waves arriving from storms 2,000 miles away" (*Ultrasonics,* 7: 30–35, 1969).

The data supporting such effects of infrasound are merely suggestive, hardly iron-clad. Typical was a study carried out by J. E. Green and F. Dunn, of the University of Illinois. They analyzed school and insurance records of the city of Chicago, for absenteeism and accidents during May 1967, and compared them with the presence of powerful storms up to 1,500 miles away, storms that very likely showered Chicago with unheard but unsettling infrasound. Their correlation was positive but weak, which is not surprising because no infrasound detectors were emplaced in Chicago, and the parameters of absenteeism and accidents are affected by many forces other than infrasound (*New Scientist,* 41: 586, 1969).

I include this section on infrasound primarily to emphasize that we detect only a small fraction of nature's spectrum of phenomena and that our state of being, our total sensory impression of nature, may well be affected by other natural forces that we have not yet learned to detect.

8

MAGNETIC DISTURBANCES

The magnetic anomalies described here are transitory—sudden deviations of the compass and jostles of the magnetometer. Permanent magnetic anomalies caused by local distortions of the earth's magnetic field (some of which are quite remarkable) are found in the companion handbook on geology.*

The transitory magnetic anomalies are of two types: (1) those for which no source can be identified and (2) those that appear associated with specific phenomena but where it is difficult to understand how the magnetic effects are produced.

Careful observers of the compass needle noted long ago that it quivered during sun-induced magnetic storms. Possibly some of the disturbances noted below are of this type, but generally they are much larger and of shorter duration than those due to magnetic storms. Their origin(s) remain mysterious.

Auroras and thunderstorms are manifestly electrical in nature, and it is conceivable that flows of electricity during these phenomena occur in such a way that they set up disturbing magnetic fields. The actual mechanism may be obscure, but the possibility is there. Earthquakes are not obviously electrical, although magnetic effects have been reported and hotly controverted for over a century. (See Chapter 5.) Piezoelectric and piezomagnetic effects may be operating in these instances. Most obscure of all are the supposed magnetic effects of meteors. The rare reports of electric shocks on the ground under high-altitude meteors fall in this class, too. It may be that intense meteor activity upsets the electrical

* Corliss, William R., *Unknown Earth: A Handbook of Geological Enigmas*, Glen Arm, Md.: The Sourcebook Project, 1980.

equilibrium of the atmosphere and the induced flow of terrestrial electricity creates the observed magnetic effects.

UNEXPLAINED MAGNETIC DISTURBANCES

The earth's geomagnetic field is restless. Our compasses reflect this activity through slight movements, usually much less than a degree in amplitude. Larger perturbations of the terrestrial field will naturally deflect compasses even more. The following observation from the M.V. *Britannic* while in the North Atlantic on September 30, 1952, is typical of the strong fluctuations expected during a severe magnetic storm. What makes the event anomalous is the fact that no global, sun-induced magnetic storms were recorded for that time period. "1932–2052 G.M.T. Abnormal magnetic variation was experienced during this period. At 1932 the deviation was 3° E., at 2024 it was 1° W. The deviation then increased to 4 1/2° W. by 2040 and decreased to the normal deviation of 3° E. at 2052. Numerous bearings of celestial bodies were obtained having both E'ly and W'ly [easterly and westerly] hour angles, and the gyro compass remained correct throughout. No abnormal static was experienced" (*Marine Observer*, 23: 148, 1953).

The next two events involve such extreme compass deviations that they must be regarded as real enigmas (assuming of course that one of the crewmen did not have a magnet in his pocket). On March 30, 1937, the S.S. *Middlesex* was steaming through the Marquesas Islands in the Pacific. ". . . between the islands of Hiva Oa and Ua Pow (Marquesas), a magnetic disturbance was experienced. The compass suddenly became very erratic, at one time pointing as much as 20° to the east of magnetic north. Within two minutes the compass-card settled down, and an azimuth showed the error to be normal again" (*Marine Observer*, 15: 6, 1936).

The second anomaly occurred on December 23, 1928, in the South Atlantic. A. R. Pearson, second officer of the S.S. *Elpenor* logged this item. "Steering by Standard Compass S. 17° E. (Error 21° W. S. 38° E. True), Steering Compass S. 22° E., both compasses were suddenly deflected 90°, North Point swinging to East, and then swung freely back to normal. Period of disturbances about three minutes" (*Marine Observer*, 6: 261, 1929).

It is always possible that ships in motion pass over highly magnetic geological deposits or man-made objects on the sea floor. However, these permanent magnetic anomalies are usually well known and marked on the charts. In any case, similar compass deflections afflict land-based compasses, too.

ELECTROMAGNETIC EFFECTS OF AURORAS

The high-altitude electrical currents that create auroral displays are accompanied by similar currents in the earth's crust, but of much lesser intensity. Such earth-currents may create electromagnetic effects, such as those described in the following item. Ernst Hartwig, who operated an electromagnetic clock at Bamberg, Germany, made the observation on October 31, 1903. "The pendulum of the clock receives an electromagnetic impulse from two accumulator cells every minute and, when the cells are in order, has a constant rate through the year. On this night, however, the pendulum was accelerated in an extraordinary manner, as if the accumulators were overcharged. On the morning of Nov. 1, Dr. Hartwig found the clock violently disturbed, the pendulum striking on both sides of the case, and the hand pointing several hours and perhaps over a whole revolution ahead, while because of the too-violent swing several-seconds intervals were skipped at a time. The accumulators had not been charged for several days past, so that it must have been an earth-current resulting from the aurora which produced the disturbance" (*Popular Astronomy*, 12: 288, 1904).

MAGNETIC ANOMALIES POSSIBLY RELATED TO EARTHQUAKES

Earthquake magnetism has had a long, controversial history. Many scientists still deny the existence of a seismomagnetic effect, despite the data presented in Chapter 5, which seem closely correlated with known quakes. Here I present excerpts from a report by S. Chapman, a long-time student of the geomagnetic field, in which he collected several observations of magnetic transients that may also be related to quakes, although they seem much too strong to be quake-generated. The first item is from the S.S. *West Holbrook*, August 3, 1926. "'While the above-named vessel was entering the Gulf of Tokyo, 6:40 P.M. A.T.S. (apparent time of ship), on the above-named date, a slight tremor was felt, as if the vessel was grounding. [The] vessel [was] shivering and a noise was heard, as if touching a rocky ledge, but no reduction in speed could be noticed.

"'Vessel heading at the time 328° P.S.C., 319° true. Deviation 3.6° west on course.

"'Bearings were immediately taken of Suno Saki Light bearing north 26° east true and Merano Hana Light bearing north 93° east true;

which placed vessel in latitude 34° 55′ north, longitude 139° 43′ 30″ east, and by chart in from 46 to 50 fathoms of water.

"'From the above position to Yokohama, the ship's compasses were acting queerly, having on northerly courses a deviation of 0.5° west: where before there had been 3° west.

"'Upon arrival in Yokohama learned that an earthquake had taken place.

"'The following morning, August 4, azimuths were taken for recording deviation. The compasses were still found to be out. On August 5 azimuths were again taken and compasses were now found to be back to normal.'

"The following report is from a ship which is provided with two entirely independent master-gyro compasses situated low down in the ship. These communicate with gyro repeaters in the navigating position for the Officer of the Watch and the steering position for the Quarter-Master. In each position there is also a magnetic compass, the one in the navigating position being known as the standard compass and the other as the steering compass. In order to check one master gyro against the other, the repeaters in the two positions are run by different masters. The report is as follows:

"'On April 22, 1928 at 18:20 G.M.T. in latitude 33° 38′ north, longitude 24° 04′ east, course 286° true—north 71° west (Standard)—a difference of 5° was noticed in the comparison between gyro and magnetic compass courses. As both standard and steering compasses were similarly affected, it was at first supposed that gyro compasses were at fault, but investigation showed both masters to be running normally, and they remained in agreement throughout—nor had any electrical changes taken place in the ship.

"'It had therefore to be assumed that for some reason the north point of the magnetic compasses had been deflected to the westward. After 10 minutes the difference between gyro and magnetic courses began to decrease, until at 19:10 G.M.T. the standard compass-course became normal again—to be followed shortly after by the steering compass.

"'As both magnetic compasses were deflected similarly, it is doubtful whether a vessel not fitted with gyro compasses would have been aware of the disturbance. Unfortunately no azimuths could be taken during the phenomenon.

"'It is noteworthy that the time of the occurrence was practically coincident with the earthquake which destroyed the town of Corinth, and that the above position is on the same magnetic meridian as that place.'

"The occurrence described . . . appears to be a quite definite instance of a large local magnetic disturbance of a temporary kind, apparently associated with an earthquake. The fact that after two days the compass-direction returned to the normal value seems to render it unlikely that the disturbance of direction was due merely to some mechanical action associated with the shock experienced by the vessel.

"It would be interesting to know how far away, and how local, was the epicentre of the earthquake referred to, and what was its intensity. It is desirable also to know whether the records of the neighboring Tokyo magnetic observatory showed any disturbance at the time; if not, then the disturbance must have been either only apparent, or, if real, extremely local, since the observatory is only a degree or two away from the position of the ship.

". . . it should [also] be noted that the Corinth earthquake occurred at 20 h. 13 m. 50 s. on April 22, 1928—that is, about two hours *after* the magnetic disturbance was noted. Hence, the latter can have nothing to do with the actual earthquake, though it might conceivably be due to the causes leading up to the quake. The ship itself experienced no shock, and its officers only learned of the earthquake next morning.

"The position of Corinth is 37.9° north, 22.9° east, and the epicentre of the earthquake of April 22, 1928, is within a degree of this; the ship must therefore have been within 4° or 5° from the epicentre.

"In another letter the ship's Commander states that there was 'no lightning or any signs of electrical activity in the atmosphere which might have explained a temporary deflection of the compass.'

* * *

"The remarkable features of the magnetic disturbance mentioned . . . are its large amount and its short duration; its amount is paralleled, in such latitudes, only during the most intense world-wide magnetic storms, which last for many hours. No such storm occurred on that date. Unfortunately there is no continuously-recording magnetic observatory within several hundred miles of Corinth, the nearest being at Helwan; at my request Mr. H. E. Hurst kindly furnished me with a tracing of the horizontal-force magnetograph for Helwan for the day in question; it showed no trace of any unusual disturbance at the time, and Mr. Hurst states that the other magnetic records were equally quiet.

"Hence, if the magnetic disturbance near Corinth was real, as seems scarcely open to doubt, it must have been much more local than are most magnetic disturbances, even when much less intense than this one. One possibility is that in the region where the ship then was, there is a large *permanent* local irregularity in the Earth's field, but it seems unlikely that so large an irregularity in such frequented waters could have escaped notice" (*Terrestrial Magnetism and Atmospheric Electricity*, 35: 81–83, 1930).

VOLCANO MAGNETISM

In the violence of a volcanic eruption, both the piezoelectric and piezomagnetic effects may contribute to the electromagnetic environment around the crater. The spewing forth of electrically charged material and the resulting play of lightning around the erupting vent likewise add to the probability of small magnetic perturbations of a local nature. But at the cataclysmic eruption of Mount Pelée on Martinique in 1902, magnetic transients were recorded thousands of miles away, as reported by L. A. Bauer. Although the Pelée eruption was powerful, there appears to be no way it could have created such long-distance magnetic effects.

"Coincident, as far as can be at present ascertained, with the time of eruption of Mont Pelée on May 8, a magnetic disturbance set in which was registered on the self-recording instruments of the two U.S. Coast and Geodetic Survey magnetic observatories, the one at Cheltenham, Maryland, seventeen miles southeast of Washington, and the other at Baldwin, Kansas, seventeen miles south of Lawrence. The preliminary reports received from Mr. L. G. Schultz, in charge of Cheltenham observatory, and Mr. W. C. Bauer, in charge of Baldwin Observatory, are sufficient to indicate that the disturbance began at practically the same instant of time at both observatories—viz., at 7 h. 54 m. St. Pierre local mean time. According to the newspaper reports the catastrophe befell St. Pierre about 8 A.M. of May 8 and it has been stated that the town clock was found stopped at 7 h. 50 m.

"Purely mechanical vibrations caused by earthquakes are often recorded by the delicately suspended magnetic needles, as for instance the Guatemalan one which was felt at Cheltenham Observatory on April 18, from about 9 h. 20 m. to 9 h. 50 m. P.M. 75th meridian mean time.

"The disturbance on May 8, however, was distinctively a magnetic and not a seismic one and hence was not recorded on seismographs. The Cheltenham magnetograms exhibit magnetic disturbances amounting at time from 0.00050 to 0.00060 c.g.s. [centimeter-gram-second] units (about 1/350 of the value of the horizontal intensity) and from 10' to 15' in declination, beginning at the time stated and continuing until midnight of the 9th. Even on the 10th tremors were still discernible. (At the time of writing the subsequent curves had not yet been received.)

"Until further information has been received from other observatories, it cannot be determined definitely whether this magnetic disturbance was due to some cosmic cause or came from within the earth's crust and was associated with the Martinique eruption. The coincidence in time is however a remarkable fact" (*Science*, 15: 873, 1902).

THUNDERSTORM MAGNETISM

On February 13, 1963, the compass of the M.V. *Dartwood*, then in the North Atlantic, was thrown off by a thunderstorm. "At 0440 GMT, the vessel encountered a violent squall, accompanied by large hailstones approximately 3/8 in. in diameter. The wind increased to force 11–12 from W., and there was a great deal of forked lightning and heavy thunderclaps; visibility was almost nil. As the storm was passing overhead, the magnetic compass was seen to be deviated 4° to the W.; it returned to its normal position after the storm moved away. Air temperature, 38° F. at 0440; 40° at 0500.

"*Note.* The following comment has been received from the Superintendent, Eskadalemuir Observatory, Dumfriesshire, Scotland:

"'The magnetic field was moderately disturbed on February 13 with a range of 20′ in declination at Eskadalemuir.'

"The deviation experienced by M.V. *Dartwood* seems much too large to be part of this disturbance, and it appears possible that it may have been due to a point discharge from the mast head. The current up the mast would be increased by the abnormal potential gradient due to the thunderstorm overhead, and by the high wind, but if this is the explanation, it is rather surprising that St. Elmo's fire was not observed; the bad weather may explain this" (*Marine Observer*, 34: 11, 1964).

POSSIBLE ELECTROMAGNETIC EFFECTS OF METEORS

The electromagnetic effects of meteor activity seem to occur at two levels, both controversial. First, meteor showers seem to induce small changes in the geomagnetic field; second, large low-level meteors may produce gross magnetic and electrical effects.

The scientific literature contains several cautious reports statistically connecting meteor showers with geomagnetic activity. This abstract from a paper by Alvin W. Jenkins, et al., exemplifies this suggestive, but hardly clear-cut work.

"A correlation between geomagnetic fluctuations and meteoric activity was reported by *Kalashnikov,* who used sensitive fluxmeters and a photographic recording technique. In his work, he noted an increase in the number of pulses in the vertical component over the dates of meteor showers. *Hawkins,* using more sensitive equipment also sensitive to the vertical component, attempted to correlate pulses with visual meteors. His results were negative, indicating only such correlation as might be expected statistically. A real discrepancy thus exists between the results of these two workers. Hawkins has pointed out, however, that Kalashni-

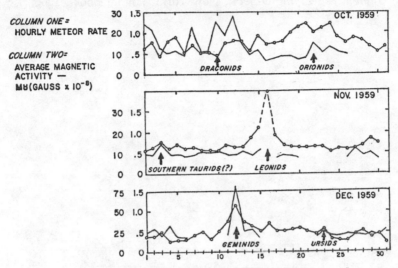

COLUMN ONE =
HOURLY METEOR RATE

COLUMN TWO =
AVERAGE MAGNETIC
ACTIVITY —
MH(GAUSS x 10⁻⁸)

Some geomagnetic fluctuations may be correlated with meteor showers.

kov's results may not be significant, since the correlation he noted is not much greater than that expected to occur accidentally. A preliminary analysis of data recently available from the IGY program concerned with subaudio fluctuations in the geomagnetic field seems to indicate that meteoric activity and the average level of the fluctuations are related" (*Journal of Geophysical Research*, 65: 1617, 1960).

Much more powerful magnetic effects were claimed by Franklin Massena, at the Itatiaia Observatory, Brazil. On July 30, 1868, he observed a brilliant meteor crossing the sky in the southwest. "This aerolite so disturbed the magnetic instruments that the declinometer turned its pole from the north toward the west and struck itself in the box where it found resistance; the horizontal magnetometer fell in its center of gravity, and finally, the compass oscillated 15° from north to west. I showed Sr. Arsenio the disturbed state of the declinometer. It is, therefore, demonstrated for physics that an aerolite has an intense action upon the north pole of magnets, powerfully attracting them" (*Scientific American*, 19: 276, 1868). It is possible, of course, that the meteor's passage and the magnetic transient were coincidental.

An even more startling effect was reported from Russia. "During the fall of one of the largest bolides, near Sichote-Alin, near Vladivostok

(USSR), an electrician on a telephone pole received a strong electric shock from disconnected wires at the instant the bolide became visible. The shock may have been due to other causes, but the possibility of strong electromagnetic effects should not be ruled out" (*Scientific Study of Unidentified Flying Objects*, New York: Bantam Books, 1969, p. 746).

The *Handbook of Unusual Natural Phenomena* is only one step in the collection, categorization, and publication of data on strange phenomena. The Sourcebook Project was created in 1974 to gather and organize information on scientific anomalies in the fields of geophysics, geology, astronomy, biology, archeology, and psychology. Individuals with information to contribute or who wish to learn more about the activities and publications of the Sourcebook Project should contact:

William R. Corliss
The Sourcebook Project
P.O. Box 107
Glen Arm, MD   21057

INDEX